3073 5913

The American Paradox

The American Paradox

Spiritual Hunger in an Age of Plenty

DAVID G. MYERS

Foreword by Martin E. Marty

Yale Nota Bene

Yale University Press   New Haven and London

First published as a Yale Nota Bene book in 2001.

Originally published in 2000 by Yale University Press.

For information about this and other Yale University Press publications, please contact:

U.S. office   sales.press@yale.edu

Europe office   sale@yaleup.co.uk

Printed in the United States of America

The Library of Congress has catalogued the hardcover as follows:

Myers, David G.

The American paradox : spiritual hunger in an age of plenty / David Myers.

p.   cm.

Includes bibliographical references and index.

ISBN 0-300-08111-1 (cloth)

1. United States–Moral conditions. 2. Social ethics–United States.
3. Communitarianism–United States.   I. Title.

HN90.M6 M94   2000

306'.0973—dc21   99-088870

ISBN 0-300-09120-6 (PBK.)

A catalogue record for this book is available from the British Library.

10   9   8   7   6   5   4   3   2   1

For tomorrow's children

Contents

Foreword

A first reading of *The American Paradox* may lead some readers—as it led me—to think, now and then, "Why don't Americans make up their minds?" Behind that there might even be another thought: "Why doesn't David Myers make up his mind?" If Americans and author Myers would simply and clearly have done that, the picture presented here would be more consistent than it appears to be. And the task of Professor Myers would have been simpler.

The story of how Americans live is, however, to say the least, mixed. Or as Myers so appropriately condenses it in his title, it is paradoxical.

If Americans were always, only, and simply materialistic and greedy, or if Myers chose to view them as such, the plot of this book could be simpler. It would make headlines. Plenty of analysts who go looking for the spiritual dimension in America and Americans' lives do skew the evidence, hide some of it, and then mount soapboxes to denounce everything that goes on in the nation as "bad faith." Such analysts usually call themselves prophets, or at least the dust jackets of their books claim that they are prophetic. To borrow from a recent book title, the headline seekers see all Americans except themselves as slouching toward Gomorrah.

Opposing the carpers are their opposite numbers, the positive thinkers, the optimists who see only the sunny side of life. They look at the same piles of evidence as do their counterparts and, also hiding some of it, proclaim that by their own standards all is well and all will be well. Such authors do not believe in dragging us through swamps of statistics and sloughs of moral despond; they will not let our true darknesses be seen as anything more than passing clouds. In the counsels of the optimists, we can trust churchgoing, book-buying, family-loving America to be spiritual.

The author before us, however, is not denunciatory, crabby, or, in those terms, prophetic. Neither is he a positive thinker, an optimist, someone who obscures from our view the heights of American exploitation or the depths of national miseries.

Given his approach, then, expect in each chapter to get an up-to-date, honest, accurate, and fair-minded presentation of a host of indicators that all is not well. Then, when he has let us glimpse the slouchers and the sloughs, Myers says, in effect, "but on the other hand . . ." and presents apparently contradictory testimony with which we have to reckon. The parts of each chapter appear in a kind of categorical and logical sequence. Yet at the end of the chapter we readers have been forced to deal with an interplay, no elements of which make full sense in isolation from their opposites.

Hence, Americans live their lives in paradoxical ways.

What impressed me, as a fifty-year chronicler of some of these American ways—I "do" religion and culture, not sex and violence—is how the data and disclosures about ways of life differ from those of, say, 1950. And yet, paradoxically, one can also observe how much continuity there is, at least in the concerns and the choice of items that cry out for measurement and that tease us into responding to ever more encompassing questions.

Myers is a social scientist, not a formal philosopher or a systematic theologian. But he does not let social sciences pull him into mere positivisms. He is a hoper, but he never lets his inclination toward hope obscure his mission as a social scientist. And after dealing with the paradoxes in his finely nuanced way, he does tilt his hand a bit and we get some glimpses of what he thinks are elements of a better society, and glances at some means he sees of producing them.

MARTIN E. MARTY
Fairfax M. Cone Distinguished Service Professor Emeritus,
The University of Chicago

Preface

While writing psychology textbooks I sometimes come across information so interesting and so humanly significant that I just can't keep
it to myself. Such feelings emerged as I tracked breathtaking cultural
changes that have occurred over our past four decades—a mere eye-
blink of time to any historian. Among my observations: From 1960 to
about 1993 we were soaring economically, especially at the upper levels, and sinking socially. To an extension of Ronald Reagan's famous
question, "Are we better off than we were 40 years ago?" our honest
answer would have been, materially yes, morally no.

Therein lies the American paradox. We now have, as average Americans, doubled real incomes and double what money buys. We have es-
presso coffee, the World Wide Web, sport utility vehicles, and caller
ID. And we have less happiness, more depression, more fragile relationships, less communal commitment, less vocational security, more
crime (even after the recent decline), and more demoralized children.

People are noticing. Seventy-six percent of Americans responding
to a late 1998 *Washington Post*/Kaiser Foundation/Harvard University
poll agreed that the country's "values and moral beliefs . . . have gotten
pretty seriously off on the wrong track"; only 21 percent see them as
"generally going in the right direction." What do you think? "Compared
to 20 years ago, do you think it is harder or not harder to raise kids to be
good people today?" If you are like 89 percent of Americans responding to this 1998 Gallup survey question, you think it is harder. And if
you are like most Americans (when reflecting on the nation's problems
for a 1999 Gallup survey), you no longer say "it's the economy, stupid";
you now see "moral problems" as the larger concern. Political leaders

of both parties are sensing our desire to move beyond increasing material prosperity to build, in Al Gore's words, "an America that is not only better off but better."

Here, it seemed to me, was profoundly important information for our national dialogue as we enter the new millennium. We cannot dodge the questions: What is the state of our culture? How are recent social trends impacting our well-being? Without trampling on our liberties, how might we reform our social ecology? What can we celebrate? What should we change?

Getting the Big Picture

As a research psychologist and writer, I am keen to inform the mind while arousing the heart. I therefore began this book not wanting to offer social commentary that was merely my own opinion. I instead wanted to share some of the surprising—and sometimes not so surprising—findings that shed light on the roots and fruits of cultural changes. Thus I wondered: by wedding scholarship with journalism, could I offer a compelling synopsis of America's social recession and of the social renewal movement that, happily, is now under way?

Other authors have focused on certain specifics: the sexual revolution, the decline of marriage and father care, the state of the nation's children, violence trends, media influences, character education, and the social consequences of faith. While I'll be drawing more extensively on psychology, my ambitious aim is to build bridges between their efforts, to connect the dots, to offer a "big picture" overview of late 20th century social trends—including the harbingers of social renewal.

Our culture's prospects for renewal are indeed brightening. We have seen a groundswell of public concern in the late 1990s, visible not only in the Million Man March, Promise Keepers' rallies, and public opinion polls but also in the discovery of common ground shared by many liberals and conservatives. Despite culture wars over gay rights, abortion, taxation, national defense, and Bill Clinton's behavior, there is shared concern for the social ecology that nurtures children and youth. The dialogue about American values has shifted from expanding personal rights to enhancing communal civility, from raising self-esteem to rousing social responsibility, from "whose values?" to "our values." The supporting voices range from Jesse Jackson to James Dobson, from Hillary Rodham Clinton to Charles Colson, and from Donna Shalala to

William Bennett. E. J. Dionne, Jr., captures the optimistic mood: "The United States is on the verge of a new era of reform similar in spirit to the social rebuilding that took place during the Progressive Era. . . . Rekindling a spirit of social reconstruction is both essential and a realistic hope."

A Psychological Science Perspective

So what is my peculiar take on all this? My perspective is not overtly political or ideological. My vocation, as one who distills psychological science for various audiences, is to pull together the emerging research and reflect on its human significance. As I report findings and draw conclusions, readers may at times feel irritated by this book's seemingly "liberal" or "conservative" slant. I resist such labels. If it is "liberal" to report the toxic consequences of materialism, economic individualism, and income inequality, then the liberalism is in the data I report. If it is "conservative" to report that sexual fidelity, co-parenting, positive media, and faith help create a social ecology that nurtures healthy children and communities, then the conservatism resides in the findings.

My concern, then, is less with whether I am being a good liberal or conservative than with assembling an accurate picture of reality. In doing so, I rely much less on compelling stories than on research findings. As an experimental social psychologist—one who studies how people view, affect, and relate to one another—I'm not much persuaded by anecdotes, testimonials, or inspirational pronouncements. When forming opinions about the social world, I tell people, beware those who tell heart-rending but atypical stories. With apologies to Mark Twain, there are three kinds of lies—lies, damned lies, and vivid but misleading anecdotes. One can marshal dramatic stories to support any contention, or its opposite. The truth of human experience, I believe, is better discerned by surveys that faithfully represent the population and control for complicating factors, and by careful experiments.

This scientific perspective is quite unlike the postmodern subjectivism that dismisses evidence as hardly more than collected biases. The scientific attitude yearns to put testable ideas to the test. Thus if we today think capital punishment does (or does not) deter crime more than other available punishments, we can utter our personal opinions, as has the U.S. Supreme Court. Or we can ask whether states with a death penalty have lower homicide rates, whether their rates have dropped after instituting the death penalty, and whether they have risen when abandoning the penalty. We can check our personal hunches against reality. In this book we will similarly put to the test much of the popular wisdom found in newspaper op-ed columns.

To be sure, pure objectivity, like pure righteousness, is an unattainable ideal. When questing for truth about controversial social issues we never leave our values at home. In looking for evidence, and in deciding what findings to report and how to report them, we are sometimes subtly steered by our hunches, our wishes, our values within. A book such as this cannot help marrying not only science with journalism but facts with values. Values-R-Us.

Indeed, social scientific detective work can be conducted with passionate purpose and with compassion for those studied. Numbers may tell the story, but ultimately you and I are interested in real people. Statistics describe reality and concrete examples bring it to life. In this book I therefore aim to offer socially important facts, and to embody them with true stories (while hiding the scholarly details in end-of-book notes).

Although I belong to a profession hardly known for its piety, my sympathies also are colored by my religious faith. In the 20th century, several pioneering social psychologists exemplified a faith-motivated drive to apply scientific social psychology to social issues. Before entering the field, Theodore Newcomb, Rensis Likert, and Goodwin Watson all studied at Union Theological Seminary. Likert, Dorwin Cartwright, and Angus Campbell studied under Kent Fellowships from the National Council on Religion in Higher Education. John Thibaut was at one time planning to be a worker priest. Gordon Allport was a devout Episcopalian who not only wrote a landmark book on prejudice but also studied the psychology of religion. Postwar research on prejudice and authoritarianism was supported by such organizations as the American Jewish Congress.

Much as the boundaries between biology and chemistry are breaking down, so some of these pioneers in their later days have argued for an integration of psychology with sociology and economics. If social psychology is to be a "science of real and whole social human beings," contends senior social psychologist Leonard Berkowitz, it must appreciate the interplay of economic, cultural, and individual influences.

The footsteps of these tough-minded but tender-hearted social psychologists define the trail that I seek to follow. Like them, my inquiry is powered by a faith-driven optimism, even as I fittingly work at a place called Hope.

My vision of the past and future is enabled by those on whose shoulders I stand. Many esteemed social science colleagues have written wonderfully helpful books about specific aspects of the social state of the nation, and I am indebted to them all: Amitai Etzioni (George Washington University), David Popenoe (Rutgers), Barbara Dafoe Whitehead (National Marriage Project), William Damon (Stanford), Martin E. P. Seligman (University of Pennsylvania), Marian Wright Edelman (Children's Defense Fund), Sylvia Ann Hewlett and Cornel West (Harvard), Robert Putnam (Harvard), Sara McLanahan and Gary Sandefur (Princeton and Wisconsin), Linda Waite (University of Chicago), David Blankenhorn (Institute for American Values), Jean Bethke Elshtain (University of Chicago), Stephanie Coontz (Evergreen State), Francis Fukuyama (George Mason), and Robert Frank (Cornell University). These scholars—and the hundreds of others on whose work I report—informed this book.

I am additionally grateful to several individuals who guided or encouraged my writing, including Gordon Bear, Jane Dickie, Robert Larzelere, David Lykken, Carol Myers, Gerald Sittser, and Wallace Voskuil. Gretchen Rumohr-Voskuil helped gather information and assisted Phyllis Vandervelde with manuscript preparation. Anna Brownson page-referenced the notes and citations at the book's end. Letha Dawson Scanzoni provided helpful freelance editing. Hope College provided a sabbatical leave during which much of my homework and writing was accomplished. Finally, at Yale University Press my wonderful editor, Susan Arellano, caught and shaped the vision for this book. With meticulous care and sensitive judgment, manuscript editor Phillip King helped tighten and polish the finished work. With the help of all these people, this is a better book than I alone could have written.

CHAPTER 1

The Best of Times, the Worst of Times

> It was the best of times, it was the worst of times, it was the age of wisdom, it was the age of foolishness, it was the epoch of belief, it was the epoch of incredulity, it was the season of Light, it was the season of Darkness, it was the spring of hope, it was the winter of despair, we had everything before us, we had nothing before us, we were all going direct to Heaven, we were all going direct the other way.
>
> —CHARLES DICKENS, *A Tale of Two Cities*

We Americans embody a paradox. We read and hear it all around us. There are those who rightly claim, "We've never had it so good. Things are going *great* in this country!" And they are right. But then there are those who wring their hands and just as rightly worry that our civilization could collapse on its decaying moral infrastructure. The best of times, the worst of times. Wisdom, foolishness. Light, darkness. Hope, despair. Dickens' words fit.

What are we to make of this seeming paradox? How can this be both the best and worst of times? And where do we go from here?

It Is the Best of Times

We are fortunate to be living when we do. Moments ago, I made a cup of tea in a microwave oven, sat down in a comfortable ergonomic office chair in my climate-controlled office, turned on my personal computer, and answered electronic mail from friends in Hong Kong and Scotland. Planning for tomorrow's trip, I check the Seattle weather forecast via the Web, then leap to a University of California survey archive to glean information for this book. Gazing through my double-glazed window, I look across a landscaped courtyard to a state-of-the-art library that feeds to my desktop screen information hidden among millions of published articles. What a different world from the one I was born into barely half a century ago—a world without broadcast television, fax machines, computers, jets, or cell phones.

The network news, cabled into my home on one of the dozens of available channels, has recently headlined new peace treaties. Northern Ireland is resolving years of strife. Russians and Americans, Israelis and Palestinians, South African blacks and whites, have taken steps toward a new world order by agreeing to turn more swords into plowshares. Communism is dying. Democracy is thriving. Military budgets are shrinking and bases are closing. Not facing (as I write) wars overseas or riots at home, we get our blood pumping with movie images of dinosaurs, extraterrestrial assaults, mutants, and icebergs.

Ethnic strife and hate crimes still haunt humanity, but in our part of the world bigotry is more gauche and diversity more accepted than ever before. The environment is under assault, but we have awakened to the perils of deforestation, ozone depletion, and global warming and are taking steps to contain the damage. (We middle-aged adults drive cars that get twice the mileage and produce a twentieth the pollution of our first cars.) Our economy has produced a growing underclass. Yet our average disposable income in constant dollars is more than double that of the mid-1950s. This enables our having, among the other accouterments of our unprecedented national wealth, twice as many cars per person today as then and our eating out two and half times as often.

More good news is bursting from all around:

- Although population has doubled since World War II, food production has tripled and food is cheaper than ever before.
- Welfare rolls are shrinking as joblessness reaches a quarter-century low.
- Inflation—the "cruelest tax"—is at a 30-year low, interest rates have moderated, the dollar rides strong, and the stock market has touched undreamed-of heights.
- The prices of cars, air travel, gasoline, and hamburgers are at record real-dollar lows. The half gallon of milk that cost the average American 39 minutes of work in 1919 now requires only 7 minutes.
- The national budget, faster than anyone dared expect, has a substantial *surplus*.
- Since the early 1990s, the AIDS death rate has plummeted.

- Over the past half century, performance on intelligence tests has been rising, and race and class differences have lessened somewhat.
- Heavy drinking rates, hard liquor consumption, and drunken driving fatalities are declining.
- New drugs are shrinking our tumors and enlarging our sexual potency.

And would any of us really wish to have braved the family life of a century ago? Without indoor plumbing? With less electricity generated each year than we now consume in a day? When trivial infections might take a life and when people feared the two leading causes of death—tuberculosis and pneumonia? (From 1900 to the present, life expectancy has risen from 47 to 76 years.)

In 1999, Joyce and Paul Bowler—a couple with a keen interest in past ways of life—were selected from among 450 applicants to Britain's Channel 4 network to spend three months with four of their children living the middle-class life of 1900 (which at the time must have seemed like a cuppa tea compared to working-class life). After just a week of rising at 5:30 each morning, preparing food like the Victorians, wearing corsets, shampooing with a mixture of egg, lemon, borax, and camphor, and playing parlor games by gaslight at night, they were "close to calling it quits." They endured. But lacking a surrounding community of other "Victorian" families, the realities of life in the early 1900s lacked the romantic appeal of *Upstairs Downstairs*.

In *The Way We Never Were: American Families and the Nostalgia Trap*, Stephanie Coontz reminds us of the way families *really* were.

Children were exploited. In Pennsylvania mines at the turn of the 20th century, 120,000 children were at work, most of whom started laboring by age 11. Children were one-fourth of the workers in southern textile mills. Seven-year-olds sometimes worked twelve-hour shifts before falling asleep on the job and being carried to bed unwashed.

Families were often broken—by death. In colonial times, mortality reduced the average length of marriage to a dozen years. Four in ten children lost a parent by age 21. As late as 1940, 1 in 10 children did not live with either parent, more than double today's 1 in 25. In 1850, when only 2 percent of the population lived past 65 and many people were migrating, few children had ties with their grandparents. Today, "for the first time in history," notes sociologist Arlene Skolnick, "the average couple has more parents living than it has children. It is also the first era when most of the parent-child relationship takes place after the child becomes an adult." Before 1900, only 4 in 10 women married, raised children, and enjoyed the empty nest with their spouse—because most women either died before marriage, never married, died before children were born or grown, or were widowed before age 50. And consider the poems unwritten, the music never composed, the philosophy never completed, because Keats died at 25, Mozart at 35, Pascal at 39.

The social safety net had gaping holes. At the beginning of the 20th century, we had no social security system. Divorced fathers were not obligated to pay child support. One in five children lived in orphanages, often because their impoverished parents could not support them.

Most people had limited educational opportunities. In the bad old days of a century ago, only half of 5- to 19-year-olds were in school (compared with more than 90 percent today). Only 3.5 percent of 18-year-olds were graduating from high school. Today, 8 in 10 adults have at least a high school education.

Women had restricted opportunities. A half century ago, only 1 in 5 Americans approved "of a married woman earning money in business or industry if she has a husband capable of supporting her." Today, 80 percent approve. Thus, 6 in 10 married women are now in the paid work force—up from 4 in 10 a half century ago and 1 in 7 a century ago. With greater economic independence, today's women are more likely to marry for love and less likely to endure abuse out of economic need. America's married women, whether employed or not, still devote twice as many hours to household tasks as do their husbands. But men's participation has doubled since 1965, putting them more often in front of the stove, behind the vacuum cleaner, and over the diaper-changing table. Today's men and women are more likely to share opportunities, responsibilities, and power.

Minorities were shunned. Within the memory of many living individuals, some public accommodations offered "colored" and "white" toilets, those with disabilities were ignored, and gays and lesbians hid from public loathing. If we have not yet achieved "the Great Society," we have improved upon yesterday's unjust society.

Ergo, however great our present problems, the past is no golden age to which we would willingly return if only we could. Yesterday was not the best of times, *today* is the best of times. Seen in the rose-tinted rearview mirror, yesterday may *seem* like a golden age. But even the wholesome '50s was the decade of McCarthyism, segregation, the Korean War, and air-raid drills and bomb shelters. Golden ages do happen, notes political scientist John Mueller. "But we are never actually *in* them," because "no matter how much better the present gets, the past gets better faster in reflection."

In his own golden age of life, my optimistic friend Sir John Templeton is one who does see the present as the best of times. In *Is Progress Speeding Up?* he concludes that things are not only getting better, they are getting better faster than ever, making this "a wonderful time to be alive!"

How true. Yet there is more to the story.

It Is the Worst of Times

We are better paid, better fed, better housed, better educated, and healthier than ever before, and with more human rights, faster communication, and more convenient transportation than we have ever known. Ironically, however, for 30-plus years—from 1960 until the early 1990s—America slid into a deepening social recession that dwarfed the comparatively milder and briefer economic recessions that often dominated our news and politics. Had you fallen asleep in 1960 and awakened in the 1990s, would you—overwhelmed by all the good tidings—feel pleased at the cultural shift? Here are some other facts that would greet you. Since 1960, as we will see,

- The divorce rate has doubled.
- The teen suicide rate has tripled.
- The recorded violent crime rate has quadrupled.
- The prison population has quintupled.
- The percentage of babies born to unmarried parents has (excuse the pun) sextupled.
- Cohabitation (a predictor of future divorce) has increased sevenfold.

Fig. 1.1 The American Paradox

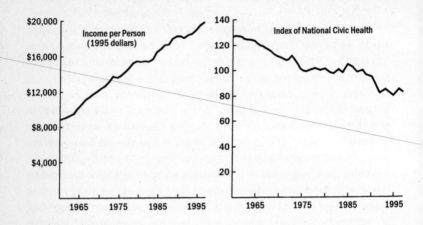

- Depression has soared—to ten times the pre–World War II level, by one estimate.

The National Commission on Civic Renewal combined social trends such as these in creating its 1998 "Index of National Civic Health"—which has plunged southward since 1960. Bertrand Russell once said that the mark of a civilized human is the capacity to read a column of numbers and weep. Can we weep for all the crushed lives behind these numbers? It is hard to argue with Al Gore: "The accumulation of material goods is at an all-time high, but so is the number of people who feel an emptiness in their lives."

At the epicenter of America's social recession are children and youth. Writing with Elizabeth Gilman, Yale psychologist Edward Zigler, co-founder of Head Start, reported a consensus among researchers: "In the past 30 years of monitoring the indicators of child well-being, never have the indicators looked so negative." Across America, children are having children and men are fathering children with little commitment to mother or child. In 1960 just over 1 in 10 children did not live with two parents. Today, a third do not. In a recent survey, American Psychological Association members rated "the decline of the nuclear family" as today's number-one threat to mental health. Urie Bronfenbrenner, a respected developmental psychologist, describes the trends starkly: "The present state of children and families in the United States represents the greatest domestic problem our nation has faced since the founding of the Republic. It is sapping our very roots." Speaking to the National Press Club in late 1998, American Psychological Association president Martin Seligman was struck by a "serious paradox": "Every statistic we have on the 'objective' well-being of young Americans is going north. And every statistic we have on their demoralization, on depression, is going in the other direction."

Facing this cultural erosion, can we—without yearning for an unreal past or squashing basic liberties—expose the corrosive social forces at work and renew our social fabric? And what are the corrosive forces? How is it that things could have gone so well materially and so poorly socially? In other ways, too, these are hardly the best of times, notes Cornell economist Robert Frank in *Luxury Fever*. Americans are spending more hours at work, fewer hours sleeping, and fewer hours with friends and family. "Traffic has grown considerably more congested; savings rates have fallen precipitously; personal bankruptcy filings are at an all-time high; and there is at least a widespread perception that employment security has fallen sharply."

Radical Individualism

Part of the explanation lies in the radical individualism familiar to us in contemporary America's pop psychology and libertarian values. Do your own thing. Seek your own bliss. Challenge authority. If it feels good, do it. Shun conformity. Don't force your values on others. Assert your personal rights (to own guns, sell pornography, do business free of regulations). Protect your privacy. Cut taxes and raise executive pay (personal income takes priority over the common good). To love others, first love yourself. Listen to your own heart. Prefer solo spirituality to communal religion. Be self-sufficient. Expect others likewise to believe in themselves and to make it on their own. Such sentiments define the heart of economic and social individualism, which finds its peak expression in modern America.

The celebration and defense of personal liberty lies at the heart of the old American dream. It drives our free market economy and underlies our respect for the rights of all. In democratic countries that guarantee what Americans consider basic freedoms, people live more happily than in those that don't. Migration patterns testify to this reality. Yet for today's radical individualism, we pay a price: a social recession that imperils children, corrodes civility, and diminishes happiness. When individualism is taken to an extreme, individuals become its ironic casualties.

To cope with the casualties at the base of the social cliffs, we can expand our social ambulance services. Or we can do as this book advises and build guardrails at the top. We can dream a new American dream—one that renews our social ecology with values and policies that balance "me thinking" with "we thinking."

What Is the New American Dream?

To counter radical individualism and cultural corrosion a new, inclusive social renewal movement is emerging: one that affirms liberals' indictment of the demoralizing effects of poverty and conservatives' indictment of toxic media models; one that welcomes liberals' support for family-friendly workplaces and conservatives' support for committed relationships; one that agrees with liberals' advocacy for children in all sorts of families and conservatives' support for marriage and co-parenting. Viewing the contest between liberal and conservative ideas, we can respond like the Dodo in *Alice's Adventures in Wonderland*: "*Everyone* has won and *all* must have prizes!"

Without suppressing our differences do we not—whether self-described liberals or conservatives—share a vision of a better world? Is it not one that rewards initiative but restrains exploitative greed? that balances individual rights with communal well-being? that respects diversity while embracing unifying ideals? that is tolerant of other cultures without being indifferent to moral issues? that protects and heals our degrading physical and social environments? In our utopian social world, adults and children will together enjoy their routines and traditions. They will have close relationships with extended family and with supportive neighbors. Children will live without fear for their safety or the breakup of their families. Fathers and mothers will jointly nurture their children; to say "He fathered the child" will parallel the meaning of "She mothered the child." Free yet responsible media will entertain us with stories and images that exemplify heroism, compassion, and committed love. Reasonable and rooted moral judgments will motivate compassionate acts and enable noble and satisfying lives.

Mapping the Quest

This dreamed-of world is, as yet, far from our real world. Still facing a large gap between the ideal and real, the advent of the new millennium is a fitting time to confront the reality of America's post-1960 social recession, to identify its roots, and to celebrate the quest for a healthier and happier American culture.

And that is my plan for this book. I begin by describing the post-1960 sexual revolution and the decline of marriage, then link these trends (and associated poverty, dislocations, and distractions) to children's plummeting well-being and to the increase in violence. Meanwhile, despite increasing affluence, Americans paradoxically were also becoming more miserable—slightly less happy and much more often depressed. Chapters 6 and 7 describe our burgeoning materialism and individualism, and the increasing rich-poor gap (the rising economic tide has lifted the yachts faster than the dinghies). These changing values and economic realities, along with demonstrably corrosive media models, have fed the social recession.

Gandhi would not have been surprised. Sixty-plus years ago he warned of "seven social sins" that can destroy a nation: politics without principle, wealth without work, commerce without morality, pleasure without conscience, education without character, science without humanity, and worship without sacrifice. The chapters to come will touch on most of these sins, showing how they push people off the social precipice—and how we can build those guardrails.

Building those guardrails requires shifting our focus from operating social ambulance services to prevention. This parallels what cities have done in shifting from firefighting to fire prevention. Rather than wait for fires and deal with the casualties, we now require fire-resistant building materials, smoke detectors, and sprinkling systems. Voila! even as the population grew, fire deaths plunged from 7,645 in 1960 to 3,761 in 1995.

One of those guardrails must be socially responsible media. In an earlier era, an awakened public consciousness sensitized us to racist media images of shuffling, dimwitted African-Americans and made such depictions gauche. This media reform reflected citizenship without censorship. Today, people are similarly awakening to the conclusive findings of research (described in Chapter 8) on how the media's false images of reality affect children's thinking and acting. As the civil rights and women's movements did earlier, today's new social ecology movement will prompt our media producers to rethink their portrayals of human relations.

Another hopeful harbinger is the renewed place of character education in America's public schools. As Chapter 9 explains, character education organizations are offering curricula for infusing character development—focused on values shared across a diverse community—into classrooms, lunchrooms, and school sports. While attending three White House conferences on character education, I have been increasingly heartened by the agreement among representatives of groups from the Children's Defense Fund to Focus on the Family—that schools should be "moral communities" in which educators work at teaching children to be both smart and good. Given the cultural corrosion and given the impossibility of value-free schools, say the new character educators, we had best get intentional about identifying and effectively teaching our shared values. There even is surprising agreement on teaching, as part of comprehensive sex education, that good and healthy sex occurs in a context of mutual commitment (a fact of life emphasized by the new nonpartisan National Campaign to Reduce Teen Pregnancy).

Finally, Chapter 10 reports a growing conviction that a loss of meaning—what Hillary Rodham Clinton has called a "spiritual vacuum"—also underlies the breakdown of civility and community. Polls, books, news magazines, and movies and television all evidence a growing spiritual hunger, as does the interest in supposed paranormal phenomena. Drawing on research and anecdote, I consider the links between faith and character, faith and altruism, and faith and social reform movements. And I suggest how social psychological principles might be harnessed by those wishing to deepen their individual or collective spirituality.

Our post-1960 trajectory therefore need not portend our future. As social consciousness rouses, more people are beginning to veer off the well-traveled road of materialism and individualism. The new American dream is pointing us toward priorities and policies that

- welcome children into families with mothers and fathers that love them and into an environment that nurtures families;

- encourage initiative and restrain exploitation, thus building a more compassionate market economy that supports and shrinks the underclass;
- protect both basic liberties and communal well-being, enabling diverse people to advance their common good;
- encourage close relationships within extended families and with supportive neighbors and caring friends—people who celebrate when you're born, care about you as you live, and miss you when you're gone;
- develop children's capacities for empathy, self-discipline, and honesty;
- provide media that offer social scripts of kindness, civility, attachment, and fidelity;
- regard relationships as covenants and sexuality not as mere recreation but as life-uniting and love-renewing;
- take care of the soul, by developing a deeper spiritual awareness of a reality greater than self and of life's resulting meaning, purpose, and hope.

Harbingers of this renewal are already emerging, like crocuses blooming at winter's end. Signs of what Everett Carll Ladd calls a "silent revolution"—a renewal of civic life—are springing up. People are beginning to understand the costs as well as the benefits of the unbridled pursuit of the old American dream—individually achieved wealth. In increasing numbers, neighborhoods are organizing, foundations are taking initiatives, youths are volunteering, scholars are discerning, faith-based institutions are tackling local problems, and civic renewal organizations are emerging. Government and corporate decision makers are becoming more agreeable to family-supportive tax and benefit policies. Supported by new gender and cross-cultural research, many of us are developing a renewed appreciation for the importance of our human bonds. A new communitarian movement offers a "third way"—an alternative to the individualistic civil libertarianism of the left and the economic libertarianism of the right. It implores us, in the words of Martin Luther King, Jr., "to choose between chaos and community," to balance our needs for independence and attachment, liberty and civility, "me thinking" and "we thinking." Therein lies the hope that, avoiding the extremes of both anarchy and repression, America will revalue her children and remember her future.

We cannot, and would not, return to the 19th century, or even the 1950s. As Alan Ehrenhalt has written, "We don't want the 1950s back. We want to edit them." Discard the patriarchy, the political bosses, and the old typewriters and beehive hairdos, but keep the safe streets, intact families, and sense of civility and community. To get there, we must build from where we are. As President Clinton told the 1998 American Association for the Advancement of Science meeting, "We must envision the future we intend to create." To understand the present and envision the future—that is what this book is about.

CHAPTER 2

The Sexual Swing

Change the way people think, and things will never be the same.
—STEVEN BIKO, South African civil rights martyr

In 1974, a virtuous Jimmy Carter told Department of Housing and Urban Development employees, "Those of you who are living in sin— I hope you'll get married." Some people hooted at Carter's fatherly advice, others admired his fidelity and integrity. By 1998, the president's fidelity and integrity seemed less an issue. Polls showed that only one-third of Americans believed Bill Clinton's initial denial of a sexual affair with 21-year-old White House intern Monica Lewinsky. Yet nearly two-thirds judged his personal moral behavior "not relevant" to how he should be judged in office. (My point concerns public attitudes, not the president's behavior.) Moreover, following the allegations Clinton's overall approval rating shot up to its highest level ever. The gist of the public reaction seemed to be: I think he exploited the power of his office in committing adultery with a wide-eyed intern barely older than his daughter—behavior for which most corporate officers, college professors, and military officers would be sacked. I think he lied about it. I'm not indifferent about this—I think his personal moral standards are the lowest of our recent presidents, for which he should be censured. But hey, boys will be boys. Clinton isn't the first president to have lied. Besides, the guy is doing his job. The economy is booming. Prosecutor Kenneth Starr should get off his back.

With astonishing speed, Western culture is changing. Change hardly is new to cultures formed by the Enlightenment and the Industrial

Revolution. But during the thin slice of years since 1960 the pace of change has accelerated. Consider one key ingredient of this new cultural revolution: the sexual revolution.

- Premarital sex, once not-okay, is now, for most, okay. In surveys by the Centers for Disease Control and Prevention in the 1990s, 4 in 10 ninth graders—who but a few years ago were more patiently awaiting adulthood—reported having had intercourse.
- Three million teenagers annually contract a sexual transmitted disease.
- The number of children having children—what Jesse Jackson has called "babies having babies"—has jumped sharply. In 1960, 92,000 unmarried teens had babies; 380,000 did in 1997. In 1960, 15 percent of births to 15- to 19-year-olds were outside of marriage. In 1997, 78 percent were.

Shame, the emotion that reveals a culture's moral norms, less often accompanies sexual transgressions. Unwed teenage parents have been admired as cheerleaders, homecoming queens and kings, and class presidents. In the adult world, recreational sex has become, in the words of a Broadway song, "just the friendliest thing two people can do." Former senator Gary Hart, who was once forced out of presidential politics by his extramarital philandering, in 1995 contemplated seeking his old Senate seat. "The whole political world has grown up," he explained, apparently believing the culture has become inured to sexual misconduct. Daniel Patrick Moynihan believes the growth is not upward. Rather, he argues, we have "defined deviancy down."

The sexual revolution has sparked a culture war in the 1990s over sex in the classroom, sex in the media, and sex on the Internet. The war also rages inside each of us, for human nature is a battlefield of opposing tendencies seeking balance. Our arousing (sympathetic) and calming (parasympathetic) nervous systems, our neural equilibrium between excitation and inhibition, our regulation of hunger and satiety, our tension between sexuality and restraint—id and superego—all involve carefully negotiated balances between opposing forces.

Cultures struggle to balance desire for sexual gratification with the need for its control. Every culture offers a mix of permissions and taboos (at the very least, a taboo against incest). Anthropologists have told us the mix has varied, supposedly from one South Pacific island where people claimed to be having nightly intercourse by age 18 to an island off the Irish coast, where married partners remained partly clothed while engaging in sex, which virtually never involved female

orgasm. In a recent survey of 4,688 unmarried Chinese students entering Hong Kong's six universities, only 2.5 percent reported having had
sexual intercourse. Only 18 students—less than one-half of one percent—reported having had sex with more than one partner. In Shanghai, too, self-restraint rather than self-gratification is the premarital
norm. Western cultures offer varying blends of their permissive Greco-
Roman heritage, which cherishes individual freedom and erotic expression, and their more restrained Judeo-Christian heritage, which values
God-given sexuality within the context of committed love.

Historical Trends

The balance point between sexual expression and restraint varies
not only across cultures but over time. In modern Europe, the late
1700s through the mid-1800s produced what historian Edward Shorter
calls "a revolution in eroticism." In Paris, prostitution tripled in the first
half of the 1800s. In France and England, the rape rate surged. Starting in the mid-1700s, the percentage of births to unmarried women
dramatically escalated, suggesting increased premarital intercourse.

But time's pendulum swings. In late 19th century England, the
family life of Queen Victoria became the social ideal. Victorianism
embraced such virtues as a sense of duty, hard work, thrift, and re-
spectable, restrained behavior. In his haphazard sampling of Americans in the 1940s, Alfred Kinsey found echoes of Victorianism. Among
women born before 1900, only 14 percent reported having had premarital intercourse by age 25.

The pendulum swung again with the sexual revolution of the 1920s.
This, too, was a time of seeming family crisis. Divorce rates rose. Birthrates fell. Sexual morality loosened. Many women coming of age in the
flapper era rebelled against their parents' Victorian sexual code. For the
first time in Western history, women's shortening skirts revealed their
legs. In the Kinsey sample, reported premarital intercourse by age 25
surged to 36 percent among women born in the decade after 1900.

During the 1950s, a decade that temporarily reversed 20th century
trends, the revolution lagged as the divorce rate dipped from its postwar highs and people married earlier, shrinking the number of passion-
filled years before marriage. "Young people were not taught how to 'say
no,'" explains Stephanie Coontz—"they were simply handed wedding
rings." Fertility increased, and the age for first parenthood fell.

Then, from 1960 to the mid-1990s, the Ozzie and Harriet interlude gave way to the great culture shift. Although the latest phase of the sexual revolution was well under way by 1969, 68 percent of Americans still told Gallup interviewers that it was "wrong for a man and a woman to have sexual relations before marriage." By 1991, people 50 and older—those whose adolescent values formed before 1960—remained in 62 percent agreement that premarital sex is wrong. Among younger generations a different story was unfolding. Just 23 percent of 18- to 29-year-olds judged premarital sex wrong. The National Opinion Research Center's annual social survey confirms the Gallup findings: In less than 30 years, sexual attitudes had undergone a sea change.

Elizabeth Winship, author since 1963 of the syndicated teen advice column "Ask Beth," illustrates: "Kids used to write me about acne, bras, long hair (boys'), short hair (girls'), nylons, tube tops, 'Mom makes me come home at 9:30!' and 'Should I kiss a boy on the first date?' Now they write me about venereal warts and condoms and suicide and drug addiction and 'Mom makes me come home at 1 A.M., and none of the other kids have to!' and 'Should I sleep with a boy on the first date? I'm 13 [12, 11, or even 10] years old.'"

Sixteen-year-old Tory speaks for many of her generation: "As long as two people love each other, there's nothing wrong with making love. I don't understand why it's only supposed to be okay if you're married. I mean why is getting married such a big deal?" Sex, in this view, is simply two good friends enjoying each other's bodies.

Seventeen magazine, which helps write sexual scripts for many of its 2 million subscribers, reflects the changing times. In the 1970s, the magazine's advice columnists (writing for girls who "don't talk to their parents," explained the editor-in-chief), offered a morality that favored the pleasures of long-term commitment over instant gratification. In the mid-1990s, their advice more often catered to radical individualism: "If you don't let somebody pressure you into having sex, why should you let somebody else pressure you into *not* having sex?" "Plenty of girls enjoy sex and want nothing more than a physical relationship," observed another columnist matter-of-factly (although without directly encouraging teen sexual activity).

When attitudes change, behaviors are often not far behind (or may even be out ahead). By 1990, 72 percent of high school seniors responding to a Centers for Disease Control "youth risk behavior" survey reported having had intercourse. Casual sex had become an alternative lifestyle, symbolized by Magic Johnson's "womanizing," Wilt Chamberlain's self-proclaimed 20,000 conquests, and William Kennedy Smith's having it on the lawn with a woman whom he misrecalled as "Cathie" (and who called him "Mike").

The Gender Gap

The pendulum swings, but a double standard endures. In a 1991 Gallup survey, almost two-thirds of young men, but only one-third of their female contemporaries, welcomed still "more acceptance of sexual freedom." A UCLA/American Council on Education survey of 267,000 new collegians in 1998 revealed a similar gender divide. "If two people really like each other, it's all right for them to have sex even if they've known each other for a very short time," agreed 54 percent of men but only 28 percent of women.

The gender gap carries over to behavior, as psychologists Russell Clark and Elaine Hatfield discovered in 1978, when they sent some average-looking student research assistants strolling across the Florida State University quadrangle. Spotting an attractive person of the other sex, the researchers would approach and say, "I have been noticing you around campus and I find you to be very attractive. Would you go to bed with me tonight?" The women all declined, some with obvious irritation ("What's wrong with you, creep, leave me alone"). But 75 percent of the men readily agreed, often with comments like "Why do we have to wait until tonight?" Somewhat astonished by the results, Clark and Hatfield repeated their study in 1982 and twice more during the AIDS era of the late '80s. Each time, virtually no women, but half or more of the men, agreed to go to bed with a stranger. The gender divide in sexual selectivity and initiative occurs worldwide. "With few exceptions anywhere in the world," cross-cultural psychologist Marshall Segall and his colleagues report, "males are more likely than females to initiate sexual activity."

Some evolutionary theorists are unsurprised: sperm are cheap, and nature has selected males who spread their genes by fertilizing many females; females, who make a greater investment in bringing a fetus to term and then nursing it, naturally invest their reproductive capital more selectively. To paraphrase Robert Hinde, men seek to reproduce widely, women wisely. And that, the evolutionists argue, helps explain the double standard that still considers Magic Johnson a hero, and puts his face on product ads, while considering a woman who has sex with countless men a tramp or a whore.

Promiscuity's Price

Is protected casual sex, psychologically speaking, safe sex? Liberated from "erotophobic" inhibitions, are consenting individuals, even if mere acquaintances, made happier by spontaneously enjoying their natural impulses, celebrating their bodies, giving and receiving pleasure? Is recreational sex—sex lite—indeed "just the friendliest thing two people can do?" Is our cultural shift from restraint to expression, from self-denial to self-gratification, from individualism to radical individualism, a net advance for human well-being? Are we recovering the refreshing self-acceptance that marked the biblical utopia of Eden, where man and woman "were both naked, and were not ashamed"? In the biblical view, sexual intimacy is, after all, a gift from the Creator who, having made male and female, judged this sexual reality as "very good." "If God created the world, He created sex," reasoned John Updike, "and one way to construe our inexhaustible sexual interest is as a form of the praise of creation."

Yet many sober minds now question the wisdom of sex without commitment. An unfulfilled Health and Human Services national health objective for the year 2000 aims to reduce the proportion of 17-year-olds who have had intercourse to under 40 percent. A new National Campaign to Reduce Teen Pregnancy aims for a 30 percent drop in pregnancy among adolescents in ten years. To see why, consider the risks associated with casual sex. Over time, increasing premarital sexual activity—more sex with more partners—has coincided with increases in sexually transmitted disease, rape, nonmarital pregnancy, cohabitation, and divorce.

Is this just a happenstance? These trends have also coincided with increases in everything from school soccer programs to restaurants. The correlations, however, occur not only over time at the societal level but across individuals. Early promiscuity helps predict an individual's statistical risk of sexually transmitted disease, sexual coercion and rape, extramarital sex, nonmarital pregnancy, cohabitation—and, for some of these reasons, the risk of future marital unhappiness and divorce. Joan Kahn and Kathryn London report a striking finding from the government-sponsored National Survey of Family Growth: among white women married between 1965 and 1983, nearly 4 in 10 nonvirgin brides, but only a quarter of today's sexual minority—virgin brides— had separated or divorced by 1988.

Like adult smokers, who overwhelmingly regret the habit they picked up as teenagers, many young adults regret their teenage sexual behavior. "I should have waited" is a common response. One recent survey invited more than 900 21-year-old New Zealanders (whose sexual patterns are similar to those of Americans) to look back on their first sexual experience. Now older and wiser, 54 percent of the young women (though only 16 percent of the men) wished they had waited longer. Among women whose first sexual experiences happened before they were 16, 70 percent wished they had waited.

National health policy discourages teenage sex partly because it yields so much sexually transmitted disease. In 1960, there were few cases of viral sexually transmitted diseases (STDs). Today, both the Alan Guttmacher Institute and the Institute of Medicine report, 12 million Americans annually contract a viral STD (not including such bacterial diseases as chlamydia, syphilis, and gonorrhea). More than 60 percent of these new infections occur in persons under 25. One-fourth—three million new cases each year—afflict teenagers.

Teenage girls' less mature biological development and fewer protective antibodies make them especially vulnerable to STD and associated risks of becoming infertile and developing certain cancers. Cervical cancer, women's second most common malignancy after breast cancer, is far more common among women who as adolescents became sexually active with multiple partners. A 1996 National Institutes of Health panel attributes this to the cellular structure of adolescents' reproductive organs.

Behind this modern epidemic is increased sexual mixing. As more people have more sex partners, the spread of STDs accelerates. Few people comprehend the mathematics of sexually transmitted disease. Imagine an island on which, up to now, all people have been virgins. Now assume that Pat has sex with nine people, each of whom similarly has sex with nine people, who in turn have sex with nine others. How many "phantom" sex partners (past partners of partners) will Pat have? Ohio State researchers Laura Brannon and Timothy Brock report that the actual number—511—is more than five times the average student's guess. If you are (microbiologically speaking) sleeping with everyone your lover has ever slept with—and with everyone your lover's lovers have slept with—the number of your phantom partners might surprise you.

The good news is that condom use greatly reduces risk of HIV transmission—a tenfold reduction, say Steven D. Pinkerton and Paul R. Abramson. The bad news is that condom users are still one-tenth as likely as those having unprotected sex to become infected. (Condoms can leak HIV.) "It is a disservice," concluded Susan Weller after assembling the available studies, "to encourage the belief that condoms *will prevent* sexual transmission of HIV." With certain other STDs that are transmitted skin to skin, condoms are less useful. Human papilloma viruses, for example, are responsible for most genital cancers.

Nonmarital Births

National health policy also discourages teenage sex because it produces so many accidental pregnancies. More than half of America's annual pregnancies—some 3.4 million of 6 million—are unintended. Thanks partly to the sexual revolution, the proportion of babies born each year to unmarried women has, as everyone by now knows, mushroomed. By the mid-1990s the trend had leveled off at a cruising altitude of 1 in 3 births. The sixfold increase since 1960 stemmed from three trends: a decreasing birthrate among married women, an increasing number of unmarried women, and (until recently) an increasing birthrate among them. The increasing nonmarital birthrate resulted from both increasing nonmarital conceptions and a halved proportion marrying before the child's birth.

There is some good news here. Almost all of the past decade's increase in births to unmarried women occurred in two-parent cohabiting unions. The bad news is that these unions are unstable (only a tenth last more than five years). Factoring in today's high divorce rate, more children than ever are experiencing family disruption.

Increasingly, then, the single-parent family arises not only from family breakup but from the failure of two-parent families to form. During the 1950s, 4 out of 5 first children were conceived by married women; during the first half of the 1990s, slightly less than half were. By the early 1990s, the total number of father-absent homes being created by unwed births, formerly a small fraction of all father-absent homes, roughly equaled the number created by divorce. Moreover, this

Fig. 2.1 Births to Unmarried Parents (% of all births)

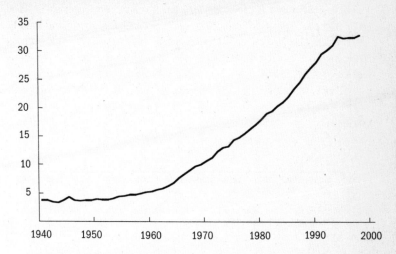

Source: National Center for Health Statistics annual "Report of Final Natality Statistics," *Monthly Vital Statistics Reports*

increasingly common 1990s-style absentee father is much more likely than a divorced father to fit the stereotype of a "deadbeat dad"—a man who is emotionally and financially unsupportive.

With this trend has come a new acceptance of single parenthood and a fading of the shame that once accompanied having an illegitimate child. In 1996 pop singer Madonna, four months pregnant with the help of her fitness instructor, who performed "the father gig" for her, was said by her publicist to be "deliriously happy." Other recent celebrity single moms by choice include Rosie O'Donnell, Michelle Pfeiffer, Donna Mills, Kate Jackson, Diane Keaton, and Jodie Foster (whom *People* described as "the perfect role model"). Detroit Lions football hero Barry Sanders, who once proclaimed his celibacy and opposition to premarital sex, later happily acknowledged that he is the father of an infant son in Dallas. "I feel great about it, it's pretty nice," he explained. "I've just changed." Responding to a 1998 *Sports Illustrated* article on NBA players fathering out-of-wedlock children, Marie Jackson, mother of Indiana Pacers point guard Mark Jackson, said, "This is a new day

Fig 2.2 First Children Conceived in Marriage

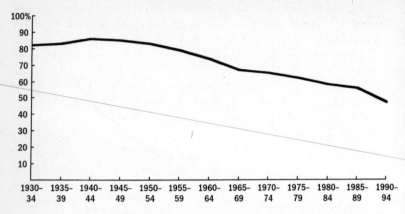

Source: Amara Bachu, "Trends in Marital Status of U.S. Women at First Birth," U.S. Bureau of the Census Population
Division Working Paper No. 20, March 1998

and a new era, and there are millions of children born out of wedlock
in society today, so why focus on these players who are just living in
what society dictates today?"

Given such examples, one can understand why 51 percent of high
school seniors in 1995 viewed having a child without being married
as "experimenting with a worthwhile lifestyle or not affecting anyone
else." Or why 7 in 10 Americans under 30 now view "having a child
without being married" as "always" or "in some situations" acceptable.
(Even in a midwestern town like Eau Claire, Wisconsin, April Schuldt,
five months pregnant, could be elected homecoming queen.) And why,
rather than marry under the shotgun, as did 60 percent of women
having a baby conceived premaritally during the early 1960s, their male
partners are now more likely to hit and run. By the early 1990s, only 24
percent of such women made it to the altar before the delivery room.

The nonmarital birth trend affects some groups more than others.
Many people "know" that most of today's nonmarital births occur
among particular population segments—blacks, teens, and women who
will receive Aid to Families with Dependent Children. But this is untrue.

Most nonmarital births occur to women in their 20s, and nearly
half of 15- to 17-year-old teenage moms are impregnated by men 20 or

older. Joe Klein tells of Charlette, who lived on the streets starting at 14 to escape an abusive mother and stepfather. Mickey, in his mid-20s, offered "to protect me, teach me things, discipline my mind. But when I told him I was pregnant, he was gone. . . . I found he had six other children, mostly with younger girls. I was naive, and he took advantage of me."

As often happens, however, the stereotypes do have a kernel of truth. The African-American nuclear family has suffered most. In 1996 the mothers of 70 percent of black newborns did not have a husband. Noting that 55 percent of black families with children under 18 are maintained by the mother (usually single, rather than divorced), former Virginia governor L. Douglas Wilder lamented that "the responsibilities of being a parent in many instances fall to the financially and emotionally deserted, single mothers." Children's Defense Fund president Marian Wright Edelman grieves that "we are on the verge of losing two generations of Black children and youths to drugs, violence, too-early parenthood, poor health and education, unemployment, family disintegration—and to the spiritual and physical poverty that both breeds and is bred by them."

Nevertheless, most nonmarital births occur among whites (who are most of the American people). Although urban populations lead the way, the nonmarital birth trend is culturewide. The proportion of nonmarital births in 1996 in my own conservative midwestern town (Holland, Michigan) lagged the national rate by a dozen years. Yet the nearly eightfold increase since 1960 (from 3 percent to 23 percent) parallels the national trend. Where inner cities have led, the rest of the nation has followed. "Indeed, with respect to the family," notes Rutgers University sociologist David Popenoe, "the characteristics of the African American family pronounced by President Johnson in 1965 to be in a state of 'breakdown' [and what Martin Luther King, Jr., called a 'social catastrophe'] are very similar to the family characteristics of America as a whole [today]!" With the white out-of-wedlock sex and birthrates now growing faster than the black rates, President Clinton argued, "we are going to have equal opportunity for all before you know it. You're laughing to keep from crying, but it's not funny, is it? We're going to see a merger of this. No more race discrimination; more than half of everybody's babies will be born where there was never a marriage. This is a disaster."

Although Clinton's critics may smirk that he, like Elmer Gantry, doth protest too much, voices from across the political spectrum similarly decry this trend, from Planned Parenthood and the Children's Defense Fund on the left to the National Research Council in the middle to Focus on the Family and the American Family Association on the right. They do so partly because it destines so many young mothers and children to lives of educational and economic impoverishment. Moreover, as we will see in Chapter 4, unwed childbearing puts children at increased risk of various social and psychological pathologies. Few anymore dispute the gist of the *Atlantic*'s best-selling issue with the theme "Dan Quayle was right." As Quayle-scorner Molly Ivins acknowledged, "He may be a doofus, but he has a point." Even Candice Bergen, who bore Murphy Brown's father-absent child to TV raves, now reflects, "None of us wanted to send out a message that fathers are dispensable."

Across Europe and North America, 1960 was the cultural turning point—a beginning of the separation of sex from marriage, leading to the separation of reproduction from marriage. Britain's sixfold increase—from 6 percent to 37 percent nonmarital births from 1960 to 1997—closely follows America's. Canada follows close on Britain and America's heels. Whatever social forces underlie this fascinating social phenomenon must be transcultural.

Yet the trend is not yet worldwide. In Japan, for instance, births outside marriage remain a rarity—1.1 percent of all births in 1994. So, too, in China, where people of both sexes rate chastity a very important quality of a potential marriage partner. It seems, then, that whatever is causing America's increasing nonmarital birth proportion is shared by other Western countries.

Does Welfare Promote Unwed Births?

Are welfare benefits the culprit? Writing for the conservative Rockford Institute, Texas banker David Hartman explains why they might be. In Texas, "an unemployed single mother of two is entitled to total benefits equivalent to $16,900 in *after-tax* income (one-third more than the federal poverty guidelines of $12,600). This income for a life of leisure can make illegitimate motherhood highly attractive to a lower-income girl desirous of leaving a poor or unhappy home." Let's set aside the questions whether a mother of two preschoolers lives "a life of leisure," or whether there is a double standard in conservatives arguing that middle-class moms should stay home to care for their young children but poor moms should not (and then complaining about inadequate supervision by poor, single parents). Was Bill Clinton correct to agree with conservatives that "there's no question [reducing welfare benefits] would be some incentive for people not to have dependent children out of wedlock"?

Surely there is practical wisdom in presuming that what we subsidize we get more of, what we penalize we get less of. Compared with individualistic Sweden, Germany—which offers greater rewards for marriage in its tax codes and employment laws—has a higher marriage rate, a lower divorce rate, and many fewer births to unwed mothers. It matters whether tax and benefit policies are family friendly or provide disincentives for marriage. In hindsight, the rule denying a needy woman support for herself and her children if an "able-bodied man" resided with her could hardly have been better calculated to discourage marriage. "These government-sponsored rules help explain why out-of-wedlock births in the black community leapt from 2.1 percent in 1960 to 69.8 percent in 1996," economist Sylvia Ann Hewlett and Afro-American studies professor Cornel West conclude in *The War Against Parents*.

Yet today's welfare benefits are no more than a very small contributor to increasing births outside marriage. There are complicating factors:

- Other industrial countries, which offer more to women and children, have lower teenage pregnancy rates. (America's rate is more than double that of the more generous European countries.)
- States like Mississippi that offer low welfare benefits tend to have *higher* nonmarital birthrates. (Mississippi, with 45 percent of its babies in 1996 born to unmarried parents, led the 50 states.)
- Women on welfare have approximately the same number of children as women not on welfare.
- Family sociologist Andrew Cherlin believes that AFDC increases may have supported the growth of single-parent families during the 1960s. But Princeton sociologist Sara McLanahan and Census Bureau researcher Lynne Casper doubt it, because during the 1960s and early 1970s the rising "illegitimacy ratio" was primarily driven by declining marital birthrates and later marriages. And all these researchers note that since the mid-1970s the nonmarital birth percentage has soared while the real value of AFDC payments has declined. From 1972 to 1992, a welfare benefit package (AFDC plus food stamps) for a family of four with no other income fell from $10,133 to $7,657 in

real, inflation-adjusted dollars, a 26 percent loss. Increased assistance from food banks, soup kitchens, and other charities have helped offset the benefit decline. But the point remains: despite lowering welfare cash incentives, we have more children of children. Such findings in 1994 led 77 poverty researchers to agree that "welfare has not played a major role in the rise of out-of-wedlock childbearing," and in 1995 the Institute of Medicine found that research does not support the popular perception that welfare programs "exert an important influence on non-marital fertility."

- Psychological studies of the behavior and thinking of teenagers engaging in unprotected sex reveal that rarely do they choose to get pregnant. Rather, often deluded by ignorance or impaired by embarrassment or alcohol, they fail to act in ways that prevent pregnancy. Thus, most unwed teenage mothers report surprise at finding themselves pregnant. (If welfare has any influence on nonmarital birthrates, it likely would be less on conception than on the rate of marriage following premarital conception—with fathers perhaps feeling less obligation to marry and provide support.)

Clearly, cultural and psychological forces other than welfare incentives are at work. And reversing the upward spiral will require cultural reforms beyond welfare reform. Moynihan, who understands that blaming welfare for the nonmarital birth increase is "nonsense," observes that "anyone who thinks that cutting benefits can affect sexual behavior doesn't know human nature."

"Regardless of one's political philosophy or moral perspective, the basic facts are disturbing," concludes a National Research Council report. "More than 1 million teenage girls in the United States become pregnant each year, just over 400,000 teenagers obtain abortions, and nearly 470,000 give birth" (nearly two-thirds of whom are unmarried). That, nearly everyone agrees, is indeed a social catastrophe.

Cohabitation

In 1958, the University of Illinois fired a professor who had suggested, through the student newspaper, the desirability of young people testing their love relationship before venturing into marriage. In 1968, Barnard College sophomore Linda Leclair moved in with her boyfriend, a Columbia University junior. In response, a student-faculty committee debated for several months before deciding that Leclair

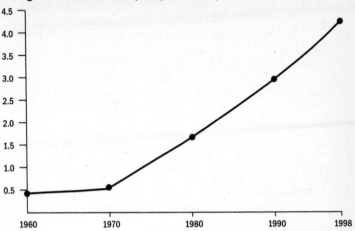

Fig. 2.3 Unmarried Couples (in millions)

could remain a student but would be denied use of the cafeteria, snack bar, and recreation room.

In today's more individualistic culture, most colleges look the other way, because cohabitation has become commonplace. In the United States cohabitation tripled during the 1970s, from a half million to 1.5 million opposite-sex couples, then doubled during the 1980s, to 2.9 million—and has continued increasing to 4.2 million as of 1998. Slightly more than half of 25- to 39-year-old baby boomer women report having cohabited. When today's brides walk down the aisle more than half meet a groom with whom they have already lived together. Indeed, the 1995 National Survey of Family Growth revealed that 47 percent of children now spend some of their first 16 years with a mother and her cohabiting partner. If she were to do it over, that's what Elizabeth Taylor would have done. "I always thought I had to get married," she said recently. "But that's passé now." This is especially so for those who live in Alaska, Vermont, and Nevada, which have the highest percentages of cohabiting partners. Folks in Alabama, Arkansas, and Utah (which have the lowest) are more likely to have their heads turned by cohabiting neighbors.

Similar trends have developed in Canada, Australia, Scandinavia, and elsewhere in Western Europe. In Canada, the number of cohabit-

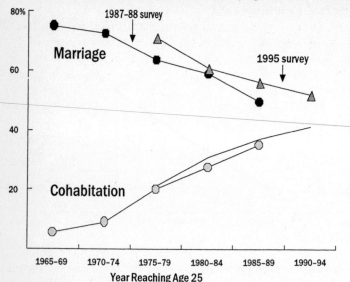

Fig 2.4 Marriage and Cohabitation Rate by Age 25

Source: National Survey of Families and Households, 1987-88, and National Survey of Family Growth, 1995, reported by Larry Bumpass et al.

ing couples rose 28 percent between 1991 and 1996. In Britain the marriage rate dropped by nearly 30 percent just during the 1980s, while the proportion of unmarried women who were cohabiting doubled, from 11 percent to 23 percent. Rabbi Jonathan Romain, noting that 18 of his previous 20 Berkshire weddings had been preceded by cohabitation, has modified his liturgy to say that "you have been sharing much together already, but this day still marks a turning point in your lives." Introducing the revised edition of *Marriage, Divorce, Remarriage* in 1992, Cherlin mused that a more truthful new title would have been *Cohabitation, Marriage, Divorce, More Cohabitation, and Probably Remarriage*.

Is it possible to find a positive side to these trends? Many cohabiting couples enjoy a close, supportive companionship. Many also are testing the marital waters. Among those who cohabit, the most common rationale is to check compatibility before marrying. Considering the doubled divorce rate since 1960, and all the hurting adults and children, wouldn't people be well advised to test drive a marriage before buying? Might not trial marriages—with less risk and less hassle if it doesn't work out—weed out unsuccessful unions before the legal pact? Aren't people who are intimately familiar with their partner's habits, desires, and lifestyle less likely to stumble into an ill-fated marriage? Asked what advice she would give her daughters about men, Sarah Ferguson, the former wife of Prince Andrew, offered, "Get to know them . . . perhaps live with them a bit" before marriage.

In a recent UCLA/American Council on Education survey of 216,000 first-year American college students, 51 percent seemed to express a similar sentiment, agreeing that "a couple should live together before marriage." From the late 1970s to 1995 agreement with a similar statement by American high school students rose from 39 percent to 58 percent. Among American adults cohabiting, more than half of both women and men say an "important" reason is to be "sure they are compatible before marriage."

Alas, the myth crumbles. Most cohabitations break up before marriage. In 1995, only 10 percent of 15- to 44-year-old women reported that their first cohabitation was still intact. But what about those who, after a trial marriage, decide to marry? Ten recent studies concur that couples who cohabit with their spouses-to-be have *higher* divorce rates than those who don't. Several studies illustrate:

- A U.S. survey of 13,000 adults found that couples who lived together before marriage were one-third more likely to separate or divorce within a decade.
- Another national study has followed 1,180 persons since 1980. By 1992, divorces had occurred among 29 percent of those who had cohabited before marriage and 13 percent of those who had not. In the 1995 National Survey of Family Growth, the corresponding divorce percentages were 26 and 15 within five years of marriage.
- A 1990 Gallup survey of still-married Americans also found that 40 percent of those who had cohabited before marrying, but only 21 percent of those who had not, said they might divorce.
- A Canadian national survey of 5,300 women found that those who cohabited were 54 percent more likely to divorce within 15 years.
- A Swedish study of 4,300 women found cohabitation linked with an 80 percent greater risk of divorce.
- And if either partner was a "serial cohabitor"—having previously cohabited with one or more others besides the spouse—the likelihood of divorce is even greater.

Family sociologists no longer debate the link between cohabitation and divorce risk. They are now trying to explain it. William Axinn at the University of Chicago and Arland Thornton at the University of Michigan find support for two possibilities. First, cohabitation attracts people who are more open to terminating unsatisfying relationships. People cohabit and sometimes divorce for the same reason—they just aren't that committed to marriage. Cohabitation is "erotic timidity," argues Maggie Gallagher. "At its core it is about anxiety, commitment with fingers crossed." It sees love as conditional rather than committed. If either partner becomes dissatisfied, he or she can seek bliss elsewhere.

People who cohabit therefore bring a more individualistic ethic to marriage, are more likely to see close relationships as temporary and fragile, are less sure that marriage is right for them, are more accepting of divorce, and are about three times more likely after marriage to have an affair. Said bluntly, the sort of person who would readily cohabit with you is a person who, when the romance fades, might be unfaithful to you and eventually leave you. Sociologists call this a *selection effect*.

There is also a second factor at work: the *causal* effect of cohabitation. The experience of cohabitation decreases endorsement of marriage and increases acceptance of divorce. Over time, those who cohabit without marriage become more approving of dissolving an unfulfilling union. This divorce-accepting attitude increases the odds of later divorce. (It also doesn't help that married people who cohabited rate their marriages as less satisfying than those who did not.)

Women, especially, have paid a price for replacing marriage with cohabitation. Over their lifetimes, women have tended to work and earn less. Thus they have more to lose by replacing a legal partnership with a no-strings-attached relationship. Upon separation or death, cohabitees have limited rights to each other's accumulated assets. The cohabitation revolution has therefore *not* supported women's quest for economic parity with men. Perhaps due to their relative youth, lesser education, greater poverty, and the presence of stepchildren, female cohabitees are also much more likely than married women to be victims of domestic violence. In Canada, they are four times more likely to be assaulted by their partner and eight times more likely to be murdered. In the United States, even after controlling for education, race, age, and gender, people who live together are 1.8 times more likely than married people to have violent arguments, reports University of Chicago sociologist Linda Waite.

Should We Live Together?

In a report for the National Marriage Project, sociologist David Popenoe and social historian Barbara Dafoe Whitehead suggest four principles for those contemplating cohabitation.

1. Consider not living together at all before marriage. There is no evidence that if you cohabit before marriage you will have a stronger marriage than if you don't, and some evidence that you are more likely to break up after marriage. Cohabitation is probably least harmful when both partners are definitely planning to marry, have formally announced their engagement, and have picked a wedding date.

2. Do not make a habit of cohabiting. Contrary to popular wisdom, you do not learn to have better relationships from having multiple cohabiting relationships. In fact, it is a strong predictor of failure in future relationships.

3. Keep cohabitation as short as possible. The longer you live together, the more likely it is that the low-commitment ethic of cohabitation will take hold—the opposite of what is required for a successful marriage.

4. Do not cohabit if children are involved. Cohabiting parents break up at a much higher rate than married parents, and the effects can be devastating and long lasting. Moreover, children of cohabiting unions are at higher risk of sexual abuse and physical violence, including lethal violence, than are children living with married parents.

Excerpted from *Should We Live Together? What Young Adults Need to Know About Cohabitation Before Marriage*, National Marriage Project, Rutgers University

Waite offers more research-based comparisons:

- Married partners tend to enhance their productivity by developing specialized skills; cohabiting partners more often do everything for themselves (being less sure of their partner's sticking around). This helps account for the "marriage premium"—men's greater earnings if married. (The selection of higher-earning men into marriage accounts for only about half the marriage premium.)
- Family members and friends are more likely to invest themselves in getting to know one's married than one's cohabiting partner, and to include the partner in activities, holidays, and financial support.
- After marrying, people often become more religiously active (especially when they have children). When cohabiting, religious involvement typically declines.
- Married dads carry weight with their children and school officials—and have legal obligations to those children—that "Mom's boyfriends" do not.
- Cohabiting couples share a sex life that is at least as active as that of mar-

ried couples their age, but they are less likely to report that their sex is physically or emotionally satisfying. Cohabiting partners are also, depending on the survey, two to five times more likely to acknowledge not being sexually faithful to their partner.

- Cohabiting people are unhappier and more vulnerable to depression—an effect partly attributed to cohabitation's insecurity.
- Married partners often support each other and share property; cohabitants usually fend for themselves. This puts cohabiting women, especially women with children, at a financial disadvantage compared with men and married women. Although cohabiting women seldom share their partner's earnings, they still do more than half the housework.

Reflecting on all these findings (which are especially true of cohabitants who are not engaged to be married), Waite surmises that cohabitation "may represent a new enslavement rather than freedom for women." She argues that society should therefore enact policies that encourage marriage—by allowing landlords to prefer married to cohabiting couples, by removing the marriage penalty from the tax code, by providing health insurance and other benefits to married couples but not to domestic partners (except for gay couples who cannot legally marry), and by reinstating common-law marriage provisions that give longtime cohabiting parents the legal rights and responsibilities of married parents.

A New Sexual Revolution?

Reflecting on these trends in teen sexuality, nonmarital births, and cohabitation one wonders: Has the historical pendulum swung to a point where the pursuit of pleasure is, ironically, amplifying misery? Between the extremes of prudery and license, is it possible for society to welcome pleasure that consecrates commitment? To affirm both intimacy and fidelity? To celebrate sexuality as part of a life-uniting and love-renewing relationship? Such are the ideals of an emerging vision of human sexuality.

Bit by bit, the facts of life assembled in this book are seeping into public consciousness. The individualism that underlies post-1960s materialism and the sexual revolution is being challenged by a new "communitarian" ethos that appreciates what social psychologists are now recognizing as our deep, ancestral "need to belong." And new ideas about character and sex education are shrinking the gap between those who believe we should teach teenagers how to do it safely and those who would teach them why they shouldn't. The new common ground, shared by James Dobson and Jesse Jackson, by Dan Quayle and Hillary Clinton, is that adolescents and the children they will eventually produce thrive best when intercourse awaits adult maturity, if not marriage. If—imagine a utopia—all adolescents were so persuaded, poverty would be reduced (as we will see in Chapter 4). Crime rates would decline (as we will see in Chapter 5). Reproductive health would be safeguarded. The risks of depression and suicide would abate. That many are not yet so persuaded makes teen pregnancy, in President Clinton's words, the nation's "most serious social problem."

Recognizing that education (especially sex education) is never value free, schools are beginning to implement abstinence-promoting comprehensive sex and family life education programs. These "abstinence plus" initiatives are modeled on effective anti-smoking education programs. They teach the facts, engage youth in practicing refusal skills, and articulate the satisfactions that accompany a secure, lifelong, close relationship. These also are among the characteristics of sex education programs eligible for $50 million annually in federal support mandated by a small section of the controversial Welfare Reform Act of 1996.

Indicators suggest that the message is reaching a growing audience, and that increasing numbers in the next generation prefer a culture of commitment—a culture that respects minority rights, women's rights, and gay and lesbian rights—and also believes that true love indeed awaits commitment. Among those indicators:

Permissive attitudes have peaked. Recent surveys showed the highest acceptance ever recorded for premarital sex (in a National Opinion Research Center survey in 1996, 44 percent declared it "not wrong at all," and 55 percent called it "not wrong" in a 1996 Gallup survey). But such acceptance seems to be leveling off, having barely changed since 1991 after three decades of sexual revolution. In a 1998 *Time*/CNN poll, 86 percent (up from 76 percent in 1977) agreed that sexual permissiveness "has led to a lot of the things that are wrong with the country these days." Dr. Laura has replaced Dr. Ruth. Wendy Shalit is promoting "a return to modesty." Among entering collegians—often the vanguard of our future—a sea change toward commitment seems under way. From 1987 to 1998, the proportion who agreed that "if two people like each other, it's all right for them to have sex even if they've known each other for a very short time" dropped from 52 percent to 40 percent. (Because peer influences on adolescents are demonstrably greater than parental influences, adolescents' changing attitudes bode well.)

Teenage sex is subsiding. The number of high school students who acknowledged in the biennial CDC youth survey having had sexual intercourse declined slightly, from 54 percent in 1991 to 48 percent in 1997. Among high school students, virgins are now the majority. Through campaigns like "True Love Waits" some 2.4 million young singles have reportedly pledged abstinence until marriage. With 38 percent of 9th graders still reporting having had intercourse, however, premature sexualization remains high.

Teenage births are ebbing. The 85 percent of adults who recently told Gallup that "the number of children being born to single parents" is a "very serious" or "critical" problem can take heart. Since its 1991 peak, the birthrate among 16- to 19-year-olds had dropped 15 percent by 1997. "Our concerted effort to reduce teen pregnancy is succeeding," exuded Secretary of Health and Human Services Donna Shalala. "The federal government, the private sector, parents, and caregivers are all helping send the same message: Don't become a parent until you are truly ready to support a child."

The racial gap is shrinking. African-American teens led the way, with a 21 percent decline in teenage birthrate. As recently as 1980, half of births to unmarried American women were to African-Americans. By 1996 one-third were. (This change is due, first, to the big increase in the percentage of white women giving birth out of wedlock and, second, to a declining birthrate among unmarried black women.)

Men's movements are revaluing commitment. Across time, across cultures, across situations, and across differing levels of education, religiosity, and peer influence, women's sexuality is more flexible and varying than men's—a phenomenon that research psychologist Roy Baumeister calls the gender difference in "erotic plasticity." This implies, he says, that "a society that needs a change in sexual behavior in order to survive or flourish would do better to target its messages and other pressures at women rather than men. . . . Women present a better prospect for achieving cultural progress than men, at least with re-

CHAPTER 3

The Past and Future of Marriage

The ranks of the optimists who think the family is alive and well have thinned considerably.

—ARLENE SKOLNICK, *Embattled Paradise*

Across time and place, human societies have nearly always included a relatively monogamous bond between men and women, and a bond between parents and their children. Despite the more indiscriminate sexual interests of human males, polygamy, though tolerated by many cultures, is the exception. Monogamy is the rule. Across the world, reports the United Nations' *Demographic Yearbook*, more than 9 in 10 people eventually marry.

"Pair-bonding is a trademark of the human animal," anthropologist Helen Fisher explains. Three recent national surveys by Gallup and the National Opinion Research Center, protecting respondents' anonymity, reveal low levels of infidelity. Contrary to speculation that half or more of married people have affairs, only about 1 in 10 married people acknowledge having had an affair during their current marriage, and about 1 in 50 acknowledge having had sex with someone other than their spouse during the previous year. Faithful attractions greatly outnumber fatal attractions. We flirt, fall in love, and marry—one person at a time.

The pioneering anthropologist Bronislaw Malinowski concurred. There is universal cultural disapproval of casual sexual unions that create a child without a responsible father. "In all human societies the father is regarded by tradition as indispensable. . . . I think that this generalization amounts to a universal sociological law." Although marriages

gard to sexuality." Yet whatever else one might think of them, Promise Keepers rallies and the Million Man March suggest that men's social and sexual consciousness can evolve. When surveyed by the *Washington Post,* 9 out of 10 attendees at the 1997 Promise Keepers rally in Washington agreed that husbands and wives should "share equally" in housework, disciplining children, and making big decisions. Moreover, these movements agree, better to be a responsible dad than a recreational cad.

Will these trends evolve into a redefinition of good sex and a revaluing of commitment? It is far easier to describe the past than to predict the future. But if all of us in religious communities, government, education, business, and the media will consider what makes for healthy societies and good lives, better times may be ahead.

may be arranged or chosen, enabled or not by a dowry or bride price, "marriage and the family have been universally viewed as [civilization's] necessary foundation," adds Elizabeth Fox-Genovese.

The two-parent arrangement makes biological sense. As babies we were all born with large, immature brains and complete dependence on others for food and safety. Historically, children of separated or uninvolved parents were therefore less likely to pass their genes along to posterity than were children whose parents cooperated to nurture them to maturity. The father had primary responsibility for hunting food, the mother for gathering food, and together they fed and protected their offspring. In later agricultural societies, diminished mobility extended the family bonds to other kin, who often lived nearby. Still, within that kin network the strongest bond was that of a man, a woman, and the children who carried their genetic investment. With industrialization, mobility increased, extended family ties waned, and the primacy of nuclear family bonds again strengthened. Francis Fukuyama sums up the anthropological evidence: "nuclear families crop up everywhere. . . . Australian Aborigines, the Trobriand Islanders of the South Pacific, Pygmies, Kalahari bushmen, and the indigenous people of the Amazon all organize themselves into nuclear families."

To an evolutionary psychologist, monogamy under all these arrangements helps children by increasing "paternal certainty" (a father's confidence that a child is his). And paternal certainty increases paternal investment in the child. For the child, having a supportive, protective father around increases survival chances—someone to provide meat and offer protection from other people and natural threats. Because there is more to bringing offspring to maturity than depositing sperm, men and women both increase the chance of leaving descendants by investing in their offspring. Ergo, love between a man and a woman has a genetic payoff.

Children reciprocate their parents' devotion. Among our early social responses—love, fear, aggression—the first and greatest is an intense bond of love. Developmental psychologists call it attachment. As infants, we soon prefer familiar faces and voices. We then coo and gurgle when our parents give us attention. By eight months, we crawl after mother or father and typically let out a wail when separated from them. Reunited, we cling. By keeping infants close to their caregivers, social attachment serves as a powerful survival impulse. Many Americans can still see in their mind's eye the compelling 1993 photograph of distraught 2 1/2-year-old Jessica DeBoer being wrenched from the only family she had known, to be returned to her biological parents.

For Jessica, the event was the psychological equivalent of parental death. And in the world's literature and lore, social historian Barbara Dafoe Whitehead argues, few events are seen as more tragic than parental death. When the Lion King–to-be is a cub, his father's death is a traumatic loss, as was Bambi's loss of his mother. Death severs the parent-child bond, depriving children of the nurturant protection of an adult who has a stake in their survival and well-being. Understanding the importance of the mother-father-child triangle, friends, relatives, and the greater community traditionally fill the breach by offering support to the widowed and their children.

Moreover, reports Cornell child development researcher Urie Bronfenbrenner, intense parent-child attachments strengthen children intellectually, emotionally, and socially. Videotape analyses reveal the intricacy and complexity of parent-infant interaction. Parents and children, given long hours of interaction, learn how to challenge and respond to each other. "Such interaction requires high levels of motivation, attentiveness, sensitivity, and persistence," says Bronfenbrenner. Such is easier to sustain given a spouse who shares the caregiving and "who assists, encourages, spells off, gives status to, and expresses admiration and affection" for his or her partner.

From time to time people have experimented with alternatives to pair bonding. Communal alternatives to marriage during the 1960s flourished and faded, with most of their members eventually marrying. Free love, unconstrained by jealousies or favorite relationships, proved unworkable. Evolutionary psychologists (who understand the reasons for sexual jealousy) are unsurprised: no community that practices unrestricted sexual relationships without anything resembling marriage has lasted for long. "The new consensus," noted feminist critic Ellen Willis, "is that the family is our last refuge, our only defense against universal predatory selfishness, loneliness, and rootlessness."

The End of Marriage?

Despite this emerging consensus, marriage has undergone serious decline. First, people are putting off marriage. The typical man isn't marrying until age 26.7 (up from 22.8 in 1960), the typical woman until

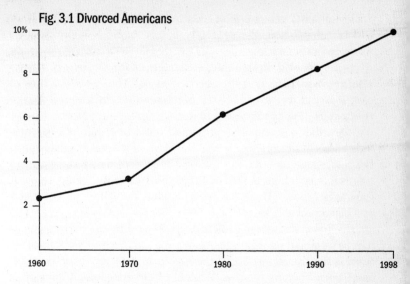

Fig. 3.1 Divorced Americans

Source: Census Bureau, "Marital Status and Living Arrangements: March 1998"

25 (up from 20.3 in 1960). As products of our times, my wife and I married in 1963 at 20 and 19, and lived on a campus that provided housing for married undergraduates. As products of their marriage-deferring times, my children, at 33, 29, and 22, are all unmarried (one is divorced), and their colleges have felt no need to offer housing for married people.

Second, people are divorcing more often—at double the 1960 rate. "We are living longer, but loving more briefly," quips Os Guinness. Although the divorce rate has now tapered off, this does not signify a renewal of marital stability, Sara McLanahan and Lynne Casper report. The divorce rate almost had to at least level off, given increased cohabitation, increased age at first marriage, and the passage of the baby boom generation through the most divorce-prone years. (Because today's counterparts to Elizabeth Taylor serially cohabit without marriage, their breakups are no longer counted as divorces. If you don't marry you can't divorce.) Nevertheless, the high plateau on which divorce continues, combined with the decline of marriage, means that currently divorced (not remarried) people are a still-increasing number of the population (from 2.9 million in 1960 to 19.4 million in 1998).

Since 1960, the percentage of divorced adults has quadrupled. If we add in cohabitation, the instability of marriagelike unions is at an American all-time high.

Is the doubled divorce rate, as some reassuringly suggest, a mere return to normality after the aberrant 1950s? The '50s was a time of early marriage (relative to the rest of the century) and lowered divorce (relative to the postwar years). But if we ignore the postwar flood of divorces, the '50s actually represented but a brief lull in a century-long climb in divorce (fig. 3.2). "The scale of marital breakdowns in the West since 1960 has no historical precedent that I know of, and seems unique," reports retired Princeton University family historian Lawrence Stone. "There has been nothing like it for the last 2,000 years, and probably longer."

Even many marriage professionals seemed by the early 1990s to have grown cold on marriage. Among the hundreds of workshops offered at the annual meeting of the American Association for Marriage and Family Therapy, observes Whitehead, "marriage rarely appears as a topic; it showed up twice in 1992 and not at all in 1993. In 1994 the association gave a major press award to a magazine article arguing that fathers are not necessary in the home. In 1995 the word 'marital' appeared only twice on the program, and 'marriage' not at all."

Well, then, does the famous rule—"half of all marriages end in divorce"—overstate the divorce rate, as others have argued? The critics are right to dispute a corollary idea, that half of all the married people around us will divorce. That's not so, because many of them married before the recent doubling of divorce and have already survived the divorce-prone early years of their marriages. Moreover, the multiple breakups of some individuals—à la Elizabeth Taylor and Mickey Rooney—inflate the divorce rate. The truth is not that half of all *people* are divorced, or will get divorced, but that half or more of all *marriages* end in divorce. Still, the truth in the 1990s is sobering: each year's 2.4 million marriages are accompanied by 1.2 million divorces.

There is a third indicator of the marital decline. As cohabitation and divorce have waxed, marriage itself has waned. Since 1960, the proportion of unmarried American adults has increased from 25 percent to 41 percent. With 80 million single adults (59 percent of whom have never married), there has been an understandable boom in singles bars, singles ministries, singles housing, and singles cruises. With so many more singles—more than twice as many as in 1960—the stigma asso-

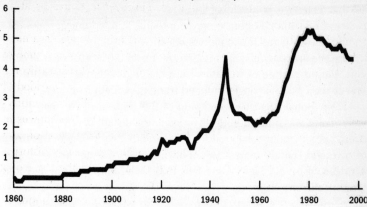

Fig. 3.2 Divorce Rate (per 1,000 population)

Sources: 1860–1956, Paul H. Jacobson, *American Marriage and Divorce* (New York: Rinehart, 1959), table 42; 1957–94, *Statistical Abstract of the United States*; 1995–97, *Monthly Vital Statistics Report*, July 28, 1998

ciated with being single has lessened. Yesterday's "spinster" is today's single professional woman.

As the stigma against divorce and single parenthood lessens, marriage becomes for many a riskier and less attractive option. "There is no human security," says pop psychologist John Bradshaw. "There is no one who will always take care of us." Why gamble on the entanglements of a fragile relationship? Why not just live together "as long as our love shall last"? And if single-parent families are as viable as two-parent families, why restrict childbearing to marriage and risk subjecting your children to the stresses of divorce?

With repeated divorce—serial monogamy or quasi polygyny—rich and powerful men tend to marry women who are progressively younger than themselves. The older the man the greater the age difference he prefers when selecting a mate. In their 20s, men prefer, and marry, women only slightly younger. In their 60s, men prefer, and marry, women averaging about 10 years younger. Thus Donald Trump leaves Ivana Trump for Marla Maples, 18 years his junior, and Johnny Carson marries four wives, each at least 6 years younger than her predecessor. Natural selection, evolutionary psychologists argue, predisposes men to feel attracted to female features associated with fertility. But in so doing, it leaves many older women and younger men without mates, thus driving up the number of unmarried. If women are attracted to rich men, and rich men to younger women, then it shouldn't surprise us that marriage is declining in an age of rich-get-richer economic policies. As author Robert Wright contends, family values proponents should advocate greater economic equality.

People are also delaying remarriage. From the late '60s to the early '80s, the proportion of women who remarried within a year after the end of their first marriages plunged from 33 percent to 16 percent.

Even Ronald Reagan, champion of the traditional Norman Rockwell family, was himself both divorced and a distant parent of his children, one of whom cohabited for a time with a rock singer. The irony of divorced "family values" Republican leaders was not lost on Garry Trudeau. Why did Newt Gingrich, Bob Dole, Pete Wilson, and Phil Gramm all leave their first wives? "Now these men are all great Americans," remarked a satirized Gingrich. "So what does that tell you? Maybe the problem isn't with us. Maybe the problem is with first wives. . . . They expect so much! Second wives are more realistic."

This is not to say divorce is always a mistake. Nearly everyone agrees that for those suffering from a partner's unrepentant hostility, unfaithfulness, or chronic irresponsibility in parenting or finances, divorce is usually prudent. Most of us do not regard marriage as a sacrament. Given an intolerable situation, divorce may be a necessary first step toward personal healing or a saner environment for one's children. Divorce is like having a leg amputated. It's bad news, the remedy of last resort, and something we all hope to avoid. But sometimes it's better than keeping the hopelessly diseased limb.

And if divorced people have participated in brokenness, who among us has not? We are all earthen vessels. We all at some time find ourselves broken—if not in our love life, then in our parenting, our friendships, or our vocations.

Trends in Marriage and Misery

Still, for most who experience it, divorce *is* brokenness—more a necessary evil than an intrinsic good. When marrying, whether for the first time or the second, nearly everyone hopes for a satisfying, enduring bond. As I explained in *The Pursuit of Happiness*, the success or failure of one's marriage is one of the most important predictors of personal well-being. Married people drink and smoke less, live longer, and earn more (a phenomenon attributed partly to healthy, successful people marrying more and partly to the motivations and social support that marriage offers). "Being divorced and a nonsmoker," notes biologist Harold Morowitz, "is slightly less dangerous than smoking a pack or more a day and staying married." He adds, facetiously, that "if a man's marriage is driving him to heavy smoking, he has a delicate statistical decision to make."

Moreover, in National Opinion Research Center surveys of more than 32,000 people since 1972, 40 percent of married adults, but only 23 percent of never-married adults, described their lives as "very happy." In repeated national surveys, happiness with marriage predicts overall happiness much better than does satisfaction with job, finances, or community. If a marriage becomes stressed, it puts people (women, especially) at risk for depression. In fact, there are few stronger predictors of happiness than a close, nurturing, equitable, intimate, lifelong companionship with one's best friend. Moreover, this marriage-happiness link occurs across ethnic groups—European-Americans, Mexican-Americans, and African-Americans. It occurs across 17 nations studied, even when controlling for health and income. And unlike married partners, cohabitants are only slightly happier than single people. To paraphrase Henry Ward Beecher, "Well-married a person is winged; ill-matched, shackled"—or, today, unshackled but still broken-hearted.

The number of broken (or empty) hearted people is on the rise. As marriage has declined, the number of depressed, despondent, downcast people has mushroomed. Moreover, National Institute of Mental Health researchers report that the risk of depression is two to four times greater for those living outside marriage. Although stress precedes divorce, distress and depression ratchet upward after divorce. Among the nonmarried, suicide rates also are elevated, both in the United States and elsewhere.

These findings partly reflect depression's toxicity. Happy people more readily attract and retain marital partners than depressed people. Misery may love company, but research on the social consequences of depression reveals that company does not love misery. A depressed (and therefore self-focused, irritable, and withdrawn) spouse or roommate is no fun to be around.

Yet "the prevailing opinion of researchers," reports University of Oslo sociologist Arne Mastekaasa, is that the association between marriage and well-being is "mainly due" to the beneficial effects of mar-

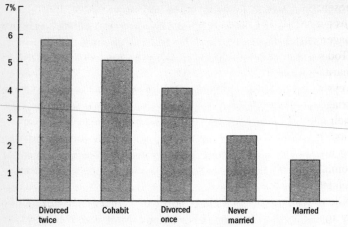

Fig. 3.3 Annual Depression Rate

Source: Lee Robins and Darrel Reiger, *Psychiatric Disorders in America* (New York: Free Press, 1991)

riage. If the happiest people marry sooner and more often, then as people age (and progressively less happy people move into marriage) the average happiness of both married and never-married people should decline. (The older, less happy newlyweds would pull down the average happiness of married people, leaving the unhappiest people in the unmarried group.) But the data do not support this prediction. Moreover, even when controlling for premarital well-being, "men who marry and stay married are less depressed than those who remain single." So, although morose people are less likely to marry, marriage mitigates against moroseness. Marital intimacy and support really do — for most people — pay emotional dividends.

We might also wonder if today's delayed marriages and doubled divorce rate weed out more unhappy marriages, leaving married couples happier than 25 years ago. Are today's couples no less happy, just freer to avoid or terminate a marriage when unhappy? If you think so, University of Texas sociologist Norval Glenn, Yale social analyst Robert Lane, and University of Nebraska sociologists Stacy Rogers and Paul Amato have independently gleaned a disconcerting fact from national surveys. Compared with back when people married more readily and divorced less readily, those in today's surviving marriages are slightly *less* likely to describe their marriage as "very happy" and are more likely to report high levels of marital conflict. The divorce change therefore represents not just an increase in bad marriages ending but in marriages going bad. For many, marriage has become a union that defies management.

Today's more divorce-accepting attitudes contribute to the decline of marital satisfaction, report Amato and Rogers from their follow-up surveys with 2,033 married persons. "The belief that an unrewarding marriage should be jettisoned may lead some people to invest less time in their marriages and make fewer attempts to resolve marital disagreements," say the researchers. Thus "greater freedom to leave unsatisfying marriages" may ironically increase the likelihood of marriages becoming unsatisfying. Divorce acceptance feeds marital unhappiness which feeds divorce.

Glenn also has followed the course of marriages that began in the early 1970s. By the late 1980s, only a third of the starry-eyed newlyweds were still married *and* proclaiming their marriages "very happy." Allowing for some overreporting of marital happiness—it's easier to tell an interviewer you've succeeded than failed in your marriage—Glenn

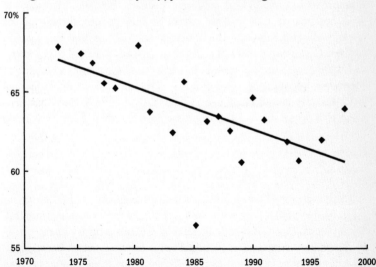

Fig. 3.4 Americans Very Happy with Their Marriage

Source: National Opinion Research Center surveys of 20,255 people

concludes that "the real proportion of those marriages that were successful . . . may well have been under a fourth." From a 1988 national survey, the Gallup Organization offered a similarly dismal conclusion: two-thirds of 35- to 54-year-olds had divorced, separated, or been close to separation.

If this pattern continues, the Gallup report concludes, "our nation will soon reach the point where the dominant experience of adults will have been marital instability." Sociologists Teresa Martin and Larry Bumpass believe it will continue—that two-thirds of today's marriages may culminate in divorce. A *New Yorker* cartoon expressed the new reality: "I'm not talking about a permanent commitment," a suitor explains to his would-be mate. "I'm talking about marriage." Others of us are more hopeful that the germinating new values revolution will increase the durability of close relationships.

This much, however, is a fact: for some reason—stay tuned—Americans are much less likely today than a generation ago to marry and live happily ever after. More often than not, sad to say, our initial euphoria mutates into a cold, loveless truce, or worse.

So, the hard truth is that most of today's marriages, begun with joy, end with the anguish of divorce, separation, or coldness. The moral: couples should neither take marital success for granted nor resign themselves to conflict and coldness. Instead, they should resolve to give their marriage at least the attention they devote to their car, by periodically refueling it, giving it occasional tuneups, and fixing what's broken. Given the impact of marital success on personal and societal well-being, we surely owe this much to ourselves and our children. Moreover, recognizing the influence of cultural views on individual attitudes, we should challenge radical individualism's view that marriage is a disposable relationship, hardly more than a big "notarized date."

Who Divorces?

Although social psychological science has given us clues to whom we're likely to fall in love with—clues that take most of a chapter in my *Social Psychology*—romantic attraction remains a pretty chancy matter. Imagine yourself as an identical twin. As you perhaps know, identical twins not only have similar traits, they also make similar choices of friends, clothes, vacations, jobs, and so on. So, if your identical twin became engaged to someone, wouldn't you (being in so many ways the same as your twin) expect to feel attracted to this person?

Surprise. In a recent University of Minnesota study of identical twins and their spouses, only half of twins recalled really liking their co-twin's selection and only 5 percent agreed "I could have fallen for my twin's fiancee." The researchers, David Lykken and Auke Tellegen, surmise that romantic love is rather like ducklings' imprinting: given repeated exposure to someone after childhood, a bond of infatuation may form with almost any available person of roughly similar background and attractiveness and who reciprocates our affections.

Whether that affection will last as long as they both shall live is, however, much more predictable. If you wanted to predict a couple's risk of divorce it would first help to know where they live. Divorce rates vary widely by country, ranging from 0.01 percent of the population annually in Bolivia, the Philippines, and Spain to 0.47 percent in the world's most individualistic and divorce-prone country, the United States. To predict a culture's divorce rates it helps to know its values. Individualistic cultures (where love is a feeling and people ask, "What does my heart say?") have more divorce than communal cultures (where love entails obligation and people ask, "What will other people say?"). "Hedonistic" marriages—those that exist to serve our individual needs and desires—tend to survive "as long as we both shall love," notes Glenn. A Hallmark card captures the hedonism: "Getting divorced can be very healthy! Watch how it improves your circulation!"

Ironically, cultures that base marriage on romantic love have the highest divorce rates. Although passionate love burns hot, it inevitably simmers down. As the marriage bond has become less sacred and economically necessary, it has become more dependent on continued romantic affection—a more fragile base for a permanent relationship. Marital commitment, studies show, is sustained not only by attraction but also by a moral conviction of the importance of marriage and by fear of the social and financial costs of breakup.

And a further irony: although one might suppose that parental conflict over divorce would be more corrosive to children in collectivist countries that frown on divorce, it seems not to be so. Instead, Carol Gohm and her University of Illinois colleagues report from a study of nearly 7,000 adults in 39 countries, "collectivism lessens the impact of divorce after a high-conflict marriage." In cultures with strong "pro-marriage norms, divorce occurs only when marital conflict is intense."

Thus when a divorce does occur in promarriage cultures, children may gain more relief.

The longer a relationship endures, the fewer its emotional ups and downs. As suggested by the rock song "Addicted to Love," the flow and ebb of romantic love follows the pattern of addictions to coffee, alcohol, and other drugs. At first, a drug gives a big kick, a high. With repetition, opponent emotions gain strength and tolerance develops. An amount that once was highly stimulating no longer gives a thrill. However, stopping the substance does not return you to where you started. Rather, it triggers withdrawal symptoms—malaise, depression, the blahs. The same often happens in love. As the passionate high cools to lukewarm, people begin to find themselves laughing more with a favorite colleague than with their partner. Their lovemaking may feel mechanical, compared to what they imagine is available elsewhere. Their felt needs for affirmation and affection may seem better met by the newer friend. The no-longer-romantic relationship becomes taken for granted—until it ends. Then the jilted lover, the widower, the divorcee, are surprised at how empty life now seems without the person they long ago stopped feeling passionately attached to. Having focused on what was not working, they stopped noticing what was.

Whether companionate love extinguishes or endures depends not only on whether one's culture prizes romantic passion but on who marries whom. We're likely to stay married if most of the following are true:

- we married after age 20
- we both grew up in stable, two-parent homes
- we dated for a long while before marriage
- we are well educated
- we enjoy a stable income from a good job
- we live in a small town or on a farm, perhaps enmeshed in an intergenerational social network
- we did not cohabit or become pregnant before marriage
- we married as virgins
- we are religiously committed and worship together
- both spouses are of similar age, faith, and education.

No one of these predictors, by itself, is essential to a stable marriage. But if none of these things are true, marital breakdown is an almost sure bet. If all are true, we are almost certain to stay together until death. A New Zealand research team led by D. M. Fergusson showed the power of these predictors in a study of 1,002 children born into two-parent families in Christchurch. During a child's first five years, family breakup was

- three times more likely if the mother was a church nonattender rather than a regular attender,
- four times more likely if the father was unskilled rather than professional, and
- six times more likely if either the mother or father was in their late teens rather than late 20s.

When they added these and other predictors together, the expected rate of family breakup ranged from a best-case prognosis (born to churchgoing, professional parents in their late 20s) of less than 1 percent to a worst-case prognosis of 99 percent.

Why Has Divorce Increased?

Divorce is less common among educated people who marry well into their 20s. Today, people are both better educated and more likely to marry in their late 20s than they were in 1960. Yet, despite these divorce-suppressing trends, the divorce rate has doubled—an ironic, important phenomenon that arouses the social-scientific detectives. To overwhelm the positive trends, some powerful social forces must be at work. Moreover, the American marriage decline—evident from increased cohabitation, later marriage, increased divorce, and the resulting drop in marriage rates—has occurred simultaneously in Europe. This multinational trend suggests that the causes of rising divorce, like the causes of increased nonmarital births, span Western cultures.

That realization may lighten our burdens of guilt. "When I go out to lecture on family history," Stephanie Coontz relates, "I sometimes feel that half the people I talk to are torturing themselves trying to figure out what *they* did wrong in their families and the other half are torturing themselves trying to figure out what their *parents* did wrong. Seeing our family pains as part of a larger social predicament means that we can let ourselves—or our parents—off the hook. Maybe our personal difficulties are not *all* our family's fault; maybe our family's difficulties are not *all* our personal fault."

Worldwide, Helen Fisher reports, the reasons men and women most often give for why they quit a marriage are adultery, sterility, and cruelty. Although such explanations locate "fault" with the other person (and most divorced people do blame their partner for the breakup), such personal faults do not explain the sevenfold increase in divorce during the past century. So what does?

Might one culprit be our more divorce-accepting attitudes? In 1951, only 51 percent of Americans agreed that "parents who don't get along should not stay together because there are children in the family." In 1985, about the time the divorce rate peaked, 82 percent agreed. And by 1994, only 15 percent thought that "parents should stay together even if they don't get along." No longer, Ellen Goodman points out, does one hear the joke from the 1970s about the 95-year-old couple who went to divorce court after 70 unhappy years of marriage. Asked by the judge why they hadn't split long ago, they replied, "We were waiting for the children to die."

But attitude changes often lag behind behavior changes. During the 1950s and early '60s, when divorce was relatively uncommon, most Americans felt that divorce laws were "not strict enough." Not until 1968, after the divorce rate increase was well under way, did more and more people begin to think that divorce should be made easier.

Might a culprit instead be easier divorce laws? Internationally, divorce rates have tended to jump after the passage of consent or no-fault divorce laws, which exemplify radical individualism by freeing either spouse to walk out on a relationship at any time for any reason (and 4 of 5 marriages do now end by the decision of one partner alone). Australia, for example, experienced a 260 percent increase in divorce following its Family Law Act of 1975. But there and elsewhere, the 1960s divorce surge was under way *before* no-fault divorce laws. Most American states did not pass no-fault divorce legislation until the 1970s and early 1980s, following the example of California's law, signed by Ronald Reagan in 1969.

Country-by-country and state-by-state analyses reveal that the switch from laws designed to protect marriage to more divorce-accepting laws did, however, further amplify increases in divorce rates. In the three years following a state's passing a no-fault divorce law, its divorce rate tended to jump (perhaps, however, because the new law speeded up divorces in the pipeline).

So, if no-fault divorce legislation was not the primary force driving the swelling divorce rate, what was? Social scientists agree that family changes are a byproduct of economic changes that few of us would want

fed by growing materialism and consumerism, were outpacing real economic growth.

Another stimulus to women's employment has been motherhood's lessening demands. In 1900, with shorter life spans, more children, and before clothes dryers, frozen foods, and wrinkle-free fabrics, only 6 percent of married women worked outside the home. Today, people live twice as long, thanks to modern medicine. They have fewer children, thanks partly to reliable birth control. They have help in rearing their children from public education, television, day care, and after school programs. The result is many more adult years free of day-long child care. And who would wish all these changes reversed?

If feminism is more a natural result than a cause of these life changes, can we say the same of the growing American individualism? Fed by a healthy respect for our social diversity, and by a valuing of self-expression and self-fulfillment, commitment to social units beyond the self have waned. Responding to a 1989 Gallup poll, 85 percent of Americans rated "having a good self-image or self-respect" as very important; none rated it unimportant. What's important has become less "we" than "me."

Ironically, David Popenoe contends, "The push for self-fulfillment, when carried to the extreme, leads not to personal freedom and happiness but to social breakdown and individual anguish." Fellow sociologists Norval Glenn and Charles Weaver agree. They suspect that "an increasingly hedonistic form of marriage is having diminished hedonistic consequences." "Real matrimony," says Catherine Wallace in *For Fidelity,* "confronts and refutes the commonplace individualism of our times because it models a human relationship that is not centered upon the emotional equivalent of cost-benefit investment calculations."

Alternatives to No-Fault Divorce

Although no-fault divorce legislation was not the main cause of rising divorce, it did express post-1960s radical individualism, by regarding "people as unencumbered individuals free from duties and responsibilities they choose to reject." "Norms of personal satisfaction are now trumping norms of relationships based on obligation," says former Clinton domestic policy aide William Galston. No-fault divorce allows one parent not only to leave the other without established cause but also to disrupt the other's parent-child relationships.

Many scholars believe that today's no-fault divorce laws, by nearly eliminating alimony, have also been financially advantageous to non-custodial parents and should therefore be reformed to better protect the economic needs of women and their dependent children. Harvard sociologist Lenore Weitzman explains that in most no-fault divorces the physical assets to be divided are no greater than one year's earnings. Thus, "If one partner builds his or her earning capacity during the marriage, while the other is a homemaker and parent, the partner whose earning capacity has developed during the marriage has acquired the major asset of the marital partnership. If that earning capacity, or the income it produces is not divided upon divorce, the two spouses are left with very unequal shares of their joint assets. This is one of the major sources of the impoverishment of women and children after divorce."

The "children first" reform advocated by Harvard family law professor Mary Ann Glendon would compel judges to consider children's needs when dividing marital property. In *Life Without Father*, Popenoe suggests "a two-tier system of divorce law: Marriages without minor children would be relatively easy to dissolve, but marriages with children would be dissolvable only by mutual agreement or on grounds that clearly involve a wrong by one party against the other, such as desertion, repeated adultery, chronic alcoholism and gambling, and physical abuse."

Others advocate a waiting period of nine months or more between the filing and granting of a divorce. This would mandate a cooling-off time for possible reconciliation and make a cultural statement about the significance of the marital commitment, at least in cases involving minor children. "It is now easier to renounce a marriage than a mortgage," writes James Q. Wilson of UCLA. "We now live in a society where it is legally easier and less risky to dump a wife than fire an employee," echoes Maggie Gallagher. "If the corporation were required to operate on the same legal principles that govern our marriage laws [enabling either party to walk away from a covenant], the economy would collapse. It is not surprising that under the same regimen, marriage is on the verge of doing just that." Much as we now allow prenuptial covenants to protect a wealthy spouse in the event of a divorce, why not allow no-divorce covenants, she wonders. Why not allow marrying couples who seek a lifelong commitment to legally bind themselves to each other, permitting divorce only in exceptional circumstances?

In 1993, the centrist Communitarian Network began advocating such "supervows."

In 1997, Louisiana, not a state famous for social innovation, brought the concept to fruition. It became the first state to allow couples who are tying the knot to choose between no-fault marriage and "covenant" marriage. (Arizona followed suit, and by 1999 similar bills had been introduced in 22 states.) Those electing covenant marriage pledge to marry only after serious deliberation, to try to resolve difficulties with counseling if either party requests it, and to limit divorce—only after a two-year work-it-out period—to circumstances of adultery, abandonment, abuse, "habitual excess," or imprisonment.

Critics object that covenant marriage contracts, which are simply ready-made prenuptial agreements, may trap unhappy couples in their misery. Communitarians respond that, feeling bound, many couples whose relationships have cooled and grown distant will now be motivated to renew their marriages. That's what many long-married people report having done, by working through rocky times with the conviction that, for better or worse, there was no walking away. Most marriages don't die of abuse or adultery. They die, says University of Washington marriage researcher John Gottman, "with a whimper, as people turn away from one another, slowly growing apart."

Critics also object that the legislation "forces" couples to choose between disposable marriages ("marriage lite") and "really mean it" marriages ("marriage plus"). Communitarians respond that, yes, the law "forces" choice, in the same sense that one's gas station does when adding a high-octane alternative to its regular gas. Giving individuals a choice they didn't have before—one that will "force" them to think about the sort of commitment they are making to each other—"is the exact opposite of coercion," observes communitarian sociologist Amitai Etzioni.

If we reinstitutionalize marriage through a covenant marriage alternative, why not also institutionalize divorce, ask feminists. "A truly feminist, pro-child divorce reform would look something like this," according to Hanna Rosin. "Dock alimony and child support automatically from the sole or primary wage-earner's paycheck, and let whoever has primary custody of the children keep the house." Surround divorce "with clear obligations and rights, supported by law, customs, and social expectations," suggests Coontz. "Closing the loopholes, and getting rid of the idea that every divorce case is a new contest in which there are no accepted ground rules will *minimize* the temptation for individuals to use divorce to escape obligations to children."

Louisiana may again lead the way. Louisiana State law professor Katherine Spaht, who drafted the model covenant marriage act, is drafting a new "Family as Community Act." At divorce or death, the act would recognize all family members—not just spouses—as stakeholders. As assets are divided and present and future income assigned, the interests of each family member would be recognized.

As the new social ecology movement gains steam, such reforms of marriage and divorce laws are increasingly being welcomed. "Should divorce in this country be easier or harder to obtain than it is now?" By late 1998, the 22 percent who said "easier" were but one-third of the 62 percent who said "harder." We can hope that marriage- and child-supporting policies will be more nuanced than merely making divorce "harder." And we must never deny the suffering that precedes many a divorce and the healing that may follow. Yet we can also welcome policies that support the ideal and strengthen the reality of the marriage covenant—of two adults enduringly committed to each other and to the welfare of their children.

The "New Familism"

Is the secret to family renewal a return to little houses on the prairie? Is it, in Katha Pollitt's words, to "bring back the whole nineteenth century: Restore the cult of virginity and the double standard, ban birth control, restrict divorce, kick women out of decent jobs, force unwed pregnant women to put their babies up for adoption on pain of social death, make out-of-wedlock children legal nonpersons"? Is it to return to the traditional nuclear family of the 1950s, to an era of housewives confined by limited notions of femininity, of black students who could only dream of opportunities closed to them, of gay men and lesbian women forced to live a charade? The very idea causes many eyes to roll at the mention of "family values." But we can skip the nostalgia trips, say pro-family sociologists like Popenoe. Genie is not going back in the bottle. The circumstances that moved men's and women's roles toward equality—the lengthening lifespan, smaller families, and equal employment opportunity—are not about to be reversed. Nor do many of us wish it. In marriages marked by shared household labor and parenting, reports sociologist Pepper Schwartz, men become more attached to their children, wives to their husbands, and husband and wife report greater friendship and sexual satisfaction. So, the past is over.

Can we, however, create new social ideals?

Can we combine the good things gained with the good things we have lost?

Can we affirm yesterday's pair-bonding and greater government support for families *and* today's more egalitarian gender roles (in "peer marriages" with shared parenting, domestic work, and decision making)?

Can we heed Etzioni's plea for a societal change "in the habits of the heart, in the ways we think about marriage and how we value it"?

Can we develop and subsidize marriage preparation courses that are effective in improving couple communication and conflict resolution and reducing marital breakdowns—and perhaps follow Florida's requiring marriage education for high school students and giving a discount of marriage license fees for those who complete an approved course?

Can we develop a new generation of marriage and family textbooks that, rather than presenting marriage as "more a problem than a solution," also present the benefits of marriage for adults and children? (The 20 existing texts analyzed by Norval Glenn devoted, on average, less than one page to the benefits of marriage for adults and twelve pages to domestic violence, three and a half pages to the effects of divorce and solo parenting on children, and seven pages to child abuse. These are all worthwhile topics, argues Glenn, but the imbalance is "both a cause and a result of a society in which marriage as an institution is growing steadily weaker.")

Can we, without suppressing our social diversity, agree that the healing of America will come as we celebrate the ideal of couples committed to each other and to their children? Can we do better than the 1996 Defense of Marriage Act, which, as Robert Wright has noted, "focused not on keeping heterosexuals married but on keeping homosexuals unmarried"?

While prohibiting housing discrimination based on race, religion, gender, or sexual orientation, should we allow landlords to have a preference for married over cohabiting male-female couples? Would such policies, along with marriage-supporting tax, welfare, and education policies, help renew marriage and families? Or would they merely return us to uncompassionate stigmatizing of single and divorced persons?

When our marriage is troubled can we remember—as those in covenant marriages surely will—that many happily married seniors have persisted through "bad marriage" times of serious friction or lovelessness—teaching us that part of a "good marriage" is loving stubbornly? Can we spread the idea that in later life such couples enjoy the satisfactions of their shared history, of the sort of comfortable honesty that accompanies security, and of mutual affection rooted in intimate knowledge of the other's needs and desires? One reason why so many couples love each other through warm times and cold is that together they love their children. "People cherish a spouse," contends evolutionary psychologist David Buss, "because that spouse is the one person on a planet of billions who has as much of an interest in the fate of their children as they do."

Can we ignite this "new familism" into a social ecology movement that transcends traditional categories of left and right? As "liberal" columnist Ellen Goodman reflected, "Words like 'liberal' and 'conservative' don't mean as much anymore, especially when we are talking about women, men and families. Is it liberal or conservative to be appalled at Tailhook, in favor of Head Start, sick of violence in the movies and worried about teen-age mothers in the community?" The old way of thinking, as Hillary Rodham Clinton has argued, pits the right wing, which says parents are to blame and government has no role to play, against the left, which excuses parental neglect, blames an abstract "society," and sees government as the solution. To "get beyond the old categories of right and left and liberal and conservative," she adds, "we're just going to have to think differently."

When social consciousness awakens and a culture redefines its values and priorities, things can change. Faced with a massive population explosion, China beginning in 1971 created educational programs, family planning services, and economic incentives in support of one-child families. In schools, children learned how one-child families would improve living standards. Birth control pills were distributed free. Awards and honorary certificates were offered to couples pledging to have only one child. Lone children enjoyed free nursery care, free medical care, and free school tuition. The mass media publicized appealing examples of one-childness. The result of this multifaceted effort? In the urban areas of China where the program was most aggressively implemented, 95 percent of today's preschool children are only children. Where there is cultural will, there is a way.

The new chorus of support for the nuclear family does transcend the labels of liberal and conservative. Its voices have included liberal Pat Schroeder and conservative William Bennett, liberal Marian Edelman of the Children's Defense Fund and conservative Gary Bauer of the Family Research Council, liberal Bill Bradley and conservative Jack Kemp, black radical Million Man Marcher Louis Farrakhan and white conservative Promise Keeper Bill McCartney. "What we are seeing," suggests Bennett, "are social antibodies reacting against a 30-year cultural virus." In a 1997 Yankelovich survey of Gen-Xers, 73 percent favored a return to more traditional standards of family life—up from 56 percent when the same question was put to baby boomers in 1977. It all adds up to "the country's newest social trend: the 'marriage movement,'" proclaimed a *USA Today* article in 1998—a "widely based, sometimes bipartisan group of researchers, academics, grassroots activists, clergy, disillusioned family therapists who think marriage therapy comes too late if at all, schoolteachers, and public officials."

These disparate voices unite in their agreement with the United Nations General Assembly's proclamation declaring the International Year of the Family: "The family constitutes the basic unit of society and therefore warrants special attention." They unite in their agreement with Popenoe and Jean Bethke Elshtain's vision of the ideal environment for children: "An enduring, two-biological-parent family that engages regularly in activities together, has many of its own routines, traditions, and stories, and provides a great deal of contact time between adults and children. The children have frequent interaction with relatives, with neighbors in a supportive neighborhood, and with their parents' world of work, coupled with no pervasive worry that their parents will break up."

CHAPTER 4

America's Children

A voice is heard in Ramah, lamentation and bitter weeping. Rachel is weeping for her children.

—JEREMIAH 31:15

Imagine that in 1960 a latter-day Rip Van Winkle lay down for a long sleep, knowing that when he awakened in the late 1990s, Americans would be enjoying doubled average incomes (in inflation-adjusted dollars), rising education, exciting new technologies, and a 50 percent increase in the proportion of adults available to provide and care for children (from fewer than two adults for every child to today's 3 to 1 ratio). Should problems arise, parents could seek help from a growing army of psychologists, social workers, and counselors, or from new drug therapies. With all this good news—more affluence, time, and sophistication to focus on proportionately fewer, more widely spaced children— might Rip not have expected improved children's well-being?

Researchers, however, agree: paradoxically, the well-being of America's children reached a modern low in the early 1990s. "Never before," declared a report by the National Association of State Boards of Education in 1990, "has one generation of American teenagers been less healthy, less cared for, or less prepared for life than their parents were at the same age." Barbara Dafoe Whitehead echoed: "This is the first generation in the nation's history to do worse psychologically, socially, and economically than its parents."

Are they right? And is American culture—in its quest for individual fulfillment—progressively devaluing children?

Judging from the number who agree that "parents who don't get along should not stay together because there are children," it seems so.

Judging from collegians' giving lower ratings (compared with the 1960s) to having children and higher ratings to demanding personal fulfillment from marriage, it seems so.

Judging from newly married couples rating personal freedom and leisure time as more important than having children, it seems so.

Judging from our paying child-care workers in the lowest tenth of wage earners (less than animal care workers in zoos), it seems so.

Judging from our government's giving people who breed horses expense deductions unavailable to those who breed children, it seems so.

Judging from the declining number of hours per week parents spend with their children, from 30 in 1965 to 17 in 1985, it seems so.

Judging from the increase in no-children apartment and condo complexes, it seems so.

Judging from the doubling of advertising on children's television and the replacement of quality network children's programming (such as *Captain Kangaroo*) with toy-based programming (such as *Mighty Morphin Power Rangers*), it certainly seems so.

Children's Poverty: Every Fifth Child

Judging from political priorities it also seems so. Thanks to the rising economic tide and new social safety net programs, poverty among all age groups declined during the 1960s. Then, during the 1970s and 1980s, taxation and entitlement policies changed to favor the elderly. Simultaneously, real hourly wages leveled off. The economic prospects —and therefore the marriage prospects—declined for young, poorly educated males. Poverty became more baby-faced, by shifting from the elderly (whose poverty rate has halved since 1970) to children (whose poverty rate increased by a third). By 1993, 40 percent of the nation's poor were children. Every fifth child lives in poverty, and nearly 1 in 3 experience "episodic poverty" (for at least two months in a year). Compared with 18 other major industrialized nations, the United States has become number one not only in basketball, billionaires, and bombs but in child poverty (not to mention divorce, teen births, economic inequality, and incarceration of its people).

In 1960, government spending for goods and services to children

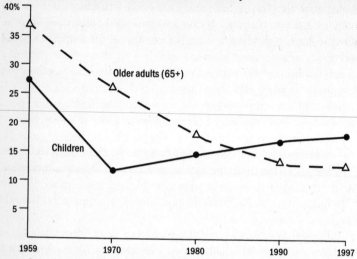

Fig. 4.1 Children and Older Adults in Poverty

Older adults (65+)

Children

1959   1970   1980   1990   1997

Source: U.S. Bureau of the Census, "Historical Poverty Tables–Persons" (www.census.gov/hhes/poverty/histpov)

(including schools) was more than double the amount spent for adults. Since then, increases in spending for adults (6.8 percent annually, adjusted for inflation) have been more than double the spending increase on children (2.9 percent annually). Thus, per person federal benefits to the elderly tower 12 to 1 over benefits to children. We are socializing the costs of growing old while privatizing the costs of child rearing, Sylvia Ann Hewlett and Cornel West argue.

The priority we give the elderly, even the rich elderly, stems from a mix of compassion, self-interest, and democracy. We provide for those unable to provide for themselves. Unlike children, however, the elderly population is increasing, and it votes. Like most people, they vote their interests, safeguarding such programs as Social Security and Medicare. They are 50 percent more likely to vote than adults with children at home. And with the American Association of Retired Persons having annual revenue 23 times that of the Children's Defense Fund, their interests are well represented. (AARP's 34 million members make it the world's largest private organization after the Catholic Church.)

We now invest 11 times more federal benefit dollars per person in those over 65 than in those under 18, who are the human capital for our future. This is despite the reality that for every senior in poverty there are four children. We have created a welfare state for the old while denying it to the young. Save now, say child advocates—like saving money by not insulating a new house—and spend later, in lost productivity, increased welfare, more police, and bloated prisons. Child poverty, for reasons we will see, is linked with this and more: more learning disabilities, more illness, more school failure, more unemployment, more home conflict, more abuse.

Children's Pathology

If we lament children's growing poverty, we shudder at their exploding pathology. Some indicators of children's well-being are troubling.

Abuse and Neglect

If a man's home is his castle, many homes today have torture chambers. Since 1976, when data were first gathered from all 50 states, the number of children reported neglected and abused has nearly *quintupled*, to 3.2 million a year. Investigation substantiates 33 percent of these cases, the National Committee for the Prevention of Child Abuse reports. In 1997, 52 percent of substantiated cases involved neglect, 26 percent physical abuse, 7 percent sexual abuse, and 15 percent emotional or unspecified forms of abuse.

These mushrooming reports partly reflect increased sensitivity to children's maltreatment and improved reporting. (Some say it also reflects a self-inflating bureaucratic reporting system that would rather blame parents for poverty and spend huge sums for custodial foster care than alleviate family poverty. Government, say Hewlett and West, is "very extravagant when it comes to replacing parents and so very mean-spirited when it comes to supporting parents.") The statistics also sometimes include multiple reports concerning the same child.

But there are good reasons to suspect that children really are more often mistreated today. Young, poor, single parents—whose numbers are growing—are more likely than mature, married parents to mistreat their children. A U.S. government study in 1996 found that children of single parents are 80 percent more at risk for abuse or neglect. A recent Canadian study of 2,447 allegedly abused children found that the proportion living in single-parent families was triple the proportion of single-parent families. Such findings led to the U.N. Secretary General's

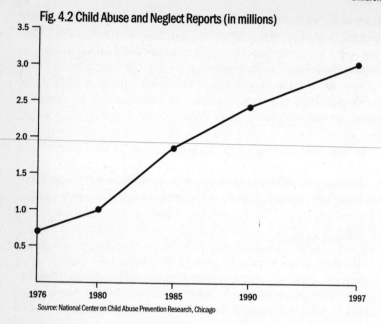

Fig. 4.2 Child Abuse and Neglect Reports (in millions)

Source: National Center on Child Abuse Prevention Research, Chicago

conclusion that "family breakdown is reflected in . . . child abuse and neglect."

Two-parent families also vary in their risk of abuse. Although usually caring and supportive, stepfathers and live-in boyfriends more often abuse children than do biological fathers, for whom selfless fatherly love comes more naturally. Although less involved than biological fathers, most stepfathers (contrary to fairy tale images of evil stepparents) are loving, caring men. Yet the incest taboo is weaker between stepfathers and stepdaughters they did not know as infants. In one study, 1 in 6 San Francisco women who had a stepfather during childhood reported being sexually abused by him, as did only 1 in 40 women who had been reared with biological fathers (despite typically having spent more years with the biological father). McMaster University researchers Martin Daly and Margo Wilson report, consistent with the fairy tale stepparent images, that infants living with stepparents are at least 60 times more likely to be murdered (nearly always by a stepfather) than those living with natural parents. Moreover, stepfathers are more likely to kill by beating the child and less likely to kill themselves afterward. "Step-relationships," they conclude, are typically "more distant, more conflictual, and less satisfying than the corresponding genetic parent-child relationships." The same is true of foster-care relationships. The clear implication: there can hardly be a better child abuse prevention program than the renewal of marriage.

To some evolutionists this brings to mind the genetic selfishness of male lions taking over a pride and killing cubs sired by the previous fathers, or male langur monkeys reportedly chasing or killing infant monkeys when taking over a troop of females. Stepfathers often lack the passionate identification with their children exhibited by other parents, and they may also at times feel irritation or jealousy over a wife's devotion to her children. They are not consciously trying to eliminate their competition for the mother's reproductive energies; they are just more easily irritated by a child they didn't father. The increasing number of transient fathers and stepchildren ("serial parenting" or "child swapping," some have called it) therefore strengthens our presumption that the surging neglect and abuse reports signify some real increase in neglect and cruelty to America's children. (Daly and Wilson report another dramatic finding: women are about four times more vulnerable to partner assault themselves if they have children sired by a previous partner. Apparently, caring for children sired by other men brings women into more frequent conflict with their new partners.)

Sadly, the sins of the fathers are often visited upon the children. The cycle of abuse is pernicious: Most abusive parents report having been neglected or battered as children. Many condemned murderers report the same. One study of 14 young men awaiting execution for juvenile crimes found that all but two had histories of brutal physical abuse.

So, do most abused children become abusive? Is today's victim predictably tomorrow's predator? No. Most abused children do not later become abusive parents or violent criminals. But 30 percent of those abused do abuse their children—a rate four times higher than the national rate of child abuse. Moreover, young children terrorized through sexual abuse or wartime atrocities (being beaten, witnessing torture, and living in constant fear) may suffer other scars—often nightmares, depression, and a troubled adolescence.

Research studies have associated childhood sexual abuse with a laundry list of pathologies: stress-related disorders such as stomachaches, headaches, and bed-wetting; substance abuse and binge eating; delinquency and suicide; sexual dissatisfaction and risky sexual behavior. When Stephanie Whitaker of Chicago was 6, an adolescent brother began sexually abusing her. Then her uncle did the same. At 14, her grandfather said he was her boyfriend and would consummate the relationship during her next overnight visit. So Stephanie had sex with a 14-year-old friend, hoping she would get pregnant and that would keep her abusers away. Her hopes were fulfilled, but only until her first child's birth.

Crime

Tragic as home-based abuse is, children report that most of the abuse they bear comes from peers. Until recently, youth-on-youth abuse was increasing. From 1960 to 1993, arrests for juvenile violent crime increased *seven*fold, from 16,000 arrests to 120,000 (during a time when the 14- to 17-year-old population, thanks to declining birthrates, crept only from 11 million to 14 million). During that time, all types of juvenile arrests soared from 475,000 to 1.74 million.

Academic Aptitude

SAT verbal scores have plunged 50 points since 1960 (the equivalent of about 8 IQ test points). Almost half that decline occurred during the 1960s and was mostly due to the increasing academic diversity of students taking the test. (Before 1960, college-bound test takers were a smaller, more elite group.) After 1970, however, the continued decline (up until the early 1980s) was mostly *not* due to changes in the number and composition of test takers. From 1966 to 1980 the number scoring 700 or above on the verbal test dropped from 33,200 to 12,300 — an effect obviously not attributable to more students taking the exam. The College Entrance Examination Board instead attributed most of the continuing decline to such factors as changed schooling, changed families, and television's progressive displacement of reading.

Psychological Disorders

Children's psychological pathology has spiraled. Eating disorders, once virtually unheard of, plague countless adolescent girls. Depression rates have soared for young adults and youths. Teenage suicide has tripled.

To explore the seeming increase in children's problems, researchers

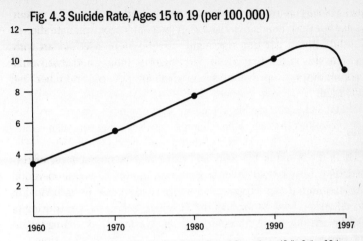

Fig. 4.3 Suicide Rate, Ages 15 to 19 (per 100,000)

Source: Victor R. Fuchs and Diane Reklis, "America's Children: Economic Perspectives and Policy Options," *Science* 255 (1992): 41–46, and *Healthy People 2000 Review, 1998–1999*

Thomas Achenbach and Catherine Howell compared the children of 1976 with those of 1989, after matching them for sex, race, social class, and age. Over the 13 years, there was an increase in the number of parents who described their children as "stubborn, sullen, or irritable." The children of 1989 were also rated as more likely to "destroy things belonging to others," lie or cheat, and have few friends or "hang around with others who get into trouble." The 3 percent of children who had received mental health services during the earlier year nearly tripled to 8 percent. Based on these reports, Achenbach and Howell believe that the number of clinically impaired children had nearly doubled, from 10 percent to 18 percent. Child watcher James Garbarino of Cornell University's Family Life Development Center concurs, saying, "Achenbach's data certainly conform to my own observations: more and more kids are in more and more trouble."

So what is the state of America's children after three decades of family change? The hard-edged truth bursts our denial. If Martin Luther King, Jr., was right to sense a "social catastrophe" three decades ago, what words can describe today's worsening crisis? Living in a culture enjoying unprecedented material abundance and unrivaled freedom to pursue one's personal bliss, America's children are plagued by social pathology. They and we, for their problems are our problems. The legacy of children's misery is spreading pathology; misery makes miserable company. The legacy is today's taxpayer-funded prisons, stuffed with six times as many inmates as in 1960. Contemporary America is creating a self-perpetuating, intergenerational cycle of nonmarital births, divorce, school dropout, poverty, and associated pathologies.

Today's children are like the easily sickened birds that miners once took into mines to warn them when gas levels were getting dangerous, says Garbarino. "They show us what is coming down the road." The legacy is the fear felt by many and expressed by our newspaper carrier Luis, an 8-year-old. Two days after an unprovoked neighborhood gang stabbing of two Hispanic teens, Luis nervously remarked, "I'm scared." Asked why, he explained: "This gang called the Crips is going to kill everybody who's Mexican, and I'm Mexican. I'm wearing these long sleeves so they can't tell."

The Decline of Father Care

Another ominous trend has accompanied our culture's increasing affluence. The proportion of children not living with two parents has increased from 12 percent to 32 percent. With a third of today's infants born to unmarried mothers and 45 percent of the rest expected to experience their parents' divorce by age 18, most of today's young children will spend part or all of their childhood apart from one of their parents. Family disruption is no longer something affecting other people and their children; increasingly, it is happening to us and our children and grandchildren. Many of them will experience a succession of family settings, disruptions, and transitions. Does it matter?

For most such children, "single-parent" means father-absent, because 5.5 times as many live with their mother as with their father. With increasing family breakup, 4 in 10 children will sleep tonight in homes without their biological fathers. (By age 17, more than half will not be living with both biological parents.) Of these, only 1 in 5 see their fathers at least weekly; ten years after their parents have broken up, the number shrinks to 12 percent. In a typical year more than 35 percent never see their fathers at all. Broken bonds with a father may also entail broken bonds with paternal grandparents.

Asked to name the "adults you look up to and admire," half of children in two-parent homes, but only 20 percent of single-parent

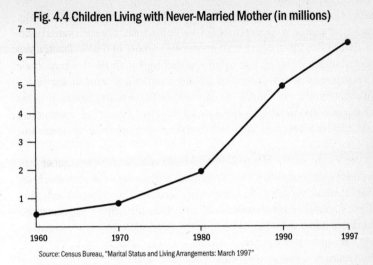

Fig. 4.4 Children Living with Never-Married Mother (in millions)

Source: Census Bureau, "Marital Status and Living Arrangements: March 1997"

children, name their father. In one national survey of children, nearly two-thirds of those living with their mother said they did not have a close relationship with their father. In Britain, too, more than half the children of divorce do not regularly see their noncustodial parent (nearly always their father). Father contact often diminishes when the mother remarries, heightening the pain and awkwardness of Dad's coming around. American mother-stepfather couples with children outnumber father-stepmother couples by a 17 to 1 ratio.

For many men, a woman and a child are a package deal, reports University of Pennsylvania sociologist Frank Furstenberg. When the relationship breaks up, "most men find it difficult to stay actively involved in their children's lives. Some men don't even try. Others make an effort and are rebuffed by the mother." When Mom remarries, Dad's coming around often becomes more painful, awkward, and infrequent. The bottom line: Divorce and nonmarital fathering impede father care (and have replaced divorce and death as the twin engines driving father absence). If we are to affirm father care we must affirm values, economic policies, and media influences that support marriage.

In her critique of individualism, Elizabeth Fox-Genovese argues that "the right to divorce has in many respects more effectively freed men from the obligation of supporting women and children than it has increased women's independence." Fathers often become like grandparents or kindly uncles—taking their children to the mall, to the movies, or out for a treat, rather than helping with homework and offering day-to-day guidance. Single moms bear most of the economic and psychological stress of providing and caring for their children. They leave one shift at work, often exhausted, to work a second shift at home (though women with husbands hardly do less domestic labor). What is more, some of the attention they and their partners once focused on their children becomes diverted to the renewal of their personal and romantic lives.

We live in an era of converging gender roles and increasing appreciation for the importance of father care. Bill Cosby's *Fatherhood,* published in 1986, sold 2 million copies in hardcover, making it the fastest selling hardcover nonfiction book in U.S. history. Spurning domestic aloofness, many men have charged into parenthood with fresh enthusiasm, attending deliveries, changing diapers, and sharing child care. Yet even in egalitarian, dual-career couples, a fact of life is that most of the child nurturing (and arranging for sitters and staying home with a sick child) still falls to Mom. The irony is that despite our celebration of fatherhood, men in general are investing less of their lives in children. We are increasingly a father-absent culture. "If there were a national index of committed fatherhood," observes Whitehead, "the fatherhood index would be falling so fast it would constitute the social equivalent of an economic crash."

The first sea change in father roles came with the Industrial Revolution, which separated work from home. In agrarian culture, fathers were on-the-job moral overseers of their children, notes Paul Taylor. Colonial child advice manuals were aimed at fathers. In the exceptional case of divorce, children often went to live with their fathers. Then, as work changed, the father became more physically distant.

Now, with the father's breadwinning responsibilities diluted, young men's family-supporting job opportunities restricted, and sexual access available outside of traditional marriage, commitment to fatherhood, especially in the economic underclass, has waned still further. Moreover, given the availability of abortion, it becomes, for many unwed biological fathers, "her choice" and responsibility if she "has the kid."

Over and over, we hear that bad things can happen in "toxic," "destructive," "dysfunctional," male-oppressed nuclear families. Today's world is scary, Stephanie Coontz grants, "but home is an even scarier place. Ninety-nine percent of kidnappers and the large majority of physical and sexual abusers of children are their parents." "We need to question the level of denial in the society when we believe that divorce results in dysfunctional adults and children," argues Diane Fassel, "while giving less weight to the numbers of intact families where affairs are common, marriages feel dead, and abuse is an everyday occurrence."

Let's set aside the easily refuted naïveté of these assumptions—that marital infidelity is commonplace, that many married people rate their marriage as unhappy, and that children of two biological parents often are abused. Granted, some intact two-parent families *are* terribly toxic, while many, many single-parent families are wonderfully nurturing. Similarly, as the tobacco industry likes to remind us, many cigarette smokers live happily into their 80s while many nonsmokers succumb to anguishing cancer deaths in their 50s. But anecdotes aside—let's not be dumb about this—does smoking (or family breakup) increase or decrease one's risk of pathology?

Said differently, should we celebrate the new family diversity? Do families come in alternate forms, each equally good? Is it harshly judgmental—a sort of cultural imperialism—not to approve all family forms? Must preferring the nuclear family—including involved biological or adoptive fathers—stigmatize struggling single parents and their children?

Actually, Whitehead reports, the "best-informed and most-articulate critics of single parenthood are single parents, particularly single mothers." I met one such eloquent person, AIDS educator Patricia Funderburk Ware of Washington, D.C., at a White House conference on character education in 1996. For 20 years, Ware was a single mom and a worker among residents of housing projects where 98 percent of households were headed by single mothers. "I don't know one single mother who has prayed, 'Dear Lord, let my child grow up to be a single parent,'" she reported. "We've been there, done that, and we know what it's like. . . . I have spoken to many audiences of single parents and received standing ovations for emphasizing the importance of marriage."

There was a time when churches banned divorced people from lay leadership, when society labeled children of the unmarried "illegitimate," when the stigma of brokenness compounded its intrinsic pain. Thankfully, such attitudes are waning. Nor should they return with a revaluing of marriage. Secure, committed, unconditional love—between a woman and a man, parents and children—is an ideal much as health is an ideal. To say health and commitment are ideals is not to judge those with broken arms, or marriages. Where there is brokenness there should be support for healing and renewal. There should also be a concern for preventing suffering—for safety-promoting structures that reduce the risk of brokenness. We need to provide an ambulance service at the base of the social cliff, yes. But we also need to build guardrails at the top. This book is about building those guardrails. As a Peruvian proverb says, "It is better to prevent than to cure."

As health is an ideal shared by those with broken and healthy bodies, so enduring love is an ideal shared by those entering a first marriage, or a second. To encourage youth to just say yes to a secure, committed, unconditional form of love needn't mean contempt or discrimination toward those who make other choices. To suggest that four hands are better than two at raising children needn't mean marginalizing struggling single parents and their children.

But are four hands in fact better than two? Does family brokenness really put children at risk? Or do family breakups and reformations, and nonmarital childbearing, represent new lifestyles that satisfy adults without harming children?

To be sure, most children of divorce and of single-parent homes develop into wonderfully happy, productive individuals. As we will see, what matters more than one versus two parents per se is the poverty, dislocation, stress, conflict, and diminished supervision that often—but not always—accompany divorce or solo parenting. (Beware social science sleight of hand, however, say marriage defenders: if they deconstruct marriage into its component benefits, they can always claim that it's the components, not the whole of marriage, that matters.)

As we shape social values and policies we confront the big question: on balance, are the sexual and divorce revolutions good, bad, or indifferent for children and their future? The National Opinion Research Center asked in a 1994 survey, "Do you agree or disagree: One parent can bring up a child as well as two parents together." Women split 50–50. Men, apparently valuing their role as fathers, *disagreed* by better than a 2 to 1 ratio. Who is right? We can reflect on this question by first looking at children's well-being, before and after 30 years of marital recession, and then comparing children of intact and divided families.

Children of Divided Families

We have seen that despite increasing American wealth, technology, education, and professional help, the well-being of children and youth has markedly declined from 1960 to the early 1990s, as indexed by levels of poverty, crime, abuse and neglect, academic difficulties, and emotional disorders. Moreover, associated with this social recession has been a marked decline in marriage, co-parenting, and father care.

So children's increasing social pathology since 1960 coincides with decreasing family solidarity, in what looks like a teeter-totter relationship: as the percentage of children living with both their natural parents has gone down, their rates of poverty, neglect, abuse, criminality, emotional disorder, and academic failure have gone up. The "liberal" risk factors of privation, joblessness, and hopelessness and the "conservative" risk factors of teen sex, unwed parents, and parental neglect all have come in the same box.

If children from intact and divided families suffer similar rates of poverty and pathology, then we could discount the impact of family disintegration. We could search instead for corrosive influences on all children. If poverty and problem behaviors occur more often among children of divorced or unwed parents than among children of intact marriages, then family breakup would become a possible culprit.

Poverty

The answers are clearest regarding poverty: Census data reveal that poverty claims 13 percent of children under age 6 living with two parents and nearly *five* times as many—59 percent—of children living with single mothers. The National Health Survey in 1988 found an even higher poverty rate among children living with never-married mothers. In one analysis, a child born to a mother who was married, older than 20, and a high school graduate had but an 8 percent chance of living in poverty; a child born to a mother who was unmarried, less than 20 years old, and not a high school graduate suffered a tenfold increased risk (79 percent) of living in poverty. Economically, not to mention psychologically, becoming an unwed mother is, says columnist Molly Ivins, "a deeply dumb thing to do."

Moreover, the phenomenon crosses national boundaries. In Canada, single-parent families comprise 12 percent of households and contain 46 percent of children in poverty. And it transcends race. Young children of white single mothers are two and a half times likelier to live in poverty than children of black married couples. Race matters, too. Children of married parents are less at risk for poverty if white. But family solidarity matters even more.

Such correlations between family status and social problems inevitably raise questions about cause and effect. Does poverty increase divorce? Or does divorce increase poverty?

It's both. The traffic between poverty and family disintegration is two-way. Poverty exacts a price. Poverty not only necessitates costly human services, which the middle class increasingly balks at paying, it entails social consequences. Poverty adds to teenagers' feelings of deprivation and degradation, and thus their eagerness to get out of their homes and get on. Young, underemployed men seldom marry. Thus, one way to support families is to raise young men's job and wage prospects, enabling them to support families. Eugene Lang in 1981 raised the prospects of 6th graders in an East Harlem school with a spontaneous offer to help pay for the college education of any of them who graduated from high school. Usually, about 1 in 4 graduated and almost none went on to college. Among these hope-filled students, 90 percent graduated and 60 percent went on to college.

But poverty is at best a partial explanation of family collapse. Starting in the early 1960s, observes Daniel Patrick Moynihan, joblessness and poverty started heading down, but marital breakdown kept going up. From 1960 to 1996 the proportion of Americans living below the poverty line decreased from 22 percent to 14 percent.

Poverty is like alcohol abuse: at any point in time it predicts various pathologies. People who live in poverty or who abuse alcohol are most at risk. Yet trends in alcohol use (which has not greatly changed since 1960) and poverty do not predict the social recession. During the depression years of the 1930s there was much more poverty, and much more family integrity.

Family disintegration also causes poverty. It costs more to run two households than one. And women's wages are still lower than men's. Thus, in one national survey, white children in families with above-the-median predivorce incomes experienced a 38 percent drop in living standards the year after a divorce. Among those with lower predivorce incomes, the 14 percent who were living in poverty before the divorce tripled to 41 percent the year after. For both women and children, Maggie Gallagher contends, "the great law of unmarriage is and remains *downward mobility.*" A 1996 Urban Institute study showed that from 1971 to 1989 the trend away from marriage accounted for "the entire rise in child poverty rates. [Thus] raising the proportion of mothers who are married would substantially reduce child poverty. . . . This evidence is about as nearly conclusive as the support for any social science proposition ever is."

Because of the collapse of alimony, the widespread failure of child support, and women's lower earnings, half the increase in child poverty in the 1980s was attributable to changes in family structure. Although government agencies are more vigorously going after deadbeat dads for child support payments, those efforts are being offset by the mushrooming number of never-married dads. Only 15 percent of never-married women with children from absent fathers receive child support payments, compared with 54 percent of divorced women. These postmodern hit-and-run fathers seldom pay support because they have little interest in either the mother or their child. In surveys, unmarried men recall having fewer offspring than unmarried women. In all, only 37 percent of the 10 million women living with children of absent fathers during 1990 were receiving any child support from these fathers. The British Rowntree Foundation discerns a similar phenomenon in the United Kingdom: "Poverty is more obviously one of the consequences of breakdown than a cause."

Such findings confirm the sad irony noted by family sociologists: although women's growing economic independence has enabled their escaping or avoiding miserable marriages, increased divorce and nonmarital births have increased many women's and children's poverty. Those who are truly concerned about poverty can therefore favor (1) a social safety net underneath the poor along with policies aimed at increasing employment and wage prospects for the underclass, and (2) the renewal of enduring marriages. The fact is, according to William Galston, "the best anti-poverty program for children is a stable, intact family." On this point Galston agrees with conservatives Charles Krauthammer (nonmarital childbearing "is the royal road to poverty") and Charles Murray (nonmarital childbearing "is the single most important social problem of our time—more important than crime, drugs, poverty, illiteracy, welfare or homelessness—because it drives everything else").

Social Problems

The social differences between children of intact and broken families are less dramatic, and certainly not huge enough to fully explain the multiplication of teen pathology. Children's well-being varies more within family types than between family types. Even in two-parent families, problems are increasing—hinting at toxic cultural forces that we will consider later. Direct parental influence, as we will also see, is overrated. Yet, University of Virginia researcher Mavis Hetherington and her colleagues conclude, divorce for whatever reason does put "children at increased risk for developing social, psychological, behavioral and academic problems."

In study after study, children of divorced parents exhibit dramatically more aggression and conduct problems than children from intact families. Best known of these studies is Judith Wallerstein's finding that half the children of 60 divorcing couples she followed in California were, on reaching young adulthood, "worried, underachieving, self-deprecating, and sometimes angry young men and women." This she attributed partly to divorcing parents "putting children on hold, attending to adult problems first. Divorce is associated with a diminished capacity to parent in almost all dimensions—discipline, playtime, physical care, and emotional support."

To most social scientists, Wallerstein's conclusions—based on a small sample of families seeking clinical help, and lacking a non-divorced control group—are less persuasive than a variety of other, less publicized findings:

- Of hard-core delinquents (overwhelmingly boys) serving in long-term correctional facilities, 7 in 10—70 percent—did not consistently live with their fathers while growing up.
- "This 70 percent figure seems to be a magic number for much social pathology," as David Lykken observes. Father-absent families accounted for approximately 7 in 10 teen runaways in 1994, 7 in 10 St. Paul, Minnesota, elementary school truants with more than twenty-two absences, and 7 in 10 antisocial boys studied at the Oregon Social Learning Center. Moreover, 7 in 10 adolescent murderers and 7 in 10 long-term prison inmates reportedly come from fatherless homes.
- In a national survey of 47,000 6th to 12th graders by the Search Institute of Minneapolis, youths from intact, two-parent homes were about half as likely to acknowledge having committed vandalism, gotten in trouble with police, stolen something, or used a weapon in the pre-

ceding 12 months. They also were half as likely to report having been physically abused or sexually abused.

- In preindustrialized societies, too, father involvement restrains male hypermasculinity and aggression. "Father-distant" cultures have the most assault and homicide. Society, as Moynihan put it in 1965, is continually beset by "invasions of barbarians"—teenage boys who become enemies of civilization unless tamed by father care and their entry into marriage and the provider role. (By one count, only 21 percent of jail inmates are married.) Speaking at Harvard two decades later, Moynihan was more persuaded than ever: "From the wild Irish slums of the 19th century Eastern seaboard to the riot-torn suburbs of Los Angeles, there is one unmistakable lesson in American history: a community that allows a large number of young men to grow up in broken families . . . never acquiring any stable relationship to male authority, never acquiring any rational expectations about the future— that community asks for and gets chaos."

Research confirms Moynihan's oft-quoted words. Even after adjusting for income, race, age, population density, and city size, juvenile violent crime is indeed more common in communities with a high proportion of one-parent families. Most fatherless boys living in a neighborhood of fatherless boys don't commit serious crime; but enough do to breed fear and suffering.

Two-parent families more successfully restrain hanging out, vandalizing, and substance abuse. A 1994 United Nations report, "Reinventing Fatherhood," illustrates: "Father Greg Boyle of Dolores Mission Church in East Los Angeles once listed the names of the first 100 gang members that came to mind and then jotted a family history next to each. All but five were no longer living with their biological fathers—if they ever had."

It's not that children from single-parent or stepparent families usually have serious problems. Most don't. We have all had or known children of divorce who are mature, loving, and successful—and children of happy marriages who are immature, hostile, or failing. Still, the stubborn fact is that children of intact families are less at risk for social problems.

Psychological Problems

The correlation between family structure and social problems is paralleled by the correlation with psychological problems. The Na-

Intact Families and Psychological Health

Data amassed from eight national surveys of adults reveal an enduring correlation between family structure and well-being. Those who grow up in intact families mature with greater well-being. As adults they are more likely to say they are "very happy" and less likely to fight and contemplate divorce if their marriage proves unhappy. In one study of 1,118 adults, divorce was barely one-third as common among couples from intact homes as among couples whose parents had both divorced. While 46 percent of adults raised by single parents end up as single parents, 77 percent of those raised in stable two-parent homes end up forming a two-parent family.

In the Search Institute's national survey of 47,000 adolescents, those living with both parents were about half as likely to report feeling "sad or depressed 'most of the time' or 'all of the time.' "

An Oregon Research Institute survey revealed that most depressed or formerly depressed western Oregon high school students live with lone parents or in stepfamilies; most never-depressed students live in two-parent families.

A recent digest of 26 Australian studies indicates that parental divorce is associated with "poor academic achievement, low self-esteem, psychological distress, delinquency, recidivism, substance use, sexual precocity, adult criminal offending, depression, and suicidal behavior."

From her ongoing studies of children of divorce, developmental psychologist Mavis Hetherington also finds that family disruption puts children at risk. She reports that the 25 percent of children of divorced or remarried couples who experience psychological disorder drops to only 10 percent among children of intact first marriages. Still, she is quick to point out, 75 percent of children of divorce are doing just fine and most will emerge as competent, well-functioning adults.

But not all. Traveling the developmental highway, some become casualties. Disrupted home backgrounds reportedly contribute to 3 in 4 teenage suicides and 4 in 5 psychiatric admissions.

tional Child Health Survey, after adjusting for differing family incomes, race, and so forth, found that the children of all forms of single-parent and stepparent families were two to three times as likely to have needed or received psychological help during the previous year. Although most children of divorce do not suffer mental health problems, they are at greater risk for them.

A research team led by Nicholas Zill has followed over time 1,147 youths participating in the government-funded National Survey of

Children. Even after controlling for sex, race, verbal ability, and parental education, youths from nondisrupted families were half as likely to have ever been treated for psychological problems (as well as half as likely to report having a poor relationship with their father *and* with their mother). When asked, "You mean a single parent can't successfully raise a child?" recent American Sociological Association president Amitai Etzioni chortled, "Sure they can. But if it were up to me, every child would have *three* parents."

Health Problems

Is a disrupted family also, as some believe, literally unhealthy? Poverty, and its links to diminished immunizations and prenatal and infant care, no doubt contributes to the greater health problems of children of never-married and divorced parents. But so do adolescent behavior differences. Children from divided families are much more likely to engage in unprotected sex, smoke cigarettes, and abuse drugs and alcohol. "These risks appear to be more pronounced for sons than for daughters of single parents," reports the National Research Council.

Thanks partly to such behavior differences, and possibly to heightened stress and risk of future divorce, parental divorce predicts a shorter life by four years. That's the conclusion drawn by Howard S.

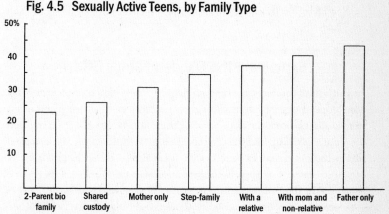

Fig. 4.5 Sexually Active Teens, by Family Type

Source: T. Luster and S. A. Small, "Youth at Risk for Teenage Parenthood," in *The State of Americans*, Urie Bronfenbrenner et al. (New York: Free Press, 1996)

Friedman and his collaborators after studying 1,284 high-IQ Californians whose lives have been followed by Stanford researchers since 1921 and whose fates were unaffected by poverty or discrimination. "In both childhood and adulthood, the trauma of divorce clearly predicted premature mortality," Friedman and his colleagues reported. A follow-up analysis suggested that the whiz kids' mortality risk stemmed partly from higher odds that their own marriages would end in divorce. Greedy morticians, it has been said, should advocate divorce.

Academic Problems

The family-structure correlates are not only social, psychological, and health related, but academic. An analysis of Census Bureau data from 115,000 15- to 24-year-olds revealed that among whites, adolescent dropout rates were 61 percent higher among those in female-headed households. Several other national surveys of thousands of youth find *doubled* dropout rates among children of single parents or stepfamilies.

Behind the numbers are real people, seen by teachers who work on education's front lines. First-grade teacher Bobbie Thomason illustrates: "I've noticed especially that little boys about age six or seven have a real hard time at school. When they don't have their father there they seem to have a real worry about it and they can't concentrate. I see it more and more the longer I teach. And I really wonder what's going to happen to this generation that's growing up, so many of them without fathers."

Explaining the Divided Family Effect

Although the facts are beyond dispute, their explanation is not. The chicken-and-egg question survives: Are children of divorce and of unwed mothers more at risk *because* of their family situation? Or are both the family breakup and the child pathology symptoms of, say, a stressed life in the economic underclass? A 1996 Robin Hood Foundation report informs us that the children of adolescent mothers are 50 percent more likely than other children to repeat a school grade and several times more likely to end up behind bars. But might this reflect nothing more than a teenage mother and child's shared genes predisposing low

Family Structure and School Performance

Do children from intact, two-parent families do better in school? The evidence:

- States with a high proportion of two-parent families also tend to have high state academic achievement scores.

- According to a National Association of Elementary School Principals study, two-parent children are twice as likely as single-parent children to be high achievers.

- After studying some 59,000 students at more than 1,000 high schools, Princeton and Johns Hopkins University researchers found that those growing up in intact families are more likely than those from single-parent and stepparent families to attend regularly, earn good grades, and stay in school.

- Among 9,915 6- to 17-year-olds responding to a recent nationally representative health survey conducted by the Census Bureau, the likelihood of having repeated a grade was about half among children of two-parent families (14 percent) as among children living with solo parents (24 percent) or grandparents (28 percent).

intelligence? Although it is indeed easy to overestimate parental influence from these correlations, *something* environmental has caused the social recession. (The human gene pool has not radically changed since 1960.)

To answer such questions, a Machiavellian scientist would prefer to randomly assign children to different family arrangements and see what develops. Back in the real world, the next best possibilities are (1) to delve into the "tangle of pathologies" and statistically extract the influence of other likely differences between intact and broken families, and (2) to follow children from before to after divorce.

Statistically Isolating the Family-Structure Factor

Shall we attribute the family-structure difference mostly to nature (heredity) or nurture (environment)? If the latter, what combination of environmental factors is responsible? Seeking answers, researchers have isolated the family effect from the tangle of interrelated factors.

In studying the family component of academic success, for example, researchers have found that after controlling for intelligence score, children of intact families score higher on various achievement tests and receive higher grades. And after adjusting for race, sex, parental education, number of siblings, and place of residence, the halved drop-out rate from two-parent families continues.

To be sure, most kids in disrupted families successfully graduate, while some of their peers in intact families drop out. Still, the statistical risk is not trivial. In the National Longitudinal Survey of Youth, for example, the adjusted risk of dropping out of high school was 29 percent among children of lone parents or stepfamilies but only 13 percent among children of two-parent households.

Several very important but underpublicized studies explore the family-structure contribution to psychological and social well-being. One Swedish study of the more than 15,000 children born in Stockholm in 1953 and still living there in 1963 found that "parental separation or divorce has negative effects on later mental health whenever it occurs and regardless of the socioeconomic status of the household." Perhaps the best available data come from Zill's summary of the National Center for Health Statistics' 1981 Child Health Survey of 15,416 randomly sampled children and from a 1988 repeat of this survey with 17,110 more children. Zill recognized that intact and broken families differ in many ways—race, children's ages, parental education, income, and family size—so he statistically adjusted scores to extract such influences. Even so, children of intact families were less likely to display antisocial and "acting out" behavior. In these national surveys of children, those living with both parents were half as likely as those living without fathers to have been suspended or expelled from school or to have had misbehavior reported by the school. In the 1988 national survey, children in intact families were, no matter what their age or race, half as vulnerable to school problems and were a third less likely to repeat a grade.

These data suggest that the social pathologies people often associate with race have more to do with family form. Control for race and you still get an effect of intact versus broken families. Control for family structure, and race hardly matters. Moreover, turn-of-the-century black families had more solidarity than today's white families. In 1925, 85 percent of Harlem's black families had an in-home father. So, although the African-American community is ground zero for the effects of today's social toxins, the problems are national human problems, not, at root, racial problems. If you want to predict risk for childhood poverty, health, and behavior problems and can ask but one ques-

Fig. 4.6 5- to 17- Year-Olds Who Have Experienced School Problems

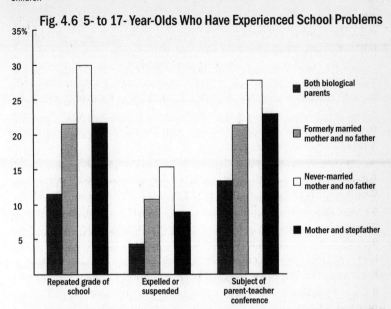

Sources: National Health Survey of 17,110 children conducted by the Census Bureau in 1988 for the National Center for Health Statistics (reported in Deborah A. Dawson, "Family Structure and Children's Health: United States, 1988," *Vital and Health Statistics Series* 10, no. 178 [1991], DHHS publication no. PHS 91-1506)

tion, ask not about the child's race. Ask whether or not the child lives with two loving, invested parents.

Following Lives Through Time

In further pursuit of possible divorce effects, a research team led by Andrew Cherlin used the second strategy, comparing children before and after divorce. This monumental but rarely discussed study began when researchers interviewed 17,414 women—the mothers of 98 percent of all British children born during the first full week of March 1958. Cherlin and his co-workers had parents and teachers rate the behavior of nearly 12,000 children as 7-year-olds and again four years later, knowing that by then some would have experienced divorce. At the second rating, boys whose parents had divorced during the four years had about one-fourth more behavior problems than those whose families remained intact.

But people wonder: are children's postdivorce problems influenced solely by the marriage breakup or also by the preexisting marital problems (divorce or no)? "Staying in an unhappy marriage is psychologically damaging," asserts University of Washington sociologist Pepper Schwartz, "and staying only for the children's sake is ultimately not in your interest or anyone else's." Happier, separated parents make for happier children is the implied theory, described by William Doherty as "psychological trickle-down." In *Creative Divorce: A New Opportunity for Personal Growth,* therapist Mel Krantzler argues that family breakup can make children more sensitive and tolerant, by stimulating "more cooperation and respect, more regard for differences as well as similarities, more opportunity for children to grow into the unique individuals they are capable of becoming."

So, rather than stay together for the sake of the children, should unhappy couples divorce for the sake of the children? (Never mind the unrealism of comparing the effects of hateful "bad marriages" to the unlikely cordiality of an ensuing "good divorce," says Maggie Gallagher. And never mind that no one ever flips the egocentric "my child will be happy if I'm happier" formula to a more child-centered "I'll be happier if my child is happy.")

The British researchers found that the apparent divorce effect was not quite halved by subtracting predivorce behavior differences between the two groups (suggesting that divorce added to the effect of predivorce problems). When again restudying the children at age 16, the researchers found that, even after adjusting for predivorce problems, the odds of scoring above the clinical cutoff for psychopathology were 39 percent greater among those whose parents had divorced in the intervening years. Predivorce misery did not fully explain postdivorce problems.

When the children had reached 23, the intrepid researchers traced and interviewed 12,537 of the original sample, enabling them to compare those who at 7 were living with two biological parents and whose parents had divorced versus not divorced by age 16. Again, controlling for predivorce family problems did not weaken the divorce effect. Moreover, among children of divorce, 45 percent had cohabited — more than double the approximately 19 percent among children of intact marriages and nearly double the 24 percent among children of families broken by a parental death. "Parental divorce seems to have stimulated a pattern of behavior characterized by early home-leaving due to conflict with parents and stepparents and early sexual activity outside marriage—leading, in this cohort, to a greater likelihood of premarital birth and cohabitation," said the researchers. "Parental death, in contrast, has a substantially weaker effect." Yet another follow-up, with 11,759 of the participants at age 33, confirmed the emotional aftermath of the chain of events that often began with parental divorce.

One conclusion of this important study: by launching children into "negative life trajectories through adolescence into adulthood," divorce predicts increased social problems. Sociologist Sara McLanahan, for ten years a single mom and an admirer of the resourcefulness and strength of single-parent families, now documents the intergenerational cycle of family disintegration. "When I first got into this research, I wanted to demonstrate that single mothers could do just as good a job of raising children as married moms. Unfortunately, the evidence led me to somewhat different conclusions."

Disentangling Family Status and Poverty

But what about income differences? Is the "family disruption effect" on academic success really just a proxy for an underlying poverty effect? Is it true, as some have argued, that "the major problem faced by single-parent families is not the lack of a male's presence, but the lack of a male income"? In their informative book, *Growing Up with a Single Parent*, McLanahan and Sandefur argue that it makes little sense to adjust for incomes when comparing family types: "We view low income as partly the *result*, as well as partly the cause, of family disruption." Whitehead offers a helpful analogy: extracting the effect of other factors that correlate with family breakup makes family structure less significant— "just as disaggregating Hurricane Andrew into wind, rain, and tides can make it disappear as a meteorological phenomenon." A "hurricane" is a package variable. Likewise, family disruption is a package variable that entails, among other things, increased risk of poverty and dislocation and diminished nurturance and supervision.

The poverty factor is itself a package variable. Youths living in father-absent homes live with lost economic resources, more poverty, and in neighborhoods with more joblessness, more violence, and a lower tax base to support schools. Like children of stepfamilies, they change residences more often and thus have disrupted routines and attachments and weaker connections to a support network of friends and neighbors. Repeatedly uprooted children, like repotted plants, have weakened roots. Like adults mourning a death, children—especially children not securely bonded to two married parents—mourn when saying goodbye to friends, classmates, teachers, ministers, home, and neighborhood. With each move, they lose their place among peers and must work to gain acceptance in a new locale. One therefore needn't attribute the divided-family effect to deficient parenting; it may instead result from a tangle of factors associated with solo parenting.

In the 1988 National Health Interview Survey of 9,915 American youths, 18 percent of kids who had moved frequently had four or more behavioral problems, as did only 7 percent of those who rarely or never had moved. Even after controlling for race and other demographic differences, those who moved frequently were 77 percent more likely to have four or more behavior problems. Poor communities with rapid population turnover typically have high violent crime rates; poor, stable communities do not. So nonmarital childbearing and family breakup increase the risk of poverty and mobility, which increase the risk of various social and psychological pathologies.

As we have already seen, risks for many social and psychological problems are nevertheless double even when controlling for income, as sociologist Douglas Downey discovered when he compared more than 18,000 eighth graders from various family backgrounds. Downey mined information gathered on these youths and their families by the National Center for Education Statistics, and he discovered that children of single mothers, whose incomes averaged about $18,000, performed more poorly in school than children of married biological parents, whose incomes averaged $51,000. With no more information than this, we couldn't know whether lower income rather than family disruption makes all the difference (even if we dismiss the effect of family breakup on household income). But Downey also took a look at children living with single fathers, whose incomes averaged $36,000 and who were more likely to be white and well educated. Despite these advantages, children of single fathers did no better in school than children of single mothers. (But compared with children of never-married parents, those living with a divorced parent "have a big edge," reports the Census Bureau. As a group, divorced parents are more educated, more likely to be homeowners, and less likely to be poor.)

Moreover, children in stepfamilies enjoy double the family income ($55,000) of children in single-parent families ($27,000) and nearly the family income of those in two-parent families ($61,000), report Mc-

Lanahan and Sandefur with more recent data. Yet "remarriage reduces nor improves a child's chances of graduating from high or avoiding a teenage birth." In general, children fare equally well whether reared by a single mom, a single dad, or a remarried mom and stepdad, and whether reared by a same-sex or other-sex parent. Such findings strengthen the conclusion we have formed from other data: family disruption puts youths at risk not only by amplifying poverty but also by corroding their general well-being. McLanahan and Sandefur offer a synopsis: "Children who grow up with only one parent are more likely to have problems in school, to drop out of school prematurely, to become teen mothers, and to have trouble finding a steady job, as compared with children who grow up with both parents. Parents . . . should realize that lack of income, and income loss associated with divorce, are responsible for about half of the disadvantages associated with living in a single-parent family, and that too little supervision and parental involvement and too much residential mobility account for most of the remaining disadvantage."

These findings strengthen our confidence in the transcultural ideal: children thrive best when raised by two parents who are enduringly committed to each other and to their child's welfare. And they remind us of a truth that ensuing chapters will explore and that many people prefer to ignore: economic and workplace policies and media influences that undermine this ideal are therefore upstream roots of poverty, abuse, educational failure, and much unhappiness.

To say that two-parent families and their surrounding environment generally work best need not demean single parents. When asked about their child-rearing values—how important is doing well at school? controlling temper? being kind?—single, divorced, and married mothers do not differ. Nor do they differ much in how much time they invest in activities like helping their children with homework. What differs much more is the engagement of present versus absentee fathers (although even married fathers devote less time than mothers to playing, working, and talking with children).

Casualties of Conflict?

To hold two-parent families up as the ideal also does not mean that they should always be preserved, or that single-parent families are all dysfunctional. Some children *are* better off when their mothers escape

Other Voices

"Families and their children are in serious trouble. . . . It is now 23 years [since the White House Conference on Children and] children and families are in even more desperate straits today."

—Founding Head Start director Edward F. Zigler

"The problems of America's young people are getting significantly worse, not better. This . . . is a national tragedy that will have a serious impact on all of us."

—National Academy of Sciences, Panel on High-Risk Youth, 1993

"Children growing up in [single-parent] households are at greater risk for experiencing a variety of behavioral and educational problems, including extremes of hyperactivity or withdrawal, lack of attentiveness in the classroom, difficulty in deferring gratification, impaired academic achievement, school misbehavior, absenteeism, dropping out, involvement in socially alienated peer groups, and, especially, the so-called 'teenage syndrome' of behaviors that tend to hang together—smoking, drinking, early and frequent sexual experience, violence, and criminal acts."

—Urie Bronfenbrenner

"Over all continents and throughout all history, no society ever thrived without family. True, there were all kinds of arrangements, from extended families to clans that helped do the parenting. In India, it is said, a child was always in somebody's arms. In Africa, we are told, it takes a whole village to raise a child. But these wondrous social fabrics gave additional support rather than replaced the nuclear family. Our society increasingly has neither."

—Amitai Etzioni

"I know of few other bodies of data in which the weight of evidence is so decisively on one side of the issue: on the whole, for children, two-parent families are preferable."

—David Popenoe

"In a society with a 50 percent divorce rate—in which a host of social pathologies can be traced directly to havoc in fatherless or broken homes—policymakers and theorists are right to place a high priority on measures aimed at keeping families intact."

—Pepper Schwartz

a conflict-ridden or abusive marriage, sometimes to an alcoholic husband. Dozens of researchers have studied marital conflict and their verdict is in. In the words of West Virginia University psychologists Patrick Davies and Mark Cummings, "destructive forms of marital conflict undermine children's feelings of emotional security." This appears to be one reason why children of a widowed parent generally fare somewhat better, especially in school, than children of other disrupted families. Death and abandonment are not social equivalents, argues father advocate David Blankenhorn. Parental death is less damaging—less rejecting, less self-blame producing, less conflict laden—than abandonment.

Parents whose marriages are more satisfying and aren't riddled with conflict are less preoccupied, less irritable, and more available to respond sensitively to their children's needs. In general, the better the marriage, the better the parent-child relations. So, yes, there is truth to the saying that the best thing you can do for your children is to make a priority of loving your mate. If, despite your best efforts, severe conflict with your spouse is overwhelming you and your children, "then divorce would generally be in children's best interest," sociologists Paul Amato and Alan Booth conclude from their studies of children growing up with family upheaval.

After divorce, the less parental conflict there is, the better off the child will be. In a "good" divorce, the separated parents live near each other, cooperate, communicate, and jointly share responsibilities and sacrifices for their children's sake. After identifying strengths of various family types, sociologists Alan Acock and David Demo conclude "that the future strength of single-parent and two-parent families rests on greater responsibility and more nurturant involvement of residential and nonresidential fathers." New programs for engaging absent fathers with their children should help. Yet parental cooperation and nurturant father care are precisely what children from one-parent families are less likely to receive, according to McLanahan and Sandefur. Stanford psychologist Eleanor Maccoby believes that conflicts with nonresidential fathers over visitation and their differing expectations help explain why father contact, though sometimes beneficial, does not predict improved adjustment among most children living with mothers. The irony is, says Blankenhorn, "The 'better' a divorce looks, the more it looks like, well, marriage . . . minus the sex."

Moreover, there are good reasons to work to save the marriage:

- Couples are more painfully aware of their marital conflict than are their children, who neither witness nor comprehend it all. (Children appear less influenced by direct parental behavior than by other influences linked with family structure.)
- About 7 in 10 divorces today—an increasing number as divorce has become more acceptable—represent the termination of low-conflict marriages that, whatever their shortcomings, are generally better for

children than divorce. The increasing termination of low-conflict marriages helps explain a surprising finding. One might suppose that children of divorce would fare better in countries where there is no longer
much stigma against divorce. In reality, children of divorce mature
with lower well-being in (individualistic) countries with a *high* divorce
rate.

- A new Dutch study of 2,517 youths reveals that those from conflicted intact families enjoy well-being that is intermediate between those from
  peaceful intact homes and those from single-parent homes.

- Recall the British study showing that children suffer worsened problems *after* their parents divorce. New research similarly has followed a
  national sample of American families through time. Again, even when
  controlling for preexisting marital conflict, divorce exacts a price on
  children.

- And recall that divorce increases economic stresses and likelihood of
  changed residence and severed attachments.

After comparing children of divorced and intact couples, Martin
Seligman reported "a very nasty picture for the children of divorce. It
used to be said that it is better for the children to have their unhappy
parents divorce than to live with two parents who hate each other. But
our findings show a bleak picture for these children: prolonged, unre-
lieved depression; a much higher rate of disruptive events; and, very
strangely, much more apparently unrelated misfortune. It would be irresponsible for us not to advise you to take these dismaying data seriously if you are thinking about divorce."

To be sure, children's responses to divorce vary. Whether they cope
well or develop behavior problems depends not only on the intensity of
parental conflict but on the children's temperament and whether they
are uprooted from familiar friends and classmates. The children who
are given lots of love and support from nearby relatives, friends, neighbors, or religious group members are less at risk for problems.

Nevertheless, concludes William Galston, "significant differences
do emerge, differences that can and should shape our understanding
of social policy." Nicholas Zill, noting that family disruption doubles
many risk factors for children, agrees: "In epidemiological terms, the
doubling of a hazard is a substantial increase. . . . The increase in risk
that dietary cholesterol poses for cardiovascular disease, for example,
is far less than double, yet millions of Americans have altered their
diets because of the perceived hazard." Lowering cholesterol levels in
a culture would not eliminate heart disease, but it would tip the odds

more toward health. Likewise, a more family-friendly culture—one in which parents could swim with rather than against the cultural current—would not eliminate broken bonds, but it would tip the odds toward greater human well-being.

Why Is Family Disruption Toxic for Children?

What factors make some family breakups toxic for children? Research is now shifting from simple comparisons of intact and nonintact biological families to studies of family dynamics that influence children. So far I have stressed one toxic effect of family disruption—increased risk of poverty and its detrimental side effects, such as dislocations and broken social bonds with friends, neighbors, and classmates.

Another potential toxin is the stress that children often experience in the midst of parental discord and separation. Children are conservative. They like things the way they've known them. They like to reread the same books, clutch the same stuffed animal, rewatch the same movies, reenact the same family traditions. They like to live in the familiar house, eat familiar foods, attend the familiar school. If you doubt it, try introducing a 10-year-old to sushi or rearranging the family-room furniture, and then watch them recoil in horror.

Attachment mechanisms bind children to their family and surroundings. And not just children: a mountain of social psychological research shows that mere repeated exposure to everything from musical selections to faces will increase liking. Shown photos of ourselves, we even prefer our familiar mirror image to an actual photo (which our friends prefer). Familiarity breeds content.

When a family divides, things change. The child's world is ripped apart. At least one of the parents moves; sometimes both do, necessitated by the economic loss. Thus, Hetherington and her colleagues report, immediately following their parents' divorce many children feel angry, resentful, and depressed. They long to have their family restored. When it doesn't happen, young children may blame themselves. Older children may exhibit heightened aggression and noncompliance. Divorce is therefore good for the therapy business.

Within two or three years, life typically regains a familiar, comfortable equilibrium. Then, often three to five years after the divorce, there may come a second dose of stress: the custodial parent's remarriage. Because 75 percent of divorced mothers and 80 percent of divorced fathers remarry, most children of divorce will gain a stepparent. Especially for girls, the new stepfather's intrusion into the home may at first be an unwelcome event, disrupting the mother-daughter relationship and requiring another period of readjustment. "Divorce" is less a single stressful event than a series of them. "Children of divorce" are therefore often children of instability, experiencing single parenting, cohabiting parenting, stepparenting—times two if they are engaged with both parents. David Popenoe, who teaches courses on marriage and family at Rutgers, has therefore "never met the child who did not want to be raised, if possible, by both biological parents who stayed together and cooperated in child rearing at least until the child's maturity (and hopefully for life)."

Books and greeting cards on divorce acknowledge the stress that separation creates for children, notes Whitehead. They often celebrate the new freedoms—the opportunities to choose your own friends and activities and fulfill your own needs. But they tell a different story for children ("I'm sorry I'm not always there when you need me"). *Dinosaurs Divorce: A Guide for Changing Families,* a popular picture book for young children undergoing family dissolution, offers advice: "If you move, you may have to say good-bye to friends and familiar places. But soon your new home will feel like the place you really belong. . . . Living with one parent almost always means there will be less money. Be prepared to give up some things. . . . Divorce may mean twice as much celebrating at holiday times, but you may feel pulled apart. . . . You may sometimes feel jealous and want your parent to yourself. Be polite to your parents' new friends, even if you don't like them at first."

The breaking of family and peer bonds does more than create stress for children. It terminates most of the moral support that parents offer each other—the nightly pillow talk celebrating or commiserating over the children, the shared decisions about privileges and discipline, the encouragement and mutual backing offered in times of conflict with a child, the relief from 24-hour responsibility. Moreover, with half as many parents around, each now burdened with maintaining a household solo and developing new relationships, supervision of the children ebbs. No wonder 50 percent of D.C.-area children of divorce said their parents spent "too little time" with them—double the 26 percent of children of married parents with the same complaint. A national study of 59,000 high school students also showed, Nan Astone and Sara McLanahan found, that those with single parents or stepparents received less encouragement and help with school work than did those living with both original parents. Woody Allen apparently thought such detachment mattered little. Contradicting those who view child rearing as a labor-intensive task, he told the *New York Times Magazine* (a year before his relationship with Mia Farrow exploded), "It's not any accomplishment to have or raise kids. Any fool can do it."

The Limits of Parents' Influence

Parental influence is "enormously powerful in determining what happens to a child," Hewlett and West contend. "Whether a child acquires discipline and self-esteem and becomes a well-adjusted, productive person is largely a function of parental input" as well as communal support. A mountain of recent evidence, however, shows that children's *personalities* (including their temperament, timidity, and aggressiveness) are less fragile and malleable than presumed by Hewlett and West—and by John Bradshaw and other family-bashing "recovery therapists" whom they rightly scorn. The evidence speaks to some important questions: Should I blame my middle-aged friends whose children have committed suicide or been in mental hospitals or prisons? Should I feel guilty for difficulties suffered by my own children? Should we pass city ordinances that punish parents for their children's misdeeds? Or does talk of wounding fragile children, through variations in the normal range of parenting, trivialize the brutality of real abuse, the force of real addictions, and the stress of family collapse?

If children's personalities are shaped by parental handling, it might be assumed that children who share the same parents should be noticeably alike. But that presumption is refuted by the most dramatic recent finding in developmental psychology. According to behavior geneticists Robert Plomin and Denise Daniels, "Two children in the same family [are on average] as different from one another as are pairs of children selected randomly from the population." This is a phenomenon recognizable to many parents who have several children, and especially to those who have several adopted children.

The claim of limited parental influence on personality is so provocative—if true, it requires dumping much of popular psychology into the trash—that it deserves explanation. The stunning findings: Adopted siblings do not develop more similar personalities if reared in the same home rather than different homes. And identical twins are not more alike in personality if reared together than if reared in separate homes. In *Nature's Thumbprint,* Peter and Alexander Neubauer illustrate.

> Identical twin men, now age thirty, were separated at birth and raised in different countries by their respective adoptive parents. Both kept their lives neat—neat to the point of pathology. Their clothes were preened, appointments met precisely on time, hands scrubbed regularly to a raw, red color. When the first was asked why he felt the need to be so clean, his answer was plain.
>
> "My mother. When I was growing up she always kept the house perfectly ordered. She insisted on every little thing returned to its proper place, the clocks—we had dozens of clocks—each set to the same noonday chime. She insisted on this, you see. I learned from her. What else could I do?"
>
> The man's identical twin, just as much a perfectionist with soap and water, explained his own behavior this way: "The reason is quite simple. I'm reacting to my mother, who was an absolute slob."

As developmental psychologist Judith Rich Harris explains in her provocative and well-argued book *The Nurture Assumption,* genetic influences explain roughly 40 to 50 percent of our individual variations in personality traits. Shared environmental influences—the home situation that siblings share—account for less than 10 percent of personality differences. If we left a group of children with their same schools, neighborhoods, and peers but switched the parents around, says Harris (referring to their temperaments and personalities, not their values), they "would develop into the same sort of adults." (Remember, schools, neighborhoods, and peers are part of the variation between the average solo-parent and two-parent family.)

Indeed, argues Harris, cultural influences, including those of peer groups, are potent. She offers examples:

- Preschoolers who disdain a certain food, despite parents' urgings, will often eat the food if put at a table with a group of children who like it.
- Children exposed to one language accent at home and another in the neighborhood will invariably end up speaking like their peers, not their parents.
- To predict whether a teenager smokes, ask not whether a parent smokes but whether the teenager has friends who smoke, who suggest its pleasures, and who offer cigarettes.
- Nazi youth group members 60 years ago mostly came from emotionally supportive middle-class homes, adds behavior geneticist David Rowe.

What corrupted them was not bad parenting but the "heavier weight" of cultural change around them.

The impact of family disruption is mostly indirect, Harris believes. First, there seems to be a genetic component. Men who propagate and split without marrying may be more impulsive and sensation seeking (and therefore crime prone) than those who propagate and stay. People who divorce may likewise be more impulsive, disagreeable, or alcoholism prone. Such traits are known to have a heritable component.

Genetic influences do not explain children's exploding pathology since 1960 (the gene pool wouldn't have radically changed in this eye-blink of history). Nor in the massive British long-term study do they readily explain the rising problems *after* parental separation. A study of 1,018 female twin pairs in 1996 revealed that the risks of family disruption are not all genetic, however. "Childhood parental loss through separation . . . substantially increased the risk" of adult alcoholism, the research team reported. Family disruptions also change the social ecology. They entail changed residences, increased poverty, decreased status, and altered peer influences. Vietnamese-American youths are more likely to exhibit high achievement if many of their friends are within their achievement-oriented ethnic group—which occurs more often for those from two-parent homes, often with an in-home grand-parent as well.

If children's psychological disorders stem more from toxic cultural and peer influences (and, yes, genetic influences) than from direct parental influence, what does this tell us? First, it tells us to agonize less about our in-home parenting style and more about the cultural va-pors seeping into our children's lives. To nurture our children well, we must care about the social environment that nurtures all children, and care about all who influence the ethos of that environment. Teachers, youth workers, and media producers and artists must appreciate the significance of their influence on youth culture. Mary Pipher is right: "Children are much more socialized by the culture than even the most conscious parent realizes."

Second, it cautions us to be less judgmental. Parents typically feel pride in their children's successes, and guilt or shame over their failures. They beam when folks offer congratulations for the child who wins an award. They wonder where they went wrong with the child who re-peatedly is called into the principal's office. Psychiatry and Freudian psychology have at times been the source of such ideas, by blaming problems from asthma to schizophrenia on "bad mothering."

Society reinforces such parent blaming. In many communities, parents can now be fined for their child's misbehavior (as if parents of troubled children weren't already suffering enough). Should we really blame the parents of Kip Kinkel (and an accomplished older sister) for his murder of them and two fellow students in the cafeteria of his Springfield, Oregon, high school in 1998? "Good parents usually have good kids. Bad parents usually have bad kids," explained a letter writer in the *Detroit Free Press*. "Do you really think those killer kids came from healthy homes? When parents fail, shame should follow them."

The extremes do confirm a power to parenting—witness the abused who become abusive, the neglected who become neglectful. University of Minnesota psychologist David Lykken agrees with Harris that parenting style matters little from the 10th to the 90th percentile. At the upper extreme, he suspects, "there are some super-parents who really do make a lasting difference, the parents who succeed in socializing the really difficult children, for example. And I am confident that the bottom ten percent, the immature, abusive, unsocialized, or simply incompetent parents (which include a large proportion of the rising tide of impoverished and overburdened single mothers) are responsible for the epidemic of crime and other social pathology that has been accelerating in this country since the 1960s."

Witness, too, the advantages to children co-nurtured by married, biological parents. Witness the documented influence of parents on their children's values, faith, and politics. (A pair of adopted children or identical twins *will* have more similar religious beliefs if reared in the same home.) Witness the remarkable academic and vocational successes of children of Asian boat people—successes attributed to close-knit, supportive, even demanding families and to the kids not yet being assimilated into American peer culture. If parents can head their kids in the right direction and see that they have friends from like-minded backgrounds, as the Amish have done with their distinct communities, then parental influence can take hold. "A bunch of people got together and decided to make Hebrew the language of their new country, and they taught their kids to speak Hebrew," observes Harris. When kids found other kids speaking Hebrew they made it their native language. Parents together achieved what parents alone couldn't (without minimizing peer contact, à la home schooling).

If the normal range of parenting styles hardly shows up in children's temperaments and personalities, then we can look skeptically on all the child-rearing recipe books, and we can dismiss the recent spate of parent-bashing books (with titles like *Toxic Parents, How to Avoid Your Parents' Mistakes When You Raise Your Children,* and *The Emotional Incest Syndrome*). We can also discount baby boomers' complaints about their overbearing mothers and emotionally distant fathers; the current generation, with its disappearing fathers, has it much worse. The rapidly declining well-being of America's youth since 1960, which genetics cannot explain, helps focus our attention on what has changed —the social ecology. Family breakdown and parental abandonment, like abuse and neglect, are huge factors. These macro-parenting factors, along with changes in peer and media influences, are the ones that matter—indeed, the only ones that matter, it now seems. The social science verdict bears repeating, because it is so important and so little known: Normal variations in well-meaning parenting matter less than most people suppose. Family collapse, and the social ecology it often entails, matters more than many suppose.

But our analysis cannot stop here, for the disintegration of nuclear families in an age of radical individualism is itself a social phenomenon in need of explanation. What are the forces corroding marriage and father commitment? Why do parents in general find parenthood more stressful than did parents in the 1950s? Why do so many parents today—single and coupled alike—feel as if they are trying to swim upstream against toxic cultural forces? And how can we renew the social values and ecology that nurture healthy, happy people?

CHAPTER 5

Violence

If we saw on this morning's news reports that a foreign power had killed 25,000 Americans or raped 106,000 American women, we would be at war by the afternoon.

—LOUIS FREEH, inaugural address as FBI director, 1993

"Dear Mr. Clinton,

"I want you to stop the killing in the city. People is dead and I think that somebody might kill me. So would you please stop the people from deading. I'm asking you nicely to stop it. I know you can do it. Do it. I now you could. Your friend, James."

So wrote 9-year-old James Darby from New Orleans on April 29, 1994. On May 8, James was killed in a drive-by shooting. As he walked home from a Mother's Day picnic with friends and family, Joseph Norfleet, 19, pulled his car alongside James and shot him in the head with a shotgun.

Not long before, Yoshihiro Hattori, a 16-year-old Japanese exchange student, went searching for a Halloween party in Baton Rouge. Showing up at the wrong house, he apparently misunderstood homeowner Rodney Peairs's command to freeze, whereupon Peairs shot and killed him. In shocked Japan, where violent crime is rare, Hattori's parents collected nearly a million signatures calling for a ban on handguns in American homes. Japanese newspapers and survival seminars taught America-bound travelers how to respond when told to "stick 'em up," "hold it," or "don't move a muscle."

Not long after, the public was stunned by a series of murders of children by fellow children as young as 7 and 8 and school shootings that from 1997 to 1999 left 29 teachers and students dead in Jonesboro, Arkansas, West Paducah, Kentucky, Pearl, Mississippi, Springfield, Oregon, and Littleton, Colorado. "Children without conscience," an alarming *People* magazine cover was headlined. President Clinton pointed an accusatory finger at violence-glorifying television and video games. The media makers pointed at negligent families.

Although Woody Allen's prediction that "by 1990 kidnapping will be the dominant mode of social interaction" has not been fulfilled, such happenings horrify us. Stunned by random carjackings, tourist assassinations on Florida highways, and children gunning down children, Americans are, in President Clinton's words, "finally coming to grips with the accumulated wave of crime and violence and the breakdown of family and community." "Something profound has happened to your country because of this," Clinton explained to Columbine High School students one month after the Littleton massacre. Crime levels remain high, but their recent declines raise hopes that civic renewal is indeed under way. Consider, then, the perceptions and reality of crime in America, and how crime trends reflect our changing social ecology.

Crime Fears

"Will my children be safe outside if I move to your neighborhood?" asks a friend who is considering a move to a home near mine in the center of our small midwestern city. "Can they walk unchaperoned to school?"

Such questions dominate many a conversation around kitchen tables and across backyards. Our fears are fanned by stories of predatory packs of rapacious teens and of tragic victims like 12-year-old Polly Klaas, abducted from her bedroom and then murdered. "This summer's craze among gangs of boys in [New York] city is 'whirlpooling,'" explains the London *Times* in depicting America's "generation of lost ideals." "Ten or 12 boys pick on a girl in one of the big municipal swimming pools, encircle her chanting rap songs with misogynist lyrics, lock arms and move in like sharks, ripping her bathing suit off and physically molesting her. There were attacks five days in a row last week. . . . The assumption that only alienated members of an underclass behave in this way towards the opposite sex is wrong. In a middle-class suburb of New Jersey, four high school footballers were convicted of raping and sexually assaulting a retarded girl with a toy baseball bat and a broom handle."

Small wonder that Americans became alarmed:

- "Crime" has become a "very serious" threat to Americans' rights and freedoms, agreed 83 percent of those responding to a recent Gallup poll. Indeed, we came to think, crime is a much greater danger than "military threat from a foreign country," which only 23 percent rated as very serious. (Curiously, though, we still devote 3.7 times as much money to national defense as to state and local police protection and corrections. We spend billions on weapons the Pentagon doesn't want, while declaring we can't afford the family supports mentioned in the next chapter.)
- Asked by *Money* to rate 43 qualities that influenced desirability when choosing a place to live, Americans rated "low crime rate" number one, surpassing clean water and air, low taxes, good schools, and affordable housing.
- Just after the 1993 crime peak, a survey of New Yorkers found that 42 percent—representing nearly 3 million people—said they had been victims of crime in the previous year. More than half a million had their houses or apartments broken into. Some 600,000 were mugged or assaulted. More than 1.5 million had their cars broken into. Surrendering, many city dwellers placed signs in their car windows saying "No radio"—pleading with thieves to look elsewhere for booty.
- A 1999 Gallup Youth Survey found 4 in 10 teenagers thinking that, at some point in their lifetimes, someone is likely to fire a gun at them. Four in ten also were fearful of walking alone at night in certain areas within a mile of their homes, and half expected at some point to be mugged.

Shortly after becoming first lady, Hillary Clinton summed up the national longing for a safer past: "I want to live in a place again where I can walk down any street without being afraid. I want to be able to take my daughter to a park at any time of day or night in the summer and remember what I used to be able to do when I was a little kid."

Crime Facts

But how bad, really, was the recent "crime epidemic"? Viewed in a long historical perspective, these were not the worst of times. Between 1550 and 1850, the original Thugs, members of a criminal fraternity in northern India, strangled more than 2 million people, claiming

to do so in the service of a goddess. Historian Lawrence Stone estimates that England's murder rate during the 1400s was 10 to 20 times
that in contemporary England and also greater than New York City's
in 1994. Then, during the 16th and 17th centuries, education, churchgoing, courtly manners, and government policing and justice increased,
and homicide decreased. Crime rates in England mushroomed during
the first half of the 1800s, then plummeted during the later 1800s. As
cultural values change, high violence rates *can* be brought down.

After 1960, the total violent crime rate reported in the FBI's annual
summation soared. Relative to 1960, the average American at the 1993
crime peak was twice as likely to be murdered, four times as likely to
report being raped, four times as likely to be robbed, and five times as
likely to be assaulted. One's risk of being murdered in 1993 was eight
times greater than in 1900. Violent crime also surged in other Western nations. In Britain, the number of violent crimes noted by police
doubled between 1984 and the peak year of 1992. Yet no other industrialized nation's homicide rate rivals America's. Canadians, for example,
are one-third as likely to be murdered. In all, 1.6 million Americans in
1997 reported to police their having been robbed, beaten, knifed, shot,
raped, or otherwise assaulted, and 18,000 more were murdered.

Each loved one lost represents a set of shocked family members and
friends, and an enduring empty spot in their hearts. Margaret Ensley's
17-year-old son, Michael, was shot and killed in his high school hallway
by a teenager who thought Michael gave him a funny look. The shooter,
said Mrs. Ensley, is now serving ten years in a youth-authority camp.
"But I have life imprisonment without the possibility of parole, because
I won't ever have my son back again. . . . When they were filling his
crypt, I said, 'Lord, let me crawl up there with him,' because the pain
was so unbearable."

In 1960, we had 3.3 police officers for every violent crime reported.
By the 1993 crime peak, we had 3.5 violent crimes reported for every
police officer. Said differently, every police officer in 1993 contended
with 11.5 times as many reported violent crimes as did his or her coun-
terpart in 1960. To restore the 1960 ratio of police officers to violent
crime, noted Adam Walinsky, would have required not 100,000 new
officers, as planned under the 1994 crime bill, but five million.

Actually, we've come a long way toward that number, by hiring 1.5
million private security guards, double the number of local, state, and
federal police officers. We also spend 64 percent more on private secu-

Fig. 5.1 Violent Crimes Reported (per 100,000)

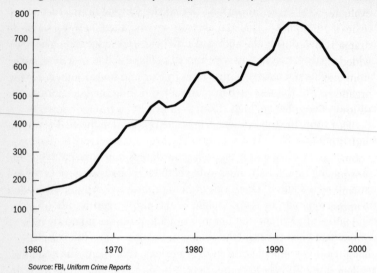

Source: FBI, *Uniform Crime Reports*

rity measures—alarms, locks, guards, and armored vehicles—than we spend on police protection. In 1960, my own place called Hope in this very nice midwestern town needed no campus police force. Today, we employ six full-time and seven part-time officers. We distribute informational warnings after every assault. And we offer a nightly shuttle service to transport students around campus.

In the mid-1990s, as the economy boomed and colleges were weathering the decline in 18-year-olds—the after-effect of the 1970s birth dearth—homicide and robbery rates eased. Experts attribute the crime decline to the aging population, increased community policing, crackdowns on gun trafficking, and the incarceration of 1.6 million Americans (who, on average, admit to a dozen crimes committed during the year before their arrest). Another partial contributor may be the doubled number of abortions in the seven years following the Supreme Court's 1973 decision. (Many of these fetuses, John Donohue and Steven Levitt remind us, would have been born into dysfunctional environments and been in their late teens in the mid-1990s.) Yet another contributor may be the pressure on police departments and precinct captains to show ever-decreasing crime statistics. If a felony crime such as burglary gets downgraded to a misdemeanor, such as vandalism or trespassing, perceived police performance (and associated evaluations) rises. Murder, however, remains an uncontested crime statistic (it is hard to hide bodies), and several urban centers have reported dramatic drops in homicide. Between 1990 and 1998, New York City added 7,000 police officers and saw the number of its murders plunge from 2,245 to fewer than 650. Boston, where inner-city ministers have organized a successful plan for cutting juvenile violence, in 1996 had its lowest murder rate in more than three decades.

Part of the crime decline may also reflect the improved economy and diminished unemployment and hopelessness. Is the economic boom, like a stretch of cool weather, masking the reality that the mosquito-producing swamp ecology still surrounds us? As global warming resumed once the atmospheric dust from Mount Pinatubo's eruption cleared, will crime rates—which tend to rise during recession and fall with economic growth—resume their climb with the next hard times? Is the recent decline "the lull before the storm," as some criminologists warn? The rebounding teenage population that will again fill colleges will also likely overstuff prisons, because males age 15 to 24 are every culture's barbarians who commit a disproportionate share of crime. Among state prisoners, their rearrest rate is nearly double that of those released when 45 or older. Cultures that have a relatively high proportion of unmarried young males (as has been true of Yugoslavia and many African countries) engage in more wars and rebellions.

With 4.3 million births in 1960, 3.1 million in 1975 (producing the shrunken population of 20-year-olds in 1995), and 4.2 million in 1990, it doesn't take a demographer to predict that, in the absence of social renewal, the national homicide rate will likely renew its upward climb. Some 40 million kids under 10 are about to become tomorrow's 15- to 24-year-olds, a record number of whom will likely be what criminologist John DiIulio calls "fatherless, godless, and jobless."

Another Perspective

We have seen that by one measure—the counting of violent crimes by local police and sheriffs, as reported in the FBI's annual *Uniform Crime Reports*—America's violent crime rate increased dramatically after 1960. Reported violent crime (homicides, rapes, assaults, and robberies per 100,000 people) *quintupled*. Moreover, in many of those years crime should have been *decreasing*, because a declining birthrate and increasing senior population mean that the next person you encounter is 25 percent less likely to be a 15- to 24-year-old male than in 1980.

By another measure—the Census Bureau's annual National Crime Victimization Survey (NCVS) for the Bureau of Justice Statistics—the violent crime rate has not increased by one iota since the first survey in 1973. True, there are many unreported crimes. The nearly 1.6 million violent crimes and nearly 12 million property crimes reported annually are only a fraction of the 44 million crimes estimated from the survey. (It takes nearly 6 million estimated violent crimes to yield those 1.6 million reports, leading to 600,000 arrests that result in 130,000 felony convictions.) Yet despite frightening TV images of violence, and despite pockets of drug-related violence, this survey of random households suggests that violent crime is not worsening. An example is women's vulnerability to rape, which the survey suggests has been decreasing since 1973, rather than increasing as the FBI count of reported rapes suggests.

So which do we believe? Our government's crime report from law enforcement agencies? Or our government's crime report from citizens? Perhaps the seeming contradiction is easily explained—the surge in reported rapes may reflect women's increasing willingness to go to the police. We could wish it were so, but the NCVS reveals no increase over time in the percentage of raped women who go to the police.

Might the surge instead reflect more recording of rape complaints by officers and dispatchers—more of whom now are women? Sociologists Gary Jensen and Maryaltani Karpos find this a more likely explanation, because the increase in women on police forces parallels the increased recording and reporting of rape.

On the other hand, the crime survey question and interview format used until recently primarily detected violent stranger rapes (not acquaintance rapes). Its screening item, after priming the person to think about vicious attacks with questions regarding being beaten up, attacked with weapons, and hit with rocks and bottles, was "Did someone try to attack you in some other way?" What is more, rapes known to police (a fraction of all rapes, everyone agrees) were nearly double the number of rapes that the NCVS estimated were reported to police. Noting these problems, rape survey expert Mary Koss is skeptical about the NCVS conclusions.

Furthermore, if the actual rape rate were steady, older women should be more likely to report ever having been raped (because of their greater years at risk). But if the rate has recently increased, today's young women should be more likely to report ever having been raped (because older women would have experienced their most vulnerable teens and twenties long ago, when rape would have been less common). It is indeed the case that younger women are more likely to report ever having been raped. Assuming that women of any age would be unlikely to forget a rape experience, this suggests that sexual violence has increased.

David Lykken offers another reason why the NCVS underestimates violence: the survey covers households, and many victims of violence live not in households but in jails, hospitals, and shelters. The mostly female interviewers may be especially reluctant to enter or make callbacks in the highest-crime neighborhoods and housing projects. This "undersampling" of crime-ridden areas "explains much of the difference" between the NCVS and FBI numbers, Lykken believes. DiIulio agrees, adding that the NCVS also counts neither crimes against children under 12 nor serial victimizations. (If a woman cannot recall how many times a man beat her, the survey counts one crime.)

It also is hard to dispute the doubled homicide rate, which has occurred despite improved emergency medicine ("turning what would have been murders in the '60s and '70s into aggravated assaults in the 1990s," as Lykken argues). Still, say the skeptics, doubled murderousness may say less about our assaultiveness than our having armed our destructive urges with so many lethal weapons (though we have also armed our capacity to save lives, thanks to modern emergency medicine). People may kill people, but they generally do it with guns, which in the past 25 years have killed nearly 800,000 (say that number slowly) Americans. About half of these deaths have been suicidal, slightly less than half homicidal, and the remainder accidental. With more than 200 millions guns at hand today, the simple but sad result is that more angry fights end as murders.

More Crime, More Prisoners

If more incarceration could solve the crime problem we should just about have it licked. In 1960, a third of a million people in America lay down to sleep each night behind bars. In 1998, six times as many—1.87 million—did so, due partly to increased violent and property crime,

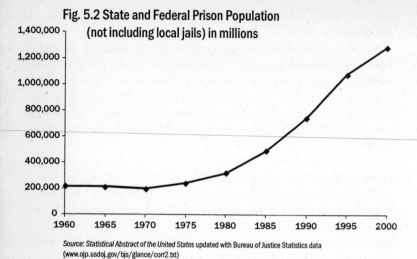

Fig. 5.2 State and Federal Prison Population (not including local jails) in millions

Source: *Statistical Abstract of the United States* updated with Bureau of Justice Statistics data (www.ojp.usdoj.gov/bjs/glance/corr2.txt)

partly to a huge increase in drug-trafficking arrests (often of people who have also been committing other crimes), and partly to mandatory sentencing. This 1 in 170 person incarceration rate tops that of all other nations and is eight to ten times that in Western Europe. Added to these 1.87 million are another 3.95 million on probation or parole, yielding a population of 5.8 million Americans under correctional supervision. And it would be even higher if William Bennett and John DiIulio had had their way and some of those 3.8 million who were set free to revictimize people were still incarcerated. (By the end of the 1990s, DiIulio shifted his emphasis to supporting urban churches rather than building more prisons. Mandatory minimum drug laws should be repealed, he now believes.)

During the 1980s we doubled our prison capacity. We upped our spending on criminal justice to some $85 billion, with more than $40 billion spent on police protection, more than $30 billion on prisons, and $10 billion on legal and judicial costs. We did so knowing that, although it costs $25,000 to incarcerate someone for a year, leaving that person on the street costs society about $46,000 in theft, damage, cash losses, and medical and lost-work expenses from personal crimes. Yet despite ever more money spent on police and prisons, our capacity to produce crime outstripped our capacity to house criminals. Even with this pace-setting rate of incarceration, the risk of being murdered has been seven to ten times greater in the United States than in most European countries.

As stranger violence has increased, arrest rates have decreased. About half of urban homicides are now stranger murders, and 80 percent of those who murder strangers get away with it. Murder the person you rob or rape and you eliminate the key witness. The net result: the arrest rate after homicides has declined from 91 percent in 1965 to 65 percent in the 1990s (58 percent in cities over one million). Thus, despite the exploding prison population—another indication that crime really has increased—our capacity to quarantine violent criminals lags behind our capacity to create them.

When a community loses a large number of its men to jails, prisons, premature deaths, and emigration, the normal 1 to 1 male-female ratio becomes imbalanced. That result is toxic to sexual commitment and marriage (and therefore ultimately to children, and not just because two-thirds of male inmates have children). Societies with a shortage of marriageable women are societies that typically value women and stress sexual morality. Societies with an oversupply of women are societies in which young males feel freer to mate with multiple partners rather than bonding with one. In such societies, explains social psychologist Paul Secord, "women experience a subjective sense of powerlessness. Divorce rates are high, illegitimate birth rates are high, and sexual libertarianism is the prevailing ethos." Thus, imprisoning large numbers of young men for long-term sentences may control crime in the short run but increase nonmarital births and associated crime in the long run. As Sing Sing inmate Hector Millan says, "prison destroys families."

Teenage Violence

Charles Conrad, age 55 and confined by multiple sclerosis to a wheelchair or walker, had no chance when burglarized and attacked by three teenage boys in his suburban Atlanta condo. From dusk till dawn, they stabbed him with a kitchen knife and barbecue fork, strangled him with a rope, and clobbered him with a hammer. Still, Conrad survived, begging the boys to shoot him and end his agony. Fearing someone would hear gunshots, they instead beat him more, poured salt in his wounds, and, when his body still twitched, threw objects at him until finally he stopped breathing. Then they took off in his van with his stereo, VCR, camcorder, and shotgun.

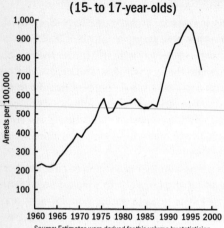

**Fig. 5.3 Arrest Rate for Juvenile Violent Crime
(15- to 17-year-olds)**

Source: Estimates were derived for this volume by statistician
Jodi M. Brown using the FBI *Uniform Crime Reports*

Big news stories like this horrific crime, and the 1997–99 spate of
school killings, need not signify big trends. But the undisputed fact is
that teen violence *has* increased. With a dozen kids dying daily from
gunshot, America has the equivalent of a Littleton massacre every day.
This increase occurred in two waves—from 1965 to 1975, and from 1985
to 1994. A National League of Cities survey of 700 communities (nearly
two-thirds of them with populations less than 50,000) in 1994 revealed
that 70 percent now assign police to patrol schools and 90 percent send
police to school athletic events. The recent surge, during which juvenile homicide doubled, brings to mind philosopher Thomas Hobbes's
description of the life of "primitive man in a state of nature"—"solitary,
poor, nasty, brutish, and short."

The peak hours for juvenile crime are now 3 to 8 P.M. Youths home
alone after school—as were 43 percent in 1970 and 71 percent in 1995
—are twice as likely to drink alcohol or take drugs. These facts motivate
many parents to seek work schedules that permit supervision, but they
also point to the wisdom of other countries that schedule secondary
schools from 9 A.M. to 4 P.M. rather than 8 to 3.

Such a schedule would also allow more students to get adequate
sleep, enabling greater alertness, better learning, and less surly and
dangerous moods. "Teens have their own biological rhythm," explains

Stanford sleep researcher William Dement, "and forcing them to adapt to an adult timetable is counter productive, causing problems both in learning and behavior." For these classic night owls, their bodies wanting to stay up and sleep late, American secondary school hours create an inevitable sleep crunch. "Teens are universally sleep deprived." Dement adds that when Edina, Minnesota, pushed back the school start time by 70 minutes, "district officials reported that students were far more awake and engaged in class, and the number of behavioral problems went down." If the need for two bus runs necessitates different starting times for elementary and secondary students, why not start the younger students (whose bedtimes are more easily controlled) earlier?

We can now sum up the violent crime facts: Despite debates over rape and assault statistics, there is little dispute over increasing homicide, exploding prison populations, or epidemic juvenile violence. Crime has dropped since 1993. But merge the still high juvenile violence rate with the rapidly increasing juvenile population and a future economic recession, and the result, some observers fear, will be a ticking crime bomb. The long-term increase and recent decrease in American violence indicate that violence is learned, not fixed in our genes. And what is learned we can potentially change with new learning.

Who Commits Crime?

Despite variations across time and place, most violent crime is committed by relatively few people. In one national survey of young offenders, 7 percent of youths perpetrated 80 percent of the violent offenses. Who are these ferocious folk? Mindful that it takes multiple ingredients to bake a cake (the flour, alone, does not cause the cake), let's consider possible biological and social ingredients of violence.

Genetic Influences

We have long known that animals of many species can be bred for aggressiveness. Sometimes this is done for practical purposes, as in the breeding of fighting cocks. Sometimes it is done for research. Finnish psychologist Kirsti Lagerspetz took normal albino mice and bred the most aggressive ones together and the least aggressive ones. After repeating the procedure for 26 generations, she had one set of fierce mice and one of placid mice.

Genetic influences naturally predispose some primates and humans likewise to be more aggressive than others. Our temperament—how intense and reactive we are—is largely something we bring with us into the world, influenced by our sympathetic nervous system's reactivity. Temperament, observed in infancy, usually endures. Thus, identical twins, when asked separately, are more likely than fraternal twins to agree on whether they have "a violent temper." And a fearless, impulsive, temper-prone child is at risk for adolescent violent behavior. Boys who exhibit little physiological arousal to scary situations are often outgoing, impulsive risk-takers who develop into "sociopaths"—manipulative, morally numbed, chronic offenders.

Testosterone "Poisoning"

As we have already noted, violence-prone people also are disproportionately young males, among whom rates of aggravated assault peak around age 18, and then decline to half that level by age 36. "We could avoid two-thirds of all crime simply by putting all able-bodied young men in cryogenic sleep from the age of 12 through 28," Lykken says. In animals, and to a lesser extent in humans, aggressiveness is influenced by the male sex hormone testosterone. Wonder of wonders, males' testosterone levels rise after puberty, and then begin falling by the mid-20s—in concert with the rise and fall of males' violent crime rates.

Compared with prisoners convicted of nonviolent crimes, those imprisoned for unprovoked violent crimes tend to have higher testosterone levels. Boys and men with high testosterone levels are more prone to delinquency, hard drug use, and aggressive responses to provocation. Drugs that diminish testosterone levels in violent human males also serve to subdue their aggressive tendencies—a fact that has led some violent sex offenders, wishing to reduce their prison terms and escape their damaging impulses, to request castration. (Although the operation is less invasive than hysterectomy, it is understandably controversial when proposed as an alternative elective punishment.)

Alcohol

Laboratory experiments confirm police experience: when people are provoked, alcohol unleashes aggression. Violent people are more likely to drink, and more likely to become aggressive when intoxicated.

In experiments, intoxicated people deliver stronger shocks or deliver more pain to supposed victims. In the real world, people who have been drinking commit at least half the violent crimes. Surveys of rapists reveal that slightly over half had been drinking before committing their offenses.

Victims, too, are often under the influence. In a recent survey of nearly 90,000 students at 171 colleges and universities, 4 in 5 students experiencing unwanted intercourse acknowledged consuming alcohol or drugs beforehand. In 65 percent of homicides, and 55 percent of in-home fights and assaults, the assailant and/or the victim had been drinking. Alcohol enhances aggressiveness in at least two ways: It reduces people's self-awareness, making them less mindful of who they are and what they value. And it reduces their ability to consider the consequences of their actions, making them less inhibited.

People who love numbers even more than I do have calculated that a 10 percent increase in alcohol consumption translates to a 9.1 percent increase in robberies and a 6.8 percent increase in rapes. They also have estimated that a 10 percent increase in the price of alcohol yields a 3 percent reduction in beer consumption and a 10 percent reduction in wine consumption. Youthful drinkers are especially price sensitive. Such numbers tell us that to reduce youthful drinking—and traffic fatalities, rapes, robberies, and adult alcoholism—we could increase the tax on alcohol. To set the actual tax rate, Bennett and DiIulio suggest, obligate alcohol users to repay society for the actual societal costs of alcohol use—the $150 billion or so in lost employment and productivity and increased medical costs.

Race

"There is nothing more painful for me at this stage in my life," reflected Jesse Jackson, "than to walk down the street and hear footsteps and start to think about robbery and then look around and see it's somebody white and feel relieved. How humiliating." The numbers validate Jackson's worries:

- Although African-Americans are but 12 percent of the American population, in 1996 they were 42 percent of those arrested for rape, 55 percent of those arrested for murder, and 58 percent of those arrested for robbery. All told, the arrest rate for violent crime was five times greater among blacks than whites. In 1995, 7 percent of African-

American males and 1 percent of European-American males were in prison.

- On any given day, about 4 in 10 African-American men in the District of Columbia are either in prison (15 percent), on probation or parole (21 percent), or being sought by police or awaiting trial (6 percent). In California, 40 percent of black men in their 20s and 5 percent of white men in their 20s are in prison, or on probation or parole.

- "Tragically, there are more young black males in prison than in college," Deborah Prothrow-Stith points out. Again, the numbers confirm: in 1991, there were 517,000 black male collegians at all levels, and some 550,000 black males behind bars.

The response among whites has been heightened fear of African-American male strangers. This fear was exploited in 1989 when news photos of the blood-splattered body of Carol Stuart appeared. Her husband, Charles Stuart, who had been shot in the stomach, reported that a black male had forced his way into their car and shot them both during a robbery. "The white middle class is now threatened by violence spilling out of the black community," was the implicit message of news coverage for weeks afterward.

But the truth is that the average white person's risk is minimal compared with the victimization of blacks. (Carol Stuart, like so many white female homicide victims, turned out to have been murdered by her white husband, who had self-inflicted his own wound to cover the crime.) Violent crime is overwhelmingly either black-on-black or white-on-white. In all of 1996, only 558 whites were killed by blacks. A white person's risk of death is eight times greater from an asthma attack. Meanwhile, 3,460 whites were murdered by whites, and 3,562 blacks by blacks. Take all the homicide victims (including those for whom the murderer is unknown) and adjust for population differences and you have a startling result: your odds of being murdered are six times greater in America if you are black rather than white.

Rev. Benjamin F. Chavis, Jr., calls this black fratricide "a life and death issue for us." Jesse Jackson has agreed, calling on African-Americans to take the "moral offensive" against violence. "More young black men die each year from gunshots than the total who have died from lynchings in the entire history of the United States," he says. "If that many blacks had been killed by whites, there would be riots everywhere. Or, if that many whites had been killed by blacks, there would be wholesale executions. But if it's black on black, there's a kind of social, cultural permissiveness." Students who wouldn't hesitate to snitch on a Klan sympathizer, "because the Klan threatens us," will not snitch on a fellow student who brings a gun to school. "But how can you be so alert, on the one hand, to a phantom of the past," asks Jackson, "and be so very vulnerable, even complicitous, to the present threat?"

So, is race per se a predictor of violence? Or is it a proxy for some other culprit factor, such as poverty? Frederick Goodwin, former director of the Alcohol, Drug Abuse, and Mental Health Administration, recalls a national survey in 1992 of young violent offenders. "There was no correlation between violence and race at all, when you took socioeconomic status out of it—in fact, black middle-class kids, we'd previously found, were less likely to abuse drugs than white middle-class kids and were more socially responsible. There *was*, however, a strong association of violence with low socioeconomic class." Violence researcher Leonard Eron and his colleagues agree: "Racial differences in homicide rates are greatly reduced or disappear when the data are controlled by income." The metropolitan areas where joblessness among young black males fell the most during the '90s were also the areas where crime fell most. Violence, then, is rather like tuberculosis, which occurs more often among African-Americans but has nothing to do with race per se. Rather, each comes with poverty, family corrosion, and associated risk factors. Rich black folks aren't at risk for TB. Poor white and black folks are.

After studying data from six major investigations, research psychologists David Rowe, Alexander Vazsonyi, and Daniel Flannery confirmed that ethnic differences in school achievement and delinquency are "no more than skin deep." The factors that influence adolescent behavior among American Hispanic, Asian, black, and white ethnic groups are "statistically indistinguishable." To the extent that family structure, peer influences, or parental education predict behavior in one ethnic group, they do so for other groups as well. In surface ways we may differ—give one group more salt and it will have more hypertension—but as members of one species we respond to the same psychological forces. We are all leaves on the same human tree.

Genetic data also hint that the race difference in violence arises from factors other than biological race differences. Only 6 percent of human genetic variation is differences among races. Only 8 percent is differences among tribes or nations within a race. The rest—more than 85 percent—is individual variation within local groups. The average genetic difference between two Icelandic villagers or between two Kenyans is much greater than the average difference between the two groups. Thus, notes geneticist Richard Lewontin, if after a worldwide catastrophe only Icelanders or Kenyans survived, the human species would suffer only "a trivial reduction" in its genetic diversity.

Not surprisingly, then, "nasty, brutish" behavior occurs across races and cultures. We have seen such behavior in Northern Ireland, the former Yugoslavia, and the Middle East. We have seen it in genocides under Hitler, Mao, Stalin, and Amin. We have seen it in wars, most notably the 55 million battle and civilian deaths occasioned by World War II. And we saw it in the fate of the generous Native Americans who saved the English colonists from starvation after their 1620 landing in Plymouth, but who eventually were nearly exterminated by European invaders. Reflecting on such species-wide barbarities, one wonders if we have projected something of ourselves into the mythical Minotaur: half human, half beast.

Culture

So far we have acknowledged the statistical fact that the odds of your being violent—or being the victim of violence—are greater if you are young, male, temperamentally reactive, alcohol-using, African-American, and poor. Yet none of these predictors explain the social recession over time.

The gene pool was not greatly different in 1960.

There were not, proportionately, fewer young males.

There was not less testosterone flowing.

There was not less alcohol use.

The black-white racial mix was not radically different.

There was not less poverty. (Since 1960, violent crime increased during times of rapid economic growth as well as during slow growth or recessionary times, suggesting that national crime trends are mostly not the result of the state of the national economy.)

What differed was the culture. The same genetic populations can produce dramatically different rates of violence in different cultural contexts. West African homicide rates are lower than the rates among Americans of West African descent. Similarly, homicide rates are much lower among Europeans than among European-Americans. America has become a crime factory. It's the culture.

Within the United States, reports University of Michigan social psychologist Richard Nisbett, the sober, cooperative white folk who settled New England and the Middle Atlantic produced a different culture than the swashbuckling, honor-preserving white folk (many of them my Scots-Irish ancestral cousins) who settled much of the South. The former were genteel farmer-artisans, the latter aggressive hunters and herders. To the present, American cities and areas that were populated by southerners have much higher white homicide rates than those populated by northerners. For example, the Texas panhandle (whose settlers came from the Upper South) has a white homicide rate four times that of Nebraska (whose settlers came from the East, Midwest, and Europe). Texas panhandle towns with little poverty have much *higher* homicide rates than Nebraska towns with considerable poverty.

It is not violence in general that southerners are more likely to exemplify, but violence that protects one's property and honor, and violence that punishes. "A man has a right to kill to defend his home," agree 18 percent of white non-southern men and 36 percent of white southern men. Thus, white southern men are twice as likely as rural midwestern white men to report having guns for protection. Southerners also more strongly support war efforts and favor disciplining by spanking (a form of discipline frequently experienced by those who later become violent).

Family

When physical health has been harmed by a noxious environment, natural scientists work to isolate the toxin. When social health has been so harmed, social scientists do the same. The possible toxins include concentrated poverty, plentiful guns, radical individualism, media portrayals of violence and infidelity, and family collapse.

For the moment, let's consider the family factor. Is there—as many have contended—a correlation between fatherlessness and violence? between unmarried girls with babies and future boys with guns? For example, do states' nonmarital birthrates predict their violent crime rates? Curious, I obtained the data for each of the 50 states and found that there is indeed a correlation. States like Utah, where families are mostly intact, tend to have low violent crime rates.

Cross-cultural data reveal a similar pattern. Cultures where child-father contact is minimal tend to be cultures with more crime. One

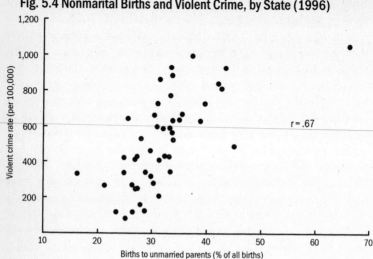

Fig. 5.4 Nonmarital Births and Violent Crime, by State (1996)

dubious theory is that boys raised by mothers may strive to avoid being feminine and overshoot in their quest for masculinity.

Comparing local communities one again finds that father-absence rates predict crime. Of 61 children murdered in Chicago during 1993, for example, 51 had unmarried teen mothers. Moreover, where families are cohesive, though poverty is great, violence is rare. San Francisco's Chinatown historically was one of the city's poorest, and safest, areas. In 1931, reports University of Newcastle upon Tyne fellow emeritus Norman Dennis, England and Wales suffered 21 percent unemployment— and 208 robberies. In 1996, after social changes paralleling those in the United States, they had less than 8 percent unemployment—and 72,000 robberies.

Finally, comparing decades we again see a correlation between father absence and crime. The dramatic upward curve in the prison population that we saw earlier in this chapter lagged 15 years behind the dramatic upward curve in the percentage of nonmarital births. In *The Antisocial Personalities,* Lykken predicted the percentage of arrests attributable to 15- to 25-year-olds from a statistic that combined their share of the population with the proportion reared without fathers. The ups and downs of their contribution to American crime across a half century mirrored this combined statistic. As a further test of the contribution of father absence to criminal risk, he applied the same analysis to white and black 15- to 25-year-olds—and discovered he could rather precisely predict their differing arrest trends since 1965. "It is not low IQ that leads a man to murder, assault, rape, and rob people," he surmised. "It is, rather, incompetent and fatherless rearing that produces sociopaths who murder, assault, rape, and rob people." And, I am sure he would now add (knowing of his appreciation for the power of peer influences), it is also the toxic environment that some-times subverts the youth of well-meaning parents in neighborhoods marked by minimal father care.

These data do not prove a family effect, because states, cultures, communities, and eras that vary in father involvement also vary in other ways. But they add to the facts of life noted in Chapter 4, such as the 7 in 10 hard-core delinquents from father-absent homes (from which Lykken has computed that the sons of single parents are at seven times greater risk of incarceration than sons reared by two biological par-ents). Other survey data indicate a less dramatic but still significant result: youths from single-parent homes are doubly likely to acknowl-edge having committed vandalism, theft, or weapon use, and to report having been physically abused.

The significance of involved fathers is confirmed in a recent study by Cynthia Harper and Sara McLanahan that followed a nationally rep-resentative sample of 6,403 boys over time. Of those who spent their teenage years in father-absent homes, three times as many had been incarcerated by their early 30s as those from father-present families. Even after controlling for race, income, residential instability, child intelligence, parental education, and urban location, a doubled risk re-mained. "For each year spent in a nonintact family, the odds of incar-ceration rise five percent," Harper and McLanahan report. And gaining a stepfather did not improve a boy's odds.

Social scientists have little difficulty conjecturing why unformed and broken two-parent families might be a root cause of violence and delinquency. Two-parent families are society's infrastructure. Marriage domesticates men and alleviates sexual competition among them. As the marriage rate among males under 25 declined (only 18 percent of today's 20- to 24-year-old males are married), their crime rate rose. Marriage also creates two extended-family circles of concern and sup-port around each child, from which flow gifts, contacts, work opportu-nities, advice, inheritances, and a kin network of attachments. Family

bonds reduce gang involvement—the most corrosive peer influence—
and inhibit delinquency.

From his quarter century of research at the Oregon Social Learning Center, Gerald Patterson observes that having two married parents
results in less stress and more positive parenting than having one. (Parenting styles, within the normal range, appear not to explain differences
among children, but the extremes of parenting do seem to matter.) Parents of delinquent youths, often beleaguered single parents, have difficulty meeting work and domestic demands *and* supervising their children and building stable new relationships. Although the parents are
well intentioned, they may lack parenting skills. Discipline consists of
screaming, hitting, or rejecting, rather than reinforcing good behavior.
Or the harried parent may assert a command ("do this" or "stop that")
to which the child responds with an argument or a temper tantrum and
the parent backs off (reinforcing the child's aggressive response). When
some children are genetically predisposed to fearless aggressiveness,
argues Lykken, diligent, patient nurturing may still shape them into
responsible adults (much as fearless, aggressive bull terriers can, with
diligent and patient training, become superb companion dogs).

In the absence of parental supervision and positive discipline, violence rarely occurs as a single impulsive act; rather, it is the culmination
of years of escalating delinquency. Stubborn defiance turns to bullying,
which blossoms into fighting, shoplifting, and lying, which grows into
predatory violence. Youths who show no signs of antisocial behavior by
age 15 are unlikely to plague society later.

Packs and Gangs

Perhaps social psychology's most reliable finding is that opposites
do *not* attract; rather, birds of a feather flock together. People gravi-
tate toward those who share their attitudes, beliefs, and backgrounds.
Most of us need look no further than our own friends to recognize
the similarity-attraction phenomenon. Similarity breeds content. So it
comes as no surprise that deviant youths, rejected by schools and by
many of their peers, often band together with others like themselves.
And as we noted in Chapter 4, peer influences on children and adolescents are life shaping.

Now stir into the social brew two other findings from social psychological research. The first is the phenomenon of *deindividuation*—the

loss of self-consciousness and therefore self-restraint in group situations that arouse people, distract them, and provide anonymity. The result can be uninhibited behavior ranging from a food fight in the dining hall or screaming at a basketball referee to vandalism or rioting. Whether in a mob, at a rock concert, at a dance, or at worship, the group loosens inhibitions. It's hard to imagine a single fan screaming at a private rock concert. The Los Angeles police officers who clobbered Rodney King with their nightsticks more than 50 times—fracturing his skull in nine places and leaving him brain damaged and missing teeth— would likely not have acted with such brutality if they had been alone. Rioters, made faceless by a mob, become free to loot. The bigger a lynch mob, the more its members lose self-awareness and become willing to commit atrocities, such as burning, lacerating, or dismembering the victim.

The second phenomenon is *group polarization*—the enhancement of shared tendencies when group members interact. I have consistently observed group polarization in some of my own experiments. In one, when prejudiced high school students discussed racial issues, their attitudes became more prejudiced. When low-prejudice students discussed the same issues, they became more tolerant.

Group polarization can have beneficial results, as when it amplifies a sought-after spiritual awareness or strengthens the mutual resolve of those in a self-help group. But it can also have dire consequences. In experiments, group decision making amplifies retaliatory responding (measured as intensity of punishing shocks delivered). In the real world, terrorism rarely erupts suddenly. Rather, it arises among people who are drawn together because of a shared grievance and become more and more extreme as they interact in isolation from moderating influences.

Ergo, when youths with shared antisocial tendencies come together in groups, the result often is social contagion: they become aroused, distracted from self, and disinhibited, and their thinking and actions polarize. Scandinavians recognize the results as "mobbing"—schoolchildren repeatedly harassing an insecure, weak schoolmate. Mobbing is a group activity. One bully alone is unlikely to taunt or attack a victim.

Americans recognize the phenomenon as gang behavior. Youths bereft of close family bonds, with low expectations of success in school and life, find in the gang a social identity and a place to belong. All of us, as what Aristotle called "social animals," define who we are partly in unique personal terms, partly in terms of our group memberships. We need to belong, to attach ourselves to something larger than self, to know who is "we" and who is "they." Our distant ancestors survived by hunting and defending themselves in groups. Out of our primal need to define a "we" comes loving families, faithful friendships, and team spirit, but also teen gangs, ethnic hostilities, and fanatic nationalism. Serb, Tamil, and Kurd represent social identities for which people are prepared to die.

Gangs offer adolescents not only identity but friendship, pride, excitement, and resources. Until gang members marry out, age out, get a job, go to prison, or die, explains Syracuse University gang expert Arnold Goldstein, they hang out. They define their turf, display their colors, challenge rivals, and, not infrequently, commit delinquent acts. And they fight. Like Serb, Tamil, and Kurd, they assault or kill over drugs, territory, honor, girls, ethnic tensions, or insults.

Guns: A Public Health Emergency

If we had allowed the motor vehicle fatality rate of 1970 to persist, we would have had 70,000 vehicle deaths in 1994. Rather than concede this much highway slaughter, we responded with improved car and highway designs, motorcycle helmet laws, and drunk driving crackdowns—and suffered "only" 42,000 vehicle deaths in 1994. Meanwhile, gun-inflicted deaths have increased from 42 percent of the number of vehicle deaths to nearly 100 percent. That, says former surgeon general C. Everett Koop, constitutes a public health emergency.

Partly in self-defense, we have armed ourselves with 220 million guns. In 1993, 42 percent of adults owned one or more guns. Given the increasing threats of intrusion, rape, and murder, are we safer with a gun in the home? Anecdotes seem to suggest so. Just ask Phil Murphy, who met a 19-year-old intruder with his rifle, enabling the police to make an arrest. Or Charmaine Klaus, who exchanged fire with a would-be robber of her convenience store. Struck in the mouth, the gunman fled to the hospital, where police arrested him. (But, of course, we can't ask those people who have died when pulling out a gun to deter a robbery, or those who have died when guns have been used during family fights.)

Although many people find vivid anecdotes like these more persuasive than dry statistics, the numbers (which together represent the universe of anecdotes) tell the truth. First, there is one's relative safety in countries that do and don't prohibit private handgun ownership. "In 1996," reports Handgun Control, Inc., "handguns murdered 2 people in New Zealand, 13 in Australia, 15 in Japan, 30 in Great Britain, 106 in Canada, 213 in Germany, and 9,390 in the United States." Anyone who has lived, as I have, in both the United Kingdom and the United States has felt the difference. Few Brits would exchange their country's gun policies for ours. (For that matter, would you rather be as safe as you would be in Britain or as safe as you are in America?) Somalia may be NRA heaven gunwise, but it has been catastrophic for Somalians (although NRA leader Neal Knox has said he would have solved the Somali crisis by giving AK-47s to Somali mothers).

Researchers have also compared sister cities with and without gun control. Vancouver, British Columbia, and Seattle, Washington, have similar populations, climates, economies, and rates of criminal activity and assault—except that Vancouver, which carefully restricts handgun ownership, has one-fifth as many handgun murders as Seattle and a 40 percent lower overall murder rate.

Researchers also have examined risks of violence in homes with and without guns. This is controversial research, because such homes may differ in many ways. One study sponsored by the Centers for Disease Control compared gun owners and nonowners of the same sex, race, age, and neighborhood. The ironic and tragic result was that those who kept a gun in the home (often for protection) were 2.7 times more likely to be murdered—nearly always by a family member or close acquaintance. There also is a fivefold increased risk of suicide in homes with guns. Other studies confirm these findings. The statistics may not apply equally in every situation, including those where people live at highest risk. Still, a gun in the home has too often meant the difference between a fight and a funeral, or between suffering and suicide.

Colt has promoted handguns to *Ladies Home Journal* readers with an image of a mother putting her boy to bed, captioned, "Self-protection is more than your right . . . it's your responsibility." This is false and deceptive advertising, complained the American Academy of Pediatrics, the American Public Health Association, and the Center to Prevent Handgun Violence. Take away the gun glut and much of the violent crime increase would evaporate overnight.

Guns are lethal for psychological as well as physical reasons. First, experiments reveal that guns can serve as "aggression cues." In one experiment by University of Wisconsin psychologist Leonard Berkowitz, children who had just played with toy guns became more willing to knock down another child's blocks. In another, angered University of Wisconsin men gave more electric shocks to their tormenter when a rifle and a revolver were nearby (supposedly leftover from a previous experiment) than when badminton racquets had been left behind. "Guns not only permit violence," surmised Berkowitz, "they can stimulate it as well. The finger pulls the trigger, but the trigger may also be pulling the finger."

Second, guns put psychological distance between aggressor and victim. Many readers will recall Stanley Milgram's famous studies of supposedly traumatic electric shocks delivered by surprisingly obedient people. One of Milgram's lessons was that remoteness from the victim facilitates such cruelty. A knife attack can be lethal. But the psychological immediacy of stabbing someone makes the act more difficult and less likely than the more distant act of pulling a trigger. Middle school principal Karen Curtner of Jonesboro, Arkansas, believed that the easy availability of guns in the South had "nothing to do" with two of her students' slaughtering four other students and a pregnant teacher (rather like saying that the lung cancer death of a two-pack-a-day smoker had nothing to do with the availability of cigarettes). Yet guns not only were the vehicle of death, they enabled Andrew Golden and Mitchell Johnson to commit their atrocity from a hillside 100 yards away.

Understanding some of these facts of life, Americans overwhelmingly favor a modest strengthening of gun laws, such as the Brady Bill's requirement of a waiting period before handgun purchases, or bans on semiautomatic assault weapons and gun purchases by juveniles. Three in four Americans, according to a 1998 Harris survey, favor more restrictions on handgun ownership. Why the political party that championed ending the tax-our-children federal deficit also has found it necessary to oppose such measures eludes even many Republicans. Is there a logical connection between supporting fiscal prudence and opposing regulation of gun show and Internet sales? Or does the explanation lie merely in pro-gun PAC contributions (mostly by the NRA to Republicans) outdoing anti-gun PAC contributions by more than 10 to 1? Under the influence of NRA lobbyists, the House of Representatives in 1996 approved renewed funding for the National Center for Injury Prevention and Control with one restriction: "None of the funds made available . . . may be used to advocate or promote gun control." And in 1998 the number of states permitting concealed weapons increased to 43.

The result is that we continue to work at disarming globally while arming domestically. We criticized our president for sending young men to armed Bosnia, where a few might be killed in peacekeeping duties, while annually tolerating the killing of many thousands of young men in armed America.

But the NRA is surely right to argue that these mild restraints on gun purchases would not significantly reduce violent crime. The thousands of people killed each year by accidental gun discharge and the thousands more killed impulsively in family and neighborhood fights will not be saved by a five-day waiting period. What we therefore need, Amitai Etzioni argues, is to consider the (for us) radical policy that is the accepted practice of nearly all other Western democracies: domestic disarmament. The initial cost would be high: buying out existing nonsporting guns at specified prices. But it would be less than the cost of continued violence, which runs up bills for medical care, lost wages, and the justice system of $135 billion per year. Not all guns would get turned in, of course, but with many fewer guns and no new ones being manufactured the black market price soon would be out of range for most youths.

Although about half of Americans favor a total ban on civilian handguns, the NRA's political might and the prospect of superpatriot vigilantes make national domestic disarmament unthinkable for now. Thus the best way to proceed, suggests Etzioni, is state by state, starting in northeastern states where most people would welcome a gun-free environment. "The rapid fall in violent crime sure to follow will make ever more states demand that domestic disarmament be extended to their region." Some cities have had success with more aggressive searches for illegal guns in cars stopped for traffic violations in high-crime areas and among youths breaking local curfews. This is one of the reasons for New York City's plummeting homicide rate. Senator Moynihan, noting that we have a two-century supply of handguns but only a four-year supply of bullets, offers an additional suggestion: prohibit the manufacture of certain types of ammunition. "Guns don't kill people," he says; "bullets do."

In the meantime, others are suggesting a massive public education campaign, akin to those against drunk driving, smoking, and unprotected sex. We have managed to reduce drunk driving and traffic fatalities, to change smoking from a glamorous habit into stinking, slow-motion suicide, and to alert people to the health risks of indiscriminate sex. So why not reframe the debate over firearms with a similar public health crusade? Why not, for example, persuade people that they and their families are safer, *much* safer, without guns for their supposed self-protection? Why not have cities and states sue gun companies for the costs incurred by their products, much as states have successfully sued tobacco companies?

Other ideas for countering violence abound:

- Build more prisons. (We have, and this has contributed to the recent crime abatement. Yet the crime rate remains high. California's get-tough quadrupling of its prison population since 1980 has had "no appreciable effect" on violent crime and only slight effects on property crime. Moreover, imprisoning huge numbers of young men contributes to imbalanced sex ratios, helping to perpetuate the vicious cycle of father absence and crime.)
- Impose a "three strikes and you're out" requirement of life in prison for those convicted of three violent crimes. (But are we really ready to pay for all the new prisons—and prison hospitals and nursing homes—we would need to house and care for senescent former muggers?)
- Although no other Western democracy permits capital punishment, deter brutal crime and eliminate the worst offenders as Iran and Iraq do—by executing them; to show that killing people is wrong, kill people who kill people. (But nearly all the cities and states with the dozen highest violent-crime rates already have the death penalty. Because most homicide is impulsive or committed under the influence of drugs or alcohol, murderers rarely calculate consequences. Moreover, says William Bennett's crime-fighting co-author John DiIulio, consider the ethics: "The death penalty as it has been administered, is administered and will likely continue to be administered is arbitrary and capricious. As a political matter, that's not likely to change. This who-shall-live state lottery is unjust both as a matter of Judeo-Christian ethics and as a matter of American citizenship. Since we can't apply it fairly, we ought to consider abolishing it.")

What matters more than a punishment's severity is its certainty. The National Research Council reports that a 50 percent increase in the probability of apprehension and incarceration reduces subsequent crime twice as much as does doubling time in prison. Even so, FBI director Louis Freeh is skeptical that tougher or swifter punishment is the ultimate answer: "The frightening level of lawlessness which has come upon us like a plague is more than a law enforcement problem. The crime and disorder which flow from hopeless poverty, unloved children, and drug abuse, can't be solved merely by bottomless prisons, mandatory sentencing, and more police." Reacting to crime after it happens is the social equivalent of putting Band-Aids on shotgun wounds.

An alternative approach is suggested by a story about the rescue of a drowning person from a rushing river. Having successfully administered first aid, the rescuer spots another struggling person and pulls her out too. After a half dozen repetitions, the rescuer suddenly turns and starts running away while the river sweeps yet another floundering person into view. "Aren't you going to rescue that fellow?" asks a bystander. "Heck no," the rescuer shouts. "I'm going upstream to find out what's pushing all these people in."

To be sure, we need police, prisons, and social workers, all of whom help us deal with the social pathologies that plague us. It's fine to swat the mosquitoes, but better to drain the swamps—by re-envisioning our culture, by challenging the "principalities and powers" that corrupt families and youth, and by renewing the moral and spiritual roots of character. If we could fight the Persian Gulf War "to protect our way of life" with no consideration of costs, says Marian Wright Edelman, then surely we can resolve to fight the economic and social forces that more certainly threaten our way of life today. The swamp-draining effort, as we will see, is under way.

CHAPTER 6

Money and Misery

> It's pretty hard to tell what does bring happiness. Poverty an' wealth have both failed.
>
> —KIN HUBBARD, *Abe Martin's Broadcast*

We have pondered four dramatic trends that have marked our cultural life since 1960: the sexual revolution, the decline of marriage, the diminishing well-being of children, and the long-term increase and short-term decrease in violence. These trends have coincided with a fifth trend: strikingly increased materialism and affluence. More and more we value having more. Compared with 1960, most of us do have more fiscal fitness. Life today is therefore paradoxical—very, very good in some ways, while distressing in others.

Increasing Materialism

Does money buy happiness? Few of us would agree. But ask us a different question—"Would a *little* more money make you a *little* happier?"—and many of us will smirk and nod. There is, we believe, some connection between wealth and well-being.

If only we had more wealth. A Roper survey asked how satisfied Americans were with 13 different aspects of their lives, including friends, house, and schooling; respondents expressed least satisfaction with "the amount of money you have to live on." When interviewers from the University of Michigan's Institute for Social Research asked what hampers the search for the good life, the most common answer was, "We're short of money." What would improve our life quality?

"More money," was the most frequent answer. According to a recent Gallup Poll, 1 in 2 women, 2 in 3 men, and 4 in 5 people earning more than $75,000 a year would like to be rich. Asked by the Roper Organization what annual income would be needed to fulfill their dreams, the average American in 1987 answered $50,000. In 1996, the response was $90,000. Think of it as today's American dream: life, liberty, and the purchase of happiness.

There is a myth that such materialism grew during the greedy 1970s and 1980s. As my colleagues in literature occasionally remind me, myths can be deeply true, as this one is. The most dramatic evidence of this "greening of America" comes from the UCLA/American Council on Education annual survey of nearly a quarter million entering collegians. Those agreeing that a "very important" reason for their going to college was "to make more money" rose from 1 in 2 in 1971 to nearly 3 in 4 in 1998. And the proportion considering it "very important or essential" that they become "very well off financially," rose from 39 percent in 1970 to 74 percent in 1998. These proportions virtually flip-flopped with those who considered it very important to "develop a meaningful philosophy of life." Materialism was up, spirituality down.

What a change in values! Among 19 listed objectives, new collegians now rank becoming "very well off financially" number one. It outranks not only developing a life philosophy but also "becoming an authority in my own field," "helping others in difficulty," and "raising a family." At the Ronald Reagan Middle School in Elgin, Illinois, principal Woodrow Wasson observes a younger form of this materialism. "They want to be doctors, lawyers, veterinarians and, of course, professional athletes. I don't remember the last time I heard somebody say they wanted to be a police officer or a firefighter. They want to do something that will make a lot of money and have a lot of prestige." To young Americans of the 1990s, money matters.

Economist Thomas Naylor could sense this intense materialism during the six years he taught corporate strategy courses at Duke University. He asked each of his students to write a personal strategic plan. "With few exceptions, what they wanted fell into three categories: money, power and things—very big things, including vacation homes, expensive foreign automobiles, yachts and even airplanes. . . . Their request to the faculty was: Teach me how to be a moneymaking machine." Little else mattered, reported Naylor, including concerns for one's family, spirituality, employees, or ethics and social responsibility.

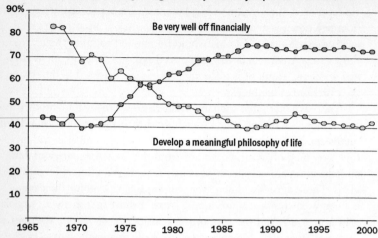

Fig 6.1 Students Entering College Who Say It Is "Very Important or Essential" To:

Source: Annual surveys of more than 200,000 new collegians, reported yearly in *The American Freshman* (Higher Education Research Institute, UCLA)

Robert Frank reports that in the late 1990s spending on luxury goods was growing four times as fast as overall spending. Thousand-dollar-a-night suites at the Palm Beach Four Seasons Hotel are booked months ahead for weddings, he reports, as are the $5,000-a-night suites at Aspen's Little Nell. The 5,000 hundred-foot yachts in this country are double the number of a decade ago, and can cost more than $10,000 per hour of use. Luxury cars (costing more than $30,000 in 1996 dollars) have shot up in the past decade from 7 percent to 12 percent of all vehicles sold. In *Luxury Fever*, Frank likens us to bull elks who compete for the social advantages of having the biggest antlers. If all their antlers were reduced by half their social hierarchy would be unchanged and they all would be safer when chased by wolves through a thick forest. If all wedding receptions were half as expensive, would we not be just as happy, and have more money to invest or give more productively?

Frank, a Cornell University economist, and psychologists Thomas Gilovich and Dennis Regan believe that economics professors are partly responsible for their students' materialism. Their nationwide survey of college professors revealed that economists, despite having relatively high salaries, were more than twice as likely as those in other disciplines to contribute no money to private charities. In response to public television appeals, most gave nothing. In laboratory monetary games, students behave more selfishly after taking economics courses. "Whoever said money can't buy happiness isn't spending it right," proclaimed a Lexus ad.

Wealth and Well-Being

Would having more money, by enabling "the good life," buy us greater well-being? As middle-class people's money goes up does their misery go down? We can triangulate on this question by asking three more specific questions.

Are Rich Countries Happier?

Surveys of several hundred thousand representatively sampled people—170,000 of whom were studied in a 16-nation study in the 1980s—reveal striking national differences in well-being. In Portugal, 1 in 10 people say they are very happy. In the Netherlands 4 in 10 people say the same. These appear to be genuine national differences, not mere variations in the connotations of the translated questions. For example, regardless of whether they are German-, French-, or Italian-speaking, the Swiss report higher well-being than their German, French, and Italian neighbors.

Comparing the countries, we find some tendency for wealthy nations to have happier, more satisfied people. The Scandinavians, for instance, are generally prosperous and happy. But there are curious reversals. The Irish during the 1980s consistently reported greater life satisfaction than the doubly wealthy West Germans. Belgians tended to be happier than their wealthier French neighbors. And the Chinese are as satisfied with life as the Japanese, who have eight times the purchasing power. Moreover, national wealth is entangled with other happiness predictors, such as civil rights, literacy, and the number of continuous years of democracy. It's not just the wealth of the Scandinavians and Swiss that matters, but their history of freedom.

The World Values Survey of 1990–91 confirmed the national differences in subjective well-being. National well-being rose with national wealth, but only up to a GNP of about $8,000 per person. "The transition from a society of scarcity to a society of security brings a dramatic increase in subjective well-being," said University of Michigan researcher Ronald Inglehart. "But (at roughly the economic level of Ire-

Fig. 6.2 National Wealth and Well-Being

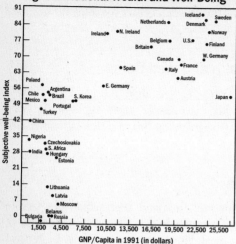

Source: Ronald Inglehart, *Modernization and Postmodernization: Cultural, Economic, and Political Change in Societies* (Princeton, N.J.: Princeton University Press, 1997), p. 62. Subjective well-being index combines measures of happiness (percentage describing themselves as "very happy" or "happy" minus those "not very happy" or "unhappy") and life satisfaction (percentage describing themselves as 7 or above on a 10-point life satisfaction scale minus those 4 or below).

land in 1990) we find a threshold at which economic growth no longer seems to increase subjective well-being. This may be linked with the fact that at this level starvation is no longer a real concern for most people. Survival begins to be taken for granted." Better (so far as happiness and life satisfaction go) to be Irish than Bulgarian. But whether one is Irish, Belgian, Norwegian, or American hardly matters.

During the mid-1980s my family and I spent a sabbatical year in the historic town of St. Andrews, Scotland. Comparing life there with life in America, we were impressed by a seeming disconnection between national wealth and well-being. To most Americans, Scottish life would have seemed Spartan. Incomes were about half those in the United States. Among families in the Kingdom of Fife surrounding St. Andrews, 44 percent did not own a car, and we never met a family that owned two. Central heating in this place not far south of Iceland was, at that time, still a luxury.

During our year there and three half-summer stays since, we enjoyed hundreds of conversations over morning coffee gatherings in my University of St. Andrews department, in church groups, and over dinner or tea in people's homes. We repeatedly noticed that, despite their simpler living, the Scots appeared no less joyful than Americans. We heard complaints about Margaret Thatcher, but never about being underpaid or unable to afford wants. With less money there was no less satisfaction with living, no less warmth of spirit, no less pleasure in one another's company.

Are Rich Americans Happier?

Within any country, such as our own, are rich people happier? In poor countries, such as Bangladesh and India, being relatively well off does make for somewhat greater well-being. Psychologically as well as materially, it is better to be high caste than low caste. We humans *need* food, rest, warmth, and social contact.

But within affluent countries, where nearly everyone can afford life's necessities, increasing affluence matters surprisingly little. In the United States, Canada, and Europe, the correlation between income and happiness is, as Inglehart noted in the 16-nation study, "surprisingly weak (indeed, virtually negligible)." Happiness is lower among the very poor. But once comfortable, more money provides diminishing returns. The second piece of pie, or the second $50,000, never tastes as good as the first. So far as happiness is concerned, it hardly matters whether one drives a BMW or, like so many of the Scots, walks or rides a bus. As David Lykken puts it based on his studies of happiness, "People who go to work in their overalls . . . are just as happy, on the average, as those in suits."

That seems to be the experience of the nearly 1,000 American teens whose experience is periodically sampled by University of Chicago psychologist Mihaly Csikszentmihalyi. Surprisingly, those from upper-middle-class backgrounds report less happiness than those from the lowest socioeconomic class. One possible explanation, according to Csikszentmihalyi (pronounced CHICK-sent-me-hi-ee), is that professional and executive parents tend to spend less time with their children than do middle- and working-class parents. "The Swedish economist Stephen Linder was the first to point out that as income and therefore the value of one's time increases, it becomes less and less 'rational' to spend it on anything besides making money—or spending it conspicuously."

Even very rich people—the *Forbes* 100 wealthiest Americans surveyed by University of Illinois psychologist Ed Diener—are only slightly happier than average. With net worths providing ample money to buy things they don't need and hardly care about, 4 in 5 of the 49 people responding to the survey agreed that "Money can increase OR decrease happiness, depending on how it is used." And some were indeed unhappy. One fabulously wealthy man said he could never remember being happy. One woman reported that money could not undo misery caused by her children's problems. When sailing on the Titanic, even first class cannot get you where you want to go.

Warren Buffett reports that Diener's findings are consistent with his own observation of billionaires. Indeed, examples of the wretched wealthy are not hard to come by: Howard Hughes, Christina Onassis, J. Paul Getty (and his heirs). "If you were a jerk before, you'll be a bigger jerk with a billion dollars," added Buffett. Thirteen-year-old Athina Roussel has a solution to the legal battles over her half-billion-dollar Onassis fortune: "If I burn the money, there will be no problem." "It would be a way to be like everybody else," her stepmother explained.

At the other end of life's circumstances are most victims of disabling tragedies. With exceptions—vicious child abuse or rape, for example— most people who suffer negative life events do not exhibit long-term emotional devastation. People who become blind or paralyzed, perhaps after a car accident, suffer the frustrations imposed by their limitations. Daily, they must cope with the challenges imposed by their disabilities. Yet, remarkably, most eventually recover a near normal level of day-to-day happiness. Thus, university students who must cope with disabilities are as likely as able-bodied students to report themselves happy, and their friends agree with their self-perceptions. "Weeping may linger for the night," observed the Psalmist, "but joy comes with the morning."

These findings underlie an astonishing conclusion from the new scientific study of happiness. As the late researcher Richard Kammann of New Zealand put it, "Objective life circumstances have a negligible role to play in a theory of happiness." People in a society where everyone lived in 4,000-square-foot houses would likely be no happier than people in a society in which everyone lived in 2,000-square-foot houses. Good events—a pay hike, winning a big game, an A on an important exam—make us happy, until we adapt. And bad events—an argument with our mate, a work failure, a social rejection—deject us, but seldom for more than a few days.

We adapt, and we also compare ourselves to our peers. Desiring the biggest antlers, we're happier making $50,000 when those around us make $40,000 than if making $60,000 while those around us make $70,000. If a rising tide lifts all boats equally, we will soon adapt and be no happier.

Feeling the short-run influence of events, people use such events to explain their happiness, all the while missing subtler but bigger influences on their long-run well-being. Noticing that an influx of cash feels good, they may accept the Hollywood, Robin Leach image of who is happy—the rich and famous. Noting their demoralization after failure, they believe success underlies happiness. Yet in less time than most people suppose, the emotional impact of significant events dissipates, Harvard social psychologist Daniel Gilbert and his colleagues argue. Faculty members being considered for tenure expect their lives would be devastated by a negative decision. In fact, five to ten years after tenure decisions are made, those denied are not noticeably unhappier than those awarded tenure. The surprising reality: we humans have an enormous capacity to adapt to fame, fortune, and affliction.

We do this by recalibrating our "adaptation levels"—the neutral points at which sounds seem neither loud nor soft, lights neither bright nor dim, experiences neither pleasant nor unpleasant. Here in Michigan on this winter day, 60 degrees would feel warm, but not when we are adapted to summer's heat. So it goes with things. Our first desktop computer, with information loaded from a cassette tape, seemed remarkable, until we got that speedier hard-drive machine, which itself became poky once we got a faster, more powerful machine. So it happens that yesterday's luxuries become today's necessities and tomorrow's relics. For 41 percent of Americans (up from 13 percent in 1973) automobile air-conditioning "is a necessity." "I cannot afford to buy everything I really need," say 39 percent of Americans earning $75,000 to $100,000 per year. (Tell that with a straight face to folks in Sudan's refugee centers.)

William Bennett, who has done much to alert us to the social recession and our need to renew values, is not exempt from the materialism of his age. In spurning a $125,000 offer to become chair of the Republican National Committee he remarked, "I didn't take a vow of poverty"—which is apparently what $125,000 felt like after making a reported $240,000 in speaking fees during just the preceding four months. But even $240,000 hardly feels like wealth to many professional athletes. "People think we make $3 million or $4 million a year," explained Texas Ranger outfielder Pete Incaviglia several years ago. "They don't realize that most of us only make $500,000."

Does Economic Growth Improve Human Morale?

We have scrutinized the American dream of achieved wealth and well-being by comparing rich and unrich countries, and rich and unrich people. That leaves the final question: over time, does happiness rise with growing affluence?

Likely not as much as might be supposed. Lottery winners appear to gain but a temporary jolt of joy from their winnings. Looking back, they feel delighted to have won. Yet the euphoria doesn't last. In fact, previously enjoyed activities like reading may become less pleasurable. Compared with the high of winning a million dollars, ordinary pleasures pale. And for some winners money's pleasures are offset by its problems. A year after Frank Capaci won a $195 million Powerball jackpot, some of his old friends were no longer talking to him, he had bought a shredder to dispose of unwanted mail, and he reportedly had gone into hiding.

On a smaller scale, a jump in our income can boost our morale, for a while. "But in the long run," argues Inglehart, "neither an ice cream cone nor a new car nor becoming rich and famous produces the same feelings of delight that it initially did. . . . Happiness is not the result of being rich, but a temporary consequence of having recently become richer." Diener's research confirms that those whose incomes have increased over a ten-year period are not happier than those whose income has not increased. Wealth is like health: although its utter absence can breed misery, having it does not guarantee happiness. Happiness is less a matter of getting what we want than of wanting what we have.

For that matter, the pain of simplification may also be short-lived. Robert Frank experienced this: "As a young man fresh out of college, I served as a Peace Corps Volunteer in rural Nepal. My one-room house had no electricity, no heat, no indoor toilet, no running water. The local diet offered little variety and virtually no meat. . . . Yet, although my living conditions in Nepal were a bit startling at first, the most salient feature of my experience was how quickly they came to seem normal. Within a matter of weeks, I lost all sense of impoverishment. Indeed, my $40 monthly stipend was more than most others had in my village, and with it I experienced a feeling of prosperity that I have recaptured only in recent years."

Our human capacity for adaptation helps explain why, despite the elation of triumph and the anguish of tragedy, lottery winners and paraplegics usually return to their preexisting happiness. "Satisfaction has a short half-life," explains University of Rochester psychologist Richard Ryan, who with Tim Kasser has studied the pursuit of wealth. The transience of monetary satisfactions explains why material wants can prove insatiable—why Imelda Marcos, living in splendor amid privation in the Philippines, could buy more shoes than she could conceivably wear. When the possessor becomes possessed by accumulating ever more possessions, the adaptation-level phenomenon has run wild.

We can also ask whether, over time, our collective happiness has floated upward with the rising economic tide. In 1940, 2 out of 5 homes lacked a shower or bathtub, 35 percent had no toilet, and heat often meant feeding wood or coal into a furnace. In 1957, when economist John Kenneth Galbraith published his influential book about the United States, *The Affluent Society*, Americans' per person income, expressed in today's dollars, was $9,000. Today it is more than $20,000, thanks to increased real wages into the early 1970s, increased working hours, increased nonwage income, and the doubling of married women's employment. Compared with 1957, we are therefore "the doubly affluent society"—with double what money buys, including twice as many cars per person, not to mention microwave ovens, big screen color TVs, home computers, and $200 billion a year spent in restaurants and bars—two and a half times our inflation-adjusted restaurant spending per person in 1960. From 1960 to 1997, the number of Americans with dishwashers zoomed from 7 percent to 50 percent, clothes dryers from 20 percent to 71 percent, and air-conditioning from 15 percent to 73 percent.

Looking through unsolicited mail order catalogs recently, my wife remarked, "You know what's become big business? It's stuff to put your stuff in." Such storage systems sell well in our neighborhood of century-old homes, built presuming less need for closets and shelving to store accumulated possessions. And to store that shelving we're building bigger houses. In 1966, 22 percent of new homes had more than 2,000 square feet; in 1994, 47 percent did. Driving around our town's new middle-class suburban developments recently, we were struck by all the three-stall garages—typically two for the cars and one for the stuff (the riding lawnmower, the boat, the bikes). In the 1950s, the average size of an entire new house was hardly bigger than today's 900-square-foot three-stall garage.

Throughout the 20th century, people of all income levels have been able to devote more time and money to having fun. In the late 1800s, MIT economist Dora Costa reports, industrial workers spent about three-quarters of their incomes on food, shelter, and clothing. By 1991, only 38 percent of average household income was dedicated to those necessities. Spending on recreation and leisure has increased, especially for home entertainment (though as the expanding cruise industry knows, on other pleasure pursuits as well). And the rich-poor discrepancy in proportion of income devoted to recreational spending is shrinking.

It's true that downsizing and recessions have contributed to the loss of 43 million jobs since 1973, with painful dislocations. But since then our economy also has created 70 million new jobs. Often, downsizing effectively reduces wages, as here in Michigan, where the automakers have shifted employment to the lower-wage payrolls of their booming supplier firms. But not all job shifts are bad. We've all heard of AT&T's laying off 40,000 workers, but few of us have heard that MCI's employment in the decade after 1985 mushroomed from 12,000 to 48,000 or Sprint's from 27,000 to 52,000. People have lost jobs to corporate mergers but found new ones in the growing smaller-company sector, including the many young technology companies. As Zoë Baird points out, the combination of inflation and unemployment is at its lowest level in 27 years.

So, believing that a little more money would make us a little happier, and having seen our affluence ratchet upward over nearly four decades, are we now happier? With even most poverty-level families today enjoying some luxuries missing from most American households a quarter century ago—color TVs, VCRs, and air-conditioning—are we happier? With all the things we now enjoy that our parents at our age missed—e-mail, suitcases on wheels, car phones, Post-it notes, CD sound systems, cosmetic surgery, computer games, and a hundred varieties of therapists—are we happier?

We are not. Since 1957, the number of people telling the University of Chicago's National Opinion Research Center that they are "very happy" has declined from 35 percent to 30 percent. Twice as rich,

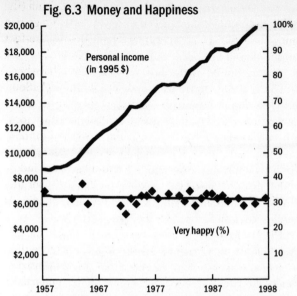

Fig. 6.3 Money and Happiness

Source: Happiness data from Richard Gene Niemi, John Mueller, and Tom W. Smith, *Trends in Public Opinion: A Compendium of Survey Data* (New York: Greenwood, 1989), and personal correspondence with Tom Smith, National Opinion Research Center; income data from *Historical Statistics of the U.S.* and *Economic Indicators*

and a little less happy. In fact, between 1956 and 1988, the number of Americans saying they were "pretty well satisfied" with their financial situation dropped from 42 percent to 30 percent.

We also are more often downright miserable. Among Americans born since World War II, depression has increased dramatically—tenfold, Martin Seligman reports. Today's 25-year-olds are much more likely to recall a time in their lives when they were despondent and despairing than are their 75-year-old grandparents, despite the grandparents having had many more years to suffer all kinds of disorder, from broken legs to the anguish of depression. Similar trends are evident in Canada, Sweden, Germany, and New Zealand. Everywhere in the modern world, it seems, more younger adults than older adults report having ever been disabled by this new great (emotional) depression.

Researchers debate the actual extent of rising depression. Do older adults simply forget long-ago depressive episodes? No, the age difference persists when people report just their recent depressive symptoms. Are younger adults just more willing to admit to such feelings? Or are they less willing to consider temporary despair a normal part of life? If so, then defining depression by other criteria—being hospitalized for depression, the duration of episodes, and so forth—should eliminate the depression age gap. But no matter how we define depression, the findings persist: young people today have grown up with much more affluence, slightly less overall happiness, and much greater risk of depression, not to mention tripled teenage suicide and all the other social pathologies we have considered. Never has a culture experienced such physical comfort combined with such psychological misery. Never have we felt so free, or had our prisons so overstuffed. Never have we been so sophisticated about pleasure, or so likely to suffer broken relationships.

These are the best of times materially, "a time of elephantine vanity and greed" observes Garrison Keillor. But they are not the best of times for the human spirit. We have bigger houses and broken homes, higher income and lower morale, more mental health professionals and less well-being. We excel at making a living but often fail at making a life.

William Bennett, no critic of free-market economies, is among those who recognize the futility of economics without ethics and money without a mission: "If we have full employment and greater economic growth—if we have cities of gold and alabaster—but our children have not learned how to walk in goodness, justice, and mercy, then the American experiment, no matter how gilded, will have failed."

The evidence leads to a startling conclusion: our becoming much better off over the past four decades has not been accompanied by one iota of increased psychological well-being. Economic growth has provided no boost to our collective morale.

Moreover, individuals who strive most for wealth tend to live with lower well-being, a finding that "comes through very strongly in every culture I've looked at," Ryan reports. Kasser, his collaborator, concludes from their studies that those who instead strive for "intimacy, personal growth, and contribution to the community" experience a higher quality of life. Ryan and Kasser's research echoes an earlier finding by H. W. Perkins: among 800 college alumni surveyed, those with "Yuppie values"—who preferred a high income and occupational success and prestige to having very close friends and a close marriage—were twice as likely as their former classmates to describe themselves as "fairly" or "very" unhappy.

We know the perils of materialism, sort of. In a nationally representative survey, Princeton sociologist Robert Wuthnow found that 89 percent of more than 2,000 participants felt that "our society is much too materialistic." *Other* people are too materialistic, that is. For 84 percent also wished they had more money, and 78 percent said it was "very or fairly important" to have "a beautiful home, a new car and other nice things."

But one has to wonder, what's the point? "Why," asked the prophet Isaiah, "do you spend your money for that which is not bread, and your labor for that which does not satisfy?" What's the point of accumulating stacks of unplayed CDs, closets full of seldom-worn clothes, garages with luxury cars? What's the point of corporate and government policies that inflate the rich while leaving the working poor to languish? What's the point of leaving huge estates for one's children, as if inherited wealth could buy them happiness, when that wealth could do so much good in a hurting world? (If self-indulgence can't buy us happiness, and cannot buy it for our kids, why not leave any significant wealth we accumulate to bettering the human condition?)

The Rest of the Story

Three hundred years ago, the philosopher-mathematician Pascal observed that no single truth is ever sufficient, because the world is complex. Any truth, separated from its complementary truth, is a half-truth. Since the late 1950s, average real personal income has doubled. It's true. Moreover, we are having fewer children to spend it on (thanks to the halved birthrate) and more discretionary income for recreation. It has been a good decade for those who manufacture cruise liners, RVs, and home entertainment systems.

But it also is true that while supervisors' and managers' portion of total national income zoomed from 16 percent to 24 percent between 1973 and 1994, production workers' share of the pie dropped by nearly the same amount. In fact, hourly workers' real wages have *declined* slightly since the early 1970s. This needn't mean that those who were low-wage workers in the early '70s have lost ground (the lower tier incorporates the influx of immigrant labor). Nevertheless, the implications for family life "are dire," Sylvia Ann Hewlett and Cornel West warn: "32 percent of all men between twenty-five and thirty-four when working full-time now earn less than the amount necessary to keep a family of four above the poverty line." Moreover, average real house-

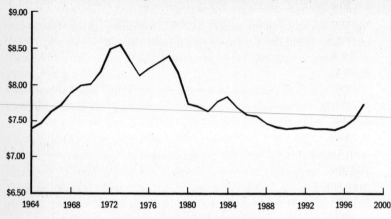

Fig. 6.4 Hourly Earnings of Production Workers (in 1982 dollars)

Source: Bureau of Labor Statistics (http://146.142.4.24/cgi-bin/surveymost)

hold income, though boosted by the increase in women's employment, has not increased as rapidly as individual income. That's because family divisions and declining marriage have spread personal income across more households. If all adults had their present income but were as likely to be married as in 1960, household income would be noticeably higher.

Inequality

There is another troubling truth. Although the economic pie has been growing, the rich (as usually happens during economic expansions) have been eating a progressively larger piece and the poor a progressively smaller one. Few of us wish for the forced equality depicted in Kurt Vonnegut's short story "Harrison Bergeron," in which talented ballerinas are burdened with sash weights and their faces masked, "so that no one, seeing a free and graceful gesture or a pretty face, would feel like something the cat drug in." Yet economic inequality is psychologically significant, because countries with large income inequality and much poverty, such as Brazil, India, and Portugal, have populations that report lower psychological quality of life than countries like Norway, the Netherlands, and Belgium, where wealth is more equally distributed.

Economists have some fancy statistical measures of income inequality. For us noneconomists, the simplest measure is the portion of all income received by the richest fifth of the population (which now includes so many billionaires that *Forbes* has stopped counting them). Since 1967, the richest fifth of households have increased their share from 43.8 percent to 49.4 percent of all income. The incomes of the richest 5 percent have swelled even faster—70 percent in real terms since 1967 (compared with 23 percent among the poorest fifth, who actually have gained nothing since 1974). As economist Glenn Loury has said, a rising tide "won't lift the sunken boats."

To make this concrete, consider families earning more than $60,000. Since 1970 (in today's dollars), their proportion has increased from approximately 20 percent to 25 percent, as has the number earning less than $20,000. The proportion in the middle has, therefore, dwindled correspondingly, from 59 percent to 50 percent. Expressed as household income, the rich-poor differences are visibly increasing.

In 1960, according to *Business Week,* the average chief executive of a major corporation earned as much as 41 factory workers. In 1996, a chief executive of a Fortune 500 company was deemed worth nearly 185 factory workers. If Louis Gerstner of IBM worked six days a week, 48 weeks a year, for his $4.6 million in 1994 salary and bonus, then he received a cool $16,000 a day—about what the average retail clerk who waited on him earned in a year. Gerstner did manage to raise that meager stipend to $13.2 million in 1995, but he got trumped by John Welch's $22 million in direct compensation from General Electric—which our $16,000 a year clerk could match by working 1,375 years.

Do big results justify big salaries? The average income of America's physicians approaches $200,000. In Britain, which has less income inequality and a health care system that costs one-third as much per person, doctors earn one-fourth as much as in the United States. Average life expectancy in both countries is 75. Of course, rich doctors can point to richer CEOs, who can defend their salaries by comparing their societal contributions with those of professional athletes. Gerstner's $4.6 million was one-tenth of Michael Jordan's $44 million in 1994. But then Jordan could look with envy on Disney chairman Michael Eisner's 1998 $575.6 million income from salary, bonus, and cashed-in options (which Holly Sklar noted could be funded by taking nearly $14 from each of the 41.7 million Florida theme-park tickets sold by Disney that year).

Since 1980, wealth, like income, has been flooding upward, not trickling down. The richest 1 percent in our egalitarian-rooted nation now own about 40 percent of the country's net wealth. Someone has calculated that Jordan made $10,000 a minute playing for the Chicago Bulls in 1998. And each time New York Mets catcher Mike Piazza comes to bat under his new $91 million, seven-year contract he will have made another $27,000, which computes to about $7,500 per pitch.

Yet the nerds beat the jocks. If Jordan took out $50 million a year and stuck it between his mattresses he would have to continue for 1,620 years to equal Bill Gates's $81 billion in Microsoft stock in August 1999. How much is $81 billion? If Gates could turn that wealth into cash and stick it between *his* mattresses, he could give away $20 million *daily* for a decade—and still have $8 billion left over (more than enough to finance his new $40 million home and anything else his heart might desire).

As conservative political analyst Kevin Phillips has said, "The 1980s were the triumph of upper America—an ostentatious celebration of wealth, the political ascendancy of the richest third of the population." Facing *Time* interviewers after being named "Man of the Year" for 1995, Newt Gingrich was up front about his mission: "to maximize the creation of wealth and the acquisition of wealth rather than the redistribution of wealth." You have to wonder if this is the economic philosophy Gingrich would pick if he had to make his choice while still in the womb—without knowing whether he would be born into privilege or poverty, whether he was white or black, whether he was endowed with exceptional native gifts or a significant disability.

Accompanying the growing economic inequality is growing economic segregation. More and more the rich live separate from the poor. Their children attend well-funded suburban schools, if not private schools. They live in enclaves with other rich. Rarely do they encounter the poor about whom they have many opinions. Old neighborhoods like the one where I live—with blocks of beautiful historic homes interspersed with those of the working poor, anchored by an elementary school where the children form an ethnic rainbow—face competition from new developments with homes and apartments at mandated price levels.

Among African-Americans, the inequality between the richest and poorest fifths is especially great. "There is more in common between two middle-class families one of which is black," Gertrude Himmelfarb claims, "than between two black families one of which is middle-class." There is, therefore, the possibility that future conflicts may erupt more between rich and poor than between ethnic groups. In a society where the top 1 percent hold assets equal to those of the bottom 40 percent, talk of revolt may flourish when the next recession hits. "Chiapas, and South American guerrillas, are not accidents of history," warns Milton Schwebel, editor of *Peace and Conflict*. "These are uncharted waters for American democracy," suggests economist Lester Thurow, referring to the growing inequality. "We are conducting an enormous social and political experiment—something like putting a pressure cooker on the stove over a full flame and waiting to see how long it takes to explode."

In the new competitive global economy nations compete for business much as low-tax states compete with high-tax states. As every national leader knows, this mandates a favorable business climate with minimal regulation, low labor costs, modest taxes, and a secure legal environment. But what is good for business in this "turbocapitalist" economy of unfettered competition may not be good for social cohesion. Because we come wired to judge our lives in comparison with others, increasing affluence at the top may demoralize those in the stable middle. "When top earners build 25,000-square-foot houses, others just below them find their own 10,000-square-foot houses no longer adequate, and so on all the way down the line," explains Robert Frank. When the rich have more to spend, you, too, eventually will need to spend more to afford the classy clothes, cars, and weddings that your family will want as they mingle with the wealthy around them.

Financial wizard George Soros is similarly concerned about the social implications of "the intensification of the profit motive" and the resulting "inequities in the distribution of wealth." "In a highly competitive, transnational market, concern for the interests of others can turn into a handicap," he argues. "What I can say with confidence is that the substitution of monetary values for all other values is pushing society toward a dangerous disequilibrium. . . . To put the matter simply, market forces, if they are given complete authority even in the purely economic and financial arenas, produce chaos and could ultimately lead to the downfall of the global capitalist system."

The growing African-American middle class has, thanks to improved job opportunities and housing desegregation, been moving out of the inner city. Chicago's South Side in the 1950s, for example, had communal neighborhoods populated by the dictates of segregation with people of all classes and incomes. The middle-class exodus from formerly stable neighborhoods has left an increasing concentration of poor African-Americans in underclass neighborhoods marked by persistent joblessness and poverty. Decreased racial segregation among the middle class has, ironically, led to increased economic segregation. For such concentrated poverty, they, and we, pay a price.

The Price of Poverty

The concentration of poor families creates high-risk settings for youth, a National Research Council report said in 1993. "Such neighborhoods are characterized by racial stratification, homelessness or very degraded housing, inadequate schools, a lack of recreational and employment opportunities, and in metropolitan areas, a high level of crime and violence. Constructing a family life that can guide children and adolescents into healthy constructive behaviors is a challenge of heroic dimensions in these settings." The challenge is exacerbated by the loss of resources needed to support churches and other community-building institutions. For family ecology, lack of money is the root of much evil.

The Children's Defense Fund, which relentlessly documents the links between children's poverty and pathology, concurs. America's 15 million poor children, it reports, are much more likely to suffer malnourishment, family stress, inferior child care, frequent moves, adolescent pregnancy, overcrowding, and death. They attend inferior schools, are more likely to drop out, to become delinquent, and to approach life with little hope. With the sense of futility comes a loss of faith in the work ethic. The moral sense takes a back seat to mere survival, aided by an underground economy.

Money may not buy happiness, but, as someone has said, it makes misery easier to live with. Having money is "better than poverty," observed Woody Allen, "if only for financial reasons." Money can buy good food, decent shelter, opportunities to learn, reduced family stress, a healthy neighborhood, preventive health care, healthy recreation, and improved economic opportunity. And, the Children's Defense Fund maintains, it would do so at less cost than the long-term price that society pays in escalating crime, welfare, and unproductivity. To ensure that few of our children live in poverty would cost us in the short run. But child-friendly priorities are an investment in our future.

The sharp-eyed reader will recall, however, that poverty and single parenthood often go hand in hand, meaning that in social science studies each of these variables tends to be a proxy for the other. In Chapter 4 we saw that although single parenthood is a major cause of poverty, family structure matters even when controlling for income. But the reverse is true as well: poverty matters even when controlling for family structure. One research team led by Greg Duncan of the University of Michigan followed 895 infants and preschoolers over five years. Its conclusion: "Family income and poverty status are powerful determinants of the cognitive development and behavior of children, even after we account for other differences—in particular family structure and maternal schooling." (There is, admittedly, another possible reason for the poverty-pathology correlation: genetic influences that put people at risk for pathology may also put them at risk for poverty. Genetics cannot, however, explain the post-1960 social megatrends.)

Moreover, poverty undermines marriage. One of the principal findings of the new science of evolutionary psychology is that females, worldwide, invest their reproductive opportunities carefully, by looking for signs of power and resources in potential mates. Men therefore strive to offer the resources that women desire, and women feel attracted to men whose wealth, power, and ambition promise resources for protecting and nurturing offspring. The high rates of unemployment and underemployment among certain groups of young men impede their chances for marriage. Young African-American women face a serious shortage of employed African-American men of similar age. "A man who can barely support himself isn't likely to look forward to taking on the responsibilities of a wife and children," psychologist Lillian Rubin contends. "Nor is a woman apt to see him as a great marriage prospect."

In *When Work Disappears: The World of the New Urban Poor,* sociologist William Julius Wilson documents the social toxicity of unemployment. It is not a coincidence that the black family has weakened during an era when African-Americans have lost so many good jobs to automation and suburbanization, he argues, or that as joblessness doubled for black men between 1960 and 1992, so did the number of female-headed black households. Here in Michigan, Detroit-area families have suffered the loss of thousands of unionized auto manufacturing jobs. (Many of those jobs have moved to smaller cities like Grand Rapids and Holland, where thousands of nonunionized workers have been hired in the past decade by newer companies that now manufacture plug-in mirrors, windows, electronic components, and mechanical systems for assembly in Detroit.)

Poverty-ridden Benton Harbor, Michigan, has led America's 3,000 largest cities with 83 percent of its families headed by single parents. Ken Parnell, a retired mechanic, responds angrily when asked why Benton Harbor has so many single parents. "Because black men can't get no jobs. Because white men got all the jobs sewed up. . . . How can you take care of your family if you can't get a job? That's it in a nutshell." More young men having a job with no future or, worse, a future with no job, means more young women having no husbands, more children without fathers, and more young men at loose ends without the civilizing responsibilities of marriage and fatherhood. Even among married couples, the odds of breakup are doubled in families where the father has no job.

So, with all these facts of life in mind, pretend some devils wanted to design a program to corrode families. They might begin by lowering the job prospects and earning power of young men. To accomplish this, they might encourage corporate CEOs to act like yesteryear's robber barons and redirect rewards to themselves. Justifying their actions with talk of freedom, they might also deregulate television, legalize gambling, structure taxes to penalize marriage, and shrink the real value of the minimum wage (which was created to be a "living family wage" that protected families and children). While this demonic river is sweeping the American family downstream, they might then beckon families to swim upstream against the cultural current, celebrate those who succeed, and blame those who drown.

The free market certainly provides incentives and has triumphed over competing economic systems. As one who is invested in the market and who sits on the advisory board of a bank and the board of directors of a food processing company, I appreciate and participate in the successes of our free-market economy. Capitalism, as Winston Churchill might have put it, is the worst economic system, except for all the others. Yet I cannot deny what even many Republicans now acknowledge: the unrestrained, profit-focused free market has corroded family values.

Unbridled capitalism, Bennett has observed, is "a problem for that whole dimension of things we call the realm of values and human relationships." "Although I have made a fortune in the financial markets," reflects Soros, "I now fear that the untrammeled intensification of laissez-faire capitalism and the spread of market values into all areas of life is endangering our open and democratic society."

In the conservative *Family in America* newsletter, Bryce Christensen says, "Americans have witnessed nothing less than an assault upon wedlock and family life. We see this assault all around us: in heavy taxation of families with children; in the systematic dismantling of the family wage formerly making it possible to support a family on a single income."

Pope John Paul and many of his bishops in Latin America and the United States are similarly concerned about the human impact of American capitalism. Like Marxism, they believe, it fails us by reducing the person to an economic dimension and by creating "a world of replaceable individuals."

Such words coming from conscientious conservatives give hope that the tide may shift from a morally untethered capitalism to a more socially responsible capitalism—one that rewards creativity and initiative but also values children and families.

Home Economics

If we really want to get serious about nurturing children, strengthening families, and improving our culture's prospects, we must turn from talking about family values to doing something—with government and corporate policies that actually value families. To praise parents who stay home to care for children and then veto a family leave bill that would have enabled them to do that without pay for 12 weeks, as George Bush did in 1992, is to talk and walk in different directions.

If we set aside culture-war issues like abortion and gay rights, we see an emerging consensus among liberals and conservatives: government and corporate policies matter, and they have not made family welfare a priority. "No government can love a child and no policy can substitute for a family's care," acknowledges a pastoral letter from the National Conference of Catholic Bishops. "But clearly families can be helped or hurt in their irreplaceable roles. Government can either support or undermine families as they cope with the moral, social, and economic stresses of caring for children."

How might we, then, improve the economic ecology for families? Imagine that we were to start over on a lush new planet. We could take today's knowledge loaded in our brains and laptop computers, but our government, economics, education, and media we would need to create afresh. Doing the work of angels rather than devils, what sort of society would we wish to create?

Might it be in some ways like our own, yet different? Perhaps having a purer democracy, uninfluenced by political contributions? Perhaps offering tax and benefit policies that reward marriage? Perhaps having a socially responsible market economy that provides incentives for achievement while protecting the natural and social environments? Perhaps having a progressive consumption tax that encourages savings, investment, and economic growth while putting a price on the accumulation of nonessential luxury goods, such as the $18,500 Range Rover child's car offered by FAO Schwarz? (Robert Frank suggests doing this by simply taxing families not on what they earn but on what they spend—which is their earnings minus their savings and perhaps their charitable giving. The tax could be made progressive with ample dependent exemptions and higher tax rates for the big spenders.)

As complete environmentalists—concerned for both natural and social environments—might we mandate "family-impact statements"? Might we want government to consider its client to be not just the individual but the family system? Remembering that a family-supportive job versus no such job affects well-being more than does high versus middle income, and that a culture's rich-poor disparity predicts its social pathology, might a family-friendly new society therefore give less priority to increasing upper incomes than to providing full employment at livable wages? (That was part of the idea behind Jack Kemp's enterprise zones, which offer investors the carrot of zero capital gains tax on businesses built and jobs created in poor neighborhoods.)

Contrast this with how we award discounted fees, fares, and prices to senior citizens. Although their average wealth greatly exceeds that of the average young parent, we give restaurant, airline, and park fee discounts to senior citizens. These amount to an implicit penalty on financially strapped young adults who must therefore pay higher fees. A 62-year-old friend tells me his favorite airline will now give him coupons to fly anywhere domestically for $270 round trip. As a sample comparison, the lowest current fare that a young couple with two 3-year-old twins would pay to fly their kids to see grandparents for a summer holiday in my home town of Seattle is $573 per person, with no discount for the children. Sorry families! My local theater likewise charges me — at 56 with an empty nest and at my earnings peak—less than it charges 30-year-olds, with their early-career wages and children at home with a babysitter. My nearest gas station has a similar senior discount. These businesses might just as well drop the price of tickets and gasoline and add a surcharge for all those under 55. Although more tactless, the effect would be identical. Shouldn't we instead be giving discounts to parents who have children at home?

Thanks partly to favoritism toward the old over the young, including the indexing of (untaxed) Social Security payments, the poverty rate of seniors is now half that of children. Such favoritism may have made sense in an age when many more seniors lived in poverty. But do such policies really express our priorities today, when for every senior in poverty we have four children? Starting afresh, it would make more sense not to devalue younger parents by charging them more than older adults.

Family-Supportive Tax and Benefit Policies

As a general rule, what we tax we get less of, what we reward we get more of. If our highways are jammed and our air polluted, we create fast lanes that reward carpooling and penalize driving solo. Commentators from the conservative Family Research Council and the Rockford Institute to the centrist Communitarian Network and the liberal Children's Defense Fund agree on at least one thing: social policies can make or break families. Government tax policies can work to provide either incentives or disincentives for marriage and family life.

In the 1950s, in some ways the golden age for the modern nuclear family, "tax policy, education policy, and housing policy worked together in powerful ways to create a society in which families were impressively strong and children flourished," observe Hewlett and West. There was an abundance of well-paying jobs, affordable housing supported by FHA and VA mortgages, a GI Bill to support higher education, a generous $6,500 dependent exemption (in 1996 dollars) to help underwrite the costs of child rearing, and a tax policy that favored married couples (by allowing them to total and split their income, with each spouse effectively taxed on half).

Beginning in the 1960s all this changed. Richard Nixon's 1969 tax reform package created a marriage penalty for certain income groups (meaning many two-income couples were better off single). Anti-father welfare policies required that there be no "man in the house." As the dependent exemption deflated, the tax rate of married couples with two children rose 43 percent between 1948 and 1984, while singles and childless couples saw no increase. Wage declines eroded young laboring men's ability to support families. And government support for home ownership diminished.

Without pretending expertise on family economics, here is a quick synopsis of proposals for how government might again foster families.

Eliminate the marriage penalty. Reverse the anti-marriage tilt in the way we tax two-income married couples, perhaps by restoring income splitting. Under current law, single-income couples pay less tax if married. But an unmarried man and woman each making $30,000 in taxable income pay some $1,000 less tax than they would on a combined $60,000 married-couple income (which is taxed in a higher bracket). "This is terrible social policy," says Dan Quayle. Eugene Steuerle of the Urban Institute agrees: removing the tax penalty for marriage will increase marriage. Economists James Alm and Leslie Whittington have estimated that a 20 percent reduction in the marriage tax would produce a 1 percent increase in the number of marriages. (Some marriage supporters advise going a step further with a "marriage encouragement" policy that would reduce taxes for couples who stay married, and an additional tax reduction for married couples who maintain guardianship of their children together.)

A friend of mine, seeing her son and his girlfriend very much in love and about to shop for a house, screws up her courage to ask why, if they're willing to make the commitment to buy a house together, they don't get married. We're not yet ready for that, the son explains, "and anyway, that's not how it's done in California. Also, there's the tax penalty."

The point to remember: tax codes are family policies.

When allocating subsidized housing and housing loans, give priority to married couples with children. So advise the sociologists and public policy experts that make up the nonpartisan Council on Families in America.

Increase incentives for self-support. Reward at-risk teens, perhaps with a cash grant, for finishing high school (preparing them for decent jobs and marriage). Increase incentives for jobless people to seek employment—by eliminating taxes on low-income workers, or increasing the Earned Income Tax Credit. President Reagan in 1986 called the Earned Income Tax Credit (which refunds taxes to the working poor), "the best anti-poverty, the best pro-family, the best job creation measure to come out of Congress." To encourage marriage, a "marriage bonus" could be additionally offered to low-income families. This would reverse the current incentives for families on public assistance, as described by Robert Rector: "The mother has a contract with the government. She will continue to receive her 'paycheck' as long as she fulfills two conditions: 1) she does not work; and 2) she does not marry an employed male. I call this the incentive system made in hell."

Increase incentives for community and child support. President Clinton's proposal in 1996 to reward adoption with a $5,000 tax credit supports adoptive families and their children. Senator Dan Coats's "Project for American Renewal" proposed similar incentives, such as a tax credit for married families receiving the Earned Income Tax Credit and a charity tax credit that would reward contributions to poverty-fighting institutions, even by those who do not itemize deductions.

Index dependent exemptions to inflation. Some federal programs, notably Social Security, are automatically adjusted to keep the real payment constant. Not so the inflation-gutted dependent exemption, which today would be worth more than $8,000 per child if indexed for inflation since World War II (not just since the 1950s). To support families, the government could restore and index the dependent exemption, under which low-income families would owe little if any tax. Proposals to raise the exemption have come from President Reagan's White House Working Group on the Family chaired by Gary Bauer (now head of the Family Research Council) and from a Progressive Policy Institute report as the top pro-family recommendation of "New Democrats." The bipartisan National Commission on Children (whose members included Bill Clinton and Marian Wright Edelman) in 1991 recommended a similar tax credit for children, as did the 1994 House Republicans' "Contract with America."

Better yet, provide a child allowance or a generous per child tax credit. Increased income exemptions give most support to those who place a higher priority on income generation than dedicating increased time to children. A European-style child allowance, on the other hand, would provide all parents (whether providing in-home care or paying for day care) with a $600 to $1,000 per child taxable cash grant. Such family-supporting tax reforms will be expensive in the short run, but less so in the long run, say child advocates, than the eventual taxes in the form of crime, welfare, and drug use that follow family collapse.

Increase the progressivity of the income tax. Allan Carlson, writing from the pro-family Howard Center for Family, Religion, and Society at the Rockford Institute, notes that a pure flat tax "is hostile to the interests of the family," because it increases the incentive to work ever longer hours outside the home. To strengthen the family, he favors establishing five income tax brackets, ranging from 10 percent to 50 percent. This change would balance the family tax cuts created by increased exemptions and child allowances or tax credits. Greater progressivity (with higher upper-income tax rates) encourages people (fathers increasingly, as couples share employment) to care for their own children rather than to work more and pay others to provide more disinterested child care.

Recouple reproduction with responsibility. Katha Pollitt of the *Nation* reports that "Newt Gingrich's Personal Responsibility Act is aimed against unmarried moms, but these women are actually *assuming* a responsibility that their babies' fathers have shirked." Recall that most teenage mothers are impregnated by men over 20. There is therefore growing support for mandatory identification of fathers as a condition for receipt of government benefits.

A good example of a better policy is the Child Support Assurance System, articulated by Columbia University social policy expert Irwin Garfinkel. This would create disincentives for hit-and-run fathering and increase support for single parents, only 40 percent of whom have received child support payments from the absent parent (usually a father). Once paternity is established, in disputed cases by DNA testing, the absent father's (or mother's) income would automatically be taxed at a rate such as 17 percent annually for one child, and 21 percent for two children. This money would be transferred to the Social Security Administration and awarded, without means testing, to the custodial parent at $2,000 a year for one dependent child, $3,000 a year for two children, and so forth.

The plan would make it harder for men to evade responsibility for their sexual behavior. It would tie men's payments directly to their income. It would transfer child support from the welfare system (which discourages work and marriage) into a self-funding Social Security program. And it would reduce bureaucracy, thanks to simplified mechanisms for collecting the money and distributing it without means testing. In this system the losers would be the men who now evade responsibility for supporting their children. The winners would be the single moms and children presently receiving no support from deadbeat dads—and all of us who would benefit from a family-supportive policy that penalizes nonmarital fatherhood.

Family-Supportive Corporate Policies

In our new utopian world, family-impact analyses will also inform socially responsible corporate policies. Business leaders will heed the Council on Civil Society's call to "recognize the moral dimensions of the decisions they make [by acting] as if their own children were the ones most directly affected by these decisions." As humane capitalists, they will recognize that the purpose of their business is not only to create products and maximize profits but to provide quality of life for their workers (their "members," as the 10,000-employee Haworth, Inc., in my town respectfully calls its employees). Supported by government incentives (without which the competitive market economy necessarily limits corporate generosity), businesses will value their workers' families and will invest in the *social* capital—the family and community networks—that nurtures the civility and trust required for a productive market economy. If companies seek honesty, industry, and competence in their workers, they had best not kill the goose that lays those golden eggs. Concern for families and communities comes most naturally from locally owned companies, whose owners and workers rub shoulders at the grocery store, in church, and at soccer games. "Why do I do what I do?" muses Haworth's founder G. W. Haworth (who 87 years ago was born in a sod house on a Nebraska homestead). "I look out my office window and see all those cars in the parking lot. All those people are depending on me to provide for their car payments, their mortgages, their livelihood."

A strengthened corporate focus on the family would do the following.

Minimize the uprooting and relocation of families with children. Companies will recognize that stable communities enable the family supports that flow from kin networks and from the social bonds formed in stable neighborhoods, churches, and schools. Thus rather than migrating in search of today's cheapest labor, companies will remain loyal to the employees and communities that have supported them.

Provide greater opportunities for parental leave. There is evidence that long hours of low-quality day care that begins in the first year of life and continues through the preschool years produces children who tend to be more insecure, disagreeable, and aggressive. This research leaves Pennsylvania State University developmental psychologist Jay Belsky "arguing for support for quality infant care for those who absolutely must have it, for policies of paid parental leave, and for occupational opportunities that turn once full-time jobs into part-time jobs during the infancy years [and] revert to their full-time status with . . . health benefits preserved."

Some European countries offer new mothers or fathers up to a year of paid leave. The United States now mandates 12 weeks of possible unpaid parental leave to workers in companies with 50 or more employees. This could be expanded to include some pay and health coverage, and gradual reentry. Summarizing research results, including from her own study following nearly 600 pregnant women in Wisconsin, research psychologist Janet Hyde believes that 12 weeks should be the minimum leave. After three months, 4 in 5 babies are sleeping through the night, the mother's energy has returned to normal, and the risk of depression is lower than among women who return to work after shorter leaves. To support women in taking such leaves (many now return sooner out of financial need), she advocates following the Canadian example of a fund, like Social Security, to which employers and employees would pay a small contribution in support of new mothers and their infants.

Relax the tension between work and family by offering flextime, compressed time, and part-time work schedules. Create new incentives for a 30-hour work week. Flextime work allows a parent to come early or late (and leave late or early) if a child is sick or the other parent is unavailable. In my community, the Donnelly Corporation, the world's largest manufacturer of auto mirrors, allows parents to stay with a sick child or attend a daytime school activity and make up the time later. Along with 19 other local corporations, Donnelly also funds a children's resource network that provides referrals to child-care providers and consultation and emergency backup services.

Compressed time schedules allow working more hours in fewer days, as might suit family needs. Job sharing and part-time arrangements, another Donnelly practice, would become more attractive if the United States, like most other industrialized countries, would mandate proportionate fringe benefits to part-time workers. As it is, low-income people (often women and minorities) often must work temporary jobs or two part-time jobs, neither with benefits, so that employers can evade responsibility for their benefits, pensions, and vacations. To save on the fringe-benefit costs of additional workers, other corporations may force employees to work overtime. As with mandating airplane and food production safety, proportional fringe benefits for part-time workers must be an enacted social policy. It cannot be left to companies whose profits in a competitive economy depend on cutting costs.

Redistributing work would simultaneously reduce overwork and underemployment. Better to downsize the work week than the work-force, says Jeremy Rifkin; better to increase leisure and family time than unemployment. Why not, for example, have two parents combine for 60 hours a week of employment (with, say, either two 30-hour jobs or one full-time and one half-time job). A recent survey of randomly selected workers nationwide also revealed a corporate benefit to family-responsive policies: regardless of whether they personally expected to gain, workers at companies with such policies felt a higher level of commitment to their worker-supportive company and were less inclined to leave.

Spreading the available work among more people working fewer hours—recreating a culture in which people work to live rather than live to work—would have multiple benefits: less jobless poverty and associated social pathology, less income gap between haves and have-nots, more relaxation, less stress, and more time for parenting. Although those who would be working fewer overtime hours may need to simplify their lives, most will do so with no long-term cost to their well-being. To encourage a more equal distribution of work, some European countries, such as France, are offering employers reduced payroll taxes as a incentive to reduce the work week. Mandating proportional fringe benefits to all would also encourage a more even distribution of work (by eliminating the incentive employers now receive to work employees overtime with little increase in fringe expenses).

There is corporate precedent for a shorter work week. During the depression the Kellogg Company supported the national union movement's recommendation of shorter weeks as a step toward fuller employment and fuller lives. Rather than employ people for three eight-hour shifts, they moved to four six-hour shifts and hired 300 additional workers. In that era, W. K. Kellogg reasoned, his families and community would benefit more from increased employment and added time than from added money. By 1984, with W. K. Kellogg long gone, the last of the six-hour shifts were abolished, with accompanying job losses and corporate fringe-benefits savings. With increasing numbers of couples wanting to share work and child care with two less-than-full-time jobs, perhaps the time has come to reinvent the Kellogg plan.

Support the familial and religious roots of virtue by minimizing Sunday work requirements. University of Iowa Writers' Workshop instructor Marilynne Robinson notes that the least prosperous among us are more often compelled to work on Sunday, often by serving in the stores, restaurants, and entertainment venues visited by those more privileged who are enjoying their weekend leisure. The net effect is to erode communal participation in family and religious activities that help nurture morality, altruism, and civility. We might better practice the tolerance for diversity that we preach, says Robinson, by respecting employees' family and religious priorities.

Allow increased home work. Where feasible, a flexible work policy would give family-oriented workers more say not only in when and how many hours they work, but where. The team of people who produce my introductory psychology textbooks are a case in point. Supported by fax machines, e-mail, telephone, and overnight express, my editor, who formerly worked with the New York publisher, now works 30 hours a week from a home office in Anchorage—with no lost time in daily travel, lessened expenses for clothing, meals, and transportation, and the publisher's saving of New York City office expenses. At home, she is free to be at work at 6 A.M., while her preschooler sleeps, and to adjust her daytime work hours around her child sitter. Much the same has been true for the book's photo editor, supporting freelance editors, and copy editor, all of whom also gain increased time available to their children. The resulting products emerge from the coordinated efforts of a team of home-based and office-based workers in a half dozen cities. Government could support this home work movement by eliminating zoning restrictions on in-home labor and easing restrictions on deductions for home office expenses.

Equitably compensate workers and executives. The socially responsible marketplace will also seek to balance the need for lucrative incentives to attract and reward outstanding executives with the need to preserve fairness and equity among employees. In my community, Herman Miller, Inc., one of the world's three largest office furniture manufacturers and regularly one of America's most admired companies in *Fortune*'s annual survey of executives, has been known for such policies. Workers have shared in company profits and over time become invested in its success as stockholders. The CEO's salary and incentive bonus compensation was limited until recently to "20 times the average annual compensation earned by the Company's regular full-time employees." (In the current competitive climate of skyrocketing executive salaries and stock options, with CEOs playing the corporate free agent market, the company has abandoned that policy in favor of more strongly rewarding the chief for achieving goals. Firms that fail to generously reward standout executives risk losing them to companies that will. Japan and Germany, where chief executives earn much lower salaries and face higher tax rates, have nevertheless provided much of America's stiffest competition.)

In response to the social recession, support for such government and corporate policies is growing. A national survey for the Task Force on Parent Empowerment revealed broad endorsement of many of these initiatives: 65 percent favor taxing married couples less than two single people with the same income (this goes beyond simply eliminating the marriage penalty); 76 percent think companies should be required to offer 12 weeks of paid leave for mothers or fathers after childbirth or adoption; 79 percent want workers to be allowed to take time off instead of extra pay for overtime; 82 percent are in favor of eliminating sales taxes on diapers, school materials, and car seats; and 82 percent say the tax exemption for dependents should be tripled, to $7,500.

With technology-aided productivity increases, corporate restructuring, and the shift to a global economy, the working world is undergoing a new revolution that will likely entail social consequences on a par with those of the Industrial Revolution. Now is therefore the time to ask: What sort of communities do we want for tomorrow? What level of joblessness and associated poverty and crime are we willing to tolerate? What priority do we wish to give children and family life in the 21st century? And, in view of our answers, what tax and incentive policies will move us toward the social world we want rather than a world we dread?

Poverty of the Spirit

Economic growth has given the average American a standard of living that is the world's envy, and a social recession that is no one's envy. Despite economic growth, our morale and social ecology have waned. In part, this social recession stems from the growing inequality, from the erosion of the "family wage" once earned by laboring young adult males, and by anti-family government and corporate policies. An awakening public now beckons politicians and executives to reinvent our tax priorities and humanize the workplace.

Yet the poverty that plagues us is not only an absolute material poverty but also a relative poverty that breeds spiritual starvation. To languish rudderless without prospects for meaningful work, surrounded by others' affluence, is a recipe for hopelessness, purposelessness, and futility. For such reasons, Martin Luther King, Jr., reminded us that "a true revolution of values" will be troubled by "the glaring contrast of poverty and wealth."

We humans have thrived under conditions of equal or greater absolute poverty. Depression-era families may have lacked the television, refrigerator, hot water, flush toilets, and food stamps of today's poor, but their families were largely intact and their neighborhoods safe. African-Americans faced worse racism, poverty, and slavery-spawned disadvantage 50 to 100 years ago, yet their husband-wife families were overwhelmingly intact. (From 1890 to 1960, 4 in 5 African-American families with children were headed by a married couple.) Calcutta's families are more wretchedly poor than America's, yet more intact. Immigrant families have typically had fewer material resources but maintained close-knit families. The problem is not racial genetics (which have not significantly changed) or absolute poverty (which is not greater today than 60 years ago) but a spirit strangled by broken attachments and surrendered hopes.

When poor but close-knit Mexican families immigrate to individualistic America, their health and well-being are generally resilient. But then as the years go by and they begin to assimilate, their risks for depression and ill health (compared with compatriots still in Mexico and more recent immigrants) begin to rise. Psychiatric researcher Javier Escobar attributes the Mexican immigrant advantage partly "to a 'protective' or 'buffering' effect of traditional culture. Traditionally, Hispanic families have been described as close-knit, extended family networks that offer a great deal of support. Also, compared with [Anglo-Americans] Mexican Americans have a higher proportion of 2-parent families and lower rates of divorce and separation."

Marian Wright Edelman recalls from a more poverty-ridden time her Baptist preacher father.

> He was not elegant, but he was educated; not rich, but richly read. He didn't care about things, he cared about thinking and thoughtfulness. He didn't care about status, but about service. He and my mother didn't leave their children any funds, but a more lasting legacy of faith. He didn't own guns because he knew goodness was more powerful, was never greedy, and was always grateful for God's amazing grace. He never hid the ugly realities of our segregated and unjust world from us, but he, my mother, and other community elders never left us children to confront that world alone. They tried to right the wrongs and teach us that the ways of the world were not the ways of God or of a purposeful life. They didn't promise us we would win all the battles we would face but instead we had to try to fight them. So we never lost hope and learned to struggle and take responsibility for ourselves and our communities because adults loved us enough to struggle with us.

The novelist Thomas Wolfe was right: You can't go home again. We cannot drive backward to that kinder, gentler (though also more impoverished and prejudiced) world of Edelman's childhood. We can only move forward. If we assume all is hopeless, we will be right. But if we can agree that prosperity must be seasoned with purpose, capital with compassion, and enterprise with equity, then maybe the best is yet to come. It has happened before. After the chaos, incivility, and greed of the Middle Ages came the Renaissance.

CHAPTER 7

Individualism and Community

This may well be mankind's last chance to choose between chaos and community.

—MARTIN LUTHER KING, JR., *Where Do We Go from Here,* 1967

Individualism is as American as baseball, hot dogs, and the fourth of July. We are a nation created by individualists. Those who willfully came here forsook their homelands and kin seeking something better for themselves. They came to found a new political order rooted in personal freedom. They came to realize the promise of individual rights to life, liberty, and the pursuit of happiness.

Once here, their individualism, and ours, has been expressed in stories of such rugged individualists as Paul Bunyan, Daniel Boone, Horatio Alger, the Lone Ranger, Luke Skywalker.

In songs: Sammy Davis, Jr., singing, "I gotta be me," Frank Sinatra crooning, "I did it my way," or Crosby, Stills, and Nash intoning, "Rules and regulations, who needs 'em. Throw 'em out the door."

In sayings: "Question authority." "Do your own thing." "If it feels good, do it." "Be true to yourself." "I owe it to myself."

In books, from *The Adventures of Huckleberry Finn* to *Looking Out for Number One,* and magazines, from *People* to *Self.*

In political rhetoric, as in Ronald Reagan declaring, "This is the age of the individual."

In popular psychology's telling us that liberating ourselves from repressive norms and mindless conformity would make for happier, more fulfilled people.

In New Age religion's seeking to connect individuals to their own inner selves rather than a transcendent God.

All post-Renaissance Western cultures to some extent express the triumph of individualism as what Elizabeth Fox-Genovese calls "*the* theory of human nature and rights." But contemporary America is the most individualistic of cultures. Asked what is special about America, one youth responding to a national survey said, "Individualism, and the fact that it is a democracy and you can do whatever you please." A comparison of 116,000 IBM employees worldwide found that Americans, followed by Australians, were indeed the most individualistic. We can glimpse this individualism in our comparatively low tax rates. Taxes advance the common good through schools, roads, parks, and health, welfare, and defense programs that serve and protect all—but at a price to individuals. And in the contest among American values, individual rights trump social responsibilities.

The French writer and statesman Alexis de Tocqueville was struck by Americans' rugged independence when he traveled the country in 1831 by steamer, stagecoach, and horseback to analyze the young democracy. To capture this independent spirit he coined the term *individualism*, which he described as "a calm and considered feeling that disposes each citizen to isolate himself from the mass of his fellows and withdraw into the circle of family and friends; with this little society formed to his taste, he gladly leaves the greater society to look after itself. . . . Such folk owe no man anything and hardly expect anything from anybody. They form the habit of thinking of themselves in isolation and imagine that their whole destiny is in their hands." An individualistic theme echoes through many of today's "success seminars" and pop psychology books: At any time we can reinvent ourselves psychologically or economically, by exercising the mind's positive power. Simply believe in your possibilities. Despite some Willy Loman–type tragedies (when believing in oneself just isn't enough), this peculiarly American idea does find support in recent studies of optimism, achievement motivation, internal "locus of control," and self-efficacy.

Individualism supports democracy by stimulating initiative, creativity, and equal rights for all individuals, Tocqueville noted. But taken to an extreme it becomes egoism, which leads a person "to think of all things in terms of himself and to prefer himself to all." Tocqueville feared that a society of such radical individualists would be vulnerable to despotism. Radical individualism corrodes the public spirit, he warned. He foresaw people, "alike and equal, constantly circling around in pursuit of the petty and banal pleasures with which they glut their souls. Each one of them, withdrawn into himself, is almost unaware of the fate of the rest." Eventually, tasks once carried out by families, churches, and communal organizations would be taken over by government, which would care for people's needs and tell people how to live.

A century and a half later, University of California sociologist Robert Bellah and his colleagues also traversed the country, interviewing Americans about their values and aspirations. Although their widely read *Habits of the Heart* and *The Good Society* have been described by fellow sociologist Andrew Greeley as "innocent of data" (at least the statistical data that persuades most of us social scientists), Bellah and company echo Tocqueville's impressions of a people who lack those habits of the heart conducive to living in community. Time and again, Bellah observed that people defined "personality, achievement, and the purpose of human life in ways that leave the individual suspended in glorious, but terrifying, isolation." Shunning conformity, commitment, and obligation, modern individualists prefer to define their own standards and do as they please.

Individualism Versus Collectivism

Some animals, like tigers, are solitary. Others, like wolves, are communal. We humans, though basically gregarious, are more variable. Some of us give priority to personal control and achievement. Others place greater value on the bonds of social intimacy and solidarity—like athletes who care more about the outcome for their team than their own performance.

Cultures, too, vary in such ways. Western cultures nurture individualism. Western literature, from the *Iliad* and *Odyssey* to *The Adventures of Sherlock Holmes,* has celebrated self-reliant individuals who act heroically or seek their own fulfillment rather than depending on others and following their expectations. Howard Roark, hero of Ayn Rand's *The Fountainhead,* succeeds in breaking free of his society's mediocrity, thanks to his individual talents and motivation. Roark, the epitome of the autonomous individual, declares, "I do not recognize anyone's right to one minute of my life. . . . I am a man who does not exist for others."

Other cultures—especially those native to Asia, Africa, and Central and South America—place a greater value on what cross-cultural psychologists call *collectivism*. Collectivist cultures give priority to the goals and welfare of their groups—their family, their clan, their work group. Their books and movies often celebrate those who resist temptations to self-indulgence and remember their social identity and social duty. When Kobe, Japan, was hit by a devastating earthquake in 1995, Western reporters were struck by the absence of looting and the orderly way people lined up for relief supplies—"as if they were waiting for a bus."

Although cultures can change—Japan, for example, is becoming more individualistic—their differences remain striking. Riding along within one's culture is like riding a bike with the wind: As it carries us along, we hardly notice it's there. When we try riding against it— violating its expectations—we feel its force. (Next time you ride a bus, try singing out loud.) We can also learn the winds of our own culture when encountering another. Seeing how "they" think and act makes us conscious of how "we" think and act. Yes, we explained to our children while living in Scotland, Europeans eat meat with the fork facing down in the left hand. But we Americans consider it good manners to cut the meat and then transfer the fork to the right hand: "I admit it's inefficient. But it's the way *we* do it."

Studies by cross-cultural psychologists help illuminate the varying cultural winds. Harry Triandis at the University of Illinois, Richard Brislin at the University of Hawaii, C. Harry Hui at the University of Hong Kong, and other researchers worldwide show us how a culture's individualism or collectivism affects its people's self-concepts, social relations, and child rearing. To better understand America's individualism, let's sample from their smorgasbord of findings.

Culture and the Self

If someone were to rip away your social connections, leaving you a solitary refugee in a foreign land, how much of your identity would remain intact?

Separated from family, friends, and community, individualists would retain their personal identity—their sense of "me," their traits, their convictions, their values. In individualistic cultures, people therefore feel free to leave jobs, communities, and churches in search of better jobs, communities, and churches. As adolescents, they struggle to separate from parents and define their personal sense of self. "Accept yourself," they hear from their culture's individualistic advice givers. Don't be "codependent" ("a psychological disorder" in which one becomes too "nurturing" and supports, loves, and stays tied to a troubled partner; in Asia, such would be a description of psychological *health*). Instead, give priority to self-expression and self-fulfillment. "The only question which matters," declared influential psychologist Carl Rogers, "is, 'Am I living in a way which is deeply satisfying to me, and which truly expresses me?'"

That libertarian vision of the good life is shared by many pop celebrities. "The heart wants what the heart wants," said Woody Allen in justifying his affair with Mia Farrow's adopted daughter. "Full freedom" and "lifestyle experimentation" are the guiding rules for Dennis Rodman, who years ago decided "to let the person inside me be free to do what he wanted to do, no matter what anybody else said or thought." His idea of the good life may not have been what Rogers had in mind, but it epitomizes individualism taken to its limits: "to live my life like a tiger in the jungle—eating whatever I want, having sex whenever I want, and running around butt naked, wild and free."

The self-esteem movement. Under the influence of Rogers and other individualistic psychologists, popular psychology treasures self-esteem as the secret to successful, happy living. If children are underachieving, unruly, unpopular, or overbearing, we assume a self-esteem deficit. The solution is to bolster their self-esteem, in part by positive affirmations that assure them they are wonderful just as they are. By the mid-1990s, thirty states had enacted more than 170 statutes promoting self-esteem. Wisconsin in 1993 directed schools to instruct students in "stress-reduction, self-improvement and self-esteem," and the same year Florida mandated curriculum revision "as appropriate, to include building self-esteem." Adults, too, can boost their self-esteem by chanting mantras like "I'm terrific" or "Every day, in every way, I'm getting better and better."

Low self-esteem does modestly correlate with drug abuse, delinquency, and underachievement. Nevertheless, psychologists William

Damon, Robyn Dawes, Mark Leary, Roy Baumeister, and Martin Seligman wonder about cause and effect. They doubt that self-esteem is
really "the armor that protects kids" from such problems. Perhaps it's
the other way around: perhaps problems and failures cause low self-
esteem. Perhaps self-esteem reflects the reality of how things are going
for us. Perhaps the best boost to self-esteem comes from hard-won
achievements.

Contrary to popular opinion, low self-esteem hardly plagues our
culture as a whole. Most Americans score well above mid-scale on tests
of self-esteem. Moreover, one of psychology's most provocative yet reliable phenomena is "self-serving bias," a scientific version of what for
centuries has been called hubris, or pride. In experiments, people accept more responsibility for good deeds than for bad, and for successes
than for failures (a phenomenon that accounts for much marital discord). In surveys, most people rate themselves as better than average on
any subjective, socially desirable dimension (from "getting along with
others" to "job performance" to "driving ability"). Our world, it seems,
is Lake Wobegon writ large—a place where "all the women are strong,
all the men are good-looking, and all the children are above average."

Self-esteem also has its dark side. Teenage males who engage in
sexual activity at an "inappropriately young age" tend to have higher
than average self-esteem. So do teen gang leaders, extreme ethnocen-
trists, and terrorists, notes Dawes, a psychologist at Carnegie Mellon
University.

Finding their favorable self-esteem threatened, people often react
by putting others down, sometimes with violence. A youth who develops a big ego, which then gets threatened or deflated by social rejection, is potentially dangerous. In one experiment, social psychologists
Brad Bushman and Roy Baumeister had 540 undergraduate volunteers
write a paragraph, in response to which another supposed student gave
them either praise ("great essay!") or stinging criticism ("one of the
worst essays I have read!"). Then each essay writer played a reaction-
time game against the other student. When the opponent lost, the
writer could assault him or her with noise of any intensity and for any
duration. After criticism, the most narcissistic people were "exception-
ally aggressive," delivering three times the auditory torture of those
with normal self-esteem. Facing failure, people high in self-esteem may
also disparage others. By perceiving other people as failing, too, they
can maintain their own sense of superiority.

"The enthusiastic claims of the self-esteem movement mostly range from fantasy to hogwash," says Baumeister, who suspects he has "probably published more studies on self-esteem than anybody else." "The effects of self-esteem are small, limited, and not all good." Those with high self-esteem, he reports, are more likely to be obnoxious, to interrupt, and to talk at people rather than with them (in contrast to the more shy, modest, self-effacing folks with low self-esteem). "My conclusion is that self-control is worth 10 times as much as self-esteem."

Do the big egos of people who sometimes do bad things conceal inner insecurity and low self-esteem? Do assertive, narcissistic people actually have a weak ego hidden by a self-inflating veneer? Many researchers have tried to find low self-esteem beneath such an outer crust, but studies of bullies, gang members, and obnoxious narcissists have turned up no sign of it. Moreover, notes Baumeister, because acknowledged low self-esteem is associated with nonviolence, we would have to say that low-self esteem predisposes violence only if hidden—in which case the cause of violence is what is *hiding* the secret insecurity, which is the veneer of *high* self-esteem. "Hidden lack of self-esteem is the New Age psychologist's ether," concludes Dawes. "The ether was a substance that was supposed to fill all space as a vehicle for the travel of light waves. It proved undetectable, and the concept was discarded when Einstein introduced the special theory of relativity. A belief in undetected low self-esteem as a cause of undesirable behavior is even less plausible; all the available evidence directly contradicts it."

It is true that people expressing low self-esteem are somewhat more vulnerable to assorted clinical problems including depression, anxiety, loneliness, eating disorders, and substance abuse. But then, says Mark Leary, people high in self-esteem are more likely to take excessive risks. Deluded by their illusory optimism, they sometimes persist in unproductive efforts. They are more often bullies.

Leary believes we all have a deep need to belong, and that self-esteem is a subjective gauge of our social functioning. Better therefore to help people succeed in their relationships (in which case self-esteem will follow) than to try to boost their self-esteem by telling them how wonderful they are. People who behave destructively may feel ignored or rejected and therefore have low self-esteem, he reasons. "To try to convince these individuals that they are, in fact, valuable, worthy, wonderful people may dissuade them from taking action to deal with the real problems as well as lead to confusion and anger. (If I'm so wonderful, why does everybody avoid me?) Such an approach tries to override the . . . natural signals that the person's social acceptance is in jeopardy, somewhat akin to trying to convince a driver to ignore the fact that the fuel gauge of the car is on 'empty.' "

The individualism of psychotherapists. America's individualism also appears in psychotherapists' assuming that problems reside inside the client's own skin, and that therapy should aim to liberate people from social straitjackets, put them "in touch with themselves," and increase their self-acceptance and self-fulfillment. Using such words as "duty," "responsibility," "should," and "must" is scorned as "musturbation." Humanistic therapist Rollo May had second thoughts about this enterprise near the end of his life, noting that "almost everyone undergoing therapy is concerned with individual gain, and the psychotherapist is hired to assist this endeavor." Therapist Fritz Perls epitomized this individualism with his Gestalt therapy "prayer":

> I do my thing, and you do your thing.
> I am not in this world to live up to your expectations,
> And you are not in this world to live up to mine.
> You are you and I am I,
> And if by chance we find each other, it's beautiful.
> If not, it can't be helped.

An alternative view of self. In collectivist cultures, where communal solidarity is prized, such words would cause people to wince. For collectivists, social networks provide one's bearings and help define who one is. To be set adrift in a foreign land would entail a greater loss to one's identity. Cross-cultural comparisons illustrate:

- Compared with American students, students in Japan and China are less likely to complete the sentence "I am . . ." with personal traits ("I am sincere," "I am confident") and more likely to declare their social identities ("I am a Keio University student," "I am the third son in my family").
- Compared with people in the West, those in the East are less likely to write autobiographies and more likely to write family histories.
- Compared with American magazine ads, Korean ads are less likely to appeal to individual interests ("She's got a style all her own") and more likely to appeal to collective interests ("We have a way of bringing people closer together").

- Compared with American schoolchildren, who express their individuality through clothing, schoolchildren in less individualistic nations display their communal solidarity by wearing school uniforms (a practice that President Clinton claims would contribute to more civility and decreased violence in America's schools).
- Advised "To thine own self be true," collectivists might respond: "Which self? My 'self-with-friend'? 'Self-at-work'? 'Self-with-parents'?" For collectivists, what's important is less "me" than "we."

Culture and Social Relations

Collectivists have fewer but more lasting relationships. Compared with North American students, university students in Hong Kong talk during a day with fewer people for longer periods. Outside this circle of familiar attachments, collectivists are more likely to act shy. In Japan more than in the United States, feeling good comes with feeling socially engaged (for example, feeling friendly rather than feeling proud).

In collectivist cultures, attachments run deep. Divorce is unusual. Employer-employee relations are marked by mutual loyalty. Valuing social solidarity, people maintain harmony by showing respect and allowing others to save face. They avoid confrontation, blunt honesty, and boasting. They stay away from touchy topics, defer to others, and display a self-effacing humility. Self-aggrandizing talk may seem like childish immaturity. Unlike America, where "the squeaky wheel gets the grease," in Japan "the nail that stands out gets pounded down."

Collectivists also do favors for one another and, remembering who has done favors for them, make reciprocation an art. In their cultures, no one is an island. The self is not independent but *interdependent*.

Culture and Child Rearing

Right from the start, Japanese and Chinese parents foster interdependence. Mother and newborn sleep, bathe, and move about together. The traditional Japanese mother carriers her child on her back for much of the first two years, a practice that may help explain why Japanese infants experience greater separation stress than do American infants.

In individualistic cultures, parents want their children to become independent and have "good judgment." They express less concern for training conformity and submissiveness (what collectivists might call "communal sensitivity and cooperation"). Schools teach children to clarify their own values so they can make good decisions for themselves. In Western restaurants, parents and children individually decide their own orders. In Western homes, adolescents open their own mail, refuse parental guidance in choosing boyfriends and girlfriends, and often seek the privacy of their own rooms. As adults they chart their own goals and separate from their parents, who already live apart from the grandparents. If a child fails, the embarrassed parents will nevertheless be able to discuss the child's problems openly.

"She had a freedom you can't get by holding her back," Jessica Dubroff's mother explained of her 7-year-old daughter's ill-fated attempt to become the youngest person to fly cross-country in 1996. "I did everything so this child could have freedom of choice, and that's what America stands for."

All this seems strange to Asian collectivists, whose parents more actively guide or decide their children's choices and whose schools are less bashful about teaching accepted cultural values. So close is the mutual identification of parent and child that the crushed parents of an errant child seldom discuss their feelings of shame.

Gender and Individualism

During the 1970s, feminism, as "the daughter of individualism," idealized androgyny—the incorporation within each individual of both masculine and feminine traits. For the androgynous person, human completeness is not a union of complementary differences but a solo act. Each man and each woman becomes a one-person band—independently capable of both assertiveness and nurturance, competitiveness and empathy, strength and sensitivity.

As gender scholarship evolved during the late 1980s and 1990s, other voices called for balance. Divorce, Barbara Dafoe Whitehead says, liberates many women from oppressive relationships, yet it also worsens their economic and domestic inequality (when it liberates men from partnership in providing, nurturing, and domestic tasks). Fox-Genovese worries that individualism, fueled by capitalism and feminism, "threatens to swing the balance between the individual and society—the balance between personal freedom and social order—wholly to the side of the individual." Lest feminism condemn "itself to the dead ends toward which individualism is now plunging," she believes it must move "individualism back to its social moorings by insisting that the rights of individuals derive from society."

Their conclusions draw strength from a newer line of studies that explore and celebrate women's social connections. After listening to women's reasoning and concerns, psychologists Nancy Chodorow, Jean Baker Miller, and Carol Gilligan have each concluded that women more than men give priority to relationships. The difference surfaces in childhood. Boys strive for independence; they define their identities in separation from their primary caregivers, usually their mothers. Girls more often welcome interdependence; they define their identities through their social connections. Boys' play often involves group activity. Girls' play occurs in smaller groups, with less aggression, more sharing, more imitation of relationships and more intimate discussion. As teens, girls spend more time with friends and less time alone than do boys.

Later experiences reinforce men's independent selves and women's more interdependent selves. Men's identities are more self-contained, women's more socially connected. Although men and women express similar self-esteem, men's is more rooted in successful independence, women's in achieving positive relationships. In conversation, men more often focus on tasks, women on relationships. In groups, men talk more to give information; women talk more to share lives, give help, or show support. Men emphasize freedom and self-reliance, women express more compassion. Among first-year college students, 5 in 10 males and 7 in 10 females say it is very important to "help others who are in difficulty." Among more than 4,000 middle-aged twins surveyed, 78 percent of the women rated their "nurturance" above men's average self-rating.

Women not only talk more about caring, they do it. They display more of what Gilligan calls "an ethic of care." Women provide most of the care to the very young and the very old. Daughters more than sons take responsibility for aging parents. In a 1989 Gallup poll, women were twice as likely as men to report talking daily with their parents. Women buy most birthday gifts and greeting cards. Women are more likely to agree that "I spend a lot of time visiting friends." Asked to provide photos that portray who they are, women include more pictures of parents and of themselves with others.

Women's caregiving extends outside the home. In most helping professions, such as social work, teaching, nursing, and child care, women outnumber men. Women are also more charitable. Among individuals leaving estates worth more than $5 million, 48 percent of women and 35 percent of men make a charitable bequest. Women's colleges have unusually supportive alumni. And in survey after survey, women also are more likely than men to support the Democratic Party's social agenda, including paying taxes to support it. In late 1995, for example, 54 percent of women but only 37 percent of men agreed that the main issue facing the nation was "social problems such as education and poverty."

When surveyed, women also are far more likely than men to describe themselves as having empathy, as being able to identify with others and feel what they feel—to rejoice with those who rejoice and weep with those who weep. Physiological measures of empathy, such as one's heart rate while seeing another's distress, reveal a much smaller gender gap than reported in surveys. Nevertheless, females are more likely to *express* empathy—to cry and to report distress when observing someone's distress.

The empathy gap may be rooted in women's skill at reading others' emotional cues. From her analysis of 125 studies of men's and women's sensitivity to nonverbal cues, psychologist Judith Hall discerned that women are generally superior at emotional decoding. Shown a two-second silent film clip of the face of an upset woman, women more accurately guess whether she is criticizing someone or discussing her divorce. Women's nonverbal sensitivity, perhaps a by-product of their less powerful roles, helps explain their greater emotional responsiveness in both depressing and joyful situations. It also helps explain why both men and women report their friendships with women to be more intimate, enjoyable, and nurturing. When they want understanding and someone to share worries and hurts with, both men and women usually turn to women.

Of course the sexes overlap. Individual men vary from fiercely competitive to gently nurturant, and so do individual women. And scientists debate what mix of nature and nurture explains the gender difference. Nevertheless, the differences provoke commentary. Some argue that affirming women's social connections applauds what should be changed. Given the lower pay associated with traditionally female caregiving occupations, such as child care, shouldn't Western women get in step with their culture's individualism? Might not women better advance their own interests by being more self-reliant? Others argue

that women's relational approach to life holds the promise of transforming power-oriented, individualistic societies into more caring communities. With the growing problems of homelessness, child neglect, loneliness, and depression, too much caring seems not to be a massive social
problem.

Women's valuing of human connections parallels the priorities of
collectivist cultures. Indeed, psychologists Kazuo Kato and Hazel Markus report, Americans and males are more likely to agree that "I always
know what I want" and "I usually make my decisions by myself," while
Japanese and females more often feel a "strong obligation" to return
favors and desire to "make a favorable impression on others." Together,
the feminist and cross-cultural scholars are forging what Markus (at
Stanford) and Shinobu Kitayama (at Kyoto University) call a new understanding of dependence: "Being dependent does not invariably mean
being helpless, powerless, or without control. It often means being
*inter*dependent." It means affecting others and being responsive to
them, giving and receiving support, confiding in them. It means seeing
oneself not as an island but as mutually attached to important others. It
means not freedom for the self but freedom from the self.

The Roots of Individualism

So, Americans—American men, especially—seem the most individualistic of people. One immediately wonders why. "Culture" helps
us describe and understand differences among different peoples, but
what explains culture?

Triandis asserts that individualistic cultures tend, first, to be more
complex. People belong to many groups, but aside from their nuclear
family don't feel extremely bound to any of them. Moreover, they
choose these groups (clubs, churches, careers, and so forth) from a buffet of possibilities, and stay or leave as meets their needs. In simpler
collectivist societies, choices are fewer. Groups—one's kin, caste, tribe,
village, nation—are more often assigned. Complexity arises from diversity. Individualistic cultures typically expose people to varying norms,
enabling them to decide for themselves which to follow. America, with
all but its native people having migrated from assorted cultures worldwide, could hardly differ more from Japan, where 99 percent of the
people are Japanese who share a common cultural history.

Social and geographical mobility also enhance individualism. Group loyalties weaken when one can easily move into new groups. What is more, rugged individualists—those most willing to leave their people and place—are the most likely pioneers. Colonization was led not by Asians, who were reluctant to cut social and family ties, but by the more individualistic Europeans (indeed, by the most individualistic of them). In America, we are their cultural heirs.

Urban settings, which offer the widest cultural buffet, nurture more individualism than rural settings. In rural settings, where one will again see people for whom one does favors, "reciprocal altruism" runs stronger. The giver can expect later to be the getter. This helps explain what happened when LeVine and his colleagues approached several thousand people in 36 cities. To assess people's helpfulness, they would drop a pen or ask for change or simulate a blind person needing help at a corner. Their finding: the smaller and less densely populated the city, the more likely people were to help. Other studies confirm that small schools, towns, churches, work teams, and dorms are all conducive to a community spirit in which people care for one another. Compared with urbanites, small-town and rural folk are more willing to relay a phone message, mail "lost" letters, cooperate with survey interviewers, help a lost child, and do small favors. As human cultures have moved from hunting-gathering to agriculture to industrialization-urbanization, individualism has replaced communalism.

Another ingredient of the individualism recipe is affluence. Affluent people can more easily afford television, which exposes them to differing and more individualistic norms, such as marrying as a romantic choice. When television comes into remote communities, individualism goes up. Television not only provides a model for individualism, it isolates people; it not only brings the world into your living room, it brings *you* out of the world and into your living room. (Actually, with 74 percent of homes now having multiple sets, it often splits families into different rooms.) If you are watching TV, you are not sitting on your porch or engaging in communal recreation. Television may be wonderful technology, but even more than air-conditioning, which also brings people indoors, it is antisocial.

More generally, affluence makes people self-sufficient, better able to live alone or to acquire needed goods and services without community support. Those born since 1950, having grown up with less scarcity, have formed values less focused on mutual survival, and more focused on self-expression. When resources are scarce or many hands are needed to make light the work—raising a barn, building a canal, harvesting and storing the crops—collectivism is more likely to flourish. In Scotland's Outer Hebrides, where sheep roam and intermingle on the hills, it takes a communal effort to round them up for shearing. Experiments on communal tasks confirm the real-life lessons: Unity grows from cooperative efforts to achieve shared goals. Rather than divide up the family chores, advised Mary Pipher, have everyone pitch in at the same time to clean up the kitchen or do the yard work.

Common predicaments also bind people together. If you have ever been snowbound together with others, harassed as part of your initiation into a group, unfairly punished by a teacher or boss, persecuted and ridiculed because of your social, racial, or religious identity, then you may recall feeling close to those with whom you shared the situation. Perhaps previous social barriers dropped as you helped one another dig out of the snow or cope with a shared threat. American patriotism and unity soared during conflicts with Germany and Japan in World War II, the Soviets during the cold war, Iran in 1980, and Iraq in 1991. Soldiers who face combat together often maintain lifelong ties with their comrades. Again, experiments illuminate the real-life experience: Having a common enemy unifies a group. When made keenly conscious of who "they" are, we also become keenly conscious of who "we" are. Few things so unite a people as a common hatred.

Finally, across time and place, individualism rises as economies become more market oriented. "Changes in the nature and organization of work under capitalism in Western industrial societies have produced a long-term shift from communal to market values and an accompanying rise of individualism," explains University of Minnesota sociologist Margaret Mooney Marini. As production shifts from families to factories and as commerce shifts from face-to-face contacts to technology-aided transactions, moral restraints subside. So do religious outlooks and values like trust and sharing that are nurtured by communal life.

According to its critics, Francis Fukuyama tells us, capitalism fuels social disorder. "By placing self-interest ahead of moral obligation, and by being endlessly innovative through the replacement of one technology by another, it destroys the bonds built up over the centuries within human communities and leaves them with nothing but naked self-interest as a source of social cohesion." "Greed is a good thing," Ivan Boesky asserted a few years before going to prison. "Individuals are fine, just keep the system from getting in their way."

This attitude helps us understand a finding that astonishes lower-income people who think that having money beyond their basic needs would enable them to give away a bigger piece of their personal pie. Repeated Gallup polls show this not to be so. People earning more than $100,000 annually give away but 2 to 3 percent of their incomes—which hardly differs from the percentage given away by people with the lowest incomes. As the economic tide has floated real incomes upward, charitable giving as a proportion of income has *not* increased. The percentage of people contributing absolutely nothing has actually grown, to 30 percent. Even Ronald Reagan, who preached voluntary generosity as an alternative to taxation, reported minimal charitable contributions. Recall, too, the relatively low charitable giving rates among economics professors and students.

To be sure, wealth can enable charity. I know this well from my participation in the market economy, which supports my family's living and giving, and from dwelling in a community in which the owners and CEOs of local industries reflect the community's strong religious values, live much like the rest of us, and have given back to the community some of the wealth derived from it. These altruistic capitalists would shudder at the self-indulgent excess of a Malcolm Forbes, who flew 700 guests to Tangiers for his birthday party, entertained them with 600 belly dancers and a 274-man honor guard, and provided 271 servants to feed them the choicest delicacies. If liberals underestimate the motivating power of self-interest, conservatives underestimate sin—the selfishness that curbs the altruism needed to care for the poor and preserve the environment.

Yet even many conservatives are sobered by what the marketplace has wrought. Don Eberly of the National Fatherhood Initiative notes that during "the roaring eighties, with exploding economic growth . . . the cultural indicators—illegitimacy, drugs, crime, and educational decline—either remained stagnant or accelerated southward." Columnist George Will chides Republicans who "see no connection between the cultural phenomena they deplore and the capitalist culture they promise to intensify; no connection between the multiplying evidence of self-indulgence and national decadence . . . and the unsleeping pursuit of ever more immediate, intense and grand material gratifications." The free market gives us low-cost computers, and cyberporn. Sociologist Daniel Bell says that capitalism is a tornado that enriches our lives yet also promotes a consumer culture, squashes small towns with Wal-Marts, and provides media models that undermine Mom, Dad, church, and community. Thus, the late Russell Kirk reminded fellow conservatives that their movement cannot be "merely a defense of industrialism and industrial free market economics." Conservatism is about "the cultivation and conservation of certain values, or it is nothing."

The Benefits and Costs of Individualism

Each way of life offers benefits, for a price. In our competitive, individualist culture, we enjoy great personal freedom. We accept credit for our successes. We take pride in our achievements. We enjoy privacy. We feel free to move about. We choose our lifestyle. We have an experimental spirit. We prize innovation and creativity. We seek and declare truth, relatively unhindered by authorities. These may be why sociologist Ruut Veenhoven finds that people live more happily in countries that guarantee basic human freedoms than in those that don't.

Individualists also affirm the dignity and worth of each person. Believing that each one is a child of God, we find it self-evident that all are created equal and "endowed by their Creator with certain unalienable Rights." We therefore are more accepting of other individuals, more likely to treat everyone with common courtesy, and less judgmental of those who differ. Triandis contrasts courteous America with his native Greece, where many secretaries come from traditional collectivist backgrounds. "When calling a typical office in Greece one gets a rather curt 'What do you want?' I have relatives and friends there, and when I call their office I am always amused by the rudeness of the first contact. But when I say 'I am Harry Triandis, your boss's cousin (or friend)' the switch is dramatic. 'How lovely to hear your voice' is the typical response!"

If extreme individualism begets self-indulgence, extreme collectivism begets intolerance. Unlike Eastern Europeans, our more individualistic country is not torn asunder by interethnic war (though we weren't much bothered by killing 100,000 Iraqis). Although I am proud of my Scottish roots, they hardly matter enough to kindle an argument, much less a fight. Unlike the Serbs who attacked, raped, and killed Bosnian Muslims as if they were hardly human, we find the collectivist idea of "ethnic cleansing" repugnant. (The former Yugoslavia scored high

on collectivism in the worldwide survey.) Because we are individualists, we no longer stone the infidels, take slaves, or stand idly by while
people starve.

Most of us probably wouldn't really rather live in prosperous but
collectivist Singapore, where laws against defamation reduce criticism
of the government to whispers, leaders of opposition parties have been
forced out of their jobs or suffered defamation suits, 1,000 people a
year are caned, the government owns the TV stations and indirectly
controls the press, official publicity regularly chides you to be more in-
dustrious, courteous, and healthy, the sale of chewing gum has been
banned, and small infractions can bring expensive penalties—littering
($625), not flushing a public toilet ($94), eating on the subway ($312).

Then again, maybe you *would* like to live in a land with no slums,
a standard of living that rivals that of the United States, with no unemployment, an environment with little pollution or litter and lots of
lush greenery, a well-planned metropolis with no traffic jams, all households with high-speed Internet connections, and a culture with almost
no drugs, pornography, or crime. Comparing his life in Singapore with
back home in strife-torn India, spice trader Sultan Ahamed speaks for
many Singaporeans: "What shall I say? This is paradise."

As collectivism in Singapore exacts costs, so does individualism in
America. Accompanying our growing individualism is more frequent
loneliness, homicide, thefts, eating disorders, and stress-related disease such as heart attacks. When individualists pursue their own ends
and all goes well, it can be rewarding, psychologist Ed Diener and his
colleagues observe. When things go badly, there is less social support.
Thus, individualistic countries often have a relatively high number of
"very happy" people (perhaps 3 in 10), *and* high suicide and homicide
rates.

Weakening Social Connections

Since the 1950s, supportive social connections and informal networks have weakened. Eye-to-eye interactions are waning, thanks
partly to drive-through food pickups, ATM machines, and e-mail. In
this era of what Robert Wuthnow calls "loose connections," people visit
one another less, belong to fewer groups, and more often live alone.
Participation is waning in scouting, Red Cross, women's clubs, and fraternal lodges. PTA membership dropped from 12 million in 1964 to

7 million in 1993. Jaycees membership is down 44 percent since 1979. We are even more often bowling apart from groups: since 1980, Harvard political scientist Robert Putnam reports, the number of bowlers has risen 10 percent, but participation in bowling leagues has dropped 40 percent. As his influential paper and important new book suggest, "bowling alone" symbolizes an increasingly atomized society.

Has group bowling, as Putnam's critics have wondered, merely shifted to other venues, such as softball? In follow-up analyses, Putnam and University of Wisconsin political scientist Steven Yonish discerned from repeated Roper surveys that the frequency of many types of community participation has declined since 1973. Moreover, the declines accelerated after 1985 and have been greater for communal activities, such as serving on a committee, than for solo activities, such as writing a letter to the paper. The shrinking percentages from 1973 to 1994 include:

Served as officer of a club or organization	–42%
Worked for a political party	–42%
Served on a committee for a local organization	–39%
Attended a public meeting on town or school affairs	–35%
Attended a political rally or speech	–34%
Made a speech	–24%
Wrote a congressman or senator	–23%
Signed a petition	–22%
Belonged to a "better government" group	–19%
Held or ran for political office	–16%
Wrote a letter to the paper	–14%
Wrote an article for a magazine or newspaper	–10%
Participated in at least one of these activities	–25%

Communal socializing also appears to be on the way out. Putnam finds that Americans in 1997 were entertaining friends and acquaintances at home 40 percent less often than in 1975, attending club meetings nearly 60 percent less often, and giving half as many dinner parties. Families are also eating together less often. In 1975, 50 percent of married Americans agreed that "our whole family usually eats dinner together"; in 1997, only 34 percent did. When we add the increasing number of single people living by themselves, "dining alone" may have doubled in the past quarter century. What we are doing more of, to replace this communal activity, is watching TV, renting videos, and Web surfing and working on our home computers.

Some of our diminishing social engagement can be attributed to work displacing other activities. More women are employed, and employed women are less engaged in social and community activities. Yet women's rising employment is only a small contributor to civic disengagement, according to Putnam, because the trends in home entertaining, club-going, and visiting with friends are equally downward among women who are not employed. (We might have hoped that men would have shifted their commitments to more equally shoulder social and community responsibilities, but that has not happened.)

Volunteerism has risen, however, Roper Center director Everett Ladd points out. (He also documents trends in charitable giving and religious participation to buttress his more bullish view of civic America.) Putnam attributes the volunteerism increase to those over 65, who are the most civic minded and whose availability is growing thanks to early retirement and longer lives. Among those born between 1950 and 1965, volunteerism actually has ebbed. People born after 1950 are less likely than those born before then to engage in various communal activities—to entertain at home, attend church, vote, and participate in clubs.

They are also less likely to feel trusting of others. Trust has declined sharply from 1960, when 55 percent told National Opinion Research Center interviewers that they felt people generally could be trusted, to 1994, when only a third said the same. Although the trust drop is imprecisely measured (because of subtle differences in these surveys), high school seniors' sense of trust has similarly declined. In 1994, 69 percent of Americans responding to a Gallup poll agreed with the statement, "These days a person doesn't really know whom he can count on." Prudential Insurance Company, once "the rock" you could count on, now wants to help you "be your own rock."

Voting, the elementary act of citizenship, also has declined. Sixty-three percent of eligible voters went to the polls in the 1960 general election; in 1996, it was 54 percent. Ron Grossman and Charles Leroux find today's more individualistic twenty- and thirty-somethings half as likely as their grandparents to join face-to-face groups, trust in others, and vote. This dramatic decline in civic engagement has occurred despite a doubled proportion of high school graduates.

There seems to be a paradox here: highly educated people are more likely to be trusting and engaged in civic groups; more people today are

Fig. 7.1 Trust in Others over Time

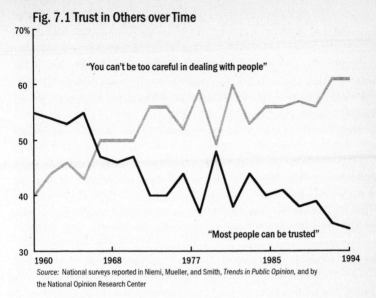

"You can't be too careful in dealing with people"

"Most people can be trusted"

70%
60
50
40
30

1960   1968   1977   1985   1994

Source: National surveys reported in Niemi, Mueller, and Smith, *Trends in Public Opinion*, and by the National Opinion Research Center

highly educated; yet civic involvement has declined sharply. Clearly, some social toxin—something powerful enough to overwhelm our increasing education—is corroding America's civic life.

Pollster Daniel Yankelovich has observed that people in the 1990s place a lower value on self-sacrifice, sexual restraint, and what we owe others out of moral obligation. During the 1980s, teenagers (especially whites) became much more accepting of people's nonmarital child-bearing as simply "doing their own thing." The army understands 1990s individualism, having replaced the communalism of "Uncle Sam wants you!" with "Be all that you can be." John F. Kennedy's "Ask not what your country can do for you" has become passé.

"Civilization is an exercise in self-restraint," said William Butler Yeats. Radical individualism undermines both restraint and concern for future generations. "Civic engagement and social connectedness are not just about warm fuzzy feelings," Putnam reminds us. Like marriage, civic connections are significant predictors of happiness and satisfaction with one's life. People who eat with friends and are active in their churches are happier than those who don't. Communities with higher levels of civic engagement tend to have less crime, lower mortality, more efficient government, and higher academic performance—regardless of the community's wealth, racial composition, or educational level.

Another price tag on individualism, argues Martin Seligman, is increased risk of depression, which has risen with it and is higher in individualistic countries. He attributes the level of depression to a cultural shift away from the "minimal self" of Yankee culture, which was concerned less with feelings than with behavior, less with freedom than with duty, and less with passions than with virtues. Seligman believes that "our epidemic of depression is a creature of [today's] maximal self," which has brought with it a "diminished sense of community and loss of higher purpose. These together proved rich soil for depression to grow in." Having foregone commitments to things larger than self (God, country, family), "where can we now turn for identity, for purpose, and for hope?" And if success is to be attributed to the individual self, then so is failure. If my career falls short of expectations, my marriage is a disappointment, and my children are flawed, well, who else is to blame? For shame. I should have tried harder, dreamed bigger, thought smarter.

Individualism and the American Family

Individualism is up, and so is family fragmentation. Is there a connection between these two trends?

If individualism does corrode family commitments, we should first expect to see that rising individualism correlates with family decline over the long run—which it does. Moreover, it doesn't require a Ph.D. to see why the values revolution of the past three decades might have had an impact on families. Hanging in the societal balance, on one side, is our valuing of self-fulfillment—insistence on our rights, cherishing personal freedom, pursuit of passion and pleasure. On the other side hangs our valuing of commitments—our sense of responsibility, our regarding permanence as a virtue, our believing that love is not just a feeling but a binding obligation. Over time, the balance has shifted toward prizing fulfillment over commitment, rights over responsibilities, wants over oughts.

Rather than viewing the self as "the servant of the marriage," social psychologist Roy Baumeister contends, "today people feel that marriage should serve the self." Thus two-thirds of Americans are unwilling to say that parents who don't get along should stay together simply because there are children. Marriage is no longer idealized as self-sacrificial love or as an enduring commitment. Bernard Farber sees the culture shifting toward "permanent availability," with adults, regardless of marital status, measuring their marriage against perceived alternatives.

The idea that a continual openness to a more satisfying partner would increase satisfaction and happiness ignores "the fact that the freedom of one spouse to leave the marriage at will is the other spouse's insecurity," sociologist Norval Glenn has remarked. And "without a reasonable degree of security, it is unlikely that a spouse will commit fully to the marriage and make the sacrifices and investments needed to make it succeed."

If individualism corrodes family commitments, we should also expect to see greater individualism linked with weaker family bonds *across cultures*—which we do. The United States is both the world's most individualistic and most divorce-prone nation. Britain is somewhat less individualistic, and it has barely half the divorce rate. (Ronald Reagan could divorce, remarry, and become president, but it was not immediately clear that Prince Charles could divorce, remarry, and become king.) Divorce rates tend to be even lower in collectivist cultures such as Japan. Collectivists demand less romance and personal fulfillment in marriage, putting the relationship under less pressure. In one survey, "keeping romance alive" was rated as important to a good marriage by 78 percent of American women and 29 percent of Japanese women.

Individualists also select mates differently, asking, "What does my heart say?" Collectivists ask, "What will other people say?" As it happens, what the heart says is a notoriously fragile foundation for long-term marital success. The high of romance may be sustained for a few months, even a couple of years. But no high lasts forever. The intense absorption in the other, the thrill of the romance, the giddy "floating on a cloud" feeling, fades. After two years of marriage, spouses express affection about half as often as when they were newlyweds. About four years after marriage the divorce rate peaks in cultures worldwide. The French have a saying for this: "Love makes the time pass and time makes love pass."

If a close relationship is to endure, it will settle to a steadier but still warm glow that social psychologist Elaine Hatfield calls "companionate love." Unlike the wild emotions of passionate love, companionate love is lower key; it's a deep, affectionate attachment.

The cooling of passionate love over time and the growing importance of other factors, such as shared values, can be seen in the feelings of those who enter arranged versus love-based marriages in India. Usha Gupta and Pushpa Singh surveyed 50 couples in Jaipur, India, and found that those who had married for love reported diminishing feelings of love if they had been married more than five years. By contrast, those in arranged marriages reported *more* love if they were not newlyweds.

After four years studying at my college, an Indonesian student returned to her collectivist roots and wrote to explain how her arranged marriage would work: "My family whom can be my cousins, uncles, and aunts would introduce me to the son of someone they know. I would only see him and talk to him once or twice or maybe more but not very often and if I like the guy I would only need to say *yes.* If I do not like the guy or I do not feel comfortable with him, I still can say *no.* I do believe if a person has a good heart, love will grow easily and beautifully." In actuality, it takes more than a good heart. It also takes the shared values, interests, and outlooks that are part of a good arranged match and that nurture companionship long after infatuation has ebbed.

If individualism corrodes family commitments we should, finally, expect to see greater individualism correlate with weaker attachments *across individuals*—which we also do. Compared with those who marry, those who cohabit have a greater desire to maintain their autonomy and a lesser need for attachment. The more people view self-actualization rather than child rearing as the purpose of partnership, the more likely they are to divorce. "We are in the business of saving individuals, not marriages," explained one marriage counselor (excluding children as stakeholders in the marital partnership). What unbridled capitalism is to economics, unfettered individualism is to human relationships.

Individualists also feel more frustration with their marriages: they criticize their partners more severely and express less marital happiness. (Is it a coincidence that so many champions of individualism —including Ronald Reagan, Newt Gingrich, and Phil Gramm—have divorced?) In their journeys around America, Robert Bellah and his colleagues observed a very nonindividualistic orientation among evangelicals, who typically assigned primacy to marriage over the self—for better or for worse, till death do us part. Even former playboy Warren Beatty now questions the self-over-commitment ethic: "My generation paid a big price . . . in terms of undeveloped family and lost family."

The Decline of the Commons

Another potential price we pay for radical individualism is its corrosion of communal well-being. Several of the problems that most threaten our human future—nuclear arms, the greenhouse effect, pollution, overpopulation, natural resource depletion—arise as various parties pursue their self-interest but do so, ironically, to their collective detriment. Any individualist can think: "It would cost me lots to buy expensive pollution controls. Besides, by itself my pollution is trivial." Many others reason similarly, and the result is fouled air and water. Thus, choices that are individually rewarding become collectively punishing when others choose the same. We therefore have an urgent dilemma: How can we reconcile the well-being of individual parties—their legitimate rights to pursue freely their personal interests—with the well-being of the community?

A metaphor for the insidious nature of social dilemmas is what ecologist Garrett Hardin called the "tragedy of the commons." He derived the name from the centrally located pasture in old English towns. The "commons" can be air, water, whales, cookies, or any shared and limited resource. If all use the resource in moderation, it may replenish itself as rapidly as it's harvested. The grass will grow, the whales will reproduce, and the cookie jar will get restocked.

Imagine 100 farmers surrounding a commons capable of sustaining 100 cows. When each grazes one cow, the common feeding ground is optimally used. But then someone reasons: "If I put a second cow in the pasture, I'll double my output, minus the mere 1 percent overgrazing." So this farmer adds a second cow. Then so does each of the other farmers. The inevitable result is the tragedy of the commons—a grassless mud field.

Many real predicaments parallel this story. Environmental pollution is the sum of many minor pollutions, each of which benefits the individual polluters much more than they could benefit themselves (and the environment) if they stopped their small pollution. We litter public places—dorm lounges, parks, zoos—but keep our personal spaces clean. And we deplete our natural resources, because the immediate personal benefits of, say, taking a long hot shower outweigh the seemingly inconsequential costs. Whalers knew others would exploit the whales if they didn't and that taking a few whales would hardly diminish the species. Everybody's business (conservation) became nobody's business.

The elements of the commons dilemma have been isolated in laboratory games. Imagine yourself as one of the Arizona State University students playing Julian Edney's Nuts Game. You and several others sit around a shallow bowl that holds ten metal nuts. The experimenter explains that your goal is to accumulate as many nuts as possible. Each of you at any time may take as many as you want, and every 10 seconds the number of nuts remaining in the bowl will be doubled. Would you leave the nuts in the bowl to regenerate, producing a greater harvest for all?

Likely not. Unless they were given time to devise and agree upon a conservation strategy, 65 percent of Edney's groups never reached the first 10-second replenishment. Often the people knocked the bowl to the floor grabbing for their share.

Like the commons dilemma, most real-life conflicts are "non-zero-sum games." The two sides' profits and losses need not add up to zero. Both can win; both can lose. Each game pits the immediate interests of individuals against the well-being of the group. Each is a social trap that shows how, even when individuals behave "rationally," harm can result. No malicious person planned for Los Angeles to be smothered in smog or for the earth's atmosphere to be warmed by a blanket of carbon dioxide.

Not all self-serving, individualistic behavior leads to collective doom. In a plentiful commons—as in the world of the 18th century capitalist economist Adam Smith—individuals who seek to maximize their own profit may also give the community what it needs: "It is not from the benevolence of the butcher, the brewer, or the baker, that we expect our dinner, but from their regard to their own interest." In today's computer, automotive, and education industries, the competition for sales and profits motivates people to make ever better products. But in those many situations that are indeed social traps, unbridled individualism can spell doom.

And that is why civilizations collect taxes (rather than trusting voluntary charity to support social and security needs), regulate whaling with an International Whaling Commission (rather than trusting individual countries and whalers), create freeway carpool lanes and mass transportation systems (that reward environmentally friendly travel), and control smoking in public places ("It is impossible for the smoker and the non-smoker to be equally free in the same railway car," observed George Bernard Shaw). Prudent restraints on individual rights enhance our collective well-being.

Authoritarian Reaction

In the beginning, individualism drives us to overthrow repressive authoritarianism. Witness the self-assertion of East Germans, Russians, and young Chinese in recent memory. Taken to a narcissistic extreme, however, the resulting social and moral chaos can trigger reactions that destroy individualism and rationality. "A society dedicated to the constant upending of norms and rules in the name of increasing individual freedom of choice will find itself increasingly disorganized, atomized, isolated, and incapable of carrying out common goals and tasks," Fukuyama argues.

One common response to the loss of shared values and beliefs is mysticism. In Britain and the United States, the founders of parapsychology were mostly people who, having lost their religious faith, were individually searching for a scientific basis for believing in the meaningfulness of life and the possibility of afterlife. In stressed Germany during the mid to late 1930s, articles on astrology increased. In the upheaval since the collapse of autocratic rule in Russia, there has come an "avalanche of the mystical, occult and pseudoscientific." "Extrasensorial" healers, astrologers, and seers fascinate the awestruck public. As one former medium said, "Wars, depressions and disaster spell prosperity for us."

The German experience alerts us to another possible response to radical individualism. "Aggregates of atomized, unbounded individuals," Amitai Etzioni warns, "are fodder for tyrannies." Democracy, as Pope John Paul II recently reminded us, requires "a shared commitment to certain moral truths about the human person and human community." When virtues erode, people look to government to provide and police order. Viewing today's tumult, Fukuyama, author of *The End of History and the Last Man,* sees the "soft authoritarianism" of countries like Singapore as a growing competitor to Western liberal democracies. Bertrand Russell foresaw the irony: "Too little liberty brings stagnation . . . too much brings chaos." And faced with chaos, people will always choose order, or even tyranny.

Communitarian Individualism

Three decades after Martin Luther King implored us to choose between chaos and community, one senses a seismic shift in our national dialogue. "Civic renewal," "the marriage movement," and "commitment" are gaining steam.

- Sociologists Robert Bellah (*Habits of the Heart*), Amitai Etzioni (*The Spirit of Community*), and Philip Selznick (*The Moral Commonwealth*) challenge contemporary individualism and remind us of the importance of social ties and social norms.
- Harvard legal scholar Mary Ann Glendon's *Rights Talk* illuminates the price we pay for translating every political dispute into the language of individual entitlement.
- The Democratic Leadership Council and its research affiliate, the Progressive Policy Institute, seek alternatives to the individualism of both Reagan-style conservatism and classical liberalism.
- President Clinton is elected with talk of a "New Covenant" of mutual responsibility between the government and the governed, between what society gives individuals and what individuals give back in voluntary service. He appoints as a domestic policy adviser political scientist William Galston, an advocate of moral and family renewal.
- Czech poet and president Vaclav Havel writes of a "single, common crisis" created by the collision of irresponsible, impersonal power and our notions of humanness and morality rooted in spirituality.
- Aleksandr Solzhenitsyn concurs. In today's philosophy, he says, "there are no higher spiritual forces above us and since I . . . am the crowning glory of the universe, then if anyone must perish today, let it be someone else, anybody, but not I, not my precious self, or those who are close to me." Whether voting on taxes or placing a value on lives near and far, most people, he laments, give priority to me and mine.
- William Bennett collects a weighty *Book of Virtues* that astonishes everyone by spending months on the best-seller list.
- Charles Colson warns that the restraints on America's individualism "have all but collapsed" and that the time has come to "reassert a sense of shared destiny as an antidote to radical individualism."
- Mayor Rudolph Giuliani has been ridiculed for his crackdown on traffic-blocking jaywalkers, surly taxi drivers, panhandlers, and strip joints, yet he is also applauded for making New York a more civil place.
- Under the leadership of German theologian Hans Kung, 24 former

heads of state in 1997 proposed "A Universal Declaration of Human Responsibilities" for United Nations endorsement as a complement to the Universal Declaration of Human Rights.

- The National Commission on Civic Renewal in its 1998 report finds common ground among Republicans and Democrats who share "concern for our country's civic condition."

- Also in 1998, the bipartisan Council on Civil Society issues *A Call to Civil Society* in response to the "nearly universal public distress about the state of our social morality." Soon after, the Penn National Commission on Society, Culture, and Community similarly decries incivility in public discourse and human relations.

The message common to these varied voices is this: as the collapse of communism shows the failure of extreme collectivism, so the American social recession shows the failure of extreme individualism. "Most civilizations die from within," observes Common Cause founder and former cabinet member John Gardner, "and are conquered less often by traitors within the gate than by traitors within the heart—loss of belief, corruption and disintegration of shared purposes." Such has been the experience of nations from Rome to the Soviet Union.

Sharing these concerns, Galston, Gardner, and several dozen other prominent citizens (including John Anderson, Betty Friedan, Richard John Neuhaus, Elliot Richardson, Lester Thurow, and Daniel Yankelovich) have signed on to a "communitarian platform" that "recognizes that the preservation of individual liberty depends on the active maintenance of the institutions of civil society" and that a "fragile social ecology" supports the family and community life that is essential to civility. Communitarians see themselves as a centrist alternative to the extremes of libertarianism and collectivism.

Typically, conservatives are economic individualists and moral collectivists. Liberals are moral individualists and economic collectivists. Communitarians advocate moral and economic policies that balance rights with communal responsibility. "Democratic communitarianism is based on the value of the sacredness of the individual, which is common to most of the great religions and philosophies of the world," explains Bellah. But it also "affirms the central value of solidarity . . . that we become who we are through our relationships." Agreeing that "it takes a village to raise a child," communitarians remind us of what it takes to raise a village.

Listen to communitarians talk about European-style child benefits,

extended parental leaves, flexible working hours, campaign finance reform, and ideas for "fostering the commons" and you'd swear they are
liberals. Listen to them talk about covenant marriages, divorce reform,
father care, and character education and you'd swear they are conservatives. In fact, communitarians see themselves not as a midpoint
between but as an alternative to the individualism-authoritarian and
liberal-conservative polarities. This "third way," as it became known in
Tony Blair's Britain, aims to synthesize some of the best ideas from both
camps.

Communitarians welcome incentives for individual initiative and
appreciate why Marxist economies have crumbled. "If I were, let's say,
in Albania at this moment," said Communitarian Network co-founder
Etzioni, "I probably would argue that there's too much community and
not enough individual rights." Even in communal Japan, Etzioni says,
he would sing a song of individuality. In the individualistic American
context, he sings a song of social order, which in times of chaos (as
in crime-plagued or corrupt countries) is necessary for liberty. Where
there is chaos in a neighborhood, people may feel like prisoners in their
homes.

Opposition to communitarians comes from civil libertarians of the
left (such as the ACLU), economic libertarians of the right (such as
the Cato Institute), and special interest libertarians (such as the NRA).
Much as these organizations differ, they are branches of the same tree
—all valuing individual rights in the contest with the common good.
The Montana Freemen who in 1996 held out for 81 days in a stand-
off with the government named their enclave Justus Township—which
was appropriate, for their circle of concern encompassed not "all of
us" but "just us." Communitarians take on all such varieties of libertarianism. Unrestrained personal freedom, they say, destroys a culture's
social fabric; unrestrained commercial freedom exploits workers and
plunders the commons. Etzioni sums up the communitarian ideal in
his *New Golden Rule:* "Respect and uphold society's moral order as you
would have society respect and uphold your autonomy."

To reflect on your own libertarian versus communitarian leanings,
consider what restraints on liberty you support: luggage scanning at
airports? smoking bans in public places? speed limits on highways? so-
briety checkpoints? drug testing of pilots and rail engineers? prohi-
bitions on leaf burning? restrictions on TV cigarette ads? regulations
on stereo or muffler noise? pollution controls? requiring seat belts and

motorcycle helmets? disclosure of sexual contacts for HIV carriers? "Megan's Laws" that mandate listing of sex offenders? outlawing child pornography? banning AK-47s and other nonhunting weapons of destruction? required school uniforms? wiretaps on suspected terrorists? fingerprinting checks to protect welfare, unemployment, and Social Security funds from fraud? All such restraints on individual rights, most opposed by libertarians of one sort or another, aim to enhance the public good.

Libertarians often object to restraints on guns, panhandlers, pornography, drugs, or business by warning that they may plunge us down a slippery slope leading to the loss of more important liberties. If today we let them search our luggage, tomorrow they'll be invading our houses. If today we censor cigarette ads on television, tomorrow the thought police will be removing books from our libraries. If today we ban handguns, tomorrow's Big Brother government will take our hunting rifles. Communitarians reply that if we don't balance concern for individual rights with concern for the commons, we risk chaos and a new fascism. Youth curfews, warrantless car searches, and raids on housing projects could herald diminishing civil liberties. The conservative movement is driven, Rabbi Barry Freundel argues, "primarily not by economics but by a sense that the moral quality of life is collapsing." When individualistic freedom becomes license breeding anarchy, an authoritarian reaction is on the horizon. As Walker Percy put it, "Weimar leads to Auschwitz."

Who, therefore, is the true defender of freedom, wonders Etzioni —those who allow radical individualism to take us toward the flash point, or those who aim to protect essential freedoms by balancing rights with responsibilities, individualism with community, liberty with fraternity?

As an antidote for the poverty cycle and a step supporting marriage, Maggie Gallagher urges an end to welfare for unmarried teenage mothers. "Instead of routinely giving custody of babies to girls too young to drive a car or sign a contract, the law should require that every baby born in America be under the guardianship of a competent adult. If the girl cannot find an adult willing to assume full legal responsibility, the baby should be placed for adoption."

Such child-protection proposals illustrate Etzioni's point: incivility will inevitably trigger efforts at reform—some wise, some extreme. The surest way to aid the extremists is to stand idly by, defending individual rights while the commons disintegrates. When a commons collapses, and when people fear for their safety, they will grasp at order. James Q. Wilson summarizes Thomas Hobbes's view of the process: "Only a sovereign power—a Leviathan—is capable of protecting every man from every other, and so to this sovereign each man surrenders his right to self-government in order to obtain that which each most desperately wants, which is to avoid a violent death."

Our Need to Belong

The communitarian movement finds its intellectual roots among sociologists who appreciate that human life everywhere, throughout history, has been lived in communities. We are, as Aristotle said, "the social animal." We become human in relationships with others—an idea first expressed in the Hebrew creation story ("It is not good that the man should be alone"). We live not as solitary beings but in family groups that are organized into larger social systems. Deprived of natural social bonds, people will recreate them by forming clubs, gangs, and support groups. Etzioni, a George Washington University sociologist, was raised in an Israeli cooperative settlement, giving him an added appreciation of the benefits of close communities.

Psychologists also have an increasing respect for community. Evolutionary psychologists contend that social bonds boosted our ancestors' survival rate. For both children and adults, bonding was adaptive. By keeping children close to their caregivers, attachments served as a powerful survival impulse. In our infancy, we therefore preferred familiar faces and voices. By eight months, we crawled after mother or father and pouted or wailed when separated from them. Reunited, we clung.

As adults, those who formed attachments were more likely to come together to reproduce and to stay together to nurture their offspring to maturity. Human bonding facilitated cooperative hunting and self-defense. In solo combat, our ancestors were not the toughest predators. But as hunters they learned that six hands were better than two. Those who foraged in groups also gained protection from predators and enemies. If those who felt a need to belong survived and reproduced most successfully, their genes would in time predominate. The result was an innately social creature.

Social psychologists Baumeister and Leary also have discerned a fundamental human need to belong—to feel connected with others in enduring, close relationships. The need to belong colors our thoughts and emotions. People spend much time thinking about their actual and hoped-for relationships. When relationships form, we often feel joy. People falling in love have been known to get cheek-aches from their ir-repressible grins. When asked "What is necessary for your happiness?" or "What is it that makes your life meaningful?" most people men-tion—before anything else—satisfying close relationships with family, friends, or romantic partners. As C. S. Lewis said, "The sun looks down on nothing half so good as a household laughing together over a meal." Dining alone is not a recipe for happiness.

Seven large investigations, each following thousands of people over years of time, reveal that close relationships also contribute to health. People who are supported by close relationships with friends, family, or members of church, work, or other groups are less likely to die pre-maturely than those with few social ties. In other studies, leukemia patients preparing to undergo bone-marrow transplants had a 54 per-cent survival rate after two years if they felt strong support from family or friends, and 20 percent survival if not. Heart disease patients had an 82 percent survival rate after five years if they were married or had a confidant, but only 50 percent if not. "Woe to one who is alone and falls and does not have another to help," said the sage of Ecclesiastes.

Much of our social behavior aims to increase our belonging—our social acceptance and inclusion. To avoid rejection, we generally con-form to group standards and seek to make favorable impressions. To win friendship and esteem, we monitor our behavior, hoping to create the right impressions. Seeking love and belonging, we spend billions on clothes, cosmetics, and diet and fitness aids—all motivated by our quest for acceptance.

People resist breaking social bonds. For most of us, familiarity breeds liking, not contempt. Thrown together at school, at summer camp, on a cross-country bus tour, people resist the group's dissolution. Hoping to maintain the relationships, they promise to call, to write, to come back for reunions. Parting, they feel distress. At the end of a mere vacation cruise, people may hug their waiter or cry when saying good-bye forever to their cabin attendant. Attachments can even keep people in abusive relationships; the fear of being alone may seem worse than the pain of emotional or physical abuse.

When something threatens or dissolves our social ties, negative emotions overwhelm us. Exile, imprisonment, and solitary confinement are progressively more severe forms of punishment. Recently bereaved people often feel that life is empty and pointless. Children reared in institutions without a sense of belonging to anyone, or locked away at home under extreme neglect, become pathetic creatures—withdrawn, frightened, speechless. Adults who are denied others' acceptance and inclusion may feel depressed. Anxiety, jealousy, loneliness, and guilt all involve threatened disruptions of our need to belong. People suffer even when bad relationships break. After such separations, feelings of loneliness and anger are commonplace. The bottom line: as we form values and decide policies, we had best be mindful not only of our basic human need to feel control but also to belong. People who have people are not only the luckiest people alive, but also the happiest and healthiest.

So we Americans are the preeminent individualists. For this we enjoy many benefits, but at what communitarians believe is an increasing cost to the social environment. We humans like to feel unique and in control of our lives, but we also are social creatures having a basic need to belong. As individuals, we therefore need to balance our needs for independence and attachment, personal control and community, individuality and social identity, freedom and order. As a society, we struggle to discover balance on that fine line of vitality between anarchy and repression. As we do so, we might recall the words of Puritan leader John Winthrop, spoken in 1630 just before his people set foot on American soil at Salem Harbor: "We must delight in each other, make others' conditions our own, rejoyce together, mourn together, labor and suffer together, always having before our eyes our community as members of the same body."

CHAPTER 8

Media, Minds, and the Public Good

What kind of country do we want?
—PHIL DONAHUE, 1993

Few things these days evoke more parental outrage than images of 3d graders watching MTV, 6th graders listening to rap lyrics glamorizing "f——ing the bitch," 9th graders learning human relations from *Rambo* and *Robocop*, or 12th graders getting their sex and intimacy education from *The Young and the Restless*, Jerry Springer trash talk, and *Freshman Fantasies* pornography. That outrage became a national obsession after Eric Harris and Dylan Klebold reportedly spent hours playing splatter games such as Doom and watching two crazy kids commit carnage in *Natural Born Killers*, prior to committing carnage at Littleton's Columbine High School. "All our children," says a palpably angry Marian Wright Edelman, "are growing up today in an ethically polluted nation where instant sex without responsibility, instant gratification without effort, instant solutions without sacrifice, getting rather than giving, and hoarding rather than sharing are the too-frequent signals of our mass media."

Psychologist James Garbarino illustrated this vulgarization by asking children to close their eyes and tell him what came to mind when he said "Mister Rogers." With smiling faces, the images spilled out: "Kind." "Gentle." "Cares about you." "King Friday." "Nice." Then he asked them to do the same with Beavis and Butthead. The looks and words change: "Nasty." "Mean." "Rude." "Hurts people." For them, Mister Rogers was history—"from our childhood," said one 8-year-old. Beavis and Butt-head were the present. "This experience crystallized for me," Garba-rino reflected, "the fact that one important feature of the social toxicity of the environment for children is the nastiness to which they are ex-posed so early in life . . . and nastiness is the last thing children need."

"Father Knows Squat," reported the *Washington Post* on how the media regularly ridicule, caricature, and marginalize parents. "Lately, I can't seem to even look at my mother without wanting to stab her repeatedly," said the lead character in the opening episode of *My So-Called Life*. Although *Father Knows Best* and *Ozzie and Harriet* were patriarchal, they did honor the parental role. "Here on primetime tele-vision were loving, hardworking parents raising their children with wis-dom and humor—solving problems, teaching values, and providing an all-important protective shield," Hewlett and West recall with a touch of nostalgia. "Themes such as family togetherness, respect for one's elders, commitment to one's spouse, and devotion to children reverber-ated like drumbeats through the culture of the day." By the century's end, however, parenting had become "a countercultural activity," they say. "It feels as though we are swimming upstream" against the cultural currents.

Are today's parents, including Edelman and Garbarino, rightly concerned? With most children now arriving at an empty home after school, does late-afternoon television fare matter? Does it matter if, in-stead of leaving our children to Beaver, we leave them to Beavis? Does viewing prime-time crime influence their thinking and acting? Does on-screen sex shape their (and our) sexual perceptions, expectations, and behavior? Do the media mold us? Mirror us? Or both?

By analyzing program content, by correlating media viewing habits with behavior, and by experiments that manipulate media exposure to discern cause and effect, social science research provides some clear and credible answers. Let's allow these answers to inform our national dialogue. And then let's see if there might be a path toward America's renewal that weaves between the rock of repressive censorship and the hard place of shameless greed.

Does Hollywood Mirror Reality?

In 1961 President Kennedy's newly appointed federal communica-tions commissioner Newton Minow challenged members of the National Association of Broadcasters to "sit down in front of your television set when your station goes on the air and stay there without a book, magazine, newspaper, profit and loss sheet, or rating book to distract you—and keep your eyes glued to that set until the station signs you off. I can assure you that you will observe a vast wasteland."

Repeating the exercise in the mid-1990s, what would broadcasters observe on their stations? Would they see social reality as in a mirror? Do today's entertainment media simply reflect the big, bad world? The answer is most definitely not. On evening dramas broadcast in the United States during the 1980s and early 1990s, and often exported to the more than 1 billion television sets around the world, only one-third of the characters were women. Fewer than 3 percent were visibly old. One percent were Hispanic. Only 1 in 10 was married.

Network programs offer about three violent acts per hour—and six times as many (18 per hour) during children's Saturday morning programs. From 1994 to 1997, the National Television Violence Study analyzed some 10,000 programs from the major networks and cable channels. Six in ten contained violence ("physically compelling action that threatens to hurt or kill, or actual hurting or killing"). During fistfights, people who go down usually shake it off and come back stronger—unlike most real fistfights that last one punch (often resulting in a broken jaw or hand). In 73 percent of violent scenes, the aggressors go unpunished. In 58 percent, the victim is not shown to experience pain. In children's programs, only 5 percent of violence is shown to have any long-term consequence; two-thirds depict violence as funny.

What does this add up to? By the end of elementary school, the average child views some 8,000 TV murders and 100,000 other violent acts. If one includes cable programming, movies, and video rentals —which together provide the biggest media change of the past decade—the violence numbers escalate, because the major networks are the relative nice guys. Premium cable channels like HBO and Showtime, offering popular films like *Die Hard 2* with its 264 deaths, are much more violent than major network programs. So is MTV. So are new Hollywood films, 65 percent of which were R-rated in 1998. Reflecting on his 22 years of cruelty counting, University of Pennsylvania media researcher George Gerbner lamented, "Humankind has had more bloodthirsty eras but none as filled with *images* of violence as the present. We are awash in a tide of violent representations the world has never seen, . . . drenching every home with graphic scenes of expertly choreographed brutality." This is indeed life as rendered by a rather peculiar storyteller, one that reflects our culture's mythology but not its reality.

Hollywood's sexual mythology is hardly a better mirror of reality. In the real world, intercourse occurs mostly among married people (because most people are married, married people have sex more often, and extramarital sex is rarer than commonly believed). In the entertainment world, implied acts of sexual intercourse overwhelmingly occur between unmarried people. In soap operas, for example, unmarried partners have outnumbered married partners 24 to 1. In the first four weeks of one recent year, seven sitcom women, including Murphy Brown, were pregnant or considering it; "only one was married—and she didn't want a child," the *New York Times* reported.

In an average prime-time hour, the three major networks offer some 15 sexual acts, words, and innuendoes—one every 4 minutes, nearly all involving unmarried persons with nary an expressed concern for birth control or sexually transmitted disease. (Those numbers are not inflated by MTV's videos or the Fox Network's sexual modeling through such programs as *Melrose Place.*) On television, impulsive couples seldom hesitate over their first deep kiss and passionate aftermath. When "they" (the young and unmarried) "do it" 20,000 times a year on television and no one gets pregnant, says Planned Parenthood, that is massive sex *dis*information. In reality, most relationships progress more awkwardly and tentatively. Through network television and MTV, Walkmans, and VCRs, the incessant sexual message, Planned Parenthood frets, is "Go for it now. . . . Don't worry about anything."

Depictions also split from reality when portraying sexual coercion. A typical sexually violent episode finds a man forcing himself upon a woman. She at first resists and tries to fight off her attacker. Gradually she becomes aroused, and her resistance melts. In pornographic films, the sequence ends with the woman in orgasmic ecstasy, pleading for more. But the same idea is often portrayed in Hollywood's more traditional fare: Dashing man grabs and forcibly kisses protesting woman. She resists, he persists. Before long, the arms that were pushing him away are clutching him tight, her passions unleashed. In *Gone with the Wind,* Scarlett O'Hara is carried to bed protesting and kicking, and wakes up singing. On ABC's *General Hospital,* Luke raped Laura, who eventually fell in love and married him, referring to the rape as "the first time we made love." Occasional fantasies aside, this is not how women normally respond to rape and other forms of sexual coercion and intimidation.

The unreality extends beyond violence and sex. In television's world, 6 percent of people have a religious identity. In America, 88 percent do. In television's world, 25 percent of people have blue-collar jobs. In America, 67 percent do. In television's world, 45 percent of beverages consumed are alcoholic. In America, 16 percent are. Hollywood may reflect our culture's mythology, but it radically distorts its reality.

Media Effects on Thinking: From Screen Images to Cerebral Scripts?

In 1945, Gallup pollsters asked Americans, "Do you know what television is?" Today, 98 percent of American homes (and a similar percentage in other industrialized nations) have a TV set. That's more than have telephones. With the average house now having 2.2 sets, America alone among the world's countries has nearly as many televisions as people. But MTV and CNN span the globe, and *Baywatch* is seen in 142 countries, so television also is creating a global pop culture.

In the average American home the set is on more than seven hours a

Fig. 8.1 Household Television Viewing (hours per day)

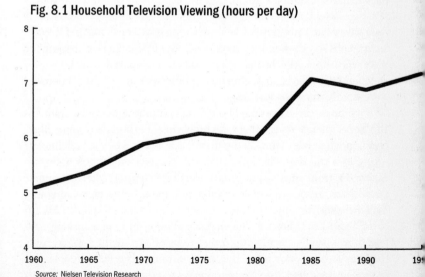

Source: Nielsen Television Research

day, with individual household members averaging three to four hours. All told, television beams its electromagnetic waves into children's eyeballs for more growing-up hours than they spend in school. More hours, in fact, than they spend in any other waking activity. From these hours —20,000 hours diverted from talking, playing, reading, and so forth— what do children learn?

Viewing Violence

Psychologists study media effects the way geologists study erosion, with experiments that discern small effects that, over time, could cumulate to big effects. By showing brutality to some children or adults but not others, they have identified two cognitive effects of viewing even a short stream of violent acts, much less a hundred thousand plus.

Viewing violence desensitizes people to cruelty. Take some emotion-arousing stimulus, perhaps an obscene word, and repeat it over and over. Over time, what will happen to your emotional arousal? Gradually, it will extinguish. What initially bothered you will bother you less and less.

After witnessing thousands of cruel acts, there is good reason to expect a similar emotional numbing. The response might well become, "I don't see why it's such a big deal. It doesn't bother me at all." This is precisely what University of Utah researcher Victor Cline and his colleagues observed when they measured the physiological arousal of 121 boys who watched a brutal boxing match. Compared with boys who watched little television, the responses of those who watched habitually were hardly more than a shrug.

Of course, these boys might differ in ways other than viewing habits. But experiments reveal that watching violence breeds a more blasé reaction when later viewing the film of a brawl or when actually monitoring two children who begin fighting (as seen on supposed closed-circuit TV from an adjacent room). Further experiments reveal a similar desensitization—a sort of psychic numbness—that grows as young men view slasher films. In one such study, researchers Charles Mullin and Daniel Linz showed University of Wisconsin men a sexually violent movie, such as *Friday the 13th,* every other day for a week. After they viewed two such films, the third film provoked less physiological arousal and seemed less violent to the inured men. And compared with men who didn't see the films, the viewers expressed less sympathy for actual domestic violence victims (shown from a PBS documentary) and rated their injuries as less severe. Ergo, watching cruelty fosters later indifference to cruelty.

Viewing violence molds our perceived reality. In their surveys of both adolescents and adults, Gerbner and his associates found that those who watch television more than four hours a day are more likely than those who watch two hours or less to exaggerate the frequency of violence in the world around them and to fear being personally assaulted. Television, Gerbner said, fosters a perception of a "mean world."

Adults can distinguish television crime from neighborhood events. Viewers of crime dramas may not be more fearful of their own neighborhood than those who don't watch these shows, but they tend to see New York, or even their own city, as a more dangerous place. Among children, television colors perceptions of more immediate surroundings. One national survey of 7- to 11-year-old children found that heavy viewers more than light viewers admitted fears "that somebody bad might get into your house" or that "when you go outside, somebody might hurt you." To one who views the world through the screen of television, the world seems more menacing.

Sexual Myths and Images

It is no secret that television and film violence desensitizes people to cruelty and makes the world seem mean (although that news has, as yet, hardly made any difference). A better kept secret is the results of newer experiments on the cognitive effects of viewing what Hillary Clinton has called a "steady diet of impulsive sexuality." We know of five such effects.

Distorted perceptions of sexual reality. Which is the more common cause of death—all forms of accidents or strokes? Do more people live in Cambodia or Tanzania? Experiments reveal an implicit rule by which the human mind makes snap judgments: If instances of something are readily available in memory, we presume the event is commonplace. Easy-to-picture events, such as accidents, therefore seem more likely than hard-to-picture events, such as strokes (which actually claim twice as many lives). With more images of Cambodians available in memory, many people think Cambodia is more populous. Actually, Tanzania has three times as many people. Likewise, because news pictures of airplane crashes are a readily available memory for most of us, we often feel greater fear in an airliner than in a car. (A Gallup survey reveals that 44 percent of flyers report feeling fear.) But perception is not reality. American travelers during the 1980s were 26 times more likely to die in a car crash than on a commercial flight covering the same distance. For most air travelers, the most dangerous part of the journey is the drive to the airport.

Even fictional happenings in novels, television, and movies leave images that later penetrate our judgments. Although I know that fatal shark attacks are about as common in the United States as airliner crashes, watching *Jaws* left me jumpy when brushing into seaweed while swimming in the Atlantic. Having seen many fictional images of marital infidelity, most people overestimate its prevalence. Although 9 in 10 people report being enduringly faithful to their spouses (98.5 percent during the previous year), they believe other people often violate their marital vows. So it goes with other erotic images of people engaging in (or discussing on talk shows) unusual sexual behaviors, such as mothers sleeping with their sons' friends. Vivid erotic images (like any emotion-arousing experience) shout "print" to the brain's memory system, making such images available as we later construct our perceived reality.

Perceived reality matters. Most university students think that other students are generally more promiscuous and less sexually responsible than themselves. Does that perception matter? Given the importance of peer influence—the tendency for peers more than parents to define behavioral norms—this indeed matters. Thus, note researchers Gina Agostinelli and David Wyatt Seal, "perceiving others' sexual attitudes as relatively permissive and less responsible can perpetuate risky sexual behavior by serving either as a permissive subjective norm in guiding one's behavior . . . or as an after-the-fact justification for one's own sexually risky behaviors." When similar misperceptions about other students' love for alcohol are corrected, alcohol use diminishes. Sex and AIDS education programs should do likewise, say Agostinelli and Seal: correct misperceptions about promiscuous norms. A more responsible entertainment industry would do the same, or would at least not create misperceptions that sex educators must reverse.

The most disturbing example of altered sexual perceptions is the rape myth—the idea that some women would welcome sexual assault, that "no" doesn't really mean No! Those of us who may not have seen movies with orgasmic rape victims can surely recall many images of strong-willed men silencing their romantic targets with forceful kisses. Usually, their persistence gets rewarded, as "No" dissolves to "Yes!" Do such fictional scripts write mental scripts onto men's and women's brains?

To find out, social psychologists Neil Malamuth and James Check showed some University of Manitoba men two nonsexual movies, while others saw two movies depicting a man sexually overcoming a woman. A week later, when surveyed by a different researcher, those who saw the films with mild sexual violence were more accepting of violence against women. The same conclusion emerges from pornography research. A social science "consensus statement" from Surgeon General Koop's Workshop on Pornography and Public Health summed it up: "Pornography that portrays sexual aggression as pleasurable for the victim increases the acceptance of the use of coercion in sexual relations."

Viewing more sexually violent slasher movies has a comparable effect. Men shown films like *The Texas Chain Saw Massacre* not only become desensitized to brutality but are more likely to view rape victims unsympathetically. College men who have viewed movies depicting a man sexually overpowering a women not only become more accepting of violence against women but report themselves a little more likely to rape if assured they could get away with it. Researchers Ed Donnerstein, Daniel Linz, and Steven Penrod invite us to imagine an evil character who wished to get people to react calmly to the torture and mutilation of women. What better advice could we give than to do pretty much what we're doing: repeatedly show people films depicting such? And then, to reinforce this learning, why not design games like Mortal Kombat, Resident Evil, and Twisted Metal that invite youths to play out their newly acquired social scripts by attacking and dismembering people?

Decreased attraction for comparatively less exciting partners. How attractive and satisfying you find a mate or romantic partner depends partly on your yardstick of comparison. In several experiments, viewing beautiful, passionate people has dampened appreciation for normal people or real-life partners. Douglas Kenrick and Sara Gutierres discovered this "contrast effect" when they had someone interrupt Montana State University men in their dormitory rooms, saying, "We have a friend coming to town this week and we want to fix him up with a date." When shown a photo of a potential date—an average-looking young woman—those who had just been watching a TV program starring three beautiful women rated her as less attractive than those who hadn't. Likewise, to men who have recently been gazing at centerfolds as part of an experiment, average women—or even their own girlfriends or wives—become less attractive. Viewing pornographic films simulating passionate sex also decreases satisfaction with one's own partner. The lingering effect of exposure to perfect "10s," or of supposed passionate ecstasy, is to make one's own partner seem more like a "6" than an "8."

The contrast effect plays on our self-image as well, leading us sometimes to feel inadequate or homely. After viewing an attractive person of the same sex, people feel less attractive than after viewing an unattractive person. To compare oneself with Sharon Stone or Leonardo DiCaprio, or with an erotic athlete, is to feel rather frumpy or lackluster. Texas A&M researcher Wendy Stock observed the contrast effect in a survey of 500 women. After viewing pornography, 42 percent said they felt bad about their bodies. A third felt sexually inadequate. A fourth felt as if sex were a performance.

Men's increased perception of women in sexual terms. Research psychologists explore how experiences "prime" our perceptions and memories. After seeing words like "adventurous," people will later, in a different context, report positive impressions of a mountain climber. If, instead, their thinking is subtly primed with negative words such as "reckless," their impressions are more negative. Likewise, watching a scary movie while home alone can prime our interpreting furnace noises as a possible intruder.

Researchers Douglas McKenzie-Mohr and Mark Zanna carried the phenomenon into the sexual arena with a simple experiment. They showed some masculine University of Waterloo men a pornographic video, while others saw a political debate. Then, supposedly as part of another experiment, a female research assistant briefly interviewed the men. Shortly thereafter another researcher asked the men to write down their recollections of the interviewer. For men primed with the sexually explicit video, 72 percent of their initial recollections concerned her physical features, compared with 49 percent among those who had seen the political debate.

Watching an erotic movie also affects men's perceptions of women's behavior. It can make a woman's friendliness seem more like a come-on. (Perhaps this helps explain the connection between Clarence Thomas's reported pornography use and his alleged sexual harassment of Anita Hill.) Music videos similarly prime viewers' thinking about sexual roles and relationships. As people heavily exposed to televised crime see the world as more dangerous, so people heavily exposed to pornography or sexually oriented rock videos see the world as more sexual.

Some couples and sex therapists see a positive side to the priming effect. Sexually explicit videos can be used to demonstrate variety and prime lovemaking. The benefit may, however, come at the price of heightened sexual expectations, which eventually increase dissatisfaction. It's a basic rule of life: the gap between aspiration and attainment defines frustration. Thus, one price of inflated expectations, of our mates and ourselves, is deflated satisfactions, which contribute to the increase in marital unhappiness and divorce.

Sexual aggression seems less serious. Over six weeks Dolf Zillmann and Jennings Bryant exposed college students to pornography—six brief sexually explicit films a week. Meanwhile, a control group viewed nonerotic films. Three weeks later, all the subjects read a newspaper report about a man convicted but not yet sentenced for raping a hitchhiker. When asked to suggest an appropriate prison term, those who had viewed the erotica recommended sentences half as long as members of the control group. For those desensitized to scenes of sexual contact, even rape no longer seemed like that big a deal. In follow-up studies, Zillmann found that after massive exposure to X-rated films, men and women also became more accepting of extramarital sex, women's sexual submission to men, and a man's seducing 12-year-old girls. Such media influences help explain "the death of outrage"—why, in 1998, the public shrugged off presidential sexual exploitation that 40 years earlier would have seemed appalling.

"Social scripts." In a new situation, unsure how to act, we often rely on culturally provided social scripts. After so many episodes of Ninja Turtles and Clint Eastwood, Sylvester Stallone, and Arnold Schwarzenegger films, youngsters may acquire such a script—a mental tape that

gets played when they face real-life conflicts. Challenged, they may "act like a man" by intimidating or eliminating the threat. After saturation viewing of sexual innuendoes and impulsive acts, youths may similarly acquire scripts they later enact in real-life relationships.

Summing up many experiments on the cognitive effects of media images, we can say this: Repeatedly viewing violence desensitizes people to violence and shapes their perceived reality. Erotic images likewise tend to distort people's perceptions of sexual reality, decrease the attractiveness of their own partners, prime men to perceive women in sexual terms, make sexual coercion seem more trivial, and provide mental scripts for how to act in sexual situations.

In such ways, "All of us who make motion pictures are teachers," George Lucas reminded the 1992 Academy Award audience, "teachers with very loud voices." "Those who tell stories hold the power in society," echoes Gerbner. "It's incumbent on [filmmakers] to realize that the films they choose to make have an effect on the workaday lives of the audience and their ability to deal with the world they inhabit," producer David Puttnam writes, reflecting on what motivated him to immortalize idealism and commitment in *Chariots of Fire*—values that have been "almost obliterated by the insidious spread of contemporary cynicism." The popular arts are not ineffectual; they color consciousness and teach us how to act.

Curiously, most folks agree that media affect the culture but deny the effect on themselves. Many parents will recall hearing this from their children: "Don't worry, Mom. Watching this doesn't affect me." This phenomenon is so robust that researchers have given it a name— "the third-person effect." Others more than us, we think, are affected by ads, political information, media violence, and social scripts. The research, however, disarms our hubris; we have met the "others" and they are us.

Media Effects on Behavior

By providing scripts and models, do the media stimulate the behaviors they depict? Or do they do the opposite—by enabling people to cathartically vent their pent-up aggressive and sexual impulses? "Seeing a murder on television can be good therapy," Alfred Hitchcock once remarked. "It can help work off one's antagonisms."

Viewing Violence and Actual Violence

Examples abound of copycat crimes. In Utah, two men murdered three people by forcing them to drink Drano. Earlier that month the men had seen the movie *Magnum Force,* depicting murder by Drano, three times in one day. Such stories may not be aberrations. In one informal survey of 208 prison convicts, 9 of 10 acknowledged learning new criminal tricks by watching crime programs, and 4 of 10 said they had attempted specific crimes seen on television. As Yogi Berra once said, "You can observe a lot just by watching."

Informal crime reports are not, however, persuasive scientific evidence. Hoping to slice the fog of contradictory claims by media critics and defenders, researchers have correlated viewing habits with behavior, and then experimentally manipulated media exposure.

Correlating viewing and behavior. To some extent, children's viewing does predict their aggressiveness. The more violent a child's television diet, the more aggressive the child. Though modest, the relationship consistently appears in studies in the United States, Europe, and Australia.

Does this indicate that watching violence increases aggressiveness? Perhaps, but it could also mean that aggressive children prefer aggressive programs. Or perhaps some underlying third factor, such as lower intelligence, predisposes some children both to prefer viewing violence and to act aggressively.

To test the "third factor" possibility, British researcher William Belson statistically pulled out such complicating influences in a study of 1,565 London boys. Compared with those who watched little violence, those who watched a great deal (especially realistic rather than cartoon violence) admitted to 50 percent more violent acts during the preceding six months (for example, "I busted the telephone in a telephone box"). When Belson extracted the influence of 22 likely third factors, such as family size, the heavy and light violence viewers still differed. He therefore surmised that the heavy viewers were indeed more violent because of their TV diet.

In a pioneering American study, Leonard Eron and Rowell Huesmann found that violence viewing predicted aggressiveness among 875 8-year-olds even after equating the children on several possible third factors. When they restudied the subjects as 19-year-olds they discovered that viewing violence at age 8 modestly predicted aggressiveness at 19, but that earlier aggressiveness did *not* predict violence viewing later. Aggression followed viewing, not the reverse. Eron and Huesmann and their colleagues confirmed these findings in follow-up studies of 758 Chicago-area and 220 Finnish youngsters. The researchers also examined the later criminal conviction records of their initial sample of 8-year-olds. At 30, those who had watched a great deal of violence as children had more often been convicted of a serious crime.

Even murder rates increase where television goes. In Canada and the United States, the homicide rate doubled between 1957 and 1974 as the first TV generation was growing up. In census regions where television came later, the homicide rate jumped later. In white South Africa, where television was not introduced until 1975, a similar near doubling of the homicide rate did not begin until after 1975. From such data University of Washington epidemiologist Brandon Centerwall surmises that, without television, violent crime today would be half what it is. This doubling of violence extends beyond crime. In one closely studied rural town where television came late, playground aggression doubled.

With such data in hand, a scientific consensus has emerged: across time and across people, watching violence predicts aggression. In 1993, the American Psychological Association's Commission on Violence and Youth declared that there is now "absolutely no doubt that higher levels of viewing violence on television are correlated with increased acceptance of aggressive attitudes and increased aggressive behavior." Eron, the commission's chairman, explains: "As a child, you see a Dirty Harry movie, where the heroic policeman is shooting people right and left. Even years later, the right kind of scene can trigger that script and suggest a way to behave that follows it. Our studies have come up with a lot of evidence that suggests that's possible." All in all, "the evidence is overwhelming," he concludes. The viewing-aggression relation "is about the same as that between smoking and lung cancer." Many who smoke don't die of lung cancer, and many who absorb countless hours playing Mortal Kombat or watching Rambo reruns will live gentle lives. (The viewing effect is most noticeable with angered or characteristically hostile individuals.) Still, the correlation is undeniable.

Fueled by the recent explosion in violent video game sales and by reports that the Paducah, Kentucky, and Littleton, Colorado, assassins treated their carnage like the splatter games they had so often played, researchers are beginning to explore the effects of repeated practice at assassinating opponents, who collapse in bloody death throes. Do mass murder simulators, such as Doom and Quake, train some kids for cruelty much as flight simulators train pilots to fly? We do know, from a recent study by psychologists Mary Ballard and Rose Wiest, that playing Mortal Kombat increases arousal and feelings of hostility as college men play it. We have good reason to doubt the rationalization of one video game CEO—that we are "violent by nature [and] need release valves." And we're not charmed by magazine ads that invite game players to "get in touch with your gun-toting, cold-blooded murdering side." But we need more research to identify what part video games might play in the genetic and ecological mix of ingredients that, in the right combination, can yield an Eric Harris.

Sexual violence and behavior. Similar results come from studies that correlate men's viewing of sexual violence with their aggression against women. It's not enough, of course, to verify that men who rape have experienced pornography. (Nearly all convicted rapists are habitual bread eaters, and some 9 in 10 consumed bread in the 24 hours before committing their violence.) So what shall we make of the finding that across the world reported rape rates increased as pornography became more widely available during the 1960s and 1970s? Is it a coincidence, researcher John Court wonders, that in places that controlled pornography, rape rates tended not to jump? In Hawaii, for example, the number of reported rapes rose ninefold between 1960 and 1974, dropped when restraints on pornography were temporarily imposed, and rose again when the restraints were lifted. (Japan, which has experienced an increase in available pornography and a decrease in sexual crimes over the past 25 years, is a notable exception to the pornography-crime correlation.)

In another correlational study, Larry Baron and Murray Straus discovered that sexually explicit magazine sales in the 50 states correlated with state rape rates. After controlling for other factors, such as the percentage of young males in each state, the correlation remained. Alaska ranked first in sales of magazines like *Hustler* and first in rape. Nevada was second on both measures.

When interviewed, Canadian and American sex offenders commonly acknowledge pornography use (although not greater exposure during childhood and adolescence). Compared with men who are not sexual offenders, Ontario rapists and child molesters have been big customers of the pornography industry. The chief U.S. postal inspector, Kenneth Hunter, reports that "approximately 30 percent of the individuals we investigate for using the mails to traffic in child pornography are or have been involved in the sexual abuse of children." The Los Angeles Police Department reports that pornography was "conspicuously present" or used in 62 percent of its extrafamilial child sexual abuse cases during the 1980s. An FBI study also reports disproportionate pornography exposure among serial killers. Tragic examples abound, such as Milwaukee mass murderer Jeffrey Dahmer—in whose apartment police found pornographic tapes.

But are the sexual offenders merely, as sex researcher John Money has suspected, using pornography "as an alibi to explain to themselves and their captors what otherwise is inexplicable"? Ted Bundy, interviewed on the eve of his execution for a series of rape-murders, gave this explanation: "The most damaging kinds of pornography [involve] sexual violence. Like an addiction, you keep craving something that is harder, harder, something which, which gives you a greater sense of excitement. Until you reach a point where the pornography only goes so far, you reach that jumping off point where you begin to wonder if maybe actually doing it would give you that which is beyond just reading it or looking at it."

Bundy is at least right about this much: it's the violence more than the sex (whether in R-rated or X-rated films) that immediately increases men's aggression against women. Ed Donnerstein discovered as much when he showed 120 men at the University of Wisconsin a neutral, an erotic, or an aggressive-erotic (rape) film. Then the men, supposedly as part of another experiment, "taught" a male or female confederate (a supposed fellow subject) some nonsense syllables by choosing how much shock to administer for incorrect answers. Especially when angered, the men who had watched the rape film gave markedly stronger shocks—but only to female victims. (The researchers appreciated the ethical questions raised by pornography experiments, and afterward they worked to debunk any rape myths the films had communicated to the subjects, then gathered data that showed their debriefings were effective.) Based on such findings, the surgeon general's conference of 21 social scientists agreed that "in laboratory studies measuring short-term effects, exposure to violent pornography increases punitive behavior toward women." Nonviolent erotica between consenting partners has multiple other effects, but in the short run it seems not to make a man more violent or hurtful.

Television viewing experiments. Defenders of the cigarette and entertainment industries object that "mere correlations" can only *suggest* cause and effect. If you get sick after eating oysters, the oysters may or may not be responsible. No correlational study can eliminate the endless list of possible third factors that could conceivably create a merely coincidental relation between viewing violence and aggression (or between smoking and lung cancer). Fortunately, there is a simple way to control for extraneous factors. Randomly assign some children to watch violence and others nonviolence. Then observe their aggressiveness. If the two groups differ, it must be due to their one difference: what they watched.

Picture this scene from a trailblazing midcentury experiment by Stanford psychologist Albert Bandura. A nursery school child is at work on a picture. An adult in another part of the room is working with some Tinker Toys. The adult then gets up and for nearly 10 minutes pounds, kicks, and throws a large inflated doll around the room, yelling, "Sock him in the nose . . . Hit him down . . . Kick him."

After observing this outburst, the child is taken to another room where there are many appealing toys. Soon the experimenter interrupts the child's play and explains that she has decided to save these good toys "for the other children." She now takes the frustrated child to an adjacent room containing a few toys, including a similar doll. When left alone, compared with children not exposed to the adult model, children who observed the aggressive outburst were much more likely to lash out at the doll.

Soon after this experiment, social psychologists Leonard Berkowitz and Russell Geen extended the findings to university students. Angered students who had viewed a violent film acted more aggressively than similarly angered students who had viewed nonaggressive films. Such experiments, coupled with growing public concern about media mayhem, prompted the surgeon general to commission 50 new studies during the early 1970s. In congressional testimony, political scientist Ithiel de Sola Pool, a onetime critic of broadcast regulation, summed up the findings: "Twelve scientists of widely different views unanimously agreed that scientific evidence indicates that the viewing of television violence by young people causes them to behave more aggressively."

Skepticism nevertheless lingered, especially among media advocates who persisted in believing that people can purge their hostilities through viewing violence. "Watching action shows cannot only be cathartic, but can encourage play," offered Margaret Loesch, Fox Children's Network president. So psychologists ran more experiments. A research team led by Ross Parke in the United States and Jacques Leyens in Belgium gave institutionalized delinquent boys a "movie week" featuring either aggressive films (such as *Bonnie and Clyde*) or nonaggressive commercial films (such as *Lily*). Their consistent finding will stun few beyond Hollywood: compared with the preceding week, fights and attacks increased sharply among boys who saw the action films.

Informed by such experiments, a 1982 National Institute of Mental Health report echoed the surgeon general's 1972 report: "The consensus among most of the research community is that violence on television does lead to aggressive behavior by children and teenagers who watch the programs." Later statements by the American Psychological Association, American Medical Association, and American Pediatric Association concurred. To be sure, the aggression provoked in these brief experiments is not assault and battery. No one alleges that folks watch movies then grab their guns. The effect is more on the scale of a shove in the dinner line, a cruel comment, a threatening gesture. And, like the gradual toxic contamination of air and water, it accumulates to a cultural climate that fosters violence. "The irrefutable conclusion," said the American Psychological Association's 1993 youth violence report, "is that viewing violence increases violence."

For any lingering doubters, Chris Boyatzis and his colleagues recently reproduced the violence effect using television's most popular—and violent—children's program, *Power Rangers*. They showed an episode to some elementary school children but not others. Immediately after viewing the episode, the viewers committed seven times as many aggressive acts per two-minute interval as the nonviewers. As in Bandura's pioneering studies, the boy viewers often precisely duplicated the characters' acts, including their flying karate kicks. Like geologic erosion, such little effects can eventually produce big results. In Norway in 1994 a 5-year-old girl was stoned, kicked, and left to freeze in the snow by playmates imitating acts seen on the show—causing it to be banned by three Scandinavian countries.

Why watching violence affects behavior. Researchers now believe these effects stem from a combination of factors—from violence-related ideas (the social scripts mentioned earlier), from excitement and arousal, from the erosion of inhibitions, and from imitation.

Arousal can heighten aggression just as it heightens all forms of social behavior. Parents see the "emotional spillover" effect as their hyped-up children sometimes waver between anger, tears, and laughter. Dozens of experiments show that adults, too, can experience a stirred-up state as one emotion or another very different one, depending on how they interpret and label it; arousal from emotions as diverse as anger, fear, and sexual excitement can spill from one to another. The arousal that lingers after an intense argument or a frightening experience may intensify sexual passion. Insult people who have just been aroused by pedaling an exercise bike or watching an exciting film and they will find it easy to misattribute their arousal to the provocation. Their feelings of anger will then be greater than those of similarly provoked people who were not previously aroused.

Viewing violence also causes disinhibition. In Bandura's experiment, the adult's punching the doll seemed to legitimize such outbursts and to lower the children's inhibitions. As television primes violence-related thoughts, inner restraints dwindle.

As dramatically evident in the *Power Rangers* experiment, the media also evoke imitation, a phenomenon familiar to elementary and junior high teachers. By observing and imitating models we learn all kinds of social behaviors. To persuade children to smoke, expose them to older kids who smoke. To encourage reading, read to children and surround them with books and people who read. To increase the odds of your children practicing your religion, worship and attend other religious activities with them. We look and we learn.

By looking at media models, children may "learn" that physical intimidation is an effective way to control others, that free and easy sex brings pleasure without the misery of unwanted pregnancy or disease, or that men are supposed to be macho and women gentle and seductive. The television industry can hardly dispute the influence of models when it persuades advertisers to fork over $29 billion a year—much of it enticing our behavior with models who eat, drink, and drive their products.

Erotica and Sexual Behavior

Social scientists have focused mainly on Hollywood's violence, not its sex. So what about the sex? We noted earlier that saturation viewing of uncommitted sex alters people's perceptions of sexual reality, diminishes their attraction to comparatively less exciting partners, primes men's perception of women in sexual terms, makes sexual aggression seem less serious, and teaches "social scripts" that may later influence their behavior in real life situations.

But does it influence behavior? Does it play any part in the decline of marriage, the corruption of childhood, and the expansion of social chaos? Except for possible spillover from sexual arousal to hostility, explicit portrayals of impulsive sex seem not to directly cause violence. But do they help foster the social conditions, such as nonmarital childbearing and family fragmentation, that breed violence?

Sexual modeling. In 1896, a film called *The Kiss* outraged moral guardians by showing a couple stealing a quick kiss. "Absolutely disgusting," said one critic. "Such things call for police action." By the 1990s, prime-time network entertainment offered sexual remarks or behavior every four minutes. From their monitoring of network programs for Planned Parenthood, Louis Harris and Associates estimated that the average viewer witnesses 14,000 sexual events annually. Nearly all involve unmarried people. An analysis of one week of network prime-time TV found that intercourse was mentioned or intimated by unmarried couples 90 times and by married couples once. Rarely are there any consequences. No one gets herpes or AIDS. No one gets pregnant. No one has to change diapers, get up in the middle of the night, or heroically struggle to socialize a fatherless child. In fact, more than two-thirds of the time (in another analysis of 220 scenes of unmarried sex) the activity is portrayed as desirable, less than 10 percent of the time as undesirable.

Developmental psychologist David Elkind wonders also about teens' "constant exposure to sexually explicit rock lyrics." He illustrates with his 11-year-old niece and a friend, who easily listed sexual songs they were familiar with, including "Let's Talk About Sex," "I Wanna

Sex You Up," "I Want Your Sex." If imagination is insufficient, MTV visualizes such images with Janet Jackson, Madonna, Robert Kelly, and others gyrating simulated sex acts. So, also, do readily accessible R-rated movies featuring teens—in which unmarried sex partners outnumber the married by a 32 to 1 ratio.

In seeking to explain today's early age of first intercourse—which most women look back on with regret—one New Zealand research team points to media depictions "of sex as glamorous, pleasurable and adult, while negative consequences and the responsibilities involved in sexual relationships are seldom portrayed." "That's putting it mildly," reflected Jane Brody. "In a currently popular movie, 'Slums of Beverly Hills,' a precocious 13-year-old decides to have sex with an older boy 'just to get it over with.' Is this the message we want to convey to American youth," the normally dispassionate *New York Times* columnist wondered, "—that sex is something you try, like rollerblading or water skiing, to see what it's like or to add to your roster of achievements?"

With 68 percent of video rental shops offering sexually explicit tapes and with 9.8 million XXX Web pages to be found through Alta Vista, pornography also has become more accessible to all ages in all places. If you've ever wondered what these X-rated films depict, curious social scientists have sampled the fare and counted the behaviors. Some titles leave little room for wondering—*Kill the Bitch, Raped School Girls, Black Bitches in Bondage.* But others are more ambiguous. So Illinois psychologist David Duncan and his associates rented and watched 50 randomly selected "adult" videos from a local video store. The average video offered 18 scenes (activity sequences in a given context), ten containing explicit sex, one-fifth of which also contained violence and 30 percent of which contained acts of degradation.

Hans-Bernd Brosius and his colleagues did a similar but more detailed content analysis of 50 pornographic videos randomly drawn from an archive of all such materials targeted to German heterosexuals during the 1980s (most were produced in the United States). Four student coders counted everything you've ever wanted to know about such films. Two-thirds of scenes were devoted to sexual activity, usually involving nude partners, lasting an average 5.28 minutes. Like TV's population of sexually active people, only 6 percent were portrayed in a committed relationship such as marriage. Intercourse occurred in 61 percent of sex scenes, fellatio in 54 percent, and cunnilingus in 40 percent. Nearly always the scene ended with the male orgasm, which usually was displayed with semen ejaculated onto the woman's body or into her mouth. Only 1 percent of women and none of the men mentioned any use of contraceptives.

Given that a growing number of adolescents and young adults rely on pornography for sexual information, Brosius and his colleagues wondered about the effect of this sex education. This is what typically is shown:

> With only a minimal preamble, the viewer encounters the characters. They are strangers, or perhaps only recent acquaintances, who—overcome by their desire for sexual pleasure and abandon—embrace one another eagerly. She is young and blond; he is older and has dark hair. Consumed by their passion, there is no need for persuasion or coercion nor time to voice any concerns about contraceptive or "safer sex" practices. She seems to understand that their intercourse will be a hurried affair of less than six minutes and initiates the sexual actions by fondling his penis or kneeling before him to perform fellatio. With his urgent need readily apparent, they shun, or at least minimize, any reciprocal genital foreplay and quickly move to coitus. The camera focuses on her, providing only fleeting glimpses of him, except for his penis. She is enraptured by his sexual excitement and, ignoring her own sexual satisfaction, is very expressive as her utterances encourage him to climax. Then, almost as swiftly as it began, their rendezvous ends when, in the heat of their passion, he graphically displays his orgasm by depositing semen onto her belly. After the briefest pauses to establish that the characters have been fulfilled and are content, the viewer is rapidly propelled into another context where some variation of the same script is enacted by innumerable other women and men.

Cable TV offers some of the same scenarios, minus the genital views. In a few moments of channel surfing in my hotel recently I stumbled across HBO's offering of a woman masturbating to the point of pleading for sex from her surprised man of the moment, who obliged by removing her remaining clothing, fondling her breasts, and performing rear-entry intercourse to mutual orgasm—all in less than five minutes. Such depictions, from X-rated videos to cable TV movies, make it hard to dispute Susan Brownmiller's observation that pornography portrays women as "anonymous, panting playthings, adult toys, dehumanized objects to be used, abused, broken and discarded." For those not sated, HBO has also offered the home audience regular exploitative programs on the sex industry, including stripper shows and *Sex Bytes*, a "sizzling" new series—advertised as "for adults only"—that "takes you into the private lives of the people who parade their sexual practices on the Internet."

Catharsis? "Viewing a porno movie could have a beneficial effect that results in releasing the pent-up energy in a harmless manner," contends a letter writer to my local paper during a controversy over neighborhood pornography peddlers. Under Freud's lingering influence, he has much company. By nearly a 2 to 1 margin, Americans during the 1980s felt that "sexual materials provide an outlet for bottled-up impulses." As ACLU president Nadine Strossen explains, "Erotic publications and videos offer an alternative sexual outlet for people who otherwise would be driven to engage in psychologically or physically risky sexual relations" and thus "serve a positive public health function."

If Strossen's pop psychology idea is right, then Nevada, with its sex industries and high consumption of sex magazines, should have a low rape rate. And viewing pornography should at least temporarily lessen sexual arousal. But the opposite is plainly so. Sexually explicit videos are an aphrodisiac; they feed sexual fantasies that fuel a variety of sexual behaviors. In the hours after watching erotic films, people become more likely to engage in masturbation and intercourse. Moreover, reports William Griffitt, studies show "increases in the frequency of sex conversations, sex fantasies, sexual desires, and sexual dreams [occur] following exposure." This result perfectly parallels the finding that theater patrons interviewed after a violent action film express greater hostility than those interviewed beforehand. Viewing aggression and sex arouses rather than discharges pent-up impulses. Still, the catharsis legend persists. As John F. Kennedy said, the "great enemy of truth" is often not the deliberate lie but the persistent, persuasive myth.

The sexual climate. Social psychologists who have studied the recipe for sexual aggression identify two key ingredients, which Malamuth calls *hostile masculinity* and *promiscuous-impersonal sex*. What makes a man sexually aggressive is not a strong sex drive or abundant sexual fantasies; a man can have strong sexual urges yet restrain their expression in celibacy or a committed, loving relationship. What's explosive is a history of unrestricted sex with many different partners — a behavior pattern that puts stress on an ongoing relationship — combined with a defensive, hostile attitude toward women.

Many sexually aggressive men acquire their hostility growing up in macho cultures or a home marked by parental fights and child abuse. Where do they acquire their scripts for promiscuous, impersonal sex? We decry impersonal or exploitative sex, unprotected sex, and teen pregnancy and its associated social pathologies. Yet these are exactly what our current media fare gives us.

Film critic Michael Medved, for 12 years the host of *Sneak Previews* on PBS, says it is "appallingly illogical" to contend "that intensely sexual material does nothing to encourage promiscuity." Child advocate Edelman agrees: "Parents alone are not responsible for the perversions of family and community values today. . . . Telling our children to 'just say no' is hypocritical and useless while parent and other adult role models send cultural messages and provide examples that 'say yes.'" "Americans once expected parents to raise their children in accordance with the dominant cultural messages," reflects Ellen Goodman. "Today they are expected to raise their children in opposition."

Studies of children's capacity for "observational learning" make such concerns understandable. Moreover, the repeated, vivid, consistent portrayal of casual sexuality, uncontested by equally potent alternative sources of sexual information, make television an ideal medium for scripting children's future sexual behaviors. MTV understands this. MTV "is a cultural force," it declared in an *Adweek* advertisement. "People don't watch it. They live it. MTV has affected the way an entire generation thinks, talks and buys." MTV's former chairman Bob Pittman explained, "At MTV, we don't shoot for the 14-year-olds, we own them."

Still, when young copycats set fires using a lighter-and-aerosol-can technique from *Beavis and Butthead*, an MTV spokesperson denied it was the program's fault and wondered, "What were the parents doing?" Motion Picture Association president Jack Valenti also excuses his industry from responsibility: "It's up to the Congress to deal with the abrasions of person and spirit that cause mayhem in the streets and fear in the neighborhoods. We all know what they are and how hard they are to deal with: Poverty. Loss of hope and family ties. Easy access to weapons. Breakdown of discipline in schools. Slackening interest in church. The tattered, scattered remnants of old-fashioned words like honor, duty, pride, compassion, sacrifice, love."

All this is true, but it is rather like the cigarette industry's deflecting responsibility for cancer to asbestos, cyclamates, and old age. Moreover, Valenti's argument begs the big question: What accounts for this social corrosion—for nonmarital childbearing, the disintegration of families, and the associated social pathologies? Blame the mosquitoes if you want, but what feeds the swamps? Judith Harris's *Nurture Assumption,* whose evidence we examined in Chapter 4, helps make the media's parent-blaming rationalizations less credible and more blatantly irresponsible.

Where Do We Go from Here?

In 1992, an upset Texas dentist, Richard Neill, orchestrated a campaign to draw attention to the social deviance on after-school talk shows hosted by Phil Donahue and others. In response to the criticism, Donahue called Neill a censor and a zealot. Pressed by Dan Rather, Donahue asked rhetorically, "What kind of country do we want?"

"That *is* the question, all right," emphasized Newton Minow and Craig LaMay in *Abandoned in the Wasteland.* "Do we want to be the kind of nation, the kind of people, who abandon their children to a state of subhuman exploitation and regard them only as customers . . . ? Americans have never debated this question; rather, they have defaulted on it." We would never allow strangers to walk into our homes and parade antisocial behavior before our children and excite their avarice for three hours a day, Minow and LaMay argue. Yet when such strangers come via television we resign ourselves to what we feel helpless to control.

Minow and LaMay speak for countless outraged parents. When *USA Weekend* invited readers to respond to the statement "Hollywood no longer reflects—or even respects—the values of most American families," 21,221 callers called to register disagreement, and a record 54,453 callers registered agreement, not to mention 400,000 unsuccessful attempts to call the jammed "agree" line (as counted by phone company computers). In President Clinton's State of the Union address in 1995, the most applauded line was the one about the damage that "comes from the incessant, repetitive, mindless violence and irresponsible conduct that permeate our media all the time."

Although Phil Donahue acknowledges that "we've got a culture in decay" and trash talk pioneer Geraldo Rivera now is "sick of the garbage that is on," media executives and apologists typically respond by advising parents simply to press the off button. "If you don't like it, don't watch it—and don't interfere with my rights to watch it." "It is vitally important that we not interfere with the rights of those who like [trash television]," counseled Ann Landers.

Such advice is either naive or disingenuous. It overestimates parental influence and underestimates the power of the cultural winds. It is equivalent to saying, "If you don't like the air pollution, don't breathe." Even if one were willing to rebuff children's pleas to watch what their friends are watching, one cannot control what they see in their friends' homes, nor the promos they see hyping off-limits programs, nor the media effect—akin to secondhand smoke—transmitted through peer values and behavior. "Very few people can sustain values at a personal level when they are continually contradicted at work, at the store, in the government, and on television," observes Stephanie Coontz. "To call their failure to do so a family crisis is much like calling pneumonia a breathing crisis. Certainly, pneumonia affects people's ability to breathe easily, but telling them to start breathing properly again, or even instructing them in breathing techniques, is not going to cure the disease."

Indeed, it just doesn't do for cynical executives to lecture parents about family viewing policies while continuing to pollute the cultural atmosphere. "When Hollywood markets the worst and tells parents to do their best, it's like shooting holes in the family boat and telling us to keep plugging," writes Ellen Goodman. "There's a point at which you just sink." And that is why the new social ecology movement expects more.

Reforming the Media

My aim as a social psychologist is not to write laws, propose regulations, or set media policies but to inform the public debate. I do, however, recoil at three tired arguments opposing efforts at media reform.

Witless argument number one is to label critics as censors. Robert Dole may have been hypocritical in excluding Republican actors like Bruce Willis and Arnold Schwarzenegger from his list of those who "poison the minds of our young people . . . for the sake of corporate profits." But his hypocrisy is exceeded by the producers and actors who, rather than engage the debate, dismiss critics as McCarthyite censors. In 1992, when a group of women organized Turn Off the TV Day, National Television Association president Peter Chrisanthopoulos objected, "Participating in national boycotts is an infringement on the network's First Amendment rights." What lovely irony, note Minow and LaMay, "that the networks, having long insisted that a parent's only constitutional recourse was to turn off the set, now view even that act as unconstitutional." When media defenders "use the First Amendment to stop debate rather than to enhance it," they reduce "our first freedom to the logical equivalent of a suicide pact."

Critics who heap shame on producers and broadcasters also have been called censors. For advocating voluntary warning labels on rock albums, Tipper Gore was vilified and accused of supporting censorship. Ice Cube granted that "the editor of *Billboard* has a right to give his opinions" about misogynist, racist, violent rap lyrics. "But when he says . . . think twice before you buy this, that's a form of censorship." The CEO of Time Warner labeled public disgust at a cop-killing rap song an attack on free speech. But whenever critics find a book or film worthless or odious, they implicitly tell us, "Skip it." And they ask the producer, who can choose from 27,000 scripts registered each year with the Writer's Guild and from countless demo tapes offered by aspiring music groups, "Why did you pick this one?" "I don't know what a critic is supposed to be doing if he or she does not write in strong terms about strong dislikes," critic Roger Rosenblatt explains. "And if that's censorship, I'll eat my hat."

Witless reaction number two is to recycle the domino theory: if we give an inch, they'll take a mile. We heard this often during the Vietnam War: "If we don't stop Communism there, it may soon spread like cancer." Well, we didn't, and it hasn't. Libertarians of left and right also wing the theory with clichés about allowing in the thin edge of the wedge, admitting the camel's nose into the tent, and the start of a slippery slope. "Let environmental and safety nuts take the federal speed limit down to 55, and next they'll want 45." "Create a seven-day waiting period or a ban on AK-47s and before you know it they'll be coming for your hunting rifles." "Raise cigarette taxes and curtail smoking in public places and soon they'll be telling us what we can eat." Pass a law curtailing TV violence, warned People for the American Way, and "curfews, newspaper censorship, book burning," and the suspension of the Constitution are not far behind. Let the government require commercial Internet sites to block access to pornography by children (as under the 1998 Child On-Line Protection Act signed into law by President Clinton) and soon a police state will be censoring the free flow of ideas.

But reasonable laws—all of which restrain our freedom—seldom cascade us down a slippery slope or trip a line of dominoes. "Not every young woman who allows herself to be kissed before marriage ends up a hooker," Etzioni chides. Credit the American people with enough sense to draw lines that respect important rights while affirming social responsibilities. Censoring slander, false advertising, cigarette ads, and pornography from network TV has not threatened *Catcher in the Rye*'s place on my library's bookshelf, much less threatened what the First Amendment was intended to protect (the expression of ideas—what Justice Oliver Wendell Holmes called "freedom for the thought that we hate"). What has curtailing the rights of child pornographers done except make it more difficult to sell child pornography?

As these examples suggest, "censorship" is a red herring. In a 1995 *Time*/CNN poll only 27 percent of Americans favored "government censorship" of sex and violence, though 66 percent approved of "more restrictions on what is shown on television." Actually, nearly all Americans favor some forms of censorship, such as on child pornography or X-rated films on prime-time TV, while supporting the free press envisioned by Thomas Jefferson. Pornography has nothing to do "with the free speech intended by the Founding Fathers," Elizabeth Fox-Genovese argues. Rather than shut off debate with cries of "slippery slope" or "censorship," let's engage the debate—as we have with gun control, environmental legislation, and drug laws. Where should we draw the line in balancing individual and communal rights? Recognizing that our individualistic culture places the burden of proof on those who would restrain individual freedoms, what are the costs and the benefits of laws and regulations?

Witless argument number three implies that if a problem has multiple causes, there's no warrant for doing anything. Cancer is mostly caused by things other than cyclamates or secondhand smoke, so why control these? Murder and rape predate guns, which hardly account for most violence, so why control guns? The cultural crisis is not mostly the media's fault, so don't imagine that a television world featuring nonviolent conflict resolution and committed love will suddenly reduce assaults and teen births. Hollywood "is not responsible for creating the problems in our society," says filmmaker Oliver Stone. Such excuses, Senator Paul Simon replies, sound suspiciously "like the National Rifle Association: 'Guns don't kill people, people kill people. We don't cause violence in the world, we just reflect it.'" "Yes, many sex criminals possess and read sexually explicit materials," acknowledged a *New*

York Times editorial opposing a Pornography Victims' Compensation Act. But, the *Times* argued (mirroring the cigarette industry's pointing to healthy smokers), "so do millions of Americans who never commit crimes of any kind."

Well, yes, we'd best not oversimplify. But if we are confronted with a serious epidemic we'd also best not be apathetic. Although the Holocaust was not mostly due to degrading anti-Semitic media stories and images, the intimidated silence of most Germans in response to such degradation enabled the social cancer to grow. All that is needed for evil to spread is for good people to do nothing. When tolerance becomes indifference, evil is uncontested.

The parallels between libertarians who favor a broad First Amendment interpretation (called liberals) and libertarians who favor a broad Second Amendment interpretation (called conservatives) is striking. Communitarians respect the First Amendment but want it balanced with the Fourteenth Amendment's guarantee of equal protection for all (women and children included) and with the Constitution's priority on our general welfare: "We the People of the United States, in Order to . . . promote the general Welfare . . . establish this Constitution for the United States of America."

Although many conservatives decry current media fare, they have the vigorous deregulation policies of the Reagan administration to thank for today's profit-driven schlock. "The marketplace will take care of children," said Mark Fowler, President Reagan's FCC chair. If children would rather watch Jerry Springer than do homework, so be it. From an average 11 hours per week of educational programming in 1980, ABC, CBS, and NBC descended to one hour a week in 1992. "Virtually overnight," report Minow and LaMay, deregulation transformed broadcasting "from a public trust into one of the hottest businesses on Wall Street. In their celebration of the bottom line and their open contempt for traditional public-interest values, broadcasters began to restructure, dismantle, or simply abandon many of the features for which the public had admired them most—news divisions, children's programs, standards-and-practices departments. The number and volume of commercials increased, and broadcasters adopted an anything-goes programming policy."

Adam Smith would not have been astonished. He described profit-motivated businesspeople much as Bob Dole described Hollywood's corporate profiteers—as "an order of men, whose interest is never exactly the same with that of the public, who have generally an interest to deceive and even to oppress the public." *Christian Century* editor James Wall put it more bluntly: "The market is a monster without values, and it will do whatever is needed to make profits." We recognize that when we impose public interest obligations on the tobacco industry, the automobile industry, and to a lesser extent the entertainment industry. Civic-minded industrialists often welcome such obligations, which enable them to add air pollution controls knowing that their competitors must bear the same costs. Lacking a mandated level playing field, those who exploit the commons can defeat their more benevolent corporate rivals.

In considering restraints on either air or airwave pollution, we weigh the harm to corporate and personal rights against the harm to societal health. Most Americans give greater weight to First Amendment freedoms than Fourteenth Amendment equal protection, to individual rights than social responsibilities. But at some point on the perniciousness scale most of us become accepting of restraints on our freedom. We accept the restrictions of open housing laws that provide equal protection to people of all races. We accept some restrictions on hate speech or on gang members' rights to roam in packs carrying chains and tire irons.

Canadian law, however, gives greater priority to equal protection. In 1992, Canada's Supreme Court upheld an obscenity law suppressing materials that subordinate, degrade, or dehumanize women. Although Canada's 1982 Charter of Rights and Freedoms guarantees freedom of expression, the court decreed that the charter's strong equality section allows limits on materials that harm women personally, harm their rights to be equal, or influence attitudes that put them at risk. Canada therefore classifies degrading forms of pornography with smelly garbage or polluting factories or unleashed dogs—as something that merits regulation because it harms the community.

Not all morality should be legislated, but sometimes communities do affirm morality with laws. Laws help "convince citizens that the community is serious about its professed standards of responsibility," William Galston urges. "From drunk driving to racial discrimination, vigorous enforcement backed by sanctions has proved essential in changing behavior." Etzioni concurs: "Without punishing those who do serious injury to our commonly held values—child abusers, toxic polluters, fathers who renege on child support, corporations who market unsafe drugs—no moral order can be sustained. We do not have to love the coercive side of the law, but we cannot fail to recognize its place as a last resort."

Should we then enact laws to prohibit violent programming when children are a large part of the viewership? require broadcasters to label violent programs? require the FCC to establish violence standards that would be enforced as a condition of license renewal? require the FCC to issue quarterly TV violence reports, identifying sponsors of violent shows? Does it make sense, asks Harvard child psychiatrist Robert Coles, to tell the tobacco companies, "Don't poison people," and then to tolerate television's poisoning of our children's minds?

Content warnings clearly are an anemic response. Alerting teens to graphic programming tends, in fact, to tantalize them, Iowa State University researchers Brad Bushman and Angela Stack report; suggest parental or viewer discretion and they will be *more* likely to watch a movie. And a national survey in 1998 showed that most adults—even in homes with children—pay little attention to ratings like "TV-PG."

Short of censorship, there is another controversial policy option: empower citizens to hold the media legally responsible for their products' effects, just as citizens can hold drug or toy companies responsible. State lawsuits against tobacco companies and city lawsuits against firearms manufacturers—seeking recompense for the medical and law-enforcement costs of cigarettes and "unreasonably dangerous" weapons—illustrate efforts to hold corporations responsible for marketing products known to be harmful. If you produce and profit from, say, a sexually violent video—an illustrated how-to manual on sexual abuse—then anyone who believes she was victimized as a result of your product could try to prove a claim against you in court.

Lawyer-writer John Grisham agrees that product liability laws should extend to media merchants. After an acquaintance of his was gunned down by two people who had watched Oliver Stone's *Natural Born Killers* for the umpteenth time before the shooting, Grisham castigated Stone: "He's an *artist* and he can't be bothered with the effects of what he produces." But let him lose a product liability suit, "and the party will be over." Civil libertarians disagree. "I do not believe, for example, that publishers of how-to books for murderers, kidnappers and thieves should be held liable for the crimes of people who read them," says Wendy Kaminer. "And, when a woman is raped I would not impose any liability on the publisher of a violent, sexually explicit magazine enjoyed by her rapist. In order to protect the right to express unpopular, provocative views and political freedom, the First Amendment should effectively prohibit third-party liability in cases involving speech."

Empowering Parents

Another debated idea—now becoming a reality—is the violence-chip requirement incorporated into the 1996 telecommunications bill. When installed in every new set, the chip will allow parents to block programs carrying designated ratings. Although the networks have, for now, elected a movie-style rating system, the Electronic Industries Association, representing television manufacturers, promises a technology that could block shows with violence, sex, or profanity at various levels, perhaps rated 0 to 5. By dialing their V-chip to numbers of their choice, parents could admit only shows that meet their criteria. The technology is cheap—adding about a dollar to the cost of a new TV. It can be as kid-proof as a pin-numbered ATM card. And it involves no government censorship—no prior restraint.

The chip is no panacea. It doesn't directly modify programming. And most parents won't use it. But some will—enough, backers suspect, to make blocked programs less appealing to advertisers (some of whom will not wish to be associated with such programs), and enough, one infers from network reactions, to make the chip a perceived threat. For NBC general counsel Richard Cotton, "This legislation turns the FCC into Big Brother." CBS Broadcast Group's former president Howard Stringer worried that "the V chip is the thin end of a wedge. If you start putting chips in the television set to exclude things, it becomes an all-purpose hidden censor." "We see [a ratings system] as beginning down the slippery slope of censorship," said Marty Franks of CBS. "Quite frankly," fretted Fox Television chairwoman Lucie Salhany, "the very idea of a V-chip scares me. I'm also very concerned about setting a precedent. Will we have an 'S-chip' [for sex]?"

These reactions expose what Adam Smith, Bob Dole, and Newton Minow warned us to expect: that corporate concern for profits exceeds concern for the public interest. The cable industry, much of whose $38 billion income in 1996 came from viewer subscriptions, supported the V-chip. The major networks, whose money comes from advertisers, resisted the chip—despite its empowering parents to do more effectively just what the networks have long advised: use the off button. For that's all the chip is—an automated off switch, an intelligent remote control. If parents want to program their chip to block gratuitous sex— or sports or news, for that matter—why should they not be free to do so? When parental control over reception gets called "censorship," then we must wonder with Lewis Carroll's Alice about the wisdom of making a word "mean so many different things."

Awakening Public Awareness: The Gauche Factor

The state has *some* power to sway individuals' moral behavior. As the civil rights era (and countless social psychological experiments) have taught us, we can, to some extent, legislate morality. After the Supreme Court's school desegregation decision in 1954, the percentage of white Americans favoring integrated schools more than doubled, and now includes nearly everyone. In the decade following the Civil Rights Act of 1964, the number of white Americans who described their neighbors, friends, co-workers, and other students as all-white declined by about 20 percent each. During this period of increasing interracial behavior, the proportion of whites who said that blacks should be allowed to live in any neighborhood increased from 65 percent to 87 percent. Racial morality has been noticeably legislated. This illustrates why we are "a government of laws" and not just of individuals. Valuing our freedom, we want limits on the laws and regulations that constrain us. Valuing civility and order, we also welcome some agreed-upon rules.

But our great need today is much less for government censorship than corporate citizenship. Morality cannot depend primarily on government decree. Mostly, it grows from the culture's moral voice. Prohibition failed because it lacked a cultural mandate. Restrictions on smoking in public places are succeeding because a long period of conversation and education helped transform public consciousness.

Pleas to Hollywood have largely fallen on deaf ears. In a *U.S. News and World Report* poll, 83 percent of the public, but only 38 percent of the Hollywood elite, expressed concern about televised portrayals of premarital sex. The media culture that American parents want piped into their homes is not what the corporate world provides. But let's not discount the power of an awakened public consciousness.

- In the 1940s, movies often depicted African-Americans as childlike, superstitious buffoons. Today such images are not illegal, they are just gauche.

- In the 1960s and 1970s, entertainment from Beatles' music to *Easy Rider* glamorized drug use. Then, during the late 1970s and 1980s, the media responded to a tidal change in cultural attitudes. Schools undertook drug education programs and the entertainment industry began portraying drugs as dangerous. From 1978 to 1991 high school seniors acknowledging marijuana use in the previous 30 days dropped from 37 percent to 11 percent (and has since rebounded somewhat as the cultural voice has relaxed).

- Even once-common gratuitous smoking largely disappeared until recently. No more Humphrey Bogart or Hedy Lamarr dragging on a cigarette. Apart from the ban on TV advertising, we did not censor portrayals of smoking. Rather, health-conscious producers, writers, and actors simply chose not to model this form of slow-motion suicide. Thanks to the enlistment of the media and other institutions in a massive public health campaign, the number of smokers dropped from 43 percent in 1972 to 27 percent in 1996. But then, in the 1990s, Hollywood again began to glamorize smoking. With Winona Ryder, Sharon Stone, Bruce Willis, and John Travolta all looking cool or rebellious dragging on a cigarette, America's teens are getting the message and becoming nicotine addicted in increasing numbers. From 1991 to 1996, smoking 10th graders have increased from 21 percent to more than 30 percent. As Hollywood's smoking has risen, fallen, and risen again, so has teen smoking in its wake.

- Responding to increased public concern for animal rights, Hollywood now vouches for the humane treatment of animals in its films and avoids showing anything that would degrade them.

- In the face of growing public concern about violent media (80 percent of people tell Gallup there is "too much violence portrayed on television" and 76 percent think TV contributes to teen pregnancy) network television lowered its violence levels during the early 1990s, though continuing to increase its portrayal of uncommitted sex. (Incredibly, only 37 percent of Hollywood executives surveyed think TV contributes to teenage pregnancy.) Although violence is still common, especially in children's programming and on cable, foreplay is displacing gunplay. But that, too, may be changing. "In some cases, we could use a few more words between 'Hello' and 'Would you sleep with me?'" said NBC Entertainment president Scott Sassa in early 1999. In remarks to the Television Critics Association, Sassa also called for more two-parent families.

Ergo, an informed and aroused public voice gets heard.

The successes of the public health campaigns to reduce drug and cigarette use suggest a two-pronged effort. First, parents, schools, and churches can offer children media awareness education. Second, we can all work to increase public consciousness of the media's part in the cultural crisis, with the aim of making barbarism and impulsive promiscuity as gauche tomorrow as racial degradation is today. Better yet, we can hope for a new generation of creative artists who will do as Joan Baez, Pete Seeger, and Peter, Paul, and Mary did in their music for the civil rights movement—give us soul-stirring songs that challenge lovelessness, greed, exploitation, and degradation and offer images of a more nurturing, selfless, spiritually sensitive, and joyful world.

Media awareness education. Parents can increase their children's media literacy. The American Psychological Association advises parents to limit their children's TV watching. Step one for any parent should be to end—right now—the increasingly common but irresponsible practice of placing televisions in children's bedrooms. Second, parents can watch programs with their children and discuss the social scripts. The cable television industry's "Voices Against Violence" initiative urges parents to "kick the glamour out of violence" by talking about it. Ask children: How would you feel if that happened to you? Could this stuff really happen—no blood on the floor, no problem jumping back up after being clobbered with a two-by-four or beaten with fists? Could this problem have been solved in some other way?

Of course, the cable industry telling us to take the glamour out of the violence they pipe into our homes is like the water department sending us polluted water with instructions on how to detoxify it. Doubting that the networks would ever "face the facts and change their programming," Eron and Huesmann taught Chicago-area children that television portrays an unreal world, that aggression is less common and effective than TV makes it seem, and that violence is wrong. When restudied two years later, these children were less influenced by violence they watched than were untrained children.

Researchers have also studied how to immunize young children so they can more effectively analyze and evaluate television commercials. This research was prompted partly by studies showing that children, especially those under 8, have trouble distinguishing commercials from programs and fail to grasp their persuasive intent, trust television advertising rather indiscriminately, and desire and badger their parents for advertised products—a finding that will astonish few parents. Children, it seems, are an advertiser's dream: gullible, vulnerable, an easy sell. Moreover, half the 20,000 ads the typical child sees in a year are for low-nutrition, often sugary foods.

Armed with such data, citizens' groups have given the advertisers of such products a chewing out: "When a sophisticated advertiser spends millions to sell unsophisticated, trusting children an unhealthy product, this can only be called exploitation. No wonder the consumption of dairy products has declined since the start of television, while soft-drink consumption has almost doubled." On the other side are the commercial interests, who claim that such ads allow parents to teach their children consumer skills and, more important, finance children's television programs. In the United States, the Federal Trade Commission has been in the middle, pushed by research findings and political pressures while trying to decide whether to place new constraints on TV ads aimed at young children.

Meanwhile, researchers have wondered whether children can be taught to resist deceptive ads. In one such effort, a team of investigators led by Norma Feshbach gave small groups of Los Angeles–area elementary school children three half-hour lessons in analyzing commercials. The children were inoculated by viewing ads and discussing them. After watching a toy ad, for example, they were immediately given the toy and challenged to make it do what they had just seen in the commercial. Such experiences helped breed a more realistic understanding of commercials.

Encouraged by such findings, a report of the Carnegie Council on Adolescent Development in 1995 urged schools "to introduce instruction and activities that contribute to media literacy." Britain, Canada, Australia, and Spain already require media literacy as part of their language arts programs. In the United States, media literacy education— supported by such organizations as the Center for Media Literacy— is in its infancy. But already New Mexico and North Carolina have included it as a basic skill in their curricula, as has the Girl Scouts, which offers three media literacy and communications badges.

Spurring a culture shift. The fundamental question for our time is what kind of culture do we want? Is it the culture we have—and were moving toward from 1960 to the early 1990s?

Of all the world's creatures, we humans are the most impressionable—the most capable of learning. That breeds hope, for what is learnable we can potentially teach. And it breeds concern, for the same potential puts us at risk for learning evil. The media's power is not intrinsically good or bad. It is like nuclear power, which can light up homes or wipe out cities. It is like persuasive power that enables us to enlighten or deceive. So how can we harness media power for good rather than evil, to create a culture we will love rather than loathe?

The answer surely will involve waving some cultural sticks. TV networks and film producers are legally free to recreate a racist Amos 'n Andy for the late 1990s, or to display anti-Semitism or celebrate gay bashing or animal torture. But they know that any bigot who did so would face moral outrage, advertiser boycott, and ultimate financial ruin. We the people are not powerless. When the revolted revolt, their voices get heard.

Of late, the revolted have spanned the political spectrum. Peggy Noonan, the former speechwriter for President Reagan, responding to rock and rap videos, heaps shame on all involved: "Really, you have to be a moral retard not to know that this is harmful, that it damages the young, the unsteady, the unfinished. You have to not care about anyone."

Marian Wright Edelman blames the moral insensitivity of the rich and famous: "If it's wrong for 13-year-old inner-city girls to have babies without the benefit of marriage, it's wrong for rich celebrities!"

Hillary Clinton has described herself as "appalled" by today's media models. Her husband, in "asking the entertainment community to reexamine itself [and its] enormous capacity to influence opinion," argued that "there's no question the cumulative impact of this banalization of sex and violence in the popular culture is a net negative for America."

Then there is liberal Democrat C. DeLores Tucker, leader of the National Political Congress of Black Women, and conservative Republican William Bennett, neither of whom are inclined to enable evil by saying nothing. After Tucker became aware of genocidal gangsta rap lyrics—"I'm thinking rape. . . . Slit her throat and watch her shake"— she bought ten shares of stock in Time Warner, which owned half of Interscope Records. At the annual meeting, she distributed lyrics and urged Time Warner executives to recite them. They didn't, but they agreed to a meeting.

A day after Tucker and Bennett met with the executives, Bennett recounted the conversation for the 1995 White House Conference on Character Building for a Democratic Civil Society. Tucker and Bennett reminded the executives of the mind-shaping power of the models children spend their time with, and asked them to read the lyrics their company was publishing—depicting sexual abuse, rape, dismemberment, and murder. When the executives again demurred, Tucker read them, then asked, "What do you think?" "That's a tough one," came the reply. "Baloney," responded Bennett, whereupon one of the executives stood up and said, "I'm not going to sit here and listen to that kind of language." Appealing to their corporate conscience, Bennett asked, "Do you have a bottom line—something you wouldn't put out?" The executives collectively could think of one rejection, an album celebrating serial killing with art by a serial killer. Fellow capitalist Bennett was heard to wonder, are these profiteers "morally disabled?"

The result of this well-publicized shaming was an embarrassed Time Warner divesting itself of Interscope (although not the pornography channels on its cable systems or other productions that would make *Time* co-founder Henry Luce roll over in his grave). Similar outrage over trash talk TV has led to lost advertising revenues and the cancellation of some shows. In late 1998, a new Forum for Responsible Advertisers—including Johnson & Johnson, Procter & Gamble, Ford, and Sears—convened to talk about ways they could use their advertising clout to promote high-quality, family-friendly programming. This is not censorship—just the economic stick of the marketplace wielded with the moral voice of the community.

The culture shift must also involve an offering of carrots. "For 30 years, our families have been under assault," President Clinton declared in a talk to 500 Hollywood executives, producers, directors, and stars. "We have to have the help of the people who determine our culture." That needn't mean projecting an unvarying image of the middle-class average to small, sleepy audiences. The successes of the *Cosby Show* in the 1980s and *Home Improvement* in the 1990s demonstrate that profits and principles can coexist.

The carrots include not only patronage of prosocial entertainment but resources that support positive programming. The presidents of the American Psychological Association, American Academy of Pediatrics, and American Psychiatric Association have written to 125 entertainment industry leaders offering assistance in understanding and reducing the harmful effects of media violence. Mediascope, an outgrowth of meetings sponsored by the Carnegie Council on Adolescent

Development, offers curricular materials for workshops and courses taken by moviemaking students.

Everything has changed, said Albert Einstein after Hiroshima and Nagasaki—except the way we think. Everything has changed again in the half century since. We enjoy unprecedented affluence and technology—with vastly expanded cable television and Internet options on the immediate horizon. Meanwhile, we have acquiesced to media models that demonstrably feed the cultural corrosion. We needn't be right-wing, anti-sex, or pro-censorship to wonder whether we cannot better balance individual liberties with social responsibility. We needn't be antibusiness to observe that there is profit to be made in the collapse of civilization. We needn't devalue the Bill of Rights to hope that, as we now look back with chagrin on degrading racial images, we might someday also look back on the time when money-grubbing film, television, and music industries entertained us with social scripts of sexual exploitation and human mutilation and annihilation. In the meantime, can we not—without violating true artistic freedom—ask our filmmakers, script writers, theater owners, advertisers, video store owners, and all the other cogs in the media monster machine: is the money really worth it?

In C. S. Lewis's *Screwtape Letters,* senior devil Screwtape counsels junior devil Wormwood, "The safest road to hell is the gradual one." As so many social psychology experiments demonstrate, succumbing to little evils paves the way for bigger ones. In complex societies, too, big evils are built of little evils. Nazi leaders were surprised at how easily they got German civil servants to handle the paperwork of the Holocaust. They were not killing Jews, of course. They were merely pushing paper. And so it is in our daily lives: the drift toward evil occurs in small steps, without any conscious intent and even without perceiving ourselves as cogs in an evil process. So it happens that nice people, good people, enable the social recession that, in the end, devastates so many lives. Can we awaken from their moral slumber those who, whether celebrities or clerks, film producers or ticket takers, conspire to define the popular culture? Must we wait, asks commentator Gregg Easterbrook, until a teenager guns down the children of studio executives in a Bel Air or Westwood high school?

Could we agree on a voluntary code declaring: "Broadcasters have a special responsibility toward children. Programs should contribute to the sound, balanced development of children. Programs involving violence should present the consequences of it to its victims and perpetrators." We have done it before. Those words are excerpted from the National Association of Broadcasters' voluntary code, abandoned in 1983—"a powerful statement of citizenship and community responsibility," according to Senator Joseph Lieberman.

And can we humanize the next generation's awareness of the real human costs of violence and impulsive or coercive sex? Can we create a culture that values kindness and civility, attachment and fidelity—a culture of commitment? "Our utopian and perhaps naive hope," say media researchers Edward Donnerstein, Daniel Linz, and Steven Penrod, "is that in the end the truth revealed through good science will prevail and the public will be convinced that these images not only demean those portrayed but also those who view them."

CHAPTER 9

Educating for a Moral Compass

> If there be righteousness in the heart,
>   there will be beauty in character.
> If there be beauty in character,
>   there will be harmony in the home.
> If there be harmony in the home,
>   there will be order in the nation.
> If there be order in the nation,
>   there will be peace in the world.
> —CONFUCIUS, *Book of Rites*

Informed people argue causes and solutions, but they no longer dispute the facts. Since 1960, Americans have been soaring materially and, until recently, sinking socially. We enjoy unprecedented peace and prosperity, liberty and longevity, technology and tolerance. We fly places we used to drive, e-mail those we used to hand write, and enjoy air-conditioned comfort where we used to swelter. And we have more children of children, more suicidal and violent teens, more demoralized and incarcerated adults, diminished civility and trust, and fewer and unhappier marriages. Voila, the American paradox.

We can attribute the social recession partly to an extreme individualism that feeds an increasing rich-poor gap and defends media models that subtly script our ideas of how to solve conflicts and relate to the other sex. And we can therefore understand that renewal requires better balancing our individualism with communitarian values, and replacing media models of barbarity and self-indulgence with models appropriate to a culture of commitment. But such a culture shift also requires a new social consciousness. To have an impact on the culture — to become the new social ecology movement — this new consciousness must feed and be fed by renewed character education in America's schools.

The Roots of Character Education

There are two restraints on evil, two reasons why citizens do good rather than bad. One is internal character, informed by a community's moral voice. The other is external rules, policed by government. More than any other form of government, James Madison argued, democracy presupposes an internal gyroscope that we call self-control. Democracy recognizes that government has insufficient carrots and sticks to make everyone act right. When the heavy hand of the state relaxed in Russia, the depleted moral infrastructure enabled increased crime. The Declaration of Independence proclaimed our rights, says James Q. Wilson, and assumed our morality. The Constitution likewise assumed that family and village life would mold character. "To educate a man in mind and not morals is to educate a menace to society," surmised Theodore Roosevelt.

If most people do not police themselves, from the inside out, we are in trouble. We can allocate yet another $30 billion to police and prisons, but no amount of money can coerce virtue. Nor do we wish for a police state, with several million officers controlling the other 275 million of us. "Only a virtuous people are capable of freedom," observed Benjamin Franklin. Freedom depends on character—on what character educator Thomas Lickona calls people's "knowing the good, loving the good, and doing the good."

For Aristotle, character was virtues—habits of the heart developed through virtuous behavior. We develop self-control as we choose to exercise self-control. For most of Western history since Aristotle, one of education's major goals has been the teaching of virtue by helping students understand, desire, and act upon consensus values. "If you ask what is the good of education," said Aristotle's teacher, Plato, "the answer is easy—that education makes good men, and that good men act nobly."

When education does not concern itself with the good, the results may be bad. Of the 14 men who attended the January 1942 Wannsee Conference and formulated the Holocaust's Final Solution, 8 had European university doctorates. And more than a few of their subordinates returned home after a day's work in the death camps to enjoy their classical music. Concluding a Harvard lecture more than 150 years ago, Ralph Waldo Emerson was prophetic: "Character is higher than intellect."

The belief that democracies needed to teach children values necessary for citizenship was an important rationale for mandatory schooling. William McGuffey's 19th century readers, which sold 122 million copies and were read by 4 in 5 schoolchildren during the 1800s and early 1900s, unabashedly offered stories featuring consensus virtues. Through "The Greedy Girl," "Advantages of Industry," and "Religion, the Only Basis of Society," McGuffey conveyed the values of middle-class America. Education's aim was not just to teach knowledge but to forge character. A teacher's mission was to help their children become both smart and good. Let such education lapse for one generation, H. Richard Niebuhr wrote, "and the whole grand structure of past achievements falls into ruins."

In England and Wales, the rate of serious criminal offenses more than tripled during the first half of the 19th century, then dropped by two-thirds during the Victorian era in the last half of the century. "The essential change that took place was a matter of values," reports Francis Fukuyama. "At the core of Victorian morality was the inculcation of impulse control in young people," aided by religion. "Victorianism was closely allied with Protestantism."

During the 20th century, as we became more culturally and religiously diverse, educators found it more difficult to proclaim the non-denominational Protestant values embraced by the previous century's curriculum. We also became aware that morality may vary with culture. This awareness led a National Education Association character education report in 1932 to ask, "Who are we, that we should attempt to tell you what you should do in order to be good?"

By the 1960s, such questions were everywhere: Is there an absolute right and wrong? Are all cultures, and their values, moral equals? Does someone have a right to presume moral judgments — and impose them on our children? Should we instead merely help students wrestle with moral dilemmas and clarify their personal values? Or, despairing of any consensus, should we avoid the subject, leaving values, virtues, and character to the home?

As we lost our resolve to teach shared values, character itself waned during the social recession. Schools took on driver education and let go of character education. "We are failing to contribute morality to the next generation and that failure is at the epicenter of our problem," declared William Galston. The current state of today's moral values is "somewhat weak" or "very weak," 78 percent of Americans lamented in a 1996 Gallup survey.

They may be right. Two-thirds of a recent national sample of high-achieving seniors in high school acknowledged copying someone else's homework, and 40 percent confessed to cheating on a quiz or test. Among a broader national sample of 10,000 high school students surveyed in 1998 by the Josephson Institute for Ethics, 70 percent admitted to cheating on an exam and 47 percent to stealing from a store in the previous year (both up from a 1992 survey). Other surveys of high school seniors reveal that the proportion who have used a cheat sheet on a test increased from 1 in 3 in 1969 to 2 in 3 in 1989. In a 1995 survey of 4,300 students at highly selective colleges, nearly two-thirds admitted to "serious" cheating on a test or written assignment. In and out of schools, civility also has waned. Los Angeles–area history teacher Connie Shepard recalls that two decades ago students responded to her "Good morning, class" with "Good morning, Miss Landers." When she recently reentered the classroom, a freckle-faced, red-haired 16-year-old responded, "Shut the f—— up, you bitch." "Value-free" education, some argue, produced value-free students.

Can We *Not* Teach Values?

But can education ever be value free? Louis Raths, Merrill Harmin, and Sidney Simon thought so. In their 1966 book *Values and Teaching,* they cautioned teachers against "moralizing, criticizing, giving values, or evaluating [or giving] hints of 'good' or 'right' or 'acceptable.'" Instead, their values-clarification approach encouraged children to choose their values, prize whatever they chose, and act accordingly. In one New Jersey high school, 15 students decided that a girl had been foolish to return $1,000 found in a purse. The counselor who led the discussion supported the girl's decision but was careful not to intrude his values. "If I come from the position of what is right and what is wrong, then I'm not their counselor," he explained to a reporter. One could hardly imagine a values education strategy more expressive of radical American individualism.

"This bit of pedagogical idiocy . . . was so at odds with common sense and the requirements of everyday life," said Wilson, "that, not surprisingly, it fell into disrepute in many quarters." Although values clarification does encourage children to align their actions with their attitudes, Harmin later granted that "our emphasis on value neutrality probably did undermine traditional morality. . . . As I look back, it would have been better had we presented a more balanced picture, had we emphasized the importance of helping students both to clarify their own personal values *and* to adopt society's moral values."

Nevertheless, individualism and relativism survive in college students' doubting the superiority of any values or morality. They have learned not to indoctrinate, not to force their values on anyone else, not to judge cultural practices they do not understand. As the New York State Regents' policy declares, each student should learn to respect and accept the "values, beliefs, and attitudes" of people who differ. Behaviors that may be wrong for me or in my culture may be right for you or in your culture.

Tolerance and respect for diversity *are* virtues (ones I implicitly promote in my own psychology texts). But are there not some core values that we do not wish to leave to personal choice? If people in another culture practice cannibalism, slavery, genocide, or clitoridectomy, is there no foundation for believing such practices are inhumane? Other countries as varying as Sweden, Japan, and Russia are not bashful about identifying and teaching their national values. Tolerance, argues Galston, "is fully compatible with the proposition that some ways of life can be known to be superior to others. It rests . . . on education or persuasion rather than coercion."

Moreover, our schools are hardly value free. In psychologist Lawrence Kohlberg's scheme of moral development, the "highest" or most "mature" stage was a morality of self-defined ethical principles (a stage we can guide children toward, it is said, by having them discuss moral dilemmas). But isn't it curious, said feminist critics, how similar this supposed moral pinnacle is to the morality of a typical individualistic Western male college professor such as Kohlberg himself? Were not his values biased against the sort of moral reasoning one finds in the communal societies of Asia and the Third World and in women, whose morality often is less a matter of abstract, impersonal principles and more a matter of caring relationships?

When accused of similarly sneaking values into my psychology textbooks, I plead guilty. My values leak through whenever I choose topics, emphases, and examples. Consider the values hidden in our labels:

Should I call sexually restrained people "erotophobic" or "sexually conservative"? Should I congratulate socially responsive people for their "social sensitivity" or disparage them for their tractable "conformity"? (Which label would you guess is preferred by psychologist-writers in our individualistic culture?)

My values guide my efforts to cultivate a sense of wonder, an attitude that respects the human creature and regards it with awe (and not as a mere machine). My values also leak through my decisions to give significant attention to topics such as cultural diversity, gender and racial prejudice, altruism, violence, individualism, peacemaking, pride, and sex and human values. If I evaded these topics I would still be making value-laden decisions. Even "active listening" and "nondirective" therapy subtly steer people in certain directions. Neutrality is impossible.

Ergo, teaching is not dispassionate. Our assumed ideas and values guide our theorizing, our interpretations, our topics of choice, and our words. In deciding what to report and how to report it, our sympathies subtly steer us. We psychology authors and teachers should, of course, remember that our books are not op-ed columns and our lecterns are not pulpits. And we must have the courage to let the chips fall where they may, even if data on sexual orientation make conservatives uncomfortable, even if data on media effects make liberals uncomfortable, and even if data from tests of parapsychological claims make New Age spiritualists uncomfortable. Still, we cannot leave our values at home.

Teachers and writers therefore needn't apologize for having deeply held convictions and values. Indeed, our values are what motivate and direct our efforts. Theologian Robert McAfee Brown says, "Beyond all rewards . . . *we write* [and teach] *because we want to change things.* We write because we have this [conviction that we] can make a difference." What greater life mission could I hope for than to do my little part, through the teaching of psychology, to restrain intuition with critical thinking, judgmentalism with compassion, and illusion with understanding? Values likewise motivate and penetrate public school teachers' story choices, disciplinary responses, and personal attitudes.

That being so, why not be open and intentional about the whole process? Why not identify and acknowledge the values we implicitly communicate and ask whether those are the values we as a community *want* to teach? Without discounting minority views, why not ask Phil

Donahue's question—What kind of country (and community) do we want?—and seek consensus on values that will take us there?

Whose Values?

"I challenge all our schools to teach character education, to teach good values and good citizenship," said President Clinton in his 1996 State of the Union address. The president was perhaps mindful of the ancient wisdom of Proverbs: "Train children in the right way, and when old, they will not stray." We can all agree with the president that a democratic civil society requires that we share some values. But then comes the inevitable question: whose values? Does the majority rule—tough luck to any minority views?

Character educators report that when diverse segments of a community come together for dialogue, workable agreements on "core values" often result. Although fundamentalists and feminists will differ on some issues, organized community dialogues typically reveal shared values that all can endorse. Three in four Americans, regardless of gender and race, agree that traditional values have grown weaker and need strengthening. In Fayetteville, North Carolina, 700 interested people gathered in a school gym to decide on what values to teach. By the end, there was consensus on seven core values that the community as a whole now solidly supports. In Colorado Springs, Antelope Trails Elementary School, which includes children from 80 religious groups including families associated with nearby Focus on the Family, has achieved broad parental support for its schoolwide character education program. In *The Youth Charter: How Communities Can Work Together to Raise Standards for All Our Children,* Stanford adolescence researcher William Damon describes a process by which whole communities can come together to hammer out principles that will guide their rearing and educating of children and youth.

The agreement should not surprise us. We saw in Chapter 4 that single, divorced, and married parents want the same things for their children. A Gallup poll in 1993 found that more than 9 in 10 parents supported schools teaching such values as the Golden Rule, caring, and racial tolerance. The teaching of honesty was endorsed by 97 percent. A follow-up poll in 1996 found more than 9 in 10 Americans supporting public schools teaching respect for others, hard work, persistence, fairness, compassion, and civility and politeness. Even most hardened criminals want their children to be good and would be "very angry" if their son or daughter committed a criminal offense.

Despite differing beliefs, faith traditions, too, share many values. In *The Abolition of Man,* C. S. Lewis in 1947 identified the morality—the seeming "natural law"—shared by the world's cultural and religious traditions. From the world's storehouse of moral stories, William Bennett discerned ten universal values (self-discipline, compassion, responsibility, friendship, work, courage, perseverance, honesty, loyalty, and faith), which he discussed in *The Book of Virtues.* The 1993 Parliament of the World's Religions affirmed "that a common set of core values is found in the teaching of the religions, and that these form the basis of a global ethic." The global ethic statement condemned "aggression and hatred," declaring, "We must treat others as we wish others to treat us. . . . We consider humankind our family. We must strive to be kind and generous. We must not live for ourselves alone, but should also serve others, never forgetting the children, the aged, the poor, the suffering, the disabled, the refugees, and the lonely." No matter what your faith tradition, those words should have a familiar ring.

The Character Counts Coalition—an alliance of almost 100 organizations representing more than 40 million Americans—offers teaching materials for six core values, called "Six Pillars of Character." These emerged from three days of discourse at a conference in 1992, where a diverse group of educators, youth leaders, and ethicists forged a consensus that a person of character

- is trustworthy (honest, promise-keeper, loyal, has integrity),
- treats people with respect (courteous, nonviolent, non-prejudiced, accepting),
- is responsible (accountable, pursues excellence, self-restrained),
- is fair (just, equitable, open, reasonable, unbiased),
- is caring (kind, compassionate, empathic, unselfish), and
- is a good citizen (law-abiding, community servant, protective of environment).

This common language—agreed upon by conservatives and liberals, religious and nonreligious leaders—has been adopted in presidential and congressional proclamations and by 38 state governors and more than 375 communities. Across our diversity, there is unity: It is better for children to resolve disputes with words than fists, better to be honest than cheat, better to be disciplined than indolent, better to be caring than self-centered. It would be a better world, we can all agree, if all children could be taught empathy for other's feelings and the self-discipline needed to restrain their impulses, to delay small gratifications now for the sake of bigger ones later. Studies show that those who learn to delay gratification become more socially responsible, academically successful, and productive.

Character Education Partnership of Alexandria, Virginia, has assembled a variety of resources for teaching character. These have been developed by such organizations as the American Institute for Character Education, the Center for the Advancement of Ethics and Character, the Center for Character Education, the Jefferson Center for Character Education, the Josephson Institute of Ethics, and the Personal Responsibility Education Program. Thanks to U.S. Department of Education grants in 1995 and 1996 for statewide character education initiatives, such programs are spreading and national surveys reveal more and more school districts involved. Forty-eight states have or are completing character education standards. Maryland, for example, calls for each of its schools to "exemplify a community of virtue in which respect, responsibility, hard work, caring, fairness, trustworthiness, and service learning are regularly modeled, expected, celebrated and taught as an integral part of the curriculum and daily school operation."

In Britain, too, "moral education" is fast becoming a national priority. Assisted by working groups with 200 advisers, the School Curriculum and Assessment Authority is proposing "greater emphasis on spiritual and moral development in teacher training and a national review of personal and social education in schools."

Anecdotes abound of the programs' positive impact. "I can see the changes in children's behavior," said a principal of one school after introducing character education. "There has definitely been a decrease in scuffling and fighting in the halls and the lunchroom." Principals who have used American Institute for Character Education materials report better attendance, improved student-teacher relationships, decreased vandalism, and improved classroom attitude.

Character educators believe that the most effective programs occur not just as occasional lessons and discussions but as comprehensive programs that engage "schools as moral communities." Such schools make moral development part of their mission. They train staff how to respond to negative behaviors. They offer school and community service opportunities. They engage children in cooperative learning activities. They have children read literature that portrays core values. They teach self-discipline, citizenship, and teamwork through their sports programs. And they evaluate teachers' effectiveness in teaching both academics and character. In *Educating for Character* and elsewhere Thomas Lickona offers a gold mine of examples:

- Molly Angelini expects courtesy from her students. If a student calls a classmate a name, she requires a written apology. When her students go to lunch, she has them greet the cafeteria workers by name and thank them as food is given them. In such ways, she aims to teach habits that show other humans respect.
- On the first day of school, Kim McConnel puts her 6th graders in groups of four to decide rules that will help the class get work done, feel safe, and "be glad we're here." After taping lists of suggested rules on the blackboard, McConnel helps the class distill "our class rules."
- The multicultural Heartwood Ethics Curriculum for Children affirms diversity *and* shared values through folk tales, legends, heroic stories, and modern classics from cultures around the world—focused, successively, on courage, loyalty, justice, respect, hope, honesty, and love. When the class finishes studying a particular character attribute, each child looks in the class mirror, asks if they have shown that attribute, and then writes a personal answer in a journal.
- One Chicago-area elementary school, troubled by fights, put-downs, and smart-mouth talk to teachers ("I don't have to listen to you!"), undertook a schoolwide "Let's Be Courteous, Let's Be Caring" initiative. A display inside the school entrance defined courtesy as saying please, thank you, you're welcome, and excuse me, being a good listener, waiting your turn, acting politely, and discussing problems. Caring was sharing, respecting others' feelings, following rules, working cooperatively, and being a good friend. These values were reinforced through photo displays, class discussions, conversations, assemblies, awards, service projects, and parent-teacher conferences. The result? Fights became rare, sharing in the lunchroom became common, a new teacher from another school was struck by the high level of respect for others, and the school received an award for excellence in both academic achievement and character development.
- Oakland, California, tested its character development program in a way that more projects should: by comparing three elementary schools in which it was implemented with three in which it was not. Through collaborative learning, the teaching of prosocial literature, a peer Buddies Program, and family-night activities, the program aims to in-

crease cooperation, friendliness, and social involvement. Outside observers not told who had participated evaluated the participants as more cooperative and friendly. And when these kids entered middle school, they displayed more self-esteem and were more active in extracurricular activities.

Many more positive examples can be found in the 1998 *Schools of Character* brochure, codeveloped by McGraw-Hill and the Character Education Partnership, and in the John Templeton Foundation's annual *Honor Roll for Character-Building Colleges.*

One subset of character education programs focuses on teaching conflict resolution and violence prevention skills to delinquent or at-risk children and youth. Counseling programs that aim to give juvenile delinquents greater insight, reported Vanderbilt University researcher Mark Lipsey after reviewing almost 500 studies of delinquency prevention, typically have little benefit beyond producing "more insightful juvenile delinquents." That may be because, as the late Barbara Jordan said, crime is a "deficit in values." Programs oriented to teaching values and social skills do more to reduce rearrest rates. Some examples:

- Aggression Replacement Training, developed by Arnold Goldstein at Syracuse University, provides schoolchildren and gang members with a 32-session program with three components: skillstreaming, which uses modeling, role playing, and skill homework to teach students how to resolve conflicts without fights; anger control, which teaches ways to deal with angry feelings; and moral reasoning, which raises awareness of justice, fairness, and concern for others' needs and rights.
- The Violence Prevention Curriculum for Adolescents, developed by Harvard psychiatrist Deborah Prothrow-Stith, uses peer mentoring, leadership training, and conflict resolution sessions to teach social skills lacking in students who pick fights or get picked on.
- A school-based bullying reduction program, developed by Dan Olweus at Norway's University of Bergen, uses supervision, rules, class discussions, and talks with parents and students. After 2,500 11- to 14-year-olds finished the program, Olweus found "marked reductions — by 50 percent or more — in bully-victims problems."
- Aided by a $600,000 federal grant in 1996, psychologist W. Rodney Hammond is establishing a training center for school-based violence prevention programs. Hammond will prepare other professionals to train teachers in how to teach youths to manage anger and conflicts.
- The Resolving Conflict Creatively Program, a K–12 violence prevention curriculum, has led to diminished classroom violence and name-

calling and improved school climate, report most RCCP teachers surveyed. David Johnson and Roger Johnson similarly put 1st-through 9th-grade children through about a dozen hours of conflict resolution training in six schools with heartening results. Before the training, most students were involved in daily conflicts — put-downs and teasing, fights over possessions or taking turns on the playground — and these nearly always resulted in a winner and a loser. After training, the children more often found win-win solutions, better mediated friends' conflicts, and retained and applied their new skills in and out of school throughout the school year. The result was a more peaceful student community and increased academic achievement.

Other strategies range from preschool programs that reduce future delinquency by promoting social competence to focused conflict resolution programs that prepare children to live in a peaceful world. Boys Town offers a comprehensive program of social skill building and education in a "family-style environment" for troubled children. "We have no walls here," says Patrick Friman, Boys Town's director of clinical research, "no lockup, no timeout rooms, no fences. I am surrounded by 600 teenage kids, some of whom have robbed, beaten, abused, and even killed others. And yet I never lock my car, never look over my shoulder — even late at night, and never even think of danger (until I leave Boys Town at night and enter Omaha where I live)."

So what's the rub? Who could object to character education? Resistance comes from three sources. One is a concern that schools, already criticized for not teaching basics, are being given yet another agenda. Let the home teach virtues, say critics, and allow the schools to focus on academics.

Actually, character educators respond, making schools into moral communities supports instruction. Values education intersects naturally with the teaching of literature and history, and with behavior management in hallways, lunchrooms, and on playgrounds. Moreover, civil classrooms and responsible students provide a hospitable context for learning. The erosion of core values is at the heart of the educational crisis and the resulting charter school and home school movements. Education, say the character educators, must therefore reassert its historic mission of transmitting habits of the heart as well as knowledge of the head.

Resistance also comes from some religious conservatives, who fear that when a politically correct educational establishment gets into the values business, their parental authority will get undermined. Will Big Brother's "tolerance" education promote the homosexual agenda or an internationalism that undermines patriotism? Phyllis Schlafly of the Eagle Forum believes that "schools were set up to teach children to read and write. That's what they ought to concentrate on."

Character educators reply that school districts are including the religious community when defining consensus values, which are congenial to all faith traditions. Moreover, some religious conservatives believe the greater problem is *a*moral education. "We can all surely agree," wrote Charles Colson to fellow evangelicals, "that our schools be required to teach basic moral concepts."

The third source of resistance is liberals who doubt the idea of universal moral standards and fear the association between values and religion. Given the nearly inevitable juxtaposition of religion and values, they would prefer teaching neither.

Character educators reply that detachment—feigned moral neutrality—is not genuinely neutral. To take no stand implicitly sends a message of minimal expectations, which children quickly pick up. Moreover, although some character educators are people of faith—Thomas Lickona makes no secret of being a devout Roman Catholic—core values can be taught without smuggling in religious beliefs.

Freedom of—or from—Religion?

The debate over religion's place in public schools is contentious. At one pole are those who wish that America's schools, like those of many other countries, would teach their religion. When my family and I lived in Scotland, my children received some religious education through their local schools, which were not restrained by a constitutional separation of church and state. Most Americans, however, are content with the First Amendment's guarantee that "Congress shall make no law respecting an establishment of religion, or prohibiting the free exercise thereof." Comparing America's religious vitality with Britain's makes the separation seem mutually beneficial to church and state. Moreover, it precludes the church's being corrupted by state power or becoming a servant to the state. And it avoids discord over differences among faiths and among conservatives and liberals within the majority Christian faith.

At the other pole are those who wish to censor mention of religion and its place in American history and values. To describe the Pilgrims' motivations for coming to the new world and their first Thanksgiving feast without mention of God or religion is to teach a false history. To describe the civil rights movement without mentioning the religious convictions of Martin Luther King, Jr., and his peers is to teach an incomplete history. To imply that the individual is "the measure of all things" and that values are subjective rather than derived from a transcendent standard, as sociologist James Davison Hunter says school curricula do, is to replace theism with egoism.

Between the extremes of teaching and censoring religion, there lies much common ground. To understand the worldviews that have shaped history, literature, art, and music, students "need to explore the place of religion," declares the Communitarian Network's position paper on character education. "Schools should chart a middle way between those who would seek to ignore the historical and social role of religion and those who would seek to make schools instruments of religion. Schools, then, have a duty *not to teach the faith but to teach about faith.*"

Hillary Clinton agrees: "I share my husband's belief that 'nothing in the First Amendment converts our public schools into religion-free zones, or requires all religious expression to be left behind at the schoolhouse door,' and that indeed religion is too important in our history and our heritage for us to keep it out of our schools." At the president's request, Secretary of Education Richard Riley and Attorney General Janet Reno issued guidelines concerning permissible religious activities in public schools. These affirm students' freedom "to express their beliefs about religion in school assignments. . . . Schools may not provide religious instruction, but they may teach *about* the Bible or other scripture (in the teaching of history or literature, for example)."

In *The Culture of Disbelief,* Yale law professor Stephen Carter asks that schools not undermine family religious values:

> Imagine that you are the parent of a child in a public school, and you discover that the school, instead of offering the child a fair and balanced picture of the world—including your lifestyle choice—is teaching things that seem to the child to prove your lifestyle an inferior and perhaps an irrational one. If the school's teachings are offensive to you because you are gay or black or disabled the chances are that the school will at least give you a hearing and, if it does not, that many liberals will flock to your side and you will find a sympathetic ear in the media. But if you do not like the way the school talks about religion, or if you believe that the school is incit-

ing your children to abandon their religion, you will probably find that the media will mock you, the liberal establishment will announce that you are engaged in censorship, and the courts will toss you out on your ear. . . . It is not that [parents] want the public schools to proselytize in their favor; it is rather that they do not want the schools to do what Dewey implied that they must, to press their own children to reject what the parents believe.

Respecting church-state separation, I do not ask that public schools assume the Christian understanding of Easter or engage their choirs in singing "Joy to the World" and "O Come All Ye Faithful" at school Christmas gatherings. But I do object to their taking over these religious holidays and substituting secular versions of them—remaking Easter into a myth about bunnies and Christmas into a celebration of a jolly fat man. If the schools cannot respect the historic meaning of these religious holidays, then could they just leave them alone? A Jew, I presume, would ask as much for Passover and Yom Kippur, a Muslim for Ramadan.

Sex Education

Consensus may be possible on core values for character education, and even on the appropriateness of schools' respecting and teaching about religion without proselytizing. But what about the culture war over sex education? Is there any common ground between those who want to teach adolescents how to do it safely and those who want to teach them why they shouldn't?

The gap between the two camps is shrinking. First, as the case becomes more compelling that teenage intercourse harms teens and society, it is becoming possible to discuss responsibility, commitment, and even abstinence without being considered right-wing. The facts are:

- Sexually transmitted disease is epidemic among younger Americans, and condoms have a known failure rate and provide little protection against certain STDs transmitted skin-to-skin. Had Magic Johnson learned the HIV status of his infected partner, he would not have put on a condom, he would have done a fast break.
- Nonmarital pregnancy impoverishes many women and puts their children at increased risk of various social and psychological pathologies.
- Psychologically as well as medically speaking, "safe sex" is an illusion for 15-year-olds.

With those elementary facts in mind, David Popenoe concludes "that the best solution to preventing adolescent sexuality with a high probability of pregnancy (and disease) rests on reestablishing the simple moral code that young people should wait until adulthood, if not marriage, before beginning a sexually active life." Popenoe has much company. It includes James Dobson and Jesse Jackson, the Quayles and the Clintons, and the Centers for Disease Control and Prevention. The CDC's national health objectives for the year 2000 include reduction in adolescent sexual intercourse: "These changes in behavior will require interventions that integrate the efforts of parents, families, schools, religious organizations, health departments, community agencies, and the media. Education programs should provide adolescents with the knowledge, attitudes, and skills they need to refrain from sexual intercourse."

But is this realistic? Given today's average age of marriage, in the mid-20s, "delay of intercourse 10 or more years beyond biological maturity . . . is contrary to practice in virtually all societies," argue sex educators Peggy Brick and Deborah Roffman. The Sexuality Information and Education Council's executive director, Debra Haffner, therefore argues for a climate "that affirms young people's sexual rights. . . . Instead of trying to reduce young people's coital experience, efforts would be more effective if they could concentrate on reducing the incidence of *unprotected coitus*. . . . Chronological age and marital status are not benchmarks for the ability to have an ethical or moral sexual relationship. . . . Adolescents who are capable of forming healthy sexual relationships must be supported." Although "virgins need our support," too, says Haffner, we'd best face the reality of adolescent sex. We should help teenagers "explore the full range of safe sexual behavior . . . [including] Necking, Massaging, Caressing, Undressing each other, Masturbation alone, Masturbation in front of a partner, Mutual masturbation." (Haffner imagines teens being like Bill Clinton, who could smoke but not inhale.)

But if the reality of early sexual activity partly reflects "value-free" sex education, say critics, is it an argument for continuing such education? When information about sex is separated from the context of human values, some students may get the idea that sexual intercourse is merely recreational activity. Diana Baumrind, a University of California child-rearing expert, suspects that adolescents interpret sex education that pretends to be "value free" as meaning that adults are neutral about adolescent sexual activity. She feels that such an implication is unfortunate, because "promiscuous recreational sex poses certain psychological, social, health, and moral problems that must be faced realistically."

Defenders of "comprehensive sex education" reply that researchers have not found any consistent effect of sex education courses on students' sexual behavior. (There's good and bad news in that finding.) So, they say, blame the culture and its sex-saturated media for the teen pregnancy and STD epidemic; don't blame the schools. Even the Centers for Disease Control contends that "for adolescents who are unwilling to refrain from sexual intercourse, programs should help to increase the use of contraceptives and condoms." Although condoms sometimes fail, especially for skin-to-skin STDs, they offer a tenfold reduction in the risk of contracting HIV from sex with an infected partner. Besides, we don't just tell kids to avoid cancer-promoting radiation by staying out of the sun. We recognize the reality of sun exposure and tell them to wear sunscreen when they go to the beach.

A more apt analogy, say critics, would be accepting the reality of drugs and giving kids clean needles, or accepting the reality of kids smoking and teaching them to use filters for safer smoking. Using pencils as models, teachers could even have students practice placing a filter over the end of one. Instead, with support from 98 percent of parents, we unhesitatingly say that smoking is stupid, self-destructive behavior. It is slow-motion suicide, assisted by the cigarette manufacturers. Without disparaging the 25 percent of Americans who are addicted to nicotine or threatening their right to smoke, health educators find the evidence sufficiently compelling to promote a smoke-free lifestyle.

New health education methods that teach the facts and actively engage youths in practicing refusal skills have effectively reduced teen smoking. One research team led by Alfred McAlister had high school students "inoculate" 7th graders against peer pressures to smoke. The 7th graders were taught to respond to advertisements implying that liberated women smoke by saying, "She's not really liberated if she is hooked on tobacco." They also acted in role plays; after being called "chicken" for not taking a cigarette, they answered with statements like, "I'd be a real chicken if I smoked just to impress you." After several such sessions during the 7th and 8th grades, the inoculated students were half as likely to begin smoking as uninoculated students at another junior high school that had an identical parental smoking rate.

Other research teams have confirmed that education-inoculation procedures reduce teenage smoking. Most newer efforts emphasize strategies for resisting social pressure. One study exposed 6th to 8th graders to antismoking films or to information about smoking, together with role plays of student-generated ways of refusing a cigarette. A year and a half later 31 percent of those who had watched the antismoking films had taken up smoking. Among those who had role-played refusing, only 19 percent had done so. Another study involved the entire 7th-grade class in a diverse sample of 30 junior high schools. It warned students about pressures to smoke and use drugs and offered them strategies for resisting. Among nonusers of marijuana, the training curbed initiation by a third; among users, it reduced usage by half.

Antismoking and drug education programs apply other persuasion principles, too. They use attractive peers to communicate information. They trigger the students' own cognitive processing ("Here's something you might want to think about"). They get the students to make a public commitment (by making a rational decision about smoking and then announcing it, along with their reasoning, to their classmates). Some of these smoking-prevention programs require only two to six one-hour class sessions, using prepared printed materials or videotapes. Today any school district or teacher wishing to use the social-psychological approach to smoking prevention can do so easily, inexpensively, and with the hope of significant reductions in future smoking rates and associated health costs.

Abstinence education programs are likewise teaching youths how to deal with pressures to have sex. In one such session, Dajahn Bievens, a San Diego Urban League health educator, challenged a 14-year-old girl that it was time to "take your panties off" or be dumped for someone who will. The girl looked him straight in the eye and firmly, as taught, simply said, "No." So he badgered her some more, saying she must be stuck-up or scared, and then pled with offers of gifts. "Stop pressuring me," she responded. "I'm not into that now. I'm into education."

Bievens was using "Postponing Sexual Involvement," developed at Atlanta's Grady Memorial Hospital as one of some fifteen abstinence curricula now available as part of a pendulum swing in sex education. Each offers lesson plans, activities, and workbook exercises. Designed for use in public schools, the curricula make no explicit use of religious arguments. The rationale is not religious morality but public health.

Early research on the abstinence education effects, like research on the initial smoking prevention programs, suggests that panaceas do not come easily. Well-intentioned efforts sometimes have little effect. The 1996 welfare reform act provided $50 million annually in matching grants for "abstinence until marriage" education programs. With all 50 states having applied for these grants, and with Congress having also allocated $6 million for a national evaluation of the programs' effectiveness, we may soon gain a better understanding of what strategies and program lengths work best, with what age groups.

A scattering of successful efforts give cause for hope. Jefferson Junior High School in Washington, D.C., used to have 12 to 15 girls pregnant each year. By the mid-1990s this was reduced to about one per year. When principal Vera White came to Jefferson, parents (90 percent single) felt they were losing the children. So parents, staff, and students together forged a five-year character development plan that focused on positive attitudes, conflict resolution, and sexual abstinence. One eight-week abstinence program, called Best Friends, focuses on friendship, love and dating, decision making, health, and STDs. The school sets high expectations for student responsibility and parent involvement. At last report Jefferson had D.C.'s highest student achievement and attendance rates and a waiting list of more than 400 students.

Sarah Brown, director of the new National Campaign to Reduce Teen Pregnancy, points to the success story of Oregon's Tillamook County, which in the mid-1980s had the state's second highest teenage pregnancy rate. Groups began meeting to discuss the problem and debate its causes. The local media spotlighted the dialogue. In the end, sex educators, church leaders, parents, family planners, and abstinence advocates agreed not to disparage one another but instead to do what they each could. Teenage parents visited classrooms. Vivid videos and presentations depicted STDs, media exploitation of sex, and date rape. By 1994, the teen pregnancy rate was cut by more than two-thirds—from 24 pregnancies per thousand 10- to 17-year-old girls to 7 per thousand—now the state's lowest rate. With success at hand, Tillamook County relaxed, Oregon public policy analysts Jeffrey Luke and Kathryn Robb Neville report. Most of the ministers turned over between 1990 and 1995, and church education programs lagged. The main school district's sex education program was condensed. Energies turned elsewhere. By 1995 the wider culture's pressures for early sexualization were less restrained, and the pregnancy rate sprang back to 15 per thousand.

Pregnancy reduction and academic success has also been boosted by outreach programs that engage teenagers as volunteers in nursing homes, elementary schools, and other community service and that coordinate their experiences with classroom life-planning discussions. One ingredient of the Tillamook success story was encouraging teens to chart their long-term future hopes.

Hoping for similar success, the New York City Board of Education in 1992 voted 4 to 3 to require that AIDS education in the classroom devote more time to abstinence than safe sex. Many AIDS educators were outraged, arguing that sexually active youths would not listen to abstinence and might miss the safe-sex message. "But if students cannot be told that abstinence is a good and desirable thing," reflected Stephen Carter

—if that simple societal value cannot be stated in the classroom without causing an uproar—then what hope is there that we can convince children that bigotry and avarice, for example, are wrong? After all, one might reasonably argue that if sexually active children will not pay attention to strong suggestions of abstinence, then children leaning toward racism may not pay attention to suggestions of tolerance and respect either. But if the message is a good one, a right one, the danger that children will tune it out is hardly sufficient reason not to try. That, I think, is why many advocates of the teaching of abstinence believe that those who object to stressing it do not really consider it a value worth stressing.

Surely, however, the dichotomy between abstinence education and comprehensive sex education is false. With 66 percent of Americans telling Gallup they favor the teaching of "sexual abstinence outside of marriage" (and surely more favoring abstinence for adolescents), most liberals and conservatives can now find common ground in supporting "abstinence-promoting comprehensive sex and family life education." One wonders of conservatives: why not provide youth with realistic information about contraception, skin-to-skin STDs, cervical cancer risks, and condom failure rates for pregnancy and HIV prevention? One wonders of liberals: why not teach the joys of saved sex—of the satisfactions that accompany a secure, lifelong, unconditionally loving relationship—a relationship free of guilt and regret, free of fears of unwanted pregnancy or disease, and free of performance worries related to comparison with other partners or losing one's mate? Why not merge family values with feminist goals, by teaching that abstinence empowers girls to fulfill their educational potential?

Such is an aim of the Chicago public schools' Cradle to Classroom program, which has offered counseling and abstinence-plus sex education to 1,959 teenage mothers since 1997. As of early 1999, not one had given birth to a second child. School officials can't specify how much abstinence, birth control, and abortion account for this dramatic result. But their delighted surprise has prompted them to expand the program's budget for the 1999–2000 school year from $2.1 million to $5 million.

Rather than narrowing sex education for other teens to either abstinence or contraception, why not embed both in a comprehensive program of family life education that documents the social recession, spells out alternative futures, and asks students to consider what kind of culture and life they want? Why not explain the impact of the sexual revolution and marriage decline on poverty and children's well-being? If we value men's involvement in child care, why not let it be known that a society of cads is a society short of good dads? (As Popenoe has written, "A man is likely to be directly involved in caring for his children if he is sure they are his . . . and he is monogamously married and emotionally close to the mother.") Why not teach youths to recognize the media's sexual scripting? And why not ask them if their generation wishes to be the one that leads toward a renewed culture of commitment—a culture that respects minority rights, women's rights, gay and lesbian rights, but also understands that in a healthy society true love waits for commitment?

For comprehensive sex and family life education, the aim is not negative—just don't do it—but positive: It aims to offer youths an attractive alternative to say "yes" to. It aims to promote the "good sex" that my ethicist colleague Allen Verhey discerns from Jewish tradition—"the 'one flesh' union of a man and a woman that gestures the commitment and covenant made in vows and carried out in fidelity." This requires teaching the personal meaning of sex in our lives. One can know every available fact about sex—that the initial spasms of male and female orgasm come at 0.8-second intervals, that the female nipples expand 10 millimeters at the peak of sexual arousal, that systolic blood pressure rises some 60 points and the respiration rate to 40 breaths per minute—but fail to understand the human significance of sexual intimacy.

Surely one significance of sexual intimacy is its expression of our deeply social nature. Sex is a socially significant act. Men and women can achieve orgasm alone, but we find greater satisfaction while embracing our loved one. Indeed, good sex—sex at its fulfilling best—is part of an enduring, totally committed and secure relationship. It is life-uniting and love-renewing. Sex, writes Maggie Gallagher, "creates people who need each other, erotically; a perpetual adult act of joining which replaces the perpetually adolescent act of breaking free." Sex is "the desire of one's body for the soul of another human being. The longing to break the boundaries of the flesh altogether, to incarnate love. . . . Sex is a living pathway of connection, an intricate web of desire that begins with lust and ends not with orgasm but with children, families . . . with love."

We cannot expect our schools alone to restore the moral infrastructure. Character is nurtured by families and supportive neighbors, churches, kin, and child-friendly media. But we can expect our schools to support the village it takes to nurture a socially fragile child into a resilient, honest, responsible, caring adult. The renaissance of character education, fueled by communities getting intentional about teaching shared values, gives hope—hope for a renewal of the delicate balance between individualism and societal well-being.

CHAPTER 10

Faith and Society

Who will lead us out of this spiritual vacuum?
—HILLARY RODHAM CLINTON, 1993

Convinced that something is awry with modern life, America's First Lady yearned for a new reformation of the human spirit. There is a "sleeping sickness of the soul," she declared in her speech at the University of Texas. We enjoy economic growth, yet paradoxically "we lack at some core level meaning in our individual lives and meaning collectively, that sense that our lives are part of some greater effort, that we are connected to one another, that community means that we have a place where we belong no matter who we are." Underneath the "hopeless girls with babies and angry boys with guns," underneath the breakdown of civility and community, underneath the alienation that marks our "acquisitive and competitive corporate culture," she said, is spiritual poverty.

America's Spiritual Hunger

Mrs. Clinton's cultural diagnosis is remarkably similar to that offered by George Bush's 1988 campaign manager, Lee Atwater, as he faced a premature death from brain cancer: "The '80s were about acquiring—acquiring wealth, power, prestige. I know. I acquired more wealth, power and prestige than most. But you can acquire all you want and still feel empty. What power wouldn't I trade for a little more time with my family? What price wouldn't I pay for an evening with friends?

It took a deadly illness to put me eye to eye with that truth, but it is a truth that the country, caught up in its ruthless ambitions and moral decay, can learn on my dime. I don't know who will lead us through the '90s, but they must be made to speak to this spiritual vacuum at the heart of American society, this tumor of the soul."

Al Gore has been similarly struck by "a spiritual crisis in modern civilization that seems to be based on an emptiness at its center and the absence of a larger spiritual purpose." Thus, he explained in declaring his presidential candidacy, "Most Americans are hungry for a deeper connection between politics and moral values; many would say 'spiritual values.'" Having solved the question of *how* to make a living, having surrounded ourselves with once unthinkable luxuries — air-conditioned comfort, CD quality sound, and fresh fruit year round — we are left to wonder *why* we live. Why run this rat race? What's the point? Why care about anything or anyone beyond myself?

This diagnosis of spiritual poverty has come from many perspectives:

- "The real problem of *modernity* is the problem of belief," observed sociologist Daniel Bell. "To use an unfashionable term, it is a spiritual crisis."
- In his Harvard commencement address, Aleksandr Solzhenitsyn deplored the Western world's material obsession and spiritual poverty. "We have placed too much hope in politics and social reforms, only to find out that we were being deprived of our most precious possession: our spiritual life."
- "There is within us a crisis, a kind of spiritual surrender," agreed Jesse Jackson. "Can we rebuild the wall (of hope)? We have the money. We have the education, but there is something within us that is in trouble." Democrat Jackson's reflections on the spiritual malaise of African-American youth are shared by Republican Alan Keyes and by academics from liberal Cornel West to neoconservative Glenn Loury.
- "There is a yawning hole in the psyche of America and Americans where our sense of common purpose, of community and connection, of hope and a spiritual satisfaction should be," echoed former *New York Times* columnist Anna Quindlen. "We liberals must acknowledge this: that while the rights of the individual are precious, at some deep level individualism alone does not suffice. And the ability of the radical right to seize and exploit the terrain of the soul has been helped immeasurably by the failure of so many of the rest of us to even acknowledge the soul's existence."

- Television producer Norman Lear concurred, saying, "At no time in my life has our culture been so estranged from spiritual values. . . . Our problems are not economic and political. They are moral and spiritual—and must be addressed on that level if real solutions are to be found."

- Rabbi Michael Lerner, editor of *Tikkun*, called "for a 'politics in the image of God,' an attempt to reconstruct the world in a way that takes seriously the uniqueness and preciousness of every human being and our connection to a higher ethical and spiritual purpose that gives meaning to our lives."

- Alienation and spiritual yearnings can also be found in popular music, as in these lyrics from Sting: "Everyone I know is lonely / and God's so far away / and my heart belongs to no one / so now some times I pray / please take this space between us / and fill it up some way." For many, Kurt Cobain's suicide symbolized such alienation and meaninglessness.

- Looking beyond America, Czech poet-president Vaclav Havel saw "the present global crisis" as "directly related to the spiritual condition of modern civilization. This condition is characterized by loss: the loss of metaphysical certainties, of an experience of the transcendental, of any superpersonal moral authority, and of any kind of higher horizon." Havel believes that "if the world is to change for the better it must start with a change in human consciousness." We must discover "a deeper sense of responsibility toward the world, which means responsibility toward something higher than self."

Are such voices harbingers of spiritual renewal? Is Nobel economist Robert Fogel right to think the United States is beginning a "Fourth Great Awakening . . . a new religious revival fueled by a revulsion with the corruptions of contemporary society"? Ronald Inglehart, a University of Michigan social scientist who follows values surveys across the Western world, discerns the beginnings of a decline in materialist values. Not only in Eastern Europe, where materialist Marxism is licking its wounds, but in the West one sees signs of a new generation maturing with decreasing concern for economic growth and strong defense, and with increasing concern for personal relationships, the integrity of nature, and the meaning of life. At the peak of her fortune and fame, with 146 tennis championships behind her and married to John Lloyd, Chris Evert reflected, "We get into a rut. We play tennis, we go to a movie, we watch TV, but I keep saying, 'John, there has to be more.' "

Changing values, lost community, and waning commitments to things greater than self motivate our quest for something more—for a vision of life that is both conservative and radical: conserving social wisdom accumulated over generations, while questioning the well-traveled road of our individualism and materialism. After two decades of rising materialism, the proportion of new collegians who rated "becoming very well off financially" as "very important or essential" peaked at 76 percent in 1987. Although this still remains top-ranked among 19 rated goals, Inglehart discerns "a renewed concern for spiritual values." Pollster George Gallup, Jr., detects the same: "One of two dominant trends in society today [along with a search for deeper, more meaningful relationships] is the search for spiritual moorings. . . . Surveys document the movement of people who are searching for meaning in life with a new intensity, and want their religious faith to grow." From 1994 to late 1998, reported Gallup, the number of Americans feeling a need to "experience spiritual growth" rose from 54 percent to 82 percent.

Vivid illustrations of this desecularization come from the Million Man March in Washington, D.C., and the Promise Keepers movement, in which millions of men have committed themselves to spiritual renewal, racial reconciliation, and a deeper, though traditionally defined, involvement in their roles as fathers and husbands. At the 1996 political conventions, Bob Dole promised to rekindle "old values" and Bill Clinton promised to "protect our values." At my college—a place called Hope—we had 40 students attending voluntary thrice-weekly chapel services during the early 1990s. By the end of the 1990s there was sometimes standing room only in the 1,000-seat college chapel.

Having "hit bottom," as Alcoholics Anonymous members would say—having faced our brokenness, with 87 percent of the public fearing that "something is fundamentally wrong with America's moral condition"—we are looking again to a higher power for something more. Although people in surveys overreport church attendance, as they do voting, religiosity seems on an upswing. Since hitting its modern low in 1993, Gallup's "Religion in America" index has been heading upward. With 96 percent of Americans believing in "God, or a universal spirit" (84 percent in a personal God accessible through prayer), we look to faith for meaning and direction.

Hoping to answer spiritual longings, authors, musicians, artists, spiritual directors, and even scientists are offering a banquet of soul food:

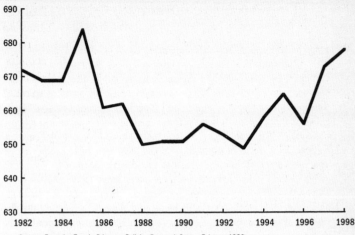

Fig 10.1 Religion in America Index (Composite eight-item score including belief in God, church attendance and membership, importance of religion)

Source: *Emerging Trends,* Princeton Religion Research Center, February 1999

- At one point in 1994, six of the top ten best-selling books explored spiritual matters. Betty Eadie was *Embraced by the Light.* Thomas Moore was taking *Care of the Soul.* Scott Peck was still taking *The Road Less Traveled* and so had made it *Further Along the Road Less Traveled.* Karen Armstrong had compiled *A History of God.* And Kathleen Norris offered an inspiring account of life and faith in *Dakota.* In 1996, God (actually *God: A Biography*) even won a Pulitzer Prize.

- *Time, Newsweek,* and *Life* have recently featured articles on God, Genesis, and the boom in angel statues, jewelry, stories, and books. In one week in April 1996, all of the journalistic Big Three—*Time, Newsweek,* and *U.S. News and World Report*—had Jesus on their covers.

- Monastic Gregorian chants sung by Benedictine monks to enhance prayer and contemplation became a surprise best-selling CD. More than a million people now annually besiege Catholic retreat centers, many to practice "centering prayers." "Spiritual formation," guided by "spiritual directors," has become common parlance for many Protestants as well.

- Each year several hundred thousand people, seeking respite from their hectic, competitive, acquisitive lives, make pilgrimage to engage the ancient Celtic spiritual tradition. The tradition is marked by deep faith, tranquil worship, and engagement with people and nature. (Genuine Celtic spirituality is not to be confused with its "escapist, romantic, nostalgic, individualistic, and self-indulgent New Age popularizations," notes Norman Shanks, leader of Scotland's Iona Community.)

- In the NFL, once rare chapel services have become "universal," and after touchdowns players have become nearly as likely to kneel as to strut.

- Movies in the 1990s from *Shadowlands* to *Dead Man Walking* have offered affirmative references to faith and God. *Touched by an Angel*, launched by CBS, went to ratings heaven and in the 1997–98 season was one of six prime-time programs with religious or spiritual themes. Still, a 1997 *TV Guide* poll found 56 percent saying religion gets not enough attention on prime-time TV (only 8 percent felt it got too much). With movies in the late 1990s about Moses (*The Prince of Egypt*), an angel (*The Preacher's Wife*), and the Dalai Lama (*Seven Years in Tibet*), Hollywood's turn to spirituality continues.

- "Science Finds God," heralded a 1998 cover story in *Newsweek* on a "Science and Spiritual Quest" gathering of 400 scientists. "Science and God: A Warming Trend?" headlined *Science*, reporting on the waning of the old science-religion conflict. New centers for the study of science and religion have sprung up. New magazines like *Science and Spirit* and *Spirituality and Health* feature mainstream science and religion. Harvard Medical School's continuing education courses on spirituality and healing have drawn nearly 2,000 health professionals and clergy members for each of the past several years. The John Templeton Foundation is now awarding $20 million annually, much of it for new science-religion courses and such projects as "Big Science Astronomy and the Spiritual Quest." We want to "rescue religion from obsolescence," declares Sir John Templeton.

- Supported by President Clinton and his attorney general and education secretary, schools are relaxing their censorship of religion's place in history and literature.

- As of August 1999, "God" could be found on 5.6 million Web sites.

Discerning Sense from Nonsense

Nature abhors a spiritual vacuum. Hungry for community, for meaning, for a sense of the transcendent, people are eager for whatever will fill the void. They may grasp at hints of the supernatural—at bizarre phenomena that seemingly defy science. Bookstore sections devoted to New Age topics and the paranormal tell us of mystical near-death experiences, people reading minds or foretelling the future, reincarnation and séances with the dead.

Angels have become especially big business, a New Age folk religion with greeting cards, tarot cards, and a spate of books about angels who seem to focus on satisfying our wants and boosting our egos. "While I relate very personally to . . . my guardian angel [whom I also consider] an aspect of my Higher Self," says Alma Daniel in *Ask Your Angels*, "I am aware of help from many other celestials who assist in different ways—facilitating my travel through the city, directing my actions in a tax audit, and so forth." "They have come to help us see our own luminous beauty," says Andrew Ramer in *Angel Answers*. This is "a supremely American revision" of the biblical concept of angels, critic Ruth Shalit points out—it is "the spirituality of self-absorption." "God and my angels want me to be happy in every way that I want to be happy," John Randolph Price assures us in *Angel Energy*.

Accepting with Shakespeare's Hamlet that there are more things in heaven and earth than are dreamt of in our philosophies—truth does often prove stranger than fiction—how can we winnow spiritual truth from irrational nonsense?

Some spiritual questions—Does God exist? Is there life beyond death?—require a leap of faith to answer (yes or no). With other spiritual claims, including some of those mentioned above, the proof is in the pudding. If someone claims to read minds or talk with the dead, put the claim to the test. This is the scientific approach long ago advocated by Moses for testing self-proclaimed prophets. "If a prophet speaks in the name of the Lord but the thing does not take place or prove true," then so much the worse for the prophet. Magician James Randi uses Moses' approach when testing those claiming to see auras around people's bodies.

RANDI: Do you see an aura around my head?

AURA-SEER: Yes, indeed.

RANDI: Can you still see the aura if I put this magazine in front of my face?

AURA-SEER: Of course.

RANDI: Then if I were to step behind a wall barely taller than I am, you could determine my location from the aura visible above my head, right?

Randi tells me that no aura-seer has agreed yet to take this simple test. For three decades, he has challenged many other would-be prophets, psychics, channelers, and out-of-body frequent flyers to similar put-up-or-shut-up tests of their supposed abilities, offering $10,000 to anyone who can demonstrate "*any* paranormal ability." The offer has recently been upped to $1.1 million with signed pledges of at least $1,000 from more than 200 other interested skeptics (myself included) in 15 countries. Still the world awaits the first reproducible psychic phenomenon, or the first individual who can reliably beat chance in reading others' minds, discerning happenings at some remote location, or solving police cases with dreams or visions.

While astronomers scoff at the naïveté of astrology, psychologists ask a different question: Does it work? Are birth dates correlated with character traits? Given someone's birth date, can astrologers surpass chance when asked to identify the person from a short lineup of different personality descriptions? Can people pick out their own horoscopes from a lineup of them? The consistent answers have been: no, no, no, and no. (Psychologists, skeptical of fortune-tellers cum fortune-takers, also have discerned and reproduced the techniques by which astrologers, palm readers, and crystal-ball gazers persuade millions of people to buy and believe their readings and advice.)

Then there are claims of reincarnation, in which 1 in 4 Americans profess to believe. Under hypnosis, fantasy-prone people who believe in reincarnation will offer vivid details of their "past lives." But they nearly always report being the same race they are now—unless the researcher has informed them that different races are common. They often report being someone famous rather than one of the more numerous unfamous. Some contradict one another by claiming to have been the same person, such as King Henry VIII. And they typically do not know things that any person of that historical time would have known. One subject who "regressed" to a "previous life" as a Japanese fighter pilot in 1940 could not name the emperor of Japan and did not know that Japan was already at war.

Does such skepticism of supernatural powers entail wholesale hostility to spirituality? Is this the very sort of scientific naturalism that has helped create the spiritual vacuum? Or does it simply challenge the sort of spirituality that sometimes gives spirituality a bad reputation?

Consider the gap between New Age and biblical spirituality. Unlike New Age and occult spirituality, biblical religions accept the reality of death, "the great enemy." Unlike Socrates drinking poison hemlock in the serene conviction that his undying soul would find release from its bodily prison, Jesus wept at the grave of his friend Lazarus—though not without hope of a "great gettin'-up morning."

Biblical religions also depart from New Age religions and the occult in believing that humans are finite creatures of the one who declares, "I am God, and there is no one like me." Biblical religions assert that God alone is omniscient (thus able to read minds and know the future), omnipresent (thus able to be in different places at once), and omnipotent (thus capable of creating or altering nature with divine power). Humans, loved by God, have dignity, but not deity.

Historically, biblical spirituality has cultivated a scientific attitude by advocating humility and by its skepticism of any self-important human authority. What matters is not my opinion or yours—we are both fallible creatures—but whatever truths are revealed in response to our questioning. Historians of science report that many of the founders of science—Blaise Pascal, Francis Bacon, Isaac Newton, and even Galileo—were people whose religious convictions led them to distrust human intuition, to feel compelled to explore the creation, and to humbly submit their ideas to the test. If, as previously supposed, nature was sacred—if nature is a divine world alive with river goddesses and sun gods—then we ought not tamper with it. But if, as the scientific pioneers assumed, it is an intelligible creation—a work to be enjoyed and managed—then let us seek its truths by observing and experimenting. And let us do so freely, knowing that our ultimate allegiance is not to human doctrine but to God alone.

Ironically, the sense of awe and bewilderment that is at the core of the religious impulse—the wonderstruck feeling that, as J. B. S. Haldane said, "the universe is not only queerer than we suppose, but queerer than we can suppose"—comes more genuinely from science than pseudoscience. This is why Carl Sagan could write that "science is not only compatible with spirituality, it is a profound source of spirituality." Poke at claims of the occult and paranormal, and time and again one is left holding a popped balloon. The more I learn about the human senses, the more convinced I am that what is truly extraordinary is not extrasensory perception, claims for which inevitably dissolve upon investigation, but rather our very ordinary moment-to-moment sensory experiences of organizing formless neural impulses into colorful sights and meaningful sounds.

As you look at someone, particles of light energy are being absorbed by your eyes' receptor cells, converted into neural signals that activate neighboring cells, which down the line transmit a million electrochemical messages per moment up to your brain. There, separate parts of your brain process information about color, form, motion, and depth, and then—somehow—converge this information to form a consciously perceived image, which is instantly compared with previously stored images and recognized as, say, your grandmother. The whole process is as complex as taking a house apart, splinter by splinter, transporting it to a different location, and then, through the efforts of millions of specialized workers, putting it back together. The material brain suddenly gives rise to consciousness. That all this happens instantly, effortlessly, and continuously is better than cool, it is truly bewildering. In explaining such phenomena in my psychology texts I empathize with Job: "I have uttered what I did not understand, things too wonderful for me."

God and Goodness

So, say many prominent voices, the social recession reflects a "spiritual vacuum," which also creates an unsatisfied hunger for mystery, an itch to experience the magical. Spiritual hunger in an age of plenty. In Britain and the United States, the founders of parapsychology were mostly people who, having lost their religious faith, were searching for a scientific basis for believing in the meaningfulness of life and the possibility of life after death.

Setting aside the irrational or refuted forms of spirituality, what remains? "If all the achievements of theologians were wiped out tomorrow," Richard Dawkins wonders, "would anyone notice the smallest difference?" The difference is what social psychologists Shalom Schwartz of Jerusalem and Sipke Huismans of Amsterdam discern as a common core of all major contemporary religions: transcendence of material concerns. "Religions encourage people to seek meaning beyond everyday existence, linking themselves to a 'ground of being' through belief and worship," they contend. "Most foster attitudes of awe, respect and humility, by emphasizing the place of the human being in a vast, unfathomable universe, and exhort people to pursue causes greater than their personal desires. The opposed orientation, self-indulgent materialism, seeks happiness in the pursuit and consumption of material goods."

The "global ethic" issued by the 1993 Parliament of the World's Religions illustrates the religious common denominator: "Every form of egoism should be rejected. . . . We must treat others as we wish others to treat us. . . . We consider humankind our family." The belief that all humans are children of God, created equal and "endowed by their Creator with certain unalienable Rights," forms the ground underneath our democratic moral consensus, notes Christopher Beem, director of the Council on Civil Society. "The roots of our nation's moral vocabulary are religious," he says. "If there is no God, we are not equal, nor are we all of inestimable value."

Similar egalitarian and communal values appeared in the new "World Faiths and Development Dialogue" initiated in 1998 by George Carey, archbishop of Canterbury, and World Bank president James Wolfensohn. "What has drawn us together is a deep moral concern for the future of human well-being and dignity. We cannot accept the suffering of so many millions of people around the world." Their sentiments echoed the "Call to the Common Ground for the Common Good" issued in 1993 by the National Council of Churches, the Synagogue Council of America, and the U.S. Catholic Conference: "The return of our national confidence must quicken our responsiveness not only to our budget deficits but more profoundly to our growing social deficits. . . . The common good is frequently diminished and sometimes destroyed by powerful currents in our national life, including . . . social forces, such as excessive individualism, materialism and consumerism. . . . It is imperative to put the welfare of the whole ahead of our own narrow interests."

But does belief in the transcendent actually correlate with living beyond self—with restrained impulsivity and materialism? Simply said, does godliness advance goodness?

Faith and Character

More than a century ago, Dostoevsky wondered, "Can civilized men believe?" Today, cultural observer Os Guinness wonders the reverse: "Can unbelieving men be civilized?" To paraphrase another of Dostoevsky's questions, "Can we be good without God?"

Of course we can, presume most Americans, 74 percent of whom answered "yes" when Gallup asked, "Can a person be a good and ethical person if he or she does not believe in God?" Moreover, religion hardly provides immunity from greed, lust, and bigotry. Examples come easily to mind of faith and *dis*honorable character—televangelist Jim Bakker with his luxurious mansions and gold-plated bathroom fixtures, Bible-quoting Ku Klux Klanners, apartheid defenders, and gay bashers, reactionary Christians who seem to equate God's will with government indifference to the poor. As Madeleine L'Engle lamented, "Christians

Reflections on Faith and Character

"Both reason and experience forbid us to expect that national morality can prevail in exclusion of religious principle."

—George Washington, presidential farewell address, 1796

"I call on all members of the faculty, as members of a thinking body, freely to recognize the tremendous validity and power of the teachings of Christ in our life-and-death struggle against the forces of selfish materialism."

—President Charles Seymour, inaugural address, Yale University, 1937

"To educate without a value system based on truth is to abandon young people to moral confusion, personal insecurity, and easy manipulation. No country, not even the most power-ful, can endure if it deprives its own children of this essential good."

—Pope John Paul II, 1993

"We are taking away the spiritual ele-ment and abandoning morality based on religious truth, counting instead on our heads and our subjective feelings to make us do what is right."

—Charles Colson, "Can We Be Good Without God?" 1993

"Civic religions, secular bodies of values, have not been able to deal with questions of ultimate values, with the meaning of life and death, with the meaning of our very existence. . . . There may be no other reliable source for understanding the human condition and for finding the meaning for one's suffering than in the spiritual realm, and within it, in religion."

—Amitai Etzioni, "Yuppie Redemption," 1994

"At the heart of our universe is a higher reality—God and his Kingdom of love— to which we must be conformed."

—Martin Luther King, Jr., "The Transformed Nonconformist"

"The taking away of God, though even in thought, dissolves all."

—John Locke

have given Christianity a bad name." The same could be said of peace-sabotaging Muslims and Jews. Every religion, every political party, and every social movement must endure those who embarrass it, who give skeptics like Richard Dawkins cause for seeing faith as "one of the world's great evils, comparable to the smallpox virus, but harder to eradicate."

Anecdotes aside—"I can counter Jim Bakker with Mother Teresa and KKK members with Desmond Tutu," responds the believer—how does faith feed character? It might do so by providing a source of values, say the religious. It might give us a convincing reason to behave morally when no one is looking. Lacking the ground of faith beneath our morality, cultural inertia may enable a lingering selflessness, but eventually the soil that feeds morality becomes depleted. "If there is no God, is not everything permissible?" asks Ivan in *The Brothers Karamazov.*

Even the 18th century French writer Voltaire, to whom Christianity was an "infamy" that deserved crushing, found the influence of faith useful among the masses. "I want my attorney, my tailor, my servants, even my wife to believe in God," he wrote, because "then I shall be robbed and cuckolded less often." He once silenced a discussion about atheism until he had dismissed the servants, lest in losing their faith they might lose their morality. Although similarly skeptical of religion, biologist E. O. Wilson likewise acknowledges that "religious conviction is largely beneficent. Religion . . . nourishes love, devotion, and above all, hope."

Was Voltaire right to presume that godliness tethers self-interest and feeds character? Seeking answers, researchers have studied not just what causes crime but what predicts virtue. Having two committed parents, a stable neighborhood, prosocial media, and schools that teach character all help. So does a spiritual sense, psychologist William Damon contends. Children are "openly receptive to spiritual ideas and long for transcendent truth that can nourish their sense of purpose and provide them with a moral mission in life," he believes. "Children will not thrive . . . unless they acquire a living sense of what some religious traditions have called *transcendence:* a faith in, and devotion to concerns that are considered larger than the self." Religiosity, he reports, "has clear benefits for children . . . enabling some children to adapt to stressful and burdensome life events."

The bipartisan National Commission on Children has concurred that religious faith strengthens children. "Through participation in a religious community—in communal worship, religious education, and social action programs—children learn and assimilate the values of their faith. For many children, religion is a major force in their moral development; for some it is the chief determinant of moral behavior." Studies confirm that religious adolescents (those who say their faith is important or who attend church) differ from those who are not religious. They are much less likely to become delinquent, to engage in promiscuous sex, and to abuse drugs and alcohol. These sharp differences seem rooted in attitudes as well as peer associations. High school seniors who attend religious services weekly, for example, tend to view a man and a woman who decide to have a child out of wedlock as "living in a way that could be destructive to society." Those who don't attend are more likely to think people are "doing their own thing and not affecting anyone else."

The faith-morality relationship extends to adulthood. Schwartz and Huismans, in their studies of Jews in Israel, Catholics in Spain, Calvinists in the Netherlands, the Orthodox in Greece, and Lutherans and Catholics in West Germany, consistently found that highly religious people tended to be less hedonistic and self-oriented. Consistent with this observation, sociologist Seymour Martin Lipset notes that charitable giving and volunteerism are higher in America than in less religious countries.

In a 1981 U.S. Values Survey, frequent worship attendance predicted lower scores on a dishonesty scale that assessed, for example, self-serving lies, tax cheating, and failing to report damaging a parked car. Moreover, cities with high churchgoing rates tend to be cities with low crime rates. In Provo, Utah, where more than 9 in 10 people are church members, you can more readily leave your car unlocked than in Seattle, where fewer than a third are. Voltaire, it seems, was on to something.

Many people sense this faith-morality correlation. If your car broke down in a crime-ridden area and some strapping teenage boys approached you, wouldn't "you feel better to know they had just come from a Bible study?" asks Rabbi Dennis Prager of Los Angeles. Still, the sharp-eyed reader may be asking another of those questions that help keep social scientists in business: Why does religion predict decreased hedonism and increased traditional morality? Is this an effect of religion per se, or of the socialization provided by religious families, which more often are undisrupted? As with the correlation between father absence and social pathology, which may be mediated by other factors like repeated uprootings, religion is an amalgam that includes devotion to a reality beyond self, a purpose for living, participation in a community with shared values, and hope for the future.

Faith and Altruism

So people of faith are, for whatever reasons, somewhat more traditionally moral—more honest and law abiding and less hedonistic.

But are they more actively compassionate? Or are they mostly self-righteous hypocrites?

People often wonder about Christianity, which has a curious history of links with both love and hate. On one side are Bible-thumping slave owners, Ku Klux Klanners, and apartheid defenders. On the other are the religious roots of the antislavery movement, the clergy's leadership of the American and South African civil rights movements, and the church's establishment of universities and Third World medical care.

A midcentury profusion of studies of religion and prejudice revealed a similarly mixed picture. On one hand, American church members expressed more racial prejudice than nonmembers, and those with conservative Christian beliefs expressed more than those who were less conservative. For many, religion seemed a cultural habit, a part of their community tradition, which also happened to include racial segregation.

On the other hand, the most faithful church attenders expressed less prejudice than occasional attenders. Clergy members expressed more tolerance and civil rights support than lay people. And those for whom religion was an end ("My religious beliefs are what really lie behind my whole approach to life") were less prejudiced than those for whom religion was a means ("A primary reason for my interest in religion is that my church is a congenial social activity"). Among church members, the devout expressed consistently less prejudice than those who gave religion lip service. "We have just enough religion to make us hate," said the English satirist Jonathan Swift, "but not enough to make us love one another."

Faith-related compassion becomes even clearer when we look at who gives most generously of time and money. *Fortune* reports that America's top 25 philanthropists share several characteristics. They are mostly self-made. They have been givers all their lives. And "they're religious: Jewish, Mormon, Protestant, and Catholic. And most attribute their philanthropic urges at least in part to their religious backgrounds."

The same appears true of the rest of us. In a 1987 Gallup survey, Americans who said they never attended church or synagogue reported giving away 1.1 percent of their incomes. Weekly attenders were two and a half times as generous. This 24 percent of the population gave 48 percent of all charitable contributions. The other three-quarters of

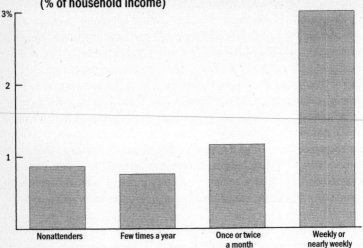

Fig. 10.2 Religious Attendance and Charitable Contributions (% of household income)

Source: Gallup survey reported in *Giving & Volunteering in the United States* (Washington, D.C.: Independent Sector, 1994)

Americans give the remaining half. Follow-up surveys in 1990, 1992, and 1994 replicated this pattern.

An estate-planning attorney at one of western Michigan's largest law firms told me that people in her highly religious area of the state are much more likely to assign part of their estate to charity than are people on the state's less religious eastern side. Much of this annual and legacy giving is not to churches. Two-thirds of the money given to secular charities comes from contributors who also give to religious organizations. (Nearly 90 percent of contributions to all causes comes from individuals, the rest mostly from bequests, foundations, and corporations.) And of the billions given to congregations, nearly half gets donated to other organizations or allocated to nonreligious programming (and that doesn't count donations of food, clothing, and shelter by most congregations).

The faith-generosity effect extends to the giving of time.

- Among the 12 percent of Americans whom George Gallup classified as "highly spiritually committed," 46 percent said they were presently working among the poor, the infirm, or the elderly—many more than the 22 percent among those "highly uncommitted."

- In a follow-up Gallup survey, charitable and social service volunteering was reported by 28 percent of those who rated religion "not very important" in their lives and by 50 percent of those who rated it "very important."
- In the 1992 Gallup survey, those not attending church volunteered 1.4 hours a week while those attending weekly volunteered 3.2 hours. The follow-up survey in 1994 found the same pattern, as did a 1996 University of Virginia national survey.
- And in yet another Gallup survey, 37 percent of those rarely if ever attending church, and 76 percent of those attending weekly, reported thinking at least a "fair amount" about "your responsibility to the poor."
- Among one notable self-giving population—adoptive parents—religious commitment is commonplace. In one national sample, 63 percent reported attending a worship service often.

Religious consciousness, it appears, does shape a larger agenda than advancing one's own private world. It cultivates the idea that my wealth and talents are gifts of which I am the steward. Spirituality promotes a "bond of care for others," says Boston College sociologist Paul Schervish. This is quite unlike the presumption of Richard Dawkins that in a universe of "blind physical forces and genetic replication, some people

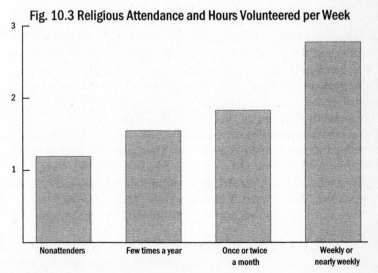

Fig. 10.3 Religious Attendance and Hours Volunteered per Week

| Nonattenders | Few times a year | Once or twice a month | Weekly or nearly weekly |

Source: Gallup survey reported in *Giving & Volunteering in the United States*

are going to get hurt, others are going to get lucky, and you won't find any rhyme or reason for it." "How convenient," responds Gregg Easter-brook, "that someone who has himself won a privileged position in life blames only a callous universe—not lack of action by persons in privileged positions—for the needs of the less fortunate. If there is higher purpose then we have obligations to one another and will be judged if those obligations go unmet."

The highest forms of altruism, psychologists Dennis Krebs and Frank Van Hesteren contend after reviewing available theory and research, are rooted in a "cosmic feeling of oneness with the universe, identification with the species, active compassion for a commonwealth of beings." Such altruism is "selfless, stemming from *agape,* an ethic of responsible universal love, service, and sacrifice that is extended to others without regard for merit." Something like the religious idea of a reality and purpose beyond self would seem foundational to such "universal self-sacrificial love."

This kind of altruism was vividly demonstrated a half century ago. With Nazi submarines sinking ships faster than the Allied forces could replace them, the troop ship SS *Dorchester* steamed out of New York harbor with 902 men headed for Greenland. Among those leaving anxious families behind were four chaplains, Methodist preacher George Fox, Rabbi Alexander Goode, Catholic priest John Washington, and Reformed Church minister Clark Poling. Some 150 miles from their destination, a submarine caught the *Dorchester* in its crosshairs. Within moments of the torpedo's impact, stunned men were pouring out from their bunks as the ship began listing. With power cut off, the escort vessels, unaware of the unfolding tragedy, pushed on in the darkness. On board, chaos reigned as panicky men came up from the hold without life jackets and leaped into overcrowded lifeboats.

As the four chaplains arrived on the steeply sloping deck they began guiding the men to their boat stations. They opened a storage locker, distributed life jackets, and coaxed the men over the side. When Petty Officer John Mahoney turned back to retrieve his gloves, Rabbi Goode responded, "Never mind. I have two pairs." Only later did Mahoney realize that the rabbi was not conveniently carrying an extra pair; he was giving up his own.

In the icy, oil-smeared water, Private William Bednar heard the chaplains preaching courage and found the strength to swim out from under the ship until he reached a life raft. Still on board, Grady Clark watched in awe as the chaplains handed out the last life jacket and then, with ultimate selflessness, gave away their own. As Clark slipped into the waters he looked back at an unforgettable sight: the four chaplains standing—their arms linked—praying, in Latin, Hebrew, and English. Other men joined them in a huddle as the *Dorchester* slid beneath the sea. "It was the finest thing I have ever seen or hope to see this side of heaven," said John Ladd, another of the 230 survivors.

Faith-based altruism is at work here in Holland, Michigan, where the Head Start Day Care program was envisioned by a prayer group at the church where it still operates. The thriving Boys and Girls Club was spawned by the Interparish Council. Habitat for Humanity construction is mostly done by church volunteers. Our community's two main nongovernmental agencies for supporting the poor—the Community Action House and the Good Samaritan Center—were begun by churches, which continue to contribute operating funds. The local theological seminary houses the community soup kitchen. Churches fund the community's homeless shelter. Annually, more than 2,000 townspeople, sponsored by thousands more—nearly all from churches—gather for a world hunger relief walk. If the churches of my community (and likely yours) shut down, along with all the charitable action they foster, we would see a sharp drop in beds for the homeless, food for the hungry, and services to children. Partners for Sacred Places, a nondenominational group dedicated to preserving old religious buildings, reports that 9 of 10 city congregations with pre-1940 buildings provide space for community programming such as food pantries, clothing closets, soup kitchens, child-care centers, recreation programs, AA meetings, and after-school activities.

As always, there are numerous exceptions—big-hearted people outside the church and miserly people of faith. Moreover, churches can become unwitting allies with low-wage industries when they rush to provide low-cost housing, food, and clothing without asking why the workers cannot afford these necessities. "In one Nebraska community," recalls David Ostendorf, director of the Center for New Community, "churches responded to the appeals by the nation's largest [meat] packer to assist new immigrant employees with affordable housing and day care, but never asked the company why the workers could not afford either one." By so doing, the churches conspired in the packer's exploitation of both workers and the community.

Still, it takes a curmudgeon to quarrel with the motives that draw people to feed the hungry, house the homeless, heal the hurting, and care for children. And mountains of data and anecdotes make it hard to dispute the conclusion of Frank Emerson Andrews that "religion is the mother of philanthropy."

Faith and Social Reform

After the internally weakened Roman Empire fell in the 5th century, chaos reigned in Europe for several hundred years. As illiterate tribes warred, literacy and civility crumbled and medieval society verged on barbarism. Rather than concede to the Dark Ages, the medieval church offered a counterculture. Disciplined monastic orders preserved literature and the scriptures, ran schools, sheltered orphans, opened hospitals, plowed fields, and practiced communal caring. "By holding on to such vestiges of civilization—faith, learning, and civility —these monks and nuns held back the night and eventually the West emerged from the Dark Ages," in Charles Colson's words. Like those monastic communities, he argues, churches today can serve as outposts of truth, decency, and civilization in the darkening culture around us.

The history of social reform movements suggests that Colson may be right. Although people of faith, as part of their culture, are often captive to their culture's norms—to individualism and materialism in contemporary America—it was people of faith who built hospitals, helped the mentally ill, staffed orphanages, brought hope to prisoners, and spread literacy.

Recall, too, how people of faith helped abolish the slave trade, lead civil rights movements, and challenge totalitarianism. In aristocratic England during the 1700s, as in America, the wealthy stood on the backs of children working in squalid conditions, and of slaves forcibly removed from their home continents and sold as chattel to masters in strange lands. But then, year by year, opposition grew. Slave trader John Newton was spiritually transformed from profiteer to pastor, abolitionist, and lyricist of "Amazing Grace." With other evangelical "enthusiasts" of the time, Newton endured the fashionable world's contempt and became a hero to politician William Wilberforce, who had likewise experienced a religious conversion. When Wilberforce considered resigning from the House of Commons, Newton along with Prime Minister William Pitt urged him to become a force for good. Wilberforce took the words to heart, believing that "Almighty God has set before me two great objectives": "the abolition of the slave trade and the reformation of [morals]."

For two decades, he eloquently pressed his case against stiff opposition. "Things have come to a pretty pass when religion is allowed to invade public life," huffed one British lord. Undaunted, Wilberforce and his community of believers persisted. They founded the Society for the Education of Africans, the Society for the Bettering of the Condition of the Poor, and the Society for the Relief of Debtors, and finally won the hearts of citizens and the Parliament. On March 25, 1807, the slave trade was banned.

It was, of course, some time later that slavery itself was abolished in England and the United States. The races were still not enjoying equal rights in 1956, when a young Martin Luther King sermonized in Montgomery, Alabama, that "standing up for the truth of God is the greatest thing in the world. . . . The end of life is to do the will of God, come what may." Only through spiritual transformation, he said, "do we gain the strength to fight vigorously the evils of the world in a humble and loving spirit."

Such hope has empowered other heroes to fight tyrannical governments. "It is no accident that the only open challenge to the totalitarian state has come from men of deep religious faith," observed the great journalist Walter Lippmann in *The Good Society*. "For in their faith they are vindicated as immortal souls, and from this enhancement of their dignity they find the reason why they must offer a perpetual challenge to the dominion of men over men." Lippmann may have overlooked people of faith who have condoned inhumanity, as did many German Christians under Hitler. Nevertheless, we cannot forget the profiles in courage:

- Theologian-pastor Dietrich Bonhoeffer enduring two years in a Nazi prison before being executed for his opposition to Hitler.
- The pastors of Le Chambon, France, whose 5,000 residents sheltered some 5,000 Jews, many of them children brought there for refuge while French collaborators elsewhere were delivering Jews to the Nazis. The people of Le Chambon, mostly descendants of a persecuted Protestant group, had been taught by their pastors to "resist whenever our adversaries will demand of us obedience contrary to the orders of the Gospel." Ordered to reveal the sheltered Jews, the head pastor refused, saying, "I don't know of Jews, I only know of human beings."

- El Salvador's only doctoral-level psychologist, Father Ignacio Martin-Baro, who after surviving six assassination attempts continued publishing data exposing Salvadoran poverty and oppression until a military death squad gunned him down along with five fellow Jesuits and two of their helpers.
- El Salvador's Archbishop Oscar Romero, felled by an assassin's bullet through his heart, reportedly just as he was finishing the words of the Eucharist: "This is my body . . . given for you . . . This is the cup of my blood . . . shed for you."
- Romanian pastor Laszlo Tokes, who having protested dictator Nicolae Ceausescu's brutal oppression, suffered being banned, harassed, beaten, and stabbed. Finally his people formed a protective human chain around his church and parsonage, igniting a revolution that in three days swept the country and toppled Ceausescu.

Contemporary American examples of moral fervor fired by a religious calling are not hard to come by. In the aftermath of her surprise best-seller, *The Measure of Our Success*, Marian Wright Edelman agreed with her publisher to write a book on children's policy. Instead, what poured out from this spiritual woman was a sampling of her own daily prayers and meditations. "My faith has been the driving thing in my life," she explained.

Many in the African-American community share Edelman's spiritually rooted passion for family renewal. "The black church is at the leading edge of the African-American community's push to influence the future of its families," observes historian Andrew Billingsley. Speaking recently to 40,000 delegates of the 8.7 million member National Baptist Convention USA—the nation's largest black organization—T. J. Jemison declared that the group would henceforth give highest priority to the family. In documenting the strength of America's 76,000 black churches as centers for community renewal, Billingsley expresses optimism that Jemison and kindred pastors just might succeed.

University of Chicago professor Don Browning has intensively studied one such church just south of the campus neighborhood where he lives. The Pentecostal Apostolic Church of God has for nearly 35 years been led by Arthur Brazier, who also heads the Woodlawn Organization's efforts to renew its ghetto neighborhood through new jobs and job training, better housing, and improved transportation. As a holiness church, Apostolic aims first to convert people, give them the gift of the Holy Spirit, and motivate them to lives of moral purity. Although politically liberal (in supporting fair housing, welfare, and affirmative action), its 10,000 members tend to be behaviorally conservative (in accepting admonitions not to drink, smoke, cheat, or have sex outside marriage).

The church's second aim is to reconstruct the black family by renewing an important role for black men. Nearly 40 percent of its parishioners are men, most under age 50. The church reminds these men that husband-wife relations are not a matter of 50–50 but "100–100." Although people from all family structures are welcome, Browning reports that the church "performs countless weddings each year, witnesses very few divorces among its congregation, sees few out-of-wedlock births among its teenagers, and supports large numbers of its children through high school and into higher education. . . . Apostolic Church even today is Woodlawn's most powerful force for social reconstruction."

Robert L. Woodson, founder of the National Center for Neighborhood Enterprise, sees examples of such religiously rooted renewal across America. The most effective community service programs, he believes, are those that satisfy "the hunger I sense in America . . . not a hunger for things but a search for meaning. . . . I'm not saying the spiritually based programs always work, only that the successful programs almost always have a spiritual base." If Cornel West is right to describe the plight of impoverished ghetto youth as "a life of horrifying meaninglessness, hopelessness, and (most important) lovelessness," then programs that attend to the inward formation of meaning, hope, and character—all words that religiously motivated caregivers comfortably speak—may indeed prove most effective. Neither Woodson nor West would be surprised at Harvard economist Richard Freeman's finding that church attendance is a "substantial" predictor of inner-city black males escaping poverty, drugs, and crime. Nor would they be surprised at the Nation of Islam's gathering nearly a million men for "moral and spiritual renewal"—in one of the safest crowds on earth, with but a single arrest throughout the day.

Vanderbilt University criminologist Byron Johnson and his colleagues have extended Freeman's finding. Most of the 40 existing religion-delinquency studies, they report, confirm that religiously involved teens are less likely to commit delinquent acts. Their own analyses have focused on 2,358 young urban black males interviewed by the National Bureau of Economic Research, on 12,686 youths followed by the National Longitudinal Survey of Youth, and on 1,725 studied over time in the National Youth Survey. In all these studies, "Most delinquent acts were committed by juveniles who had low levels of religious commitment. Those juveniles whose religiosity levels were in the middle to high levels committed very few delinquent acts." Even when controlling for other factors, such as socioeconomic level, neighborhood, and peer influences, kids who went to church rarely were delinquent.

Teen by teen, block by block, neighborhood by neighborhood, many inner city pastors have been harnessing the power of moral and spiritual renewal. Boston's police commissioner has shared credit for the city's recent crime drop and five years with only one youth gun death with the "Ten-Point Coalition" of churches organized by Rev. Eugene Rivers III to evangelize gang members and drug traffickers, walk the streets, and offer "high octane" faith-based programs in preparing young men to be fathers. Rivers, a former gang member and now pastor of a Pentecostal church, explains, "We knew that the presence of the Divine in a child's life makes that child feel differently about himself because it is the Divine that establishes the sacredness of the human experience." John DiIulio, who also directs the Partnership for Research on Religion and At-Risk Youth, is documenting the influence of these "super-preachers" on youths he once called "super-predators." He attributes their influence to the "four Ms"—their monitoring, mentoring, and ministering, all grounded in a moral understanding of the nature of the problem.

Faith-rooted social services are spreading outside of urban centers. In Michigan, "Holland and surrounding Ottawa County has come closer than any community in America to the implicit goal of the national welfare overhaul put in place last year," reports the *Washington Post*. "Every able-bodied welfare recipient here has found a job." Social service officials accomplished this with the support of 50 local churches—and their member carpenters, doctors, mechanics, teachers, attorneys, and retirees. When Sylvia Ornelas, a mother of four, was connected with Hardewyk Christian Reformed Church, people helped her with school shopping, buying a used car, locating an apartment, and securing a job. When her husband reentered her life, Pastor Andrew Gorter provided the couple with marital counseling.

Those of us who live in Holland are aware that the level of success experienced here might be specific to communities like ours with lots of active churches and virtually no unemployment. In communities where the ratio of poor people per church is higher and the employment rate is lower, churches may be overwhelmed by the needs. Yet not only Michigan but other states such as Mississippi and Texas are now partnering with churches in weaving the social safety net.

Might this new partnership between government and religious nonprofit organizations develop while preserving the government's religious neutrality? Ronald Sider, Heidi Rolland, and Stephen Monsma believe it can. To be neutral, federal funds would need to be equally available toward those of any faith or none and without any direct support of an organization's religious mission. But such support could still allow the organization to offer a faith component. So long as faith-based programs are nondiscriminatory and noncoercive, DiIulio argues, "it makes good practical and moral sense to strive to keep the 'faith' in 'faith-based'" programs.

Such partnership has happened before and is happening still. When the GI Bill gave veterans educational support they could take it to a secular school or a school of any religious persuasion, and so can today's lower-income college students who receive Pell grants. Likewise, parents are free to take federal vouchers for child-care services to whatever provider (sectarian or not) they believe would best meet their child's needs. Drug addicts might be given similar freedom to redeem rehabilitation vouchers at nonsectarian or sectarian nonprofit agencies. If a Muslim addiction recovery program that included a spiritual transformation component proved effective, addicts could be at liberty to elect it for themselves. Michigan has contracted with the Salvation Army to provide services for the homeless (not including any spiritual counseling, which is privately funded). In Texas, Arlington's Tillie Burgin provides 500 families a day with food, clothing, day care, medical care, and after-school programs through Mission Arlington, where she also offers Bible studies.

Colson claims that former inmates of São Paulo's Humaita Prison, which is run by his Prison Fellowship religious organization, experience a mere 4 percent recidivism rate. This compares, he says, with 75 percent recidivism among other Brazilian and American prisons. Setting aside our natural skepticism about such a spectacular claim—I, too, am from Missouri—assume for the moment that Colson's mix of vocational training, character-building classes, and religious instruction is even half as effective as he believes and could be successfully replicated in the United States. If so, should federal or state governments provide funding for Prison Fellowship (or Muslim or other religious organizations, for that matter) to run alternative prisons, in which prisoners could elect to be incarcerated?

Such questions deserve debate among those who believe that society has a compelling interest in government supporting the most effective programs, without religious favoritism, and those who favor the separation of state from even the nonreligious component of religion-affiliated nonprofits. Conservatives seem to welcome the diversion of government funds to faith-based programs, but so do some liberals. "Some of the best antipoverty work I've seen has come from faith-based agencies," said Senator Paul Wellstone of Minnesota in voting for the "charitable choice" provision in the 1996 welfare reform bill (before voting against the final bill). "I don't see the First Amendment as so rigid that it prevents us from contracting with people who are getting the job done right," added Senator Bob Kerrey of Nebraska. In 1998, President Clinton unveiled a "values-based violence prevention initiative" making $2.2 million in grants to foster collaboration between faith-based groups and police and community organizations. "The faith community has an important role to play" in bringing down juvenile crime, the president declared. In 1999, Al Gore and George W. Bush kicked off their presidential campaigns with bipartisan support of funds for nondiscriminatory "faith-based" social services.

Regardless of the outcome of this debate, the contribution of church and synagogue to social renewal must also be prophetic. It must not only care for the casualties at the base of the cliffs but also call for guardrails at the top. In Britain, which is entering a parallel national debate over "the moral and spiritual decline of the nation," George Carey opened "an unprecedented debate on morality" in the House of Lords in 1996 by decrying the decline of moral order and spiritual purpose and the tendency to view moral judgments as mere private taste. Jonathan Sacks, England's chief rabbi, supported his compatriot by saying:

> The power of the Judaeo-Christian tradition is that it charts a moral reality larger than private inclination. . . . It suggests that not all choices are equal: some lead on to blessing, others to lives of quiet despair. . . .
>
> It may be that religious leaders can no longer endorse, but instead must challenge the prevailing consensus—the role of the prophet through the ages. In which case the scene is set for a genuine debate between two conflicting visions—between those who see the individual as a bundle of

impulses to be gratified and those who see humanity in the image of God; between those who see society as a series of private gardens of desire and those who make space for public parts which we do not own but which we jointly maintain for the sake of others and the future. No debate could be more fundamental, and its outcome will shape the social contours of the 21st century.

Renewing Faith

"America, you must be born again!" declared Martin Luther King, Jr., not long before his death. Speaking in the church where King preached his last sermon, President Clinton recounted progress since then, yet warned that we may "still fail unless we meet the great crisis of the spirit that is gripping America today." Reacting against the religious right's identification with conservative Republican politics, a coalition of 80 "progressive evangelical" Protestants, Catholics, and people of Orthodox faith nevertheless agreed with them "that the crisis we face in this country is indeed a spiritual one."

King, Clinton, and the religious right and left would surely have acknowledged that religion is a mixed bag. It motivates good, yet has also been used as justification for apartheid, limiting women's rights, gay bashing, ethnic cleansing, and war. For all sorts of cruel deeds, noted William James, "Piety is the mask"—a mask that sometimes portrays lovely expressions while hiding ugly motives. In almost every country, leaders invoke religion to sanctify the present order. As chaplain to the air crews that bombed Hiroshima, Nagasaki, and other Japanese civilian targets, Father George Zabelka provided religion's blessing for their missions of devastation. Years later he came to regret it. "The whole structure of the secular, religious, and military society told me clearly that it was all right to 'let the Japs have it.' God was on the side of my country."

For many, however, religion is more a mark of group identity than of genuine piety. In the midst of conflict, people may identify themselves as Serbian Orthodox or Protestant and yet be unable to identify any of Jesus' Beatitudes (blessed are the merciful, the meek, the peacemakers, and those who hunger and thirst for righteousness). On balance, godliness seems more often linked with character, altruism, and social reform. In *The Pursuit of Happiness* I documented links between faith and joy as well. In Europe and North America, religiously

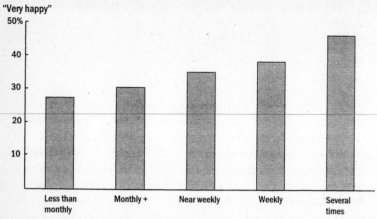

Fig. 10.4 Religious Attendance and Happiness

"Very happy"

| | Less than monthly | Monthly + | Near weekly | Weekly | Several times |

Source: 34,706 participants in General Social Surveys, National Opinion Research Center, 1972–96

active people report greater happiness. In one Gallup survey, highly spiritual people (who agreed, for example, with the statement "My religious faith is the most important influence in my life") were twice as likely as those lowest in spiritual commitment to declare themselves very happy. Other surveys find that happiness and life satisfaction rise with strength of religious affiliation and frequency of worship attendance. One statistical digest of research among the elderly found that one of the best predictors of life satisfaction is religiousness.

Studies have also probed the connection between faith and coping with a crisis. Compared with religiously inactive widows, recently widowed women who worship regularly report more joy in their lives. Compared with irreligious mothers of disabled children, those with a deep religious faith are less vulnerable to depression. Those with a strong faith also recover greater happiness after suffering divorce, unemployment, or serious illness.

If faith advances both social health and personal happiness, is this an argument for belief? Shortly before he died, Carl Sagan asked Martin Gardner if he believed in God because it made him "feel good." "I replied that this was exactly right," recalled Gardner, "though the emotion was deeper than the way one feels good after three drinks. It is a way of escaping from a deep-seated despair." Although this pragmatic argument for taking a leap of faith is worth pondering, the key issue for belief should be truth. If belief in God were known to be true, though occasionally discomfiting, what honest person would want to disbelieve? If known to be untrue but an opiate for the masses, what honest person would want to believe?

If God does not exist, one might still argue that faith is prudent— better to believe in *something* beyond the self. Or lacking belief in God, we could seek to live as if we did. But surely a knowingly make-believe faith would be one that pales alongside the robust faith of those who think their cosmic vision really captures transcendent truth. Truth, and one's confidence in it, matters.

Leaving theologians and atheists to duke it out over the ancient what-is-truth question, we are left with the fact that 96 percent of Americans affirm the reality of God and 87 percent claim religion is at least "fairly important" in their own lives. Given such belief, can the social and personal significance of faith motivate our giving it priority in our personal and communal lives? I should think so. Since we do believe in God, we should try to live as though we did.

How, then, might the 96 percent of us deepen our individual and collective spirituality? How might we extend our God concept beyond times of crisis? How might we increase the mere 13 percent whom Gallup judges to "have a 'transforming faith,' manifested in measurable attitudinal and behavioral ways"? To the library of recent books on spiritual formation, I add three insights derived from social psychological research.

Belief follows behavior. One of social psychology's premier lessons is that we are as likely to act ourselves into a way of thinking as to think ourselves into action. Not only do we often stand up for what we believe, we also come to believe more strongly in what we have stood up for. In experiment after experiment, people who speak or write on behalf of an idea become more convinced of it. Saying becomes believing.

Likewise, people induced to harm a supposed innocent victim— by making cutting comments or delivering electric shocks—will often later disparage their victim. "If the King destroys a man, that's proof to the King it must have been a bad man," says Thomas Cromwell in Robert Bolt's *A Man for All Seasons*. Little evils, too, corrode the conscience, paving the way for greater ones. Thus, men in training to be torturers have first been engaged as guards outside interrogation cells, then as inside guards, then as questioners and torturers. What we do, we gradually become.

Fortunately, the principle works for good, too. In the years following school desegregation and the 1964 Civil Rights Act, white Americans expressed diminishing racial prejudice. As we interacted more with those of other races, our attitudes improved. And as we came to act more alike across America—thanks to more uniform national standards against discrimination—we began to think more alike. Experiments confirm that moral action strengthens conscience, and that doing favors for another person often leads us to like the person more. We love people for the good we do them as well as for the good they do us. Thus Jewish tradition advises dealing with anger by giving a gift to the object of your rage. Evil acts shape the self, but so do moral acts.

As social psychologists explore the interplay between attitudes and behavior, so the Jewish-Christian tradition reminds us of the interplay between faith and action. Like chicken and egg, each generates the other. Faith feeds action: Ezekiel, Isaiah, Jeremiah, and Paul each undergo a spiritual transformation that produces new behavior. But faith also follows action. In the Old Testament, the Hebrew word for *know* is usually a verb, something one does. To know love, one must not only know about love, one must *act* lovingly.

Philosophers and theologians note how faith grows as people act on what little faith they have. Rather than insist that people believe before they pray, Talmudic scholars would tell rabbis to get them to pray and then their belief will grow. "The proof of Christianity really consists in 'following,'" declared Soren Kierkegaard. To attain faith, said Pascal, "follow the way by which [the committed] began; by acting as if they believed, taking the holy water, having masses said, etc. Even this will naturally make you believe." C. S. Lewis concurred: "Believe in God and you will have to face hours when it seems *obvious* that this material world is the only reality; disbelieve in Him and you must face hours when this material world seems to shout at you that it is not all. No conviction, religious or irreligious, will, of itself, end once and for all [these doubts] in the soul. Only the practice of Faith resulting in the habit of Faith will gradually do that."

Faith is like love. When we hoard it, it shrivels. When we live and express it, it grows. So, to deepen faith—or any attitude or conviction—we had best not sit passively, waiting for conviction to overtake us.

Rather, enact what little faith we have. "Ask yourself," advised Lewis, " 'If I were sure that I loved God, what would I do?' When you have found the answer, go and do it."

Group amplification. Educational researchers have observed a curious phenomenon: Over time, initial differences between groups of college students often grow. If the first-year students at one college tend to be more intellectually oriented than those at another, their difference will likely be amplified by the time they are seniors. Similarly, if students who join fraternities and sororities are politically more conservative than those who don't, the political attitude gap between the two groups will probably widen as they progress through college.

This enhancement of a group's prevailing tendencies—called group polarization—occurs in the laboratory when people in small groups discuss attitudes that most of them favor or oppose. For example, George Bishop and I discovered that when prejudiced high school students discussed racial issues with other like-minded students, their attitudes became even more prejudiced. When low-prejudice students discussed the same issues, they became more tolerant.

Group polarization can have dire consequences. From their analysis of terrorist organizations around the world, psychologists Clark McCauley and Mary Segal found that the terrorist mentality does not erupt suddenly. Rather, it arises among people who have come together because of a grievance and who become more and more extreme as they interact in isolation from moderating influences. But groups can also amplify desired tendencies, as when people strengthen one another in self-help groups. "The more we get together, the slimmer we'll be," was the theme of one weight-loss group. Through fellowship with kindred spirits, people also heighten their religious identity. As Thomas à Kempis advised, "a devout communing on spiritual things sometimes greatly helps the health of the soul, especially when men of one mind and spirit in God meet and speak and commune together."

Throughout their history, the Jewish and Christian traditions have affirmed that faith grows from life in a worshipping community. Communal images abound: "We are the church," "where two or three are gathered," "members of one body," "bearing one another's burdens," supported by "the ties that bind." It's tough to remain a minority of one, to sustain a purely private faith, to hold to one's Amish convictions if living alone in Los Angeles. For the members of early Christian cell groups, for members of religious orders, and for all believers, conviction and commitment grow when shared. The ancient Catholic dictum "outside the church there is no salvation" anticipated social psychological wisdom about our need to belong and about the strength found in community.

As further evidence, consider the findings of a national Gallup survey analyzed by sociologist Robert Wuthnow. Religious individualists—those who said they develop their own spirituality independent of any church—were less likely than those within the church to value caring for the needy and to contribute time to charitable activities. The more often people claimed to experience divine love, the more time they volunteered, *if* they attended church regularly. Other studies confirm, says Wuthnow, "that spirituality begins to move people toward being compassionate only when a threshold of involvement in some kind of collective religious activity has been reached."

As described in Chapter 7, we live in a culture and time marked by unprecedented individualism. Baby-boomer spirituality is often private and self-defined. It asserts what most Americans today believe—that people can be good Christians or Jews alone, apart from any church or synagogue. Individualists prefer to go it alone, home-brewing their beliefs and values apart from the historic wisdom of communities of faith.

Robert Bellah illustrated today's religious individualism by quoting part of an interview with a young nurse, Sheila. "I believe in God," she explained. "I'm not a religious fanatic. I can't remember the last time I went to church. My faith has carried me a long way. It's Sheilaism. Just my own little voice."

Such do-it-yourself piety is not only thinner—less likely to yield compassionate action—it also has contributed to the decline of traditional denominations, notes University of Massachusetts sociologist N. J. Demerath III. Many people attribute the decline of mainline Protestant membership to reactions against its liberalism. Evidence discounts this. Presbyterian giving did not decline after the controversial defense fund was established on behalf of black radical Angela Davis. Moreover, youths who left the mainline churches have not flocked to conservative churches. Rather, they tend to have been liberals who merely drifted away, caught up in their culture's valuing of freedom and autonomy. Individualism is a "centrifugal organizational force," says

Demerath, leading people away from commitment and community and toward privatization.

Make youth a priority. A curious fact of life is that many attitudes vary with age. In Chapter 2, for example, we saw that 62 percent of people over 50 consider premarital sex wrong, as do only 23 percent of those 18 to 29. There are two possible explanations for this age gap. One is a life-cycle explanation: attitudes change (in this case, become more conservative) as people grow older. The other is a generational explanation: the attitudes older people adopted when they were young persist; a generation gap develops because today's young people are adopting different attitudes.

UCLA psychologist David Sears reports that the evidence "almost invariably" supports the generational explanation. When surveying and resurveying groups of younger and older people over several years, and when studying how much people change when moving into new situations, researchers have found that older people's attitudes are more durable. Although we never stop learning, attitudes and worldviews formed during the teens and early twenties tend to persist.

A striking example: During the 1930s and early 1940s, students at Vermont's Bennington College—women from privileged, conservative families—encountered a free-spirited environment led by a left-leaning young faculty. One of those faculty, social psychologist Theodore Newcomb, later denied the faculty was trying to make "good little liberals" out of its students. Nevertheless, they succeeded. The students became much more liberal than was typical of those from their backgrounds. Moreover, attitudes formed at Bennington endured. A half century later, the Bennington women, now seventyish, voted Democratic by a 3 to 1 margin in the 1984 presidential election, while other seventyish college-educated women were voting Republican by a 3 to 1 margin. The views embraced in the impressionable years of transition to adulthood had survived a lifetime of wider experience.

Experiences during adolescence and early adulthood are formative partly because they make deep and lasting impressions. When University of Michigan researchers Howard Schuman and Jacqueline Scott asked people to name the one or two most important national or world events of the previous half century, most recalled something from their teens or early twenties. For those who experienced the Great Depression or World War II as 16- to 24-year-olds, those events overshadowed the civil rights movement and the Kennedy assassination of the early '60s, the Vietnam War and moon landing of the late '60s, and the women's movement of the '70s, each of which imprinted themselves on the minds of those who experienced them as 16- to 24-year-olds.

When setting priorities, rabbis, priests, and pastors should bear in mind the impressionability of the teens and early twenties. Given the limits of parental influence and the great socializing power of peer culture, they should recognize the significance of their potential influence on the ethos of neighborhood youth culture.

Regrettably, few in the clergy do make youth a priority, although it's understandable. It is difficult work, sometimes without visible rewards. Young people provide little praise for well-delivered messages, few words of thanks for pastoral calls, and more than a few exasperating moments. They don't hire and pay clergy members, set their budgets, or write their job descriptions. So it is not surprising that seminaries and churches focus most of their time and resources on adults, often leaving youths to ill-equipped volunteers or temporary interns.

"Too many congregations are not child- and family-friendly," Edelman laments. "Religious congregations need to examine their service and witness for our children and families. Too many family and youth ministries are weak or are limited to one day of worship. What is there for the young people to do in your congregation and community during the week? On Friday and Saturday nights? During the summer months?"

A half century ago a group of Jewish leaders led by Mordecai Kaplan of the Jewish Theological Seminary of America decided to use those summer months. They envisioned a summer-long camp program that would contest Jewish children's assimilation into the surrounding culture. Camp Ramah, as they called it, offered sports and activities, but also intensive education and formation in Jewish life, through daily prayer and 90 minutes of religious instruction six days a week. A half century later, and with half a dozen thriving camps plus feeder day camps for 8- to 10-year-olds, the project has produced two generations of leaders for Conservative Judaism, report Ellen and Dana Charry. So why not offer Christian kids a similar summer break from the vulgarity around them and a program to help them "become more embedded in their baptismal identity than in popular culture"?

As Chicago's Pentecostal Apostolic Church of God reminds us, the church's first concern is not social work but developing spiritual roots for its followers. However, as it succeeds in guiding the spiritual formation of its children and youths, it will help renew the world as well. Gandhi understood: "If we are to teach real peace in this world and if we are to carry on a real war against war, we shall have to begin with children." And if religious communities are to advance America's renewal, they must begin by giving priority to the spiritual formation of their children.

Epilogue

Come my friends,
'Tis not too late to seek
a newer world.
—ALFRED, LORD TENNYSON, *Ulysses*, 1842

At the dawn of a new millennium we stand where two roads diverge. One continues down the well-traveled track of radical individualism and materialism leading toward a deepened cultural crisis. As "me thinking" continues to prevail over "we thinking," as the rich-poor gap continues to widen, as the media continue to promote coercive human relations and uncommitted sex, as marriage continues to disintegrate, as children's well-being continues to nosedive, and if violence rebounds with the next recession, calls for imposed order will likely increase.

But this 1960-to-early-1990s trajectory is not our inevitable destiny, as demonstrated by past efforts to project the social future from current trajectories.

- "The family, in its old sense, is disappearing from our land, and not only our free institutions are threatened but the very existence of our society is endangered," warned a contributor to the *Boston Quarterly Review*—in 1859. Despite this dire prediction from a pre-Victorian period of family decline, the family regrouped and survived.
- In 1962, *Look* magazine invited scholars and national leaders to foretell the America of 1987. Along with predictions of 500-mile-per-hour carplanes and automated kitchens were descriptions of family life that projected Ozzie and Harriet into a happy future. "Linda (the wife)

runs her home with extreme good taste and manages her children with serene authority. But she does not try to run or manage her husband." There was no forecast of revolutionary changes in sexual behavior, family life, or gender roles. Indeed, the sexual revolution, women's movement, and gay liberation movement were all unpredicted by the crystal ball of early-1960s mainstream social science. Social scientists can describe the world once it is here much better than we can predict it.

- A "Beyond the Year 2000" special issue of *Time* in 1992 predicted, "The family of the 21st century may have a robot maid, but the chances are good that it will also be interracial or bisexual, divided by divorce, multiplied by remarriage, expanded by new birth technologies—or perhaps all of the above. Single parents and working moms will become increasingly the norm, as will out-of-wedlock babies, though there will surely be a more modern term for them." But this is, once again, merely a projection of recent trends.

However, there is also a less traveled road we are beginning to steer toward. As the slumbering public consciousness awakens, something akin to the earlier social reform movements—the civil rights movement, the feminist movement, the environmental movement—seems to be germinating. "Anyone who tunes in politics even for background music can tell you how the sound has changed," observes Ellen Goodman. Yesterday's shouting match over family values has become today's choir, she says. When singing about children growing up without fathers, "Politicians on the right, left and center may not be hitting exactly the same notes, but like sopranos, tenors and baritones, they're pretty much in harmony." We are recognizing that liberals' risk factors (poverty, inequality, hopelessness) and conservatives' risk factors (early sexualization, unwed parenthood, family fragmentation) all come in the same package. What Winston Churchill said after the Battle of El Alamein could as well be said of the new social ecology movement: "Now this is not the end. It is not even the beginning of the end. But it is, perhaps, the end of the beginning."

History would encourage our hopes for renewal. "This country has gotten itself into a crisis that is unprecedented, that has no equivalent," Daniel Patrick Moynihan proclaims. "But then this country has no equivalent. We have done things in the past that no one would have believed." We have ventured into space. We have bested communism. We even recovered from the crime, intemperance, and family decline that marked the early 1800s and the 1920s.

Moreover, we have strengths to build upon. We have economic abundance, unlike in the Great Depression. We are not threatened by external enemies as during World War II. Our country is not nearly as chaotic as Bosnia. We are not starting from scratch as did the founders. When our national security has been threatened, as it is today, "we the people" have always found the resolve to plan, sacrifice, meet the hardships, and come together in common cause, even as we once came together "to form a more perfect Union, establish Justice, insure domestic Tranquility, provide for the common defense, promote the General Welfare, and secure the Blessings of Liberty to ourselves and our Posterity."

As we come together again on the common ground of concern for our children and their future, let us imagine the culture we aspire to. Whatever our differences, most of us wish for the culture envisioned in Chapter 1—a culture that

- welcomes children into families with mothers and fathers that love them, and an environment that nurtures families,
- rewards initiative and restrains exploitative greed, thus building a strong economy that shrinks the underclass,
- balances individual liberties with communal well-being,
- encourages close relationships within extended families and with supportive neighbors and caring friends, people who celebrate when you're born, care about you as you live, and miss you when you're gone,
- values our diversity while finding unity in shared ideals,
- develops children's capacities for empathy, self-discipline, and honesty,
- provides media that offer social scripts of kindness, civility, attachment, and fidelity,
- regards relationships as covenants and sexuality not as mere recreation but as life-uniting and love-renewing,
- takes care of the soul, by developing a deeper spiritual awareness of a reality greater than self and of life's resulting meaning, purpose, and hope.

So we face that fork in the road. We have, as Solzhenitsyn said in concluding his commencement address at Harvard, "reached a major watershed in history, equal in importance to the turn from the Middle Ages to the Renaissance. It will demand from us a spiritual blaze; we shall have to rise to a new height of vision, to a new level of life, where our physical nature will not be cursed, as in the Middle Ages, but even more importantly, our spiritual being will not be trampled upon, as in the Modern Era."

This ascension is similar to climbing to the next anthropological stage. No one on earth has any other way left—but upward.

Those who take this upward road—those who live remembering the future—will fulfill the ancient prophecy of Isaiah: "You shall raise up the foundations of many generations; you shall be called the repairer of the breach, the restorer of streets to live in."

Notes

Preface

p. ix Wrong track: Richard Morin, "*Washington Post*/Henry J. Kaiser Family Foundation/Harvard University Studies of Political Values," presented at the Communitarian Summit, Washington, D.C., February 1999.

ix Raising kids: *Gallup Poll Monthly,* July 1998, p. 30.

ix "Moral problems": *Emerging Trends,* March 1999, p. 1.

x Public opinion polls: Asked "Which concerns you more, the nation's moral problems or the nation's economic problems?" 53 percent of Americans said "moral problems," 42 percent said "economic problems" (Gallup Poll, in *Emerging Trends,* March 1997, Princeton Religion Research Center); 78 percent rated "the state of moral values in the country today" as "somewhat weak" or "very weak."

xi E. J. Dionne, Jr.: *Community Works: The Revival of Civil Society in America* (Washington, D.C.: Brookings Institution, 1998), pp. 13–14.

xii History of social psychology: See Bertram H. Raven, "Reflections on Interpersonal Influence and Social Power in Experimental Social Psychology," in *Reflections on One Hundred Years of Experimental Social Psychology,* ed. Aroldo Rodrigues and Robert Levine (New York: Basic, 1999).

xiii Leonard Berkowitz: "On the Changes in U.S. Social Psychology: Some Speculation," in *Reflections on One Hundred Years,* ed. Rodrigues and Levine.

Chapter 1: The Best of Times, the Worst of Times

p. 2 Bigotry gauche: See the chapter on "Prejudice" in my *Social Psychology,* 6th ed. (New York: McGraw-Hill, 1999).

3 Life expectancy: 1900 data, *Historical Statistics of the United States, Colonial Times to 1970* (Washington, D.C.: Bureau of the Census, 1976); 1996 data, *Statistical Abstract of the United States, 1998* (Washington, D.C.: Bureau of the Census, 1998), Table 128.

3 Joyce and Paul Bowler: Nicholas Hellen and Simon Trump, "Victorian TV Family Fails Test of Time," *Sunday Times* (London), August 15, 1999.

3 Stephanie Coontz: *The Way We Never Were: American Families and the Nostalgia Trap* (New York: Basic, 1992).

3 Arlene Skolnick: *Embattled Paradise: The American Family in an Age of Uncertainty* (New York: Basic, 1991), p. 154. Skolnick also provides the 1850 statistic given in the previous sentence (p. 153), and the data for the following sentence (p. 166).

4 Graduation rates: *Historical Statistics of the U.S., Colonial Times to 1970*, pt. 1 (Washington, D.C.: Bureau of the Census, 1976).

4 8 in 10 (over age 25): *Statistical Abstract of the United States, 1998*, Tables 264, 265.

4 Women earning money: R. G. Niemi, J. Mueller, and Tom W. Smith, *Trends in Public Opinion: A Compendium of Survey Data* (New York: Greenwood, 1989).

4 Gender opinions: John P. Robinson, "Who's Doing the Housework?" *American Demographics* (December 1988): 24–28, 63.

5 John Mueller: "The Catastrophe Quota: Trouble After the Cold War," *Journal of Conflict Resolution* 38 (1994): 355–75.

5 John M. Templeton: *Is Progress Speeding Up?* (Radnor, Pa.: Templeton Foundation Press, 1997), p. 2.

6 Index of National Civic Health: *A Nation of Spectators* (the final report of the National Commission on Civic Renewal, 1998). The index averages 22 trend lines, each set at 100 for 1974. The components are political (e.g., voter turnout), trust (in others and government), memberships and contributions, security (crime and fear), and family well-being (divorce and nonmarital births).

6 Al Gore: *Earth in the Balance* (Boston: Houghton Mifflin, 1992), pp. 221–22.

6 Edward F. Zigler and Elizabeth P. Gilman, "An Agenda for the 1990s: Supporting Families," in *Rebuilding the Nest: A New Commitment to the American Family,* ed. D. Blankenhorn, S. Bayme, and J. B. Elshtain (Milwaukee, Wis.: Family Service America, 1990.)

6 Children not living with two parents: In 1960, 88 percent of children lived with two parents. In 1998, 68 percent did (48.6 million of 71.4 million children). These are Bureau of the Census survey data reported in *Sta-*

tistical Abstract of the United States, 1998, Tables 85, 86, and "Marital Status and Living Arrangements, March 1998."

6 American Psychological Association members: *Survey of American Psychological Association Members* (Washington, D.C.: American Psychological Association, 1990).

6 Urie Bronfenbrenner: Quoted in Hillary Rodham Clinton, *It Takes a Village* (New York: Simon and Schuster, 1995).

7 Robert Frank: *Luxury Fever: Why Money Fails to Satisfy in an Era of Excess* (New York: Free Press, 1999), p. 92.

9 Fire deaths: *Statistical Abstract of the United States, 1985,* Table 116, and *Statistical Abstract of the United States, 1998,* Table 148.

11 Everett Carll Ladd: *Silent Revolution: The Rebirth of America's Civic Life and What It Means for All of Us* (New York: Free Press, 1998).

11 Alan Ehrenhalt: "Where Have All the Followers Gone?" in *Community Works: The Revival of Civil Society in America,* ed. E. J. Dionne, Jr. (Washington, D.C.: Brookings Institution Press, 1998), p. 96.

12 Bill Clinton: "Catalyzing Scientific Progress," *Science* 279 (1988): 1111.

Chapter 2: The Sexual Swing

p. 12 Jimmy Carter: Quoted in David Whitman, "Was It Good for Us?" *U.S. News & World Report,* May 19, 1997, pp. 57–64.

12 Polls: *Time*/CNN polls, *Time,* February 2 and February 16, 1998, p. 27.

12 Clinton moral standards: Given a multiple choice test with the names of the last nine presidents, 56 percent of the public named President Clinton as having the lowest moral standards, and 77 percent thought he should be censured if not impeached. In citing these figures, Roper Center director Everett C. Ladd contests the idea that Americans were indifferent to Clinton's moral failings ("The Communitarian Spirit and Contemporary America," remarks to the Communitarian Summit, Washington, D.C., February 1999).

14 Ninth graders: About 4 in 10 ninth graders (somewhat less for girls, more for boys) report having had sexual intercourse. Centers for Disease Control, "Sexual Behavior Among High School Students—United States, 1990," *Morbidity and Mortality Weekly Report* 40 (January 3, 1992): 885–87, and "Trends in Sexual Risk Behaviors Among High School Students—United States, 1991–1997," *Morbidity and Mortality Weekly Report* 47 (September 18, 1998): 749–52.

14 Teens and STDs: Alan Guttmacher Institute, *Sex and America's Teenagers,* 1994, p. 38.

14 380,000: S. J. Ventura, R. N. Anderson, J. A. Martin, and B. L. Smith, "Births and Deaths: Preliminary Data for 1997," *National Vital Statistics Reports* 47, no. 4 (Hyattsville, Md.: National Center for Health Statistics, 1998).

14 "Friendliest thing": Quoted in Francis Canavan, "The Sexual Revolution, Explained," *New Oxford Review,* November 1993.

14 Gary Hart: Quoted in Gertrude Himmelfarb, "America's Moral Diversity," *New York Times,* September 6, 1995.

14 Cultural variations in sex: Clellan S. Ford and Frank A. Beach, *Patterns of Sexual Behavior* (New York: Harper & Row, 1951); J. C. Messenger, "Sex and Repression in an Irish Folk Community," in *Human Sexual Behavior,* ed. D. S. Marshall and R. C. Suggs (New York: Basic, 1971).

15 Hong Kong students: M. S. Fan, J. H. Hong, M. L. Ng, L. K. C. Lee, P. K. Lui, and Y. H. Choy, "Western Influences on Chinese Sexuality: Insights from a Comparison of the Sexual Behavior and Attitudes of Shanghai and Hong Kong Freshmen at Universities," *Journal of Sex Education and Therapy* 21 (1995): 158–66.

15 "Revolution in eroticism": Edward Shorter, "Illegitimacy, Sexual Revolution, and Social Change in Modern Europe," in *The American Family in Social-Historical Perspective,* ed. Michael Gordon (New York: St. Martin's, 1973).

15 Kinsey: Alfred C. Kinsey, Wardell B. Pomeroy, Clyde E. Martin, and Paul Gebhard, *Sexual Behavior in the Human Female* (Philadelphia: Saunders, 1953), p. 298.

15 Flapper era: Arlene Skolnick, *Embattled Paradise: The American Family in an Age of Uncertainty* (New York: Basic, 1991), pp. 20, 43.

15 Stephanie Coontz: *The Way We Never Were: American Families and the Nostalgia Trap* (New York: Basic, 1992), p. 39.

16 Premarital sex opinions: Larry Hugick and Jennifer Leonard, "Sex in America," *Gallup Poll Monthly,* October 1991, pp. 60–73.

16 Elizabeth C. Winship: Quoted in Martin Marty, "The TV Made Me Do It," *Context,* February 15, 1995, p. 3.

16 Tory: Quoted in Lillian B. Rubin, " 'People Don't Know Right from Wrong Anymore,' " *Tikkun* 9, no. 1 (1994): 15–18, 83–87.

16 *Seventeen* editor-in-chief: Caroline Miller, quoted in L. Smith, "Magazine Opens Dad's Eyes: Stafford Schools Take *Seventeen* Off Shelves While Reviewing Complaint," *Washington Post,* April 2, 1995.

16 *Seventeen* content analysis: Laura M. Carpenter, "From Girls into Women: Scripts for Sexuality and Romance in *Seventeen* Magazine, 1974–1984," *Journal of Sex Research* 35 (1998): 158–68. The quotes are

taken from June 1994, p. 118, and February 1994, p. 62. The 1994 editors were not, however, encouraging active sexuality, notes Carpenter.

16 Youth risk behavior survey: Centers for Disease Control, "Sexual Behavior Among High School Students."

17 UCLA/American Council on Education survey: Linda J. Sax, Alexander W. Astin, William S. Korn, and Kathryn M. Mahoney, *The American Freshman: National Norms for Fall 1998* (Los Angeles: Higher Education Research Institute, UCLA, 1998).

17 Russell D. Clark III and Elaine Hatfield: "Gender Differences in Willingness to Engage in Casual Sex," *Journal of Psychology and Human Sexuality* 2 (1989): 39–55. Follow-up experiments: Russell D. Clark III, "The Impact of AIDS on Gender Differences in Willingness to Engage in Casual Sex," *Journal of Applied Social Psychology* 20 (1990): 771–82.

17 Marshall H. Segall, P. R. Dasen, John W. Berry, and Y. H. Poortinga: *Human Behavior in Global Perspective: An Introduction to Cross-Cultural Psychology* (New York: Pergamon, 1990), p. 244.

18 John Updike: "The Deadly Sins/Lust: Even the Bible Is Soft on Sex," *New York Times Book Review*, June 20, 1993.

18 National health objective: Centers for Disease Control, "Sexual Behavior Among High School Students."

18 National Campaign to Reduce Teen Pregnancy: Reported by its director, Sarah Brown, in remarks to the Third Annual White House Conference on Character Education, June 7, 1996.

18 Promiscuity and rape: Neil M. Malamuth et al., "Characteristics of Aggressors Against Women: Testing a Model Using a National Sample of College Students," *Journal of Consulting and Clinical Psychology* 59 (1991): 670–81.

18 Premarital sex and marital unhappiness: Michael D. Newcomb and Peter M. Bentler, "Impact of Adolescent Drug Use and Social Support on Problems of Young Adults: A Longitudinal Study," *Journal of Abnormal Psychology* 97 (1988): 64–75.

18 National Survey of Family Growth: Joan R. Kahn and Kathryn A. London, "Premarital Sex and the Risk of Divorce," *Journal of Marriage and the Family* 53 (1991): 845–55. Kahn and London remind us that the correlation between nonvirginity and later divorce may not be cause and effect; it may instead result from other factors, such as a willingness to break traditional norms.

19 New Zealand study: Reported in *British Medical Journal*, 1998, and discussed by Jane Brody, "Teen-Agers and Sex: Younger and More at Risk," *New York Times*, September 14, 1998.

19 STDs: *Facts in Brief* (New York: Alan Guttmacher Institute, 1993), and Institute of Medicine report by Thomas R. Eng and William T. Butler, eds., *The Hidden Epidemic: Confronting Sexually Transmitted Disease* (Washington, D.C.: National Academy Press, 1997).

19 Teenage girls' vulnerability: *Sex and America's Teenagers* (New York: Alan Guttmacher Institute, 1994).

19 Cervical cancer: National Institute of Health report released April 4, 1996, and reported by the Associated Press.

19 Laura A. Brannon and Timothy C. Brock: "Perilous Underestimation of Sex Partners' Sexual Histories in Calculating Personal AIDS Risk," paper presented to the American Psychological Society convention, 1994. The mathematics here are more complicated than you might suppose, assuming that each of Pat's partners is accruing phantom partners at the same rate she is.

20 Steven D. Pinkerton and Paul R. Abramson: "Condoms and the Prevention of AIDS," *American Scientist* 85 (1997): 364–73.

20 Condom failure: Susan Weller, "A Meta-Analysis of Condom Effectiveness in Reducing Sexually Transmitted HIV," *Social Science and Medicine* 36, no. 12 (1993): 1635–44.

20 Condoms and other STDs: Medical Institute for Sexual Health, "Condoms Ineffective Against Human Papilloma Virus," *Sexual Health Update* 2 (April 1994).

20 3.4 million unintended pregnancies: Philip Elmer-DeWitt, *Time,* August 12, 1991, p. 52.

20 Good news, bad news: Larry Bumpass and Hsien-Hen Lu, "Trends in Cohabitation and Implications for Children's Family Contexts," Center for Demography and Ecology, University of Wisconsin, Madison, Working Paper 98-15, 1998.

20 Maritally conceived first births: The Census Bureau reports the marital status of women when conceiving their first child as follows: 82.8 percent married in 1950–54; 79.1 percent married in 1955–59; 47.2 percent married in 1990–94 (Amara Bachu, "Trends in Marital Status of U.S. Women at First Birth, 1930 to 1994," U.S. Census Bureau, Population Division Working Paper No. 20, March 1998).

21 Barry Sanders: Associated Press, "Lions' Sanders Admits Paternity," *Holland (Mich.) Sentinel,* September 27, 1994.

21 Marie Jackson: Chris Broussard, "Pro Players' Mothers Help Their Children, and Themselves," *New York Times,* August 24, 1998.

22 51 percent: Monitoring the Future Survey, Survey Research Center, University of Michigan.

22 7 in 10: Richard Morin, comments on *"Washington Post*/Henry J. Kaiser Family Foundation/Harvard University Studies of Political Values," presented at the Communitarian Summit, Washington, D.C., February 1999. Among all adult Americans in August 1998, 57 percent felt "having a child without being married" was always or in some situations acceptable, and 41 percent felt it was either "unacceptable, but should be tolerated by society" or "unacceptable and should not be tolerated."

22 April Schuldt: Lena Williams, "Pregnant Teenagers Are Outcasts No Longer," *New York Times,* December 2, 1993.

22 Nonmarital births in 20s: In 1992, there were 1,225,800 births to unmarried women, 55 percent of whom were in their 20s, 27 percent of whom were 15 to 19, and 10 percent of whom were in their 30s. *Statistical Abstract of the United States, 1995* (Washington, D.C.: Bureau of the Census, 1995), Table 94.

22 15- to 17-year-olds: A recent National Center for Health Statistics survey of nearly 10,000 15- to 49-year-old mothers indicates about half of births to 15- to 17-year-old girls are fathered by men 20 and over. A 1988 National Maternal and Infant Health Survey found that 39 percent of 15-year-old mothers, 47 percent of 16-year-olds, and 55 percent of 17-year-olds had babies fathered by men 20 and over (*Trends in the Well-Being of America's Children and Youth, 1996* [Washington, D.C.: U.S. Department of Health and Human Services], p. 177).

23 Joe Klein: "The Predator Problem," *Newsweek,* April 29, 1996, p. 32.

23 70 percent of black births: National Center for Health Statistics data reported by Steven A. Holmes, "Birth Rate for Unmarried Black Women Is at 40-Year Low," *New York Times,* July 1, 1998.

23 L. Douglas Wilder, "On Our Own: The Black Family," *The Responsive Community* 1 (1991): 3–5.

23 Marian Wright Edelman: *The Measure of Our Success: A Letter to My Children and Yours* (Boston: Beacon, 1992), p. 15.

23 David Popenoe, "The American Family Crisis," *National Forum* 75, no. 3 (summer 1995): 17.

23 President Clinton: Remarks by the president to the National Baptist Convention, New Orleans, September 9, 1994.

24 Molly Ivins: Quoting an earlier column in "Arts Critic Bob Dole Is Right and Wrong," Creators Syndicate, *Grand Rapids Press,* June 7, 1995.

24 Candice Bergen: "Soundbites," *TV, etc.,* October 1994, p. 3.

24 Britain's nonmarital births: *Annual Abstract of Statistics, 1999* (London: HMSO).

24 Japanese nonmarital births: Sheryl WuDunn, " 'Unwed' Remains a Dirty Word in Japanese," *Detroit Free Press,* March 14, 1996.

24 China and chastity: David M. Buss and David P. Schmitt, "Sexual Strategies Theory: An Evolutionary Perspective on Human Mating," *Psychological Review* 100 (1993): 204–32.

24 David A. Hartman: "Destroying the Family in the Lone-Star Welfare State," *The Family in America* 10 (October 1995): 3–5.

25 Bill Clinton: Quoted in Michael Kramer, "The Myth About Welfare Moms," *Time,* July 3, 1995, p. 21.

25 Sweden and Germany: "The Family: Home Sweet Home," *Economist,* September 9, 1995, pp. 25–26.

25 Sylvia Ann Hewlett and Cornel West: *The War Against Parents* (Boston: Houghton Mifflin, 1998), p. 40.

25 State welfare spending and nonmarital birthrates: Shirley L. Zimmerman, *Family Policies and Family Well-Being* (Newbury Park, Calif.: Sage, 1992), p. 158. Mississippi nonmarital birth data in *Monthly Vital Statistics Report* 46, no. 11 (June 30, 1998), Table 19.

25 Number of children: Craig N. Shealy, "From *Boys Town* to *Oliver Twist:* Separating Fact from Fiction in Welfare Reform and Out-of-Home Placement of Children and Youth," *American Psychologist* 50 (1995): 565–80.

25 AFDC benefits declining: David T. Ellwood and Lawrence H. Summers, "Poverty in America: Is Welfare the Answer or the Problem?" in *Fighting Poverty: What Works and What Doesn't,* ed. Sheldon H. Danziger and Daniel H. Weinberg, rev. ed. (Cambridge: Harvard University Press, 1986), pp. 134–35.

25 Welfare fall since 1972: Sara McLanahan and Gary Sandefur, *Growing Up with a Single Parent* (Cambridge: Harvard University Press, 1994), pp. 139–40.

26 77 researchers and Institute of Medicine: "Welfare and Out-of-Wedlock Births: A Research Summary," letter signed in 1994 by 77 social scientists (available from the American Psychological Association Public Policy Office, Washington, D.C. 20002); S. S. Brown and L. Eisenberg, eds., *The Best Intentions: Unintended Pregnancies and the Well-Being of Children and Families* (Washington, D.C.: National Academy Press, 1995). Both are cited, along with pertinent evidence, in Brian L. Wilcox, Jennifer K. Robbennolt, Janet E. O'Keeffe, and Marisa E. Pynchon, "Teen Nonmarital Childbearing and Welfare: The Gap Between Research and Political Discourse," *Journal of Social Issues* 52 (1996): 71–90.

26 Teenagers' ignorance and impairment: In eight surveys, fewer than half

the adolescents could correctly identify the safe and risky times of the menstrual cycle (D. M. Morrison, "Adolescent Contraceptive Behavior: A Review," *Psychological Bulletin* 98 [1985]: 536–68). Sexually active teens are typically alcohol-using teens (National Research Council, *Risking the Future: Adolescent Sexuality, Pregnancy, and Childbearing* [Washington, D.C.: National Academy Press, 1987]).

26 Surprise at pregnancy: Jeanne Brooks-Gunn and Frank E. Furstenberg, Jr., "Adolescent Sexual Behavior," *American Psychologist* 44 (1989): 249–57.

26 Moynihan: Quoted in Kramer, "The Myth About Welfare Moms."

26 National Research Council: *Risking the Future,* p. 1.

26 University of Illinois professor: Harry C. Triandis, *Social Behavior and Culture* (New York: McGraw-Hill, 1994).

26 Linda Leclair story: Charles Kaiser, *1968 in America* (New York: Weidenfeld and Nicholson, 1988), cited in Skolnick, *Embattled Paradise,* p. 75.

27 Cohabitation trends: Neil G. Bennett, Ann K. Blanc, and David E. Bloom, "Commitment and the Modern Union: Assessing the Link Between Premarital Cohabitation and Subsequent Marital Stability," *American Sociological Review* 53 (1988): 127–38; Larry L. Bumpass and James A. Sweet, "National Estimates of Cohabitation," *Demography* 26 (1989): 615–25. The 1960 to 1990 data are reported in "Marital Status and Living Arrangements, March 1990," *Current Population Reports,* Series P-20, no. 450 (Washington, D.C.: Bureau of the Census, 1991). The 1998 data are Census Bureau statistics from the "Marital Status and Living Arrangements, March 1998" report.

27 More than half cohabited: Brad Edmondson, "New Lifestage: Trial Marriage," *Forecast,* October 1997 (using National Center for Health Statistics data). Available at www.demographics.com/publications/fc/97_fc/9710_fc/fc07106.htm. A 1996 Gallup poll found that about half of married 18- to 29-year-olds reported living together before their marriage (*Gallup Poll Monthly,* September 1995, p. 19).

27 Brides, grooms, and cohabitation: Bumpass and Lu, "Trends in Cohabitation and Implications for Children's Family Contexts."

27 Elizabeth Taylor: *Poz* magazine, quoted in *Time,* October 20, 1997, p. 21.

27 Similar trends: Larry L. Bumpass, James A. Sweet, and Andrew Cherlin, "The Role of Cohabitation in Declining Rates of Marriage," *Journal of Marriage and the Family* 53 (1991): 913–27.

27 Canada: "1996 Census: Marital Status, Common-Law Unions, and Families," Statistics Canada (www.statcan.ca/daily/english/97104/d97014.htm).

28 British cohabitation: Office of Population Censuses and Surveys, Social
Survey Division, *General Household Survey, 1991* (London: HMSO,
1993).

28 Andrew J. Cherlin: *Marriage, Divorce, Remarriage,* rev. ed. (Cambridge:
Harvard University Press, 1992), p. vii.

28 To check compatibility: Bumpass, Sweet, and Cherlin, "Role of Cohabitation in Declining Rates of Marriage."

29 Sarah Ferguson: Associated Press, "Estranged Royal Keeps a Stiff Upper
Lip," *Holland (Mich.) Sentinel,* December 8, 1994.

29 College survey on trial marriage: Nan Astin, William S. Korn, and E. R.
Berz, *The American Freshman: National Norms for Fall 1989* (a report
of the Cooperative Institutional Research Program sponsored by the
American Council on Education), Los Angeles, Calif.: Higher Education Research Institute, Graduate School of Education, UCLA, 1989.
In the 1994 National Opinion Research Center General Social Survey
of adult Americans, only 41 percent disagreed that "It's a good idea
for a couple who intend to get married to live together first." The rest
either agreed (33 percent) or expressed no opinion.

29 High school survey: Monitoring the Future Surveys, conducted by the
Survey Research Center, University of Michigan, and reported in the
National Marriage Project's *The State of Our Unions, 1999.* The survey
statement was: "It is usually a good idea for a couple to live together
before getting married in order to find out whether they really get
along."

29 Among American adults cohabiting: In the 1987–88 National Survey
of Families and Households, 51 percent of males and 56 percent of
females declared this an important reason; 18 and 16 percent, respectively, said it was not an important reason (Bumpass, Sweet, and
Cherlin, "Role of Cohabitation in Declining Rates of Marriage").

29 Cohabitation still intact: Edmondson, "New Lifestage."

29 Cohabitation and divorce rates, American surveys: Alan Booth and David
Johnson, "Premarital Cohabitation and Marital Success," *Journal of
Family Issues* 9 (1988): 255–72; E. Lowell Kelly and James J. Conley,
"Personality and Compatibility: A Prospective Analysis of Marital
Stability and Marital Satisfaction," *Journal of Personality and Social
Psychology* 52 (1987): 27–40; Michael D. Newcomb, "Cohabitation and
Marriage: A Quest for Independence and Relatedness," in *Family Pro-
cesses and Problems: Social Psychological Aspects,* ed. Stuart Oskamp
(Newbury Park, Calif.: Sage, 1987); Alfred DeMaris and K. Vaninadha
Rao, "Premarital Cohabitation and Subsequent Marital Stability in the
United States: A Reassessment," *Journal of Marriage and the Family*

54 (1992): 178–90; Elizabeth Thomson and Ugo Colella, "Cohabitation and Marital Stability: Quality or Commitment?" *Journal of Marriage and the Family* 54 (1992): 259–67; Samuel S. Janus and Cynthia L. Janus, *The Janus Report on Sexual Behavior* (New York: John Wiley, 1993), pp. 176–78; Bumpass and Sweet, "National Estimates of Cohabitation," pp. 615–25; Paul R. Amato, "Explaining the Intergenerational Transmission of Divorce," *Journal of Marriage and the Family* 58 (1996): 628–40 ("29 and 13 percent" data by personal e-mail).

29 Cohabitation and divorce rates, Canadian survey: T. R. Balakrishnan et al., "A Hazard Model Analysis of the Covariates of Marriage Dissolution in Canada," *Demography* 24 (1987): 395–406; S. S. Halli and Z. Zimmer, "Common Law Union as a Differentiating Factor in the Failure of Marriage in Canada, 1984," *Social Indicators Research* 24 (1991): 329–45; James M. White, "Reply to Comment by Professors Trussell and Rao: A Reanalysis of the Data," *Journal of Marriage and the Family* 51 (1989): 540–44; David R. Hall, "Marriage as a Pure Relationship: Exploring the Link Between Premarital Cohabitation and Divorce in Canada," *Journal of Comparative Family Studies* 28 (1996): 1–12.

29 Cohabitation and divorce rates, Swedish study: Bennett, Blanc, and Bloom, "Commitment and the Modern Union," pp. 127–38. The British *General Household Survey* of 1989 likewise found that "unions which began with cohabitation and proceeded to first marriage were *more* likely to end within 10 years than first marriages without a period of premarital cohabitation" (London: HMSO, 1991).

29 Serial cohabitors: Alfred DeMaris and William MacDonald, "Premarital Cohabitation and Marital Instability: A Test of the Unconventionality Hypothesis," *Journal of Marriage and the Family* 55 (1993): 399–407.

30 Explaining cohabitation-divorce association: William G. Axinn and Arland Thornton, "The Relationship Between Cohabitation and Divorce: Selectivity or Causal Influence?" *Demography* 29 (1992): 357–74.

30 Maggie Gallagher: *The Abolition of Marriage* (Washington, D.C.: Regnery, 1996), pp. 167–68.

30 Three times more likely: Renata Forste and Koray Tanfer, "Sexual Exclusivity Among Dating, Cohabiting, and Married Women," *Journal of Marriage and the Family* 58 (1996): 33–47. The result comes from young adult women only (surveyed in the 1991 National Survey of Women).

30 Attitude changes with cohabitation: William G. Axinn and Jennifer S. Barber, "Living Arrangements and Family Formation Attitudes in Early Adulthood," *Journal of Marriage and the Family* 59 (1997): 595–611.

30 Married people who cohabitated: "Couples who give their marriage a

lower grade—that is, B or below—are more likely to say they lived together before marriage than are those who give their marriage an A" (*Gallup Poll Monthly*, September 1996, p. 19).

30 Canadian cohabitees: Data summarized by Margo I. Wilson and Martin Daly, "Male Sexual Proprietariness and Violence Against Wives," *Current Directions in Psychological Science* 5 (1996): 2–7.

30 Linda J. Waite: "Cohabitation: A Communitarian Perspective," Communitarian Network, Washington, D.C., 1999. See also Linda J. Waite and Maggie Gallagher, *The Case for Marriage* (Cambridge: Harvard University Press, 2000). The U.S. domestic violence data were analyzed by Waite from the 1987–88 National Survey of Families and Households.

33 President Clinton: Quoted in David Whitman, "Was It Good for Us?" *U.S. News & World Report*, May 19, 1997, pp. 57–64.

33 National Opinion Research Center survey: 1996 survey, reported in Tom Smith, "Social Change in America, 1972–1996," *Social Indicators Network News*, winter 1997, pp. 1–3. Gallup: *Gallup Poll Monthly*, June 1996, p. 35.

33 *Time*/CNN poll: Bruce Handy, "How We Really Feel About Fidelity," *Time*, August 31, 1998, pp. 52–53.

34 52 percent to 42 percent: *The American Freshman: National Norms for Fall 1998*, the UCLA/ACE annual surveys of some quarter million entering collegians.

34 CDC youth survey: "Trends in Sexual Risk Behaviors Among High School Students."

34 2.4 million: *Sexual Health Update*, winter 1998, p. 2, from the Medical Institute for Sexual Health, Austin, Texas.

34 85 percent of adults: CNN/*USA Today*/Gallup Poll, conducted May 9–12, 1996.

34 Teenage births ebbing: National Center for Health Statistics numbers are, for 1991, 62.1 births per 1,000 15- to 19-year-olds; for 1997, 52.9 (*National Vital Statistics Reports* 47, no. 12 [December 17, 1998]). The 1997 figure was revised to 52.3 in an NCHS report, April 28, 1999.

34 Donna Shalala: NCHS press release, April 30, 1998.

34 Racial gap shrinking: *Statistical Abstract of the United States, 1997*, Table 97. Also, *Monthly Vital Statistics Report* 46, no. 11(S) (June 30, 1998), Table 17.

34 Roy Baumeister: "Gender Differences in Erotic Plasticity: The Female Sex Drive as Socially Flexible and Responsive," *Psychological Bulletin*, in press.

Chapter 3: The Past and Future of Marriage

p. 36 Helen E. Fisher, "After All, Maybe It's Biology," *Psychology Today*,
March/April, 1993, pp. 40-45, 82 (excerpted from her book *Anatomy
of Love: The Natural History of Monogamy, Adultery, and Divorce*,
New York: Norton, 1992).

36 Low levels of infidelity: While premarital sex has increased dramatically,
extramarital sex has not, although popular articles, books, and films—
not to mention the escapades of national political leaders—would
have us believe that affairs are commonplace. Two-thirds of married
men and half of married women have had an affair, declared Joyce
Brothers in a 1990 *Parade* magazine article. Shere Hite believed the
number even higher—75 percent of women married more than five
years responding to her questionnaire. Influenced by such claims, and
perhaps by their own sexual fantasies, only a fourth of people surveyed
recently by Gallup believed that most married people are faithful. Yet,
reports Gallup, 9 in 10 Americans say they've not had sex with anyone
other than their spouse during their present marriage. The National
Opinion Research Center reports that during any given year only "1.5
percent of married people have a sex partner other than their spouse."
In another national survey, sponsored by the National Institute on
Alcohol Abuse and Alcoholism, 3.6 percent of married respondents
reported sex with more than one partner in the previous year, 6 percent in the previous five years. Thus, the sexual revolution seems not
to have greatly affected marital fidelity.

36 Bronislaw Malinowski: From *Sex, Culture, and Myth*, 1930, quoted in
Marriage in America: A Report to the Nation (New York: Council on
Families in America, 1995), p. 12, and David Popenoe, *Life Without
Father* (New York: Free Press, 1996), p. 36.

37 Elizabeth Fox-Genovese: "Thoughts on the History of the Family," in
The Family, Civil Society, and the State, ed. C. Wolfe (Lanham, Md.:
Rowman & Littlefield, 1998), pp. 4, 8.

37 Nuclear and extended families in history: See Robert F. Winch and Rae
Lesser Blumberg, "Societal Complexity and Familial Organization," in
Selected Studies in Marriage and the Family, ed. Robert F. Winch and
Louis Wolf Goodman (New York: Holt, Rinehart and Winston, 1968).

37 Francis Fukuyama: *The Great Disruption: Human Nature and the Reconstitution of Social Order* (New York: Free Press, 1999).

38 World's literature and lore: Barbara Dafoe Whitehead, "Dan Quayle Was
Right," *Atlantic*, April 1993, pp. 47-84.

38 Urie Bronfenbrenner: "Discovering What Families Do," in David
Blankenhorn, Steven Bayme, and Jean Bethke Elshtain, *Rebuilding the*

Nest: A New Commitment to the American Family (Milwaukee, Wis.: Family Service America, 1990).

38 Communes: Arlene Skolnick, *Embattled Paradise: The American Family in an Age of Uncertainty* (New York: Basic, 1991), p. 95.

38 Evolutionary psychologists: Alan Page Fiske, Shinobu Kitayama, Hazel Rose Markus, and Richard E. Nisbett, "The Cultural Matrix of Social Psychology," in *The Handbook of Social Psychology*, ed. D. Gilbert, S. Fiske, and G. Lindzey, 4th ed. (New York: McGraw-Hill, 1998).

38 Ellen Willis: *Beginning to See the Light* (New York: Knopf, 1981), p. 150, cited in Skolnick, *Embattled Paradise*, p. 95.

38 Typical (median) age at first marriage: U.S. Bureau of the Census, Current Population Reports, Series P-20, no. 461, *Marital Status and Living Arrangements, March 1991* (Washington, D.C.: U.S. Government Printing Office, 1992), p. 5; updated with 1997 marriage data (Bureau of the Census, *Marital Status and Living Arrangements, March 1998*).

39 Os Guinness: *The American Hour: A Time of Reckoning and the Once and Future Role of Faith* (New York: Free Press, 1993), p. 309.

39 Sara McLanahan and Lynne Casper: "The American Family in 1990: Growing Diversity and Inequality," unpublished manuscript, Princeton University, 1994.

40 All-time high: Larry Bumpass and Hsien-Hen Lu, "Trends in Cohabitation and Implications for Children's Family Contexts," Center for Demography and Ecology, University of Wisconsin, Madison, Working Paper 98-15, 1998.

40 Lawrence Stone: "The Road to Polygamy," *New York Review*, March 2, 1989, pp. 12–15, cited in Popenoe, *Life Without Father*, p. 22.

40 Barbara Dafoe Whitehead: *The Divorce Culture* (New York: Vintage, 1998), p. 190.

40 Proportion married: *Statistical Abstract of the United States, 1994*, Table 58, updated with Bureau of the Census, *Marital Status and Living Arrangements, March 1998*.

41 John Bradshaw: *Treating Love: The Last Great Stage of Growth* (New York: Bantam, 1992), p. 342, quoted in Maggie Gallagher, *The Abolition of Marriage* (Washington, D.C.: Regnery, 1996), p. 109.

41 Marital age gaps: Douglas T. Kenrick and R. C. Keefe, "Age Preferences in Mates Reflect Sex Differences in Reproductive Strategies," *Behavioral and Brain Sciences* 15 (1992): 75–133.

42 Robert Wright: "Our Cheating Hearts," *Time*, August 15, 1994, pp. 44–52.

42 Percentage remarrying within a year (from a national survey of 57,900 15- to 44-year-old women): Kathryn A. London, "Cohabitation, Mar-

riage, Marital Dissolution, and Remarriage: United States, 1988. Data from the National Survey of Family Growth," *Advance Data,* Vital and Health Statistics of the National Center for Health Statistics, report no. 194, January 4, 1991.

42 Marriage, health, and earnings: Linda J. Waite, "Social Science Finds: 'Marriage Matters,'" *Responsive Community,* summer 1996, pp. 26-35.

43 Harold Morowitz: Quoted in James L. Lynch, *The Broken Heart: The Medical Consequences of Loneliness* (New York: Basic, 1977), pp. 45-46.

43 Marriage and happiness: I gleaned these 1972 to 1994 data from www.icpsr.umich.edu. See also Norval Glenn and Charles N. Weaver, "The Changing Relationship of Marital Status to Reported Happiness," *Journal of Marriage and the Family* 50 (1988): 317-24; and Walter R. Gove, Carolyn B. Style, and Michael Hughes, "The Effect of Marriage on the Well-Being of Adults: A Theoretical Analysis," *Journal of Family Issues* 11 (1990): 4-35. For a summary of Western European surveys, see Ronald Inglehart, *Culture Shift in Advanced Industrial Societies* (Princeton: Princeton University Press, 1990).

43 Happiness with marriage predicts happiness: Correlation of .47 dwarfs the .27 to .29 range of the other predictive correlations in General Social Surveys from 1972 to 1994, reports Robert E. Lane, "Searching for Lost Companions in the Groves of the Market," paper presented to the Understanding Quality of Life: Enjoyment and Suffering conference, Princeton, N.J., November 1996.

43 Marriage stress and depression: Frank D. Fincham, Steven R. H. Beach, Gordon T. Harold, and Lori N. Osborne, "Marital Satisfaction and Depression: Different Causal Relationships for Men and Women?" *Psychological Science* 8 (1997): 351-57.

43 European-Americans, etc.: Keith D. Parker, Suzanne T. Ortega, and Judy VanLaningham, "Life Satisfaction, Self-Esteem, and Personal Happiness Among Mexican and African Americans," *Sociological Spectrum* 15 (1995): 131-45.

43 17 nations studied, cohabitants' happiness: Steven Stack and J. Ross Eshleman, "Marital Status and Happiness: A Seventeen-Nation Study," *Journal of Marriage and the Family* 60 (1998): 527-36.

43 Distress after divorce: Frederick O. Lorenz et al., "Married and Recently Divorced Mothers' Stressful Events and Distress: Tracing Change Across Time," *Journal of Marriage and the Family* 59 (1997): 219-32.

43 Marriage and suicide: G. Hoyer and E. Lund, "Suicide Among Women Related to Number of Children in Marriage," *Archives of General Psychiatry* 50 (1993): 134-37; Arne Mastekaasa, "Age Variations in the Sui-

cide Rates and Self-Reported Subjective Well-Being of Married and Never Married Persons," *Journal of Community and Applied Social Psychology* 5 (1995): 21–39; S. Stack, "Marriage, Family, Religion, and Suicide," in *Assessment and Prediction of Suicide*, ed. R. Maris, A. Berman, J. Maltsberg, and R. Yufits (New York: Guilford, 1992).

43 Depressed people not fun: Ian H. Gotlib, "Interpersonal and Cognitive Aspects of Depression," *Current Directions in Psychological Science* 1 (1992): 149–54; Cris Segrin and James Price Dillard, "The Interactional Theory of Depression: A Meta-Analysis of the Research Literature," *Journal of Social and Clinical Psychology* 11 (1992): 43–70.

43 Arne Mastekaasa: "Age Variations in Suicide Rates."

44 Marriage and men's depression: Allan V. Horwitz, Helene Raskin White, and Sandra Howell-White, "Becoming Married and Mental Health: A Longitudinal Study of a Cohort of Young Adults," *Journal of Marriage and the Family* 58 (1997): 895–907.

44 Disconcerting fact from national surveys: Norval Glenn, "The Social and Cultural Meaning of Contemporary Marriage," in *The Retreat from Marriage*, ed. Bryce Christensen (Rockford, Ill.: Rockford Institute, 1990), and "The Course of Marital Success and Failure in Five American 10-Year Marriage Cohorts," *Journal of Marriage and the Family* 60 (1998): 569–76; Lane, "Searching for Lost Companions"; Stacy J. Rogers and Paul R. Amato, "Is Marital Quality Declining? The Evidence from Two Generations," *Social Forces* 75 (1997): 1089–1100.

45 Paul R. Amato and Stacy J. Rogers: "Do Attitudes Toward Divorce Affect Marital Quality?" *Journal of Family Issues* 20 (1999): 69–86.

45 Norval Glenn: "The Recent Trend in Marital Success in the United States," *Journal of Marriage and the Family* 53 (1991): 261–70. After studying the 1985 U.S. government population survey, Teresa Castro Martin and Larry L. Bumpass similarly estimated that two-thirds of recent marriages are destined for divorce or separation ("Recent Trends in Marital Disruption," *Demography* 26 [1989]: 37–51).

46 Gallup report: Diane Colasanto and James Shriver, "Mirror of America: Middle-Aged Face Marital Crisis," *Gallup Report*, no. 284, May 1989, pp. 34–38.

46 Teresa Martin and Larry Bumpass: "Recent Trends in Marriage Disruption."

47 David T. Lykken and Auke Tellegen: "Is Human Mating Adventitious or the Result of Lawful Choice? A Twin Study of Mate Selection," *Journal of Personality and Social Psychology* 65 (1993): 56–68.

47 International divorce comparisons: Harry C. Triandis, *Culture and Social Behavior* (New York: McGraw-Hill, 1994).

47 Norval Glenn: "Social and Cultural Meaning of Contemporary Marriage."

47 Hallmark card: Quoted in Karla B. Hackstaff, "The Rise of Divorce Culture and Its Gendered Foundations," *Feminism and Psychology* 3 (1993): 363-68.

47 Romantic love and divorce: Robert Levine, Suguro Sato, Tsukasa Hashimoto, and Jyoti Verma, "Love and Marriage in Eleven Cultures," *Journal of Cross-Cultural Psychology* 26 (1995): 554-71.

47 Marital commitment: Jeffrey M. Adams and Warren H. Jones, "The Conceptualization of Marital Commitment: An Integrative Analysis." *Journal of Personality and Social Psychology* 47 (1997): 1177-96.

47 Carol L. Gohm: with Shigehiro Oishi, Janet Darlington, and Ed Diener, "Culture, Parental Conflict, Parental Marital Status, and the Subjective Well-Being of Young Adults," *Journal of Marriage and the Family* 60 (1998): 319-34.

48 Emotional ups and downs: Ellen Berscheid, Mark Snyder, and Allen M. Omoto, "Issues in Studying Close Relationships: Conceptualizing and Measuring Closeness," in *Review of Personality and Social Psychology*, ed. C. Hendrick, vol. 10 (Newbury Park, Calif.: Sage, 1989).

48 Stopped noticing: J. Carlson and Elaine Hatfield, *The Psychology of Emotion* (Fort Worth, Tex.: Holt, Rinehart & Winston, 1992).

48 Predictors of stable marriage: T. R. Balakrishan et al., "A Hazard Model Analysis of the Covariates of Marriage Dissolution in Canada," *Demography* 24 (1987): 395-406; Colasanto and Shriver, "Mirror of America"; Tim B. Heaton and E. L. Pratt, "The Effects of Religious Homogamy on Marital Satisfaction and Stability," *Journal of Family Issues* 11 (1990): 191-207; Gay C. Kitson, Karen Benson Babri, and Mary Joan Roach, "Who Divorces and Why: A Review," *Journal of Family Issues* 6 (1985): 255-93; Jay D. Teachman, Karen A. Polonko, and John Scanzoni, "Demography of the Family," in Marvin B. Sussman and Suzanne K. Steinmetz, *Handbook of Marriage and the Family* (New York: Plenum Press, 1987); Matt McGue and David T. Lykken, "Genetic Influence on Risk of Divorce," *Psychological Science* 3 (1992): 368-73; Joan R. Kahn and Kathryn A. London, "Premarital Sex and the Risk of Divorce," *Journal of Marriage and the Family* 53 (1991): 845-55.

48 D. M. Fergusson, L. J. Horwood, and F. T. Shannon: "A Proportional Hazards Model of Family Breakdown," *Journal of Marriage and the Family* 46 (1984): 539-49.

49 European family trends: Andrew Cherlin and Frank F. Furstenberg, Jr., "The Changing European Family: Lessons for the American Reader," *Journal of Family Issues* 9 (1988): 291-97; David Popenoe, "Family

Decline in the Swedish Welfare State," *Public Interest* 102 (winter 1991): 65–77.

49 Stephanie Coontz: *The Way We Never Were: American Families and the Nostalgia Trap* (New York: Basic, 1992), p. 287.

49 Helen Fisher: *Anatomy of Love: The Natural History of Monogamy, Adultery, and Divorce* (New York: Norton, 1992).

50 Blaming partner for breakup: Janice D. Gray and Roxane Cohen Silver, "Opposite Sides of the Same Coin: Former Spouses' Divergent Perspectives in Coping with Their Divorce," *Journal of Personality and Social Psychology* 59 (1990): 1180–91.

50 82 percent agreed: Norval D. Glenn, "The Family Values of Americans" (New York: Institute for American Values, 1991), p. 6, cited in David Popenoe, "The Family Condition of America," Brookings Institution Seminar paper, March 1992.

50 Stay together: National Opinion Research Center (University of Chicago) survey, January to May 1994, reported by *American Enterprise*, July/August 1995, p. 104.

50 Ellen Goodman: "Call to Uplift Marriage Leaves Love Out of It," Washington Post Writers Group, *Grand Rapids Press*, April 11, 1995.

50 Divorce attitudes lag divorce behavior: Coontz, *Way We Never Were*, p. 167.

50 One partner alone: "Four out of five marriages ended unilaterally," report Frank F. Furstenberg, Jr., and Andrew J. Cherlin in *Divided Families: What Happens to Children When Parents Part* (Cambridge: Harvard University Press, 1991), pp. 21–22.

50 Australian divorce: Ailsa Burns, "Mother-Headed Families: An International Perspective and the Case of Australia," *Social Policy Report* (Society for Research in Child Development) 6, no. 1 (1992): 1–22.

50 Divorce in no-fault states: Paul A. Nakonezny, Robert D. Shull, and Joseph Lee Rodgers, "The Effect of No-Fault Divorce Law on the Divorce Rate Across the 50 States and Its Relation to Income, Education, and Religiosity," *Journal of Marriage and the Family* 57 (1995): 477–88. This analysis challenges an earlier report that no-fault divorce laws had no effect (Gerald C. Wright, Jr., and Dorothy N. Stetson, "The Impact of No-Fault Divorce Law Reform on Divorce in American States," *Journal of Marriage and the Family* 40 [1978]: 575–80). For worldwide data, see Ailsa Burns and Cath Scott, *Mother-Headed Families and Why They Have Increased* (Hillsdale, N.J.: Erlbaum, 1994), p. 1.

51 Great Plains counties: Don E. Albrecht, "The Industrial Transformation of Farm Communities: Implications for Family Structure and Socioeconomic Conditions," *Rural Sociology* 63 (1998): 51–64.

51 Amish: Quoted in Mart Fritz, "Cultural Crossroads," *Grand Rapids Press,* July 10, 1998.

51 Women's employment and earnings: *Statistical Abstract of the United States, 1997,* Tables 625 and 663.

51 Andrew J. Cherlin: *Marriage, Divorce, Remarriage,* rev. ed. (Cambridge: Harvard University Press, 1992), p. 51.

51 Sara McLanahan and Lynne Casper, "Growing Diversity and Inequality in the American Family," in *State of the Union: America in the 1990s,* ed. R. Farley, vol. 2, *Social Trends* (New York: Russell Sage Foundation, 1995), p. 39.

52 Judith Stacey: "The New Family Values Crusaders," *Nation,* July 25/August 1, 1994, pp. 119-22.

52 Traditionalism and low divorce: Letitia Anne Peplau, Charles T. Hill, and Zick Rubin, "Sex Role Attitudes in Dating and Marriage: A 15-Year Follow-Up of the Boston Couples Study," *Journal of Social Issues* 49 (1993): 31-52.

52 Approval of women's working: National Opinion Research Center surveys reported by Richard Gene Niemi, John Mueller, and Tom W. Smith, *Trends in Public Opinion: A Compendium of Survey Data* (New York: Greenwood, 1989), and Tom W. Smith, personal correspondence.

52 Dropping wages since 1973: Sylvia Ann Hewlett and Cornel West, *The War Against Parents* (Boston: Houghton Mifflin, 1998).

52 Victor R. Fuchs and Diane M. Reklis: "America's Children: Economic Perspectives and Policy Options," *Science* 255 (1992): 41-46.

53 David Popenoe: "Family Condition of America."

53 Norval D. Glenn and Charles N. Weaver: "Changing Relationship of Marital Status to Reported Happiness."

53 Catherine Wallace: *For Fidelity* (New York: Knopf, 1998), p. 67.

53 Unencumbered individuals: Hewlett and West, *The War Against Parents.*

53 William Galston: Quoted in Kim A. Lawton, " 'No Fault' Divorce Under Assault," *Christianity Today,* April 8, 1996, pp. 84-87.

54 Divorce law reform: Mary Ann Mason, "The De-Regulation of Family Law: In Whose Best Interests?" *Responsive Community* 3 (spring 1993): 43-51.

54 Financial inequality of divorce: Lenore J. Weitzman, *The Divorce Revolution: The Unexpected Social and Economic Consequences for Women and Children in America* (New York: Free Press, 1985); Lenore J. Weitzman, "Why Divorce Laws Are Impoverishing Women and Children," in *How Does Divorce Affect the Family?* ed. D. L. Bender (San Diego: Greenhaven); and Marilyn Coleman and Lawrence H.

Ganongh, "Financial Responsibility for Children Following Divorce and Remarriage," *Journal of Family and Economic Issues* 13 (winter 1992): 445–55.

54 Mary Ann Glendon: *Abortion and Divorce in Western Law* (Cambridge: Harvard University Press, 1987).

54 Popenoe: *Life Without Father,* pp. 222–23

54 James Q. Wilson: *The Moral Sense* (New York: Free Press, 1993), p. 249.

54 Maggie Gallagher: *Abolition of Marriage,* pp. 146, 149, 250.

55 22 states: Katherine Spaht, "New Pro-Family Policies: Covenant Marriage and Children First," presented at the Communitarian Summit, Washington, D.C., February 1999.

55 John Gottman: Quoted in Hara Estroff Marano, "Rescuing Marriages Before They Begin," *New York Times,* May 28, 1997.

55 Amitai Etzioni: "Marriage with No Easy Outs," *New York Times,* August 13, 1997.

55 Hanna Rosin: Quoted in Ashton Applewhite, "Don't Blame No-Fault Divorce" (www.intellectualcapital.com/issues/97/1030/icpro.asp).

55 Stephanie Coontz: *The Way We Really Are* (New York: Basic, 1997), p. 107.

56 Family as Community Act: Spaht, "New Pro-Family Policies."

56 Divorce harder: Richard Morin, "*Washington Post*/Henry J. Kaiser Family Foundation/Harvard University Studies of Political Values," presented at the Communitarian Summit, Washington, D.C., February 1999.

56 Katha Pollitt: "Bewildered and Bothered," *New York Times,* July 22, 1993.

57 Pepper Schwartz: "Peer Marriage," *Responsive Community,* summer 1998, pp. 48–60.

57 Amitai Etzioni: "How to Make Marriage Matter," *Time,* September 6, 1995, p. 76.

57 Marriage preparation courses: For a quick synopsis of some well-researched possibilities, see Marano, "Rescuing Marriages Before They Begin."

57 Norval Glenn: *Closed Hearts, Closed Minds: The Textbook Story of Marriage* (New York: Council on Families, Institute for American Values, 1997).

57 Robert Wright: "The False Politics of Values," *Time,* September 9, 1996, pp. 42–45.

58 Loving stubbornly: "A good marriage is often not so much a matter of choosing carefully as of loving well—and stubbornly," writes Maggie Gallagher (*Abolition of Marriage,* p. 111).

58 David Buss: "Evolutionary Science Ponders: Where Is Fancy Bred?" *New York Times,* June 1, 1999.

58 Ellen Goodman: In syndicated newspapers, March 16, 1993.

58 Hillary Clinton: Quoted in Anna Quindlen, "Hillary Clinton in Search of New Image," *New York Times,* May 1994.

58 The China experiment: B. G. Rosenberg and Qicheng Jing, "A Revolution in Family Life: The Political and Social Structural Impact of China's One Child Policy," *Journal of Social Issues* 52 (1996): 51–69.

59 Diverse voices in one chorus: For examples, see Steven A. Holmes, "Unlikely Union Arises to Press Family Issues," *New York Times,* May 1, 1992; David Broder, "The Evidence Comes In—Dan Quayle Was Right," Washington Post Writers Group, *Grand Rapids Press,* March 24, 1993.

59 Social antibodies: William Bennett, "The National Prospect," *Commentary,* November 1995, pp. 29–30.

59 Yankelovich: Reported by Kendal Hamilton and Pat Wingert, "Down the Aisle," *Newsweek,* July 29, 1998, pp. 54–57.

59 Marriage movement: Karen S. Peterson, "Making 'I Do' Harder to Undo," *USA Today,* July 21, 1998.

59 David Popenoe and Jean Bethke Elshtain: "Some Fundamental Propositions About Marriage and the Family in America," draft discussion statement for the Council on Families in America, undated.

Chapter 4: America's Children

p. 60 Adult-to-child ratio: Victor R. Fuchs and Diane M. Reklis, "America's Children: Economic Perspectives and Policy Options," *Science* 255 (1992): 41–46, reports that between 1960 and 1990 the number of children remained at 64 million, while the number of people age 18 and over increased from 117 million to 183 million. By 1995, the United States had grown to a projected 68.5 million children and 193.5 million adults—a ratio of 2.82 adults per child.

60 Researchers agree: Edward F. Zigler and Elizabeth P. Gilman, "An Agenda for the 1990s: Supporting Families," in *Rebuilding the Nest: A New Commitment to the American Family,* ed. D. Blankenhorn, S. Bayme, and J. B. Elshtain (Milwaukee, Wis.: Family Service America, 1990).

60 "Never before": National Commission on the Role of the School and the Community in Improving Adolescent Health, *Code Blue: Uniting for Healthier Youth* (Alexandria, Va.: National Association of State Boards of Education, 1990).

60 Barbara Dafoe Whitehead: "Dan Quayle Was Right," *Atlantic,* April 1993, p. 84.

61 51 to 82 percent: Norval D. Glenn, "The Family Values of Americans," Institute for American Values, 1991, p. 6, cited in David Popenoe, "The Family Condition of America: Cultural Change and Public Policy," in *Values and Public Policy,* ed. Henry J. Aaron, Thomas E. Mann, and Timothy Taylor (Washington, D.C.: Brookings Institution, 1994), p. 111.

61 Today's collegians: Rachel Roseman Barich and Denise B. Bielby, "Rethinking Marriage: Change and Stability in Expectations, 1967–1994," *Journal of Family Issues* 17 (1996): 139–69.

61 Today's newlyweds: A. G. Neal, H. T. Groat, and J. W. Wicks, "Attitudes About Having Children: A Study of 600 Couples in the Early Years of Marriage," *Journal of Marriage and the Family* 51 (1989): 313–28.

61 Hours parents spend with children: John P. Robinson, "Who's Doing the Housework?" *American Demographics* (December 1988): 24–28, 63.

61 40 percent of the poor: In 1993, there were 15,727,000 children among 39,265,000 people below the poverty line (U.S. Bureau of the Census, *Statistical Abstract of the United States, 1995,* Table 747).

61 Episodic poverty: 32.4 percent rate for 1994, reports a U.S. Census Bureau report by Mary Naifeh, "Dynamics of Economic Well-Being, Poverty 1993–1994: Trap Door? Revolving Door? Or Both?" *Current Population Reports: Household Economic Studies,* July 1998, P70-63.

61 United States is number one: Andrew L. Shapiro, *We're Number One: Where America Stands—and Fails—in the New World Order* (New York: Vintage, 1992). Divorce and teen births: Urie Bronfenbrenner, "The State of Americans: This Generation and the Next," address to the American Psychological Association convention, 1996. Economic inequality (ratio of worker earnings at 90th and 10th percentiles): Peter Gottschalk and Timothy Smeeding, "Cross-National Comparisons of Levels and Trends in Inequality," Luxembourg Income Study Working Paper 126, July 1995, cited in James Carville, *We're Right, They're Wrong* (New York: Simon & Schuster, 1996), p. 85.

62 12 to 1 and socializing costs of growing old: Sylvia Ann Hewlett and Cornel West, *The War Against Parents* (Boston: Houghton Mifflin, 1998).

62 50 percent more likely and AARP revenues: Elizabeth Gleick, "The Children's Crusade," *Time,* June 3, 1996, pp. 31–35.

62 Elderly get 11 times what children receive: Peter G. Peterson and Neil Howe, *On Borrowed Time: How the Growth in Entitlement Spending Threatens America's Future* (San Francisco: ICS Press, 1988), p. 11.

63 Poverty links: "Consequences of Poverty for Children and Families," a

1995 research brief sponsored by the Society for Research in Child Development, Society for Research on Adolescence, International Society for Infant Studies, and Division 7, American Psychological Association. David C. Rowe and Joseph L. Rodgers note that existing studies seldom disentangle possible genetic and environmental differences between the poor and not-poor ("Poverty and Behavior: Are Environmental Measures Nature and Nurture?" and "Poverty and Behavior: A Response to a Critique of a Critique of a Special Issue," *Developmental Review* 17 [1997]: 358–75, 394–406).

63 Child abuse and neglect: National Committee for the Prevention of Child Abuse reports of April 1992 and 1998 reveal that child abuse cases have increased every year since 1976, from 669,000 to 3.1 million (Deborah Daro and Karen McCurdy, "Current Trends in Child Abuse Reporting and Fatalities: The Results of the 1991 Annual Fifty-State Survey," and Ching-Tung Lung and Deborah Daro, "Current Trends in Child Abuse Reporting and Fatalities: The Results of the 1997 Annual Fifty State Survey" [Chicago: National Center on Child Abuse Prevention Research, 1992 and 1998]).

63 Blame parents for poverty: Hewlett and West, *The War Against Parents*, pp. 109–20.

63 Growing sensitivity: L. Gordon, *Heroes of Their Own Lives* (New York: Viking, 1988).

63 Mistreat children: Jay Belsky, "Etiology of Child Maltreatment: A Developmental-Ecological Analysis," *Psychological Bulletin* 114 (1993): 413–34.

63 1996 government study: "Child Abuse Doubles in Seven Years," Associated Press report of Department of Health and Human Services study released September 1996 (*Grand Rapids Press*, September 19, 1996).

63 Canadian study: Nico Trocme, Debra McPhee, and Kwok Kwan Tam, "Child Abuse and Neglect in Ontario: Incidence and Characteristics," *Child Welfare* 74 (1995): 563–72.

63 Secretary General: Report of the Secretary General to the Forty-Eighth Session of the United Nations General Assembly, Item 110, "Social Development Including Questions Relating to the World Social Situation and to Youth, Aging, Disabled Persons and the Family," August 19, 1993, p. 38.

64 Stepfathers and boyfriends more often abuse: Jan Faust, Melissa K. Runyon, and Maureen C. Kenny, "Family Variables Associated with the Onset and Impact of Intrafamilial Childhood Sexual Abuse," *Clinical Psychology* 15 (1995): 443–56; Leslie Margolin, "Child Abuse by

Mothers' Boyfriends: Why the Overrepresentation?" *Child Abuse and Neglect* 16 (1992): 541–51.

64 San Francisco study: Diana E. H. Russell, "The Prevalence and Seriousness of Incestuous Abuse: Stepfathers vs. Biological Fathers," *Child Abuse and Neglect* 8 (1984): 15–22.

64 Martin Daly and Margo Wilson: Summarized, with data, by Ann Gibbons, "Really Wicked Stepparents," *Science* 261 (1993): 987.

64 "Step-relationships more distant": Martin Daly and Margo Wilson, "Violence Against Stepchildren," *Current Directions in Psychological Science* 5 (1996): 77–81.

65 Foster care abuse: Donna Mack, *The Assault on Parenthood* (New York: Simon & Schuster, 1997), p. 67.

65 Langur monkeys: Carl Zimmer, "First Kill the Babies," *Discover*, September 1996, pp. 73–78.

65 Women vulnerable to partner assault: Martin Daly and Margo Wilson, "Evolutionary Psychology and Marital Conflict: The Relevance of Stepchildren," in *Sex, Power, Conflict*, ed. D. M. Buss and N. M. Malamuth (New York: Oxford University Press, 1996). Daly and Wilson report another dramatic finding: women are about four times more vulnerable to partner assault themselves if they have one or more children sired by a previous partner (when compared with those who have children only with their present partner). Apparently, such women's caring for their children sired by other men (who themselves may now be subject to abuse) brings them into more frequent conflict with their new partners.

65 Abusive parents: R. S. Kempe and C. C. Kempe, *Child Abuse* (Cambridge: Harvard University Press, 1978).

65 Condemned murderers: D. O. Lewis, J. H. Pincus, B. Bard, E. Richardson, L. S. Prichep, M. Feldman, and C. Yeager, "Neuropsychiatric, Psychoeducational, and Family Characteristics of 14 Juveniles Condemned to Death in the United States," *American Journal of Psychiatry* 145 (1988): 584–89.

65 Abused become abusive: J. Kaufman and E. Zigler, "Do Abused Children Become Abusive Parents?" *American Journal of Orthopsychiatry* 57 (1987): 186–92; Cathy S. Widom, "Does Violence Beget Violence? A Critical Examination of the Literature," *Psychological Bulletin* 106 (1989): 3–28, and "The Cycle of Violence," *Science* 244 (1989): 160–66.

65 Wartime torture: K. A. Kendall-Tackett, L. M. Williams, and D. Finkelhor, "Impact of Sexual Abuse on Children: A Review and Synthesis of Recent Empirical Studies," *Psychological Bulletin* 113 (1993): 164–80.

65 Sexual abuse: Melissa A. Polusny and Victoria M. Follette, "Long-Term Correlates of Child Sexual Abuse: Theory and Review of the Empirical Literature," *Applied and Preventive Psychology* 4 (1995): 143–66; Tori DeAngelis, "Research Documents Trauma of Abuse," American Psychological Association *Monitor,* April 1995, p. 34.

65 Stephanie Whitaker: Sarah Nordgren, "Sex Abuse Called First Step to Teen Pregnancy," Associated Press release (*Holland Sentinel,* September 17, 1995).

66 Peer abuse: Anne-Marie Ambert, "Toward a Theory of Peer Abuse," in *Sociological Studies of Children,* ed. A. M. Ambert, vol. 7 (Greenwich, Conn.: JAI Press, 1995).

66 Juvenile violent crime: FBI annual *Uniform Crime Reports.*

66 About 8 IQ points: The SAT and the Stanford-Binet and Wechsler intelligence tests are all academic aptitude tests. A 50-point decline (from the mid 470s to the mid 420s) on the SAT scale of 200 to 800 represents one-half of the 100-point standard deviation of scores. Intelligence tests have a 15-to-16-point standard deviation. Thus, a corresponding standard-deviation decline would be about 8 points.

66 Number scoring 700 or above: Nicholas Zill and Carolyn C. Rogers, "Recent Trends in the Well-Being of Children in the United States and Their Implications for Public Policy," in *The Changing American Family and Public Policy,* ed. Andrew J. Cherlin (Washington, D.C.: Urban Institute Press, 1988), pp. 64–65.

66 College Entrance Examination Board: *On Further Examination: Report of the Advisory Panel on the Scholastic Aptitude Test Score Decline* (New York: College Entrance Examination Board, 1977).

67 Achenbach and Howell: "Are American Children's Problems Getting Worse? A Thirteen-Year Comparison," *Journal of the American Academy of Child and Adolescent Psychiatry* 32 (1993): 1145–54.

67 James Garbarino: "Growing Up in a Socially Toxic Environment: Life for Children and Families in the '90s," in *Nebraska Symposium on Motivation,* ed. Gary B. Melton (Lincoln: University of Nebraska Press, 1995). Also see James Garbarino, *Raising Children in a Socially Toxic Environment* (San Francisco: Jossey-Bass, 1995).

68 James Garbarino: Quoted by Associated Press, May 12, 1995, based on a talk in East Lansing, Michigan (*Holland Sentinel*).

68 12 percent to 32 percent: From 1960 to 1998, the proportion of children living with two parents decreased from 88 percent to 68 percent ("Living Arrangements of Children Under 18 Years Old: 1960 to the Present," U.S. Bureau of the Census table accessed via WWW, 1995;

updated to 1998 with "Marital Status and Living Arrangements, March 1998").

68 Most of today's young children: Sara McLanahan and Gary Sandefur, *Growing Up with a Single Parent* (Cambridge: Harvard University Press, 1994), pp. 2–3. Donald J. Hernandez, chief of the Census Bureau's Marriage and Family Statistics Branch, projects that 46 percent of whites and 80 percent of blacks who were children in the 1980s will live with fewer than two parents by age 17 ("Children's Changing Access to Resources: A Historical Perspective," *Social Policy Report* 8, no. 1 [spring 1994]: 1–23).

68 Father-absent: In 1998, 32 percent of America's 71 million children did not live with two parents ("parents" includes both biological parents and stepparents). Of children living with a single parent (16 percent with their father, 84 percent with their mother), 39 percent lived with a never-married parent, 36 percent with a divorced parent, 21 percent with a spouse-absent parent, and 4 percent with a widowed parent (Bureau of the Census, "Marital Status and Living Arrangements, March 1998").

68 4 in 10 children: In 1990, 70 percent of children lived in two-parent families, 83 percent of which involved a biological mother and father or a stepmother and biological father. Thus 58 percent of all children were living with their biological father. Another 4 percent lived with a single-parent father. (*Statistical Abstract of the United States, 1994,* Tables 72, 79.)

68 More than half: Donald J. Hernandez, *America's Children* (New York: Russell Sage Foundation, 1993), p. 71.

68 Ten years after: 1988 National Survey of Families and Households, reported in Judith A. Seltzer, "Relationships Between Fathers and Children Who Live Apart: The Father's Role After Separation," *Journal of Marriage and the Family* 53 (1991): 79–101.

68 Never see father: Data from 1981 Census Bureau survey of over 15,000 children, Judith A. Seltzer and Susan M. Bianchi, "Children's Contact with Absent Parents," *Journal of Marriage and the Family* 50 (1988): 663–77. The 1988 National Survey of Families and Households shows slightly higher rates of father contact—27 percent as often as weekly, 29 percent never (Seltzer, "Relationships Between Fathers and Children Who Live Apart"). Reporting from the same data source, Mary Ann Mason and Jane Mauldon report that half of children of single mothers see their fathers yearly or more often ("The New Stepfamily Requires a New Public Policy," *Journal of Social Issues* 52 [1996]: 11–27).

69 Two-thirds of those living with their mother: James L. Peterson and
      Nicholas Zill, "Marital Disruption, Parent-Child Relationships, and
      Behavior Problems in Children," *Journal of Marriage and the Family*
      48 (1986): 295–307.

69 Britain: "Home Sweet Home," *Economist,* September 9, 1995, pp. 25–27.

69 17 to 1 ratio: *Statistical Abstract of the United States, 1994,* Table 78.

69 Frank F. Furstenberg: Quoted in Paul Taylor, "Why More and More
      Fathers Are Drifting Away," *Grand Rapids Press,* June 11, 1992.

69 Elizabeth Fox-Genovese: *Feminism Without Illusions: A Critique of Indi-
      vidualism* (Chapel Hill: University of North Carolina Press, 1991),
      p. 20.

70 Hardly do less: Alan C. Acock and David H. Demo, *Family Diversity and
      Well-Being* (Thousand Oaks, Calif.: Sage, 1994).

70 Cosby's *Fatherhood* sales: Andrew J. Cherlin, "The Changing American
      Family and Public Policy," in *The Changing American Family and Pub-
      lic Policy,* ed. Andrew J. Cherlin (Washington, D.C.: Urban Institute
      Press, 1988), p. 14.

70 Fathers' participating: Eleanor E. Maccoby, "Divorce and Custody: The
      Rights, Needs, and Obligations of Mothers, Fathers, and Children,"
      Nebraska Symposium on Motivation, vol. 42 (Lincoln: University of
      Nebraska Press, 1995).

70 Barbara Dafoe Whitehead: *The Divorce Culture* (New York: Vintage,
      1997), p. 154.

70 Paul Taylor: "Why More and More Fathers Are Drifting Away."

70 Stephanie Coontz: *The Way We Never Were: American Families and the
      Nostalgia Trap* (New York: Basic, 1992), p. 207.

71 Diane Fassel: *Growing Up Divorced: A Road to Healing for Adult Chil-
      dren of Divorce* (New York: Simon & Schuster, 1991).

71 Barbara Dafoe Whitehead: "Time for Kitchen-Table Language About
      Children," *Des Moines Register,* July 26, 1991.

71 Patricia Funderburk Ware: Remarks to the Communitarian Network's
      Family Life and Sex Education Task Force at the 1996 White House
      Conference on Character Education, and in correspondence (Octo-
      ber 9, 1996).

72 Some marriage defenders: For example, Maggie Gallagher, *The Aboli-
      tion of Marriage: How We Destroy Lasting Love* (Washington, D.C.:
      Regnery, 1996), p. 41.

72 NORC result: "Single-Parent Families," *American Enterprise,* July/August
      1995, p. 101.

73 13 percent and 59 percent in poverty: U.S. Bureau of the Census, *Statistical Abstract of the United States, 1994,* Table 729.

73 Poverty rate among children of never-married: Deborah A. Dawson, "Family Structure and Children's Health: United States, 1988," *Vital and Health Statistics, Series 10, Data From the National Health Survey, No. 178* (Hyattsville, Md.: National Center for Health Statistics, DHHS Publication No. PHS 91-1506).

73 Risk of poverty: Data from the National Health Interview Survey reported in Nicholas Zill and Christine Winquist Nord, *Running in Place: How American Families Are Faring in a Changing Economy and an Individualistic Society* (Washington, D.C.: Child Trends, 1994), p. 16.

73 Molly Ivins: Creators Syndicate column, September 11, 1995 (*Grand Rapids Press*).

73 Canada: "Breakdown of Family Blamed for Child Poverty," *Toronto Star,* March 23, 1999.

74 Transcends race: In 1992, 46 percent of mother-only white children and 19 percent of married-couple black children lived in poverty (*Statistical Abstract of the United States, 1994,* Table 729).

74 Poverty's price: See Greg J. Duncan and Jeanne Brooks-Gunn, eds., *Consequences of Growing Up Poor* (New York: Russell Sage Foundation, 1997).

74 Eugene Lang: I Had a Dream Foundation (http://www.ihad.org/), 1998.

74 Daniel Patrick Moynihan: "The Great Transformation," *American Enterprise,* January/February 1995, pp. 38–41.

74 Poverty decrease: *Statistical Abstract of the United States, 1995,* Table 749, updated with *Poverty in the United States, 1996,* Current Population Reports, P60-198.

74 Alcohol use: Alcohol use increased during the 1970s but declined during the 1980s. Also, consumption since 1980 has shifted away from distilled spirits, declining from 3.0 to 1.9 gallons per person annually (*Statistical Abstract of the United States, 1994,* Table 227).

75 Tripled to 41 percent: Greg J. Duncan and Saul D. Hoffman, "Economic Consequences of Marital Instability," in *Horizontal Equity, Uncertainty, and Economic Well-Being,* ed. Martin David and Timothy Smeeding (Chicago: University of Chicago Press, 1985); see also S. Wayne Duncan, "Economic Impact of Divorce on Children's Development: Current Findings and Policy Implications," *Journal of Clinical and Child Psychology* 23 (1994): 444–57.

75 Maggie Gallagher: *The Abolition of Marriage,* p. 95.

75 Urban Institute Study: Robert I. Lerman, "Effect of Family Structure on

Child Poverty and Income Inequality," *The Urban Institute Policy and Research Report* (summer–fall 1996).

75 Half the increase in child poverty: David J. Eggebeen and Daniel T. Lichter, "Race, Family Structure, and Changing Poverty Among American Children," *American Sociological Review* 56 (1991): 801–17.

75 Support payments: Census Bureau data reported in Zill and Nord, *Running in Place*, pp. 7–8.

75 Surveys of unmarried men: Frank Furstenberg, Jr., "Good Dads — Bad Dads: Two Faces of Fatherhood," in *The Changing American Family and Public Policy*, ed. Andrew J. Cherlin (Washington, D.C.: Urban Institute, 1988), pp. 201–2; cited in David Popenoe, *Life Without Father* (New York: Free Press, 1996), p. 25.

75 Rowntree Foundation: *Economist*, September 9, 1995, pp. 26–29.

75 William Galston: "A Liberal-Democratic Case for the Two-Parent Family," *Responsive Community* 1 (1990–91): 14–26.

75 Charles Krauthammer and Charles Murray: "The Scourge of Illegitimacy," *Reader's Digest*, March 1994, pp. 49–53.

76 Social differences less dramatic: Paul B. Amato and Bruce Keith, "Parental Divorce and the Well-Being of Children: A Meta-Analysis," *Psychological Bulletin* 110 (1991): 26–46.

76 Variation within: Acock and Demo, *Family Diversity and Well-Being*, pp. 214, 230.

76 Hetherington: E. Mavis Hetherington, Margaret Stanley-Hagan, and Edward R. Anderson, "Marital Transitions: A Child's Perspective," *American Psychologist* 44 (1989): 303–12. See also E. Mavis Hetherington and W. Glenn Clingempeel, "Coping with Marital Transitions: A Family Systems Perspective," *Society for Research in Child Development Monographs* 57, no. 227 (1992): 1–240.

76 In study after study: Summarized by John H. Grych and Frank D. Fincham, "Interventions for Children of Divorce: Toward Greater Integration of Research and Action," *Psychological Bulletin* 111 (1992): 434–54.

76 Judith Wallerstein: "The Long-Term Effects of Divorce on Children: A Review," *Journal of the American Academy of Child and Adolescent Psychiatry* 30 (1991): 349–60.

76 "Putting children on hold": Judith Wallerstein, *Second Chances: Men, Women, and Children a Decade After Divorce* (New York: Ticknor and Fields, 1989), p. 7.

76 70 percent: Allen J. Beck, Susan A. Kline, and Lawrence A. Greenfeld,

"Survey of Youth in Custody, 1987," U.S. Department of Justice, Bureau of Justice Statistics Special Report, 1988.

76 David Lykken: *Happiness* (New York: Golden Books, 1999), p. 163.

76 Adolescent murders and long-term inmates: Data provided by the National Fatherhood Initiative and reported in Popenoe, *Life Without Father,* p. 63.

76 Search Institute: Peter L. Benson and Eugene C. Roehlkepartain, *Youth in Single-Parent Families* (Minneapolis: Search Institute, 1993).

77 "Father-distant" cultures: Popenoe, *Life Without Father,* pp. 156–57. Popenoe draws on B. B. Whiting and J. W. M. Whiting, *Children of Six Cultures: A Psychocultural Analysis* (Cambridge: Harvard University Press, 1975), and P. Draper and H. Harpending, "Father Absence and Reproductive Strategy: An Evolutionary Perspective," *Journal of Anthropological Research* 38 (1982): 255.

77 21 percent of inmates: Calculation by David Courwright, reported in Popenoe, *Life Without Father,* p. 75.

77 "Asks for and gets chaos": Daniel Patrick Moynihan, *Family and Nation: The Godkin Lectures, Harvard University* (New York: Harcourt Brace Jovanovich, 1986), p. 9.

77 Two-parent crime control: McLanahan and Sandefur, *Growing Up with a Single Parent,* p. 137.

77 Father Greg Boyle: "Reinventing Fatherhood," Occasional Papers Series, no. 14, International Year of the Family (Vienna: United Nations, 1994). Quote is attributed to Nina J. Easton, "Life Without Father," *Los Angeles Times Magazine,* June 14, 1992, p. 15.

78 Nicholas Zill: with Donna Ruane Morrison and Mary Jo Coiro, "Long-Term Effects of Parental Divorce on Parent-Child Relationships, Adjustment, and Achievement in Young Adulthood," *Journal of Family Psychology* 7 (1993): 91–103.

78 More likely to say "very happy": Norval Glenn and Kathryn B. Kramer, "The Psychological Well-Being of Adult Children of Divorce," *Journal of Marriage and Family* 47 (1985): 905–12; Alan Booth and John N. Edwards, "Transmission of Marital and Family Quality Over the Generations: The Effect of Parental Divorce on Unhappiness," *Journal of Divorce* 12 (1989): 41–58.

78 If marriage proves unhappy: Pamela S. Webster, Terri L. Orbuch, and James S. House, "Effects of Childhood Family Background on Adult Marital Quality and Perceived Stability," *American Journal of Sociology* 101 (1995): 404–32.

78 Study of 1,118 adults: Paul R. Amato, "Explaining the Intergenerational

Transmission of Divorce," *Journal of Marriage and the Family* 58 (1996): 628–40.

78 46 percent and 77 percent: Urie Bronfenbrenner, "The State of Americans: This Generation and the Next," address to the American Psychological Association, 1996. For more information on family structures linked with nonmarital births (with income controlled), see Lawrence L. Wu, "Effects of Family Instability, Income, and Income Instability on the Risk of a Premarital Birth," *American Sociological Review* 61 (1996): 386–406.

78 Search Institute: Peter L. Benson and Eugene C. Roehlkepartain, *Youth in Single-Parent Families* (Minneapolis: Search Institute, 1993).

78 Oregon Research Institute: Peter M. Lewinsohn, Robert E. Roberts, John R. Seeley, Paul Rohde, Ian H. Gotlib, and Hyman Hops, "Adolescent Depression: II. Psychosocial Risk Factors," unpublished manuscript, 1995.

78 Australian studies: Bryan Rodgers, "Social and Psychological Well-Being of Children from Divorced Families: Australian Research Findings," *Australian Psychologist* 31 (1996): 174–82.

78 E. Mavis Hetherington: "Families in Transition: Divorce and Remarriage," address to the Midwestern Psychological Association convention, May 5, 1995.

78 Teenage suicides and psychiatric admissions: Jean Bethke Elshtain, "Family Matters: The Plight of America's Children," *Christian Century,* July 14–21, 1993, pp. 710–12, quoting Karl Zinsmeister, "Growing Up Scared," *Atlantic,* June 1990, pp. 49–66.

79 Amitai Etzioni: Remarks to the Third Annual White House Conference on Character Education, June 7, 1996.

79 Adolescent health behaviors: National Research Council, Commission on Behavioral and Social Sciences and Education, Panel on High-Risk Youth, *Losing Generations: Adolescents in High-Risk Settings* (Washington, D.C.: National Academy Press, 1993), p. 49.

80 Howard S. Friedman: with Joan S. Tucker, Joseph E. Schwartz, Carol Tomlinson-Keasey, Leslie R. Martin, Deborah L. Wingard, and Michael H. Criqui, "Psychosocial and Behavioral Predictors of Longevity: The Aging and Death of the 'Termites,'" *American Psychologist* 50 (1995): 69–78.

80 Follow-up study: Joan S. Tucker et al., "Parental Divorce: Effects on Individual Behavior and Longevity," *Journal of Personality and Social Psychology* 73 (1997): 381–91.

80 Census Bureau: From an analysis by Hauser and Phang reported in National Research Council, *Losing Generations,* pp. 50–51.

80 Doubled dropout rates: McLanahan and Sandefur, *Growing Up with a Single Parent*, pp. 40–43.

80 Bobbie Thomason: Quoted on *All Things Considered,* National Public Radio, January 17, 1995, transcript 1730.

80 Robin Hood Foundation: "Teen Pregnancy Costs U.S. $29 Billion a Year," Associated Press, *Grand Rapids Press,* June 14, 1996.

80 Academic problems: Grych and Fincham, "Interventions for Children of Divorce."

81 States with high proportion: Paul E. Barton, *America's Smallest School: The Family* (Princeton, N.J.: Educational Testing Service, 1992).

81 School principals study: Karl Zinsmeister, "Growing Up Scared," *Atlantic,* June 1990, p. 52.

81 Princeton/Johns Hopkins study: Nan Marie Astone and Sara S. McLanahan, "Family Structure, Parental Practices, and High School Completion," *American Sociological Review* 56 (1991): 309–20.

81 Repeating grade: David Wood, Neal Halfon, Debra Scarlata, Paul Newacheck, and Sharon Nessim, "Impact of Family Relocation on Children's Growth, Development, School Function, and Behavior," *Journal of the American Medical Association* 270 (1993): 1334–38; Nicholas Zill, "Behavior, Achievement, and Health Problems Among Children in Stepfamilies: Findings from a National Survey of Child Health," in *Impact of Divorce, Single Parenting, and Stepparenting on Children,* ed. E. Mavis Hetherington and Josephine D. Arasteh (Hillsdale, N.J.: Erlbaum, 1988), p. 344.

82 National Longitudinal Survey: McLanahan and Sandefur, *Growing Up with a Single Parent,* p. 41.

82 Stockholm study: Duncan W. G. Timms, *Family Structure in Childhood and Mental Health in Adolescence* (Stockholm, Sweden: Department of Sociology, University of Stockholm, 1991), p. 93, quoted in Popenoe, *Life Without Father,* p. 58.

82 Nicholas Zill: "Behavior, Achievement, and Health Problems Among Children in Stepfamilies: Findings from a National Survey of Child Health," in *Impact of Divorce, Single Parenting, and Stepparenting on Children,* ed. E. Mavis Hetherington and Josephine D. Arasteh (Hillsdale, N.J.: Erlbaum, 1988). The 1988 survey is summarized in Dawson, "Family Structure and Children's Health."

82 School suspension and misbehavior: Peterson and Zill, "Marital Disruption, Parent-Child Relationships."

82 Harlem: David T. Lykken, "Fatherless Rearing Leads to Sociopathy," *Behavioral and Brain Sciences* 18 (1995): 563–64.

83 Highest risk: See, for example, National Research Council, *Losing Generations*, p. 52.

83 British 7-year-olds: Andrew J. Cherlin et al., "Longitudinal Studies of Effects of Divorce on Children in Great Britain and the United States," *Science* 252 (1991): 1386–89.

84 Pepper Schwartz: "When Staying Is Worth the Pain," *New York Times*, April 4, 1995, quoted in Popenoe, *Life Without Father*, p. 209.

84 William J. Doherty: Quoted in Whitehead, *The Divorce Culture*, p. 89.

84 Mel Krantzler: *Creative Divorce: A New Opportunity for Personal Growth* (New York: Signet, 1974), p. 211, quoted in Whitehead, *The Divorce Culture*, p. 87.

84 Maggie Gallagher: *The Abolition of Marriage*.

84 Age 23: Andrew J. Cherlin, Kathleen E. Kiernan, and P. Lindsay Chase-Lansdale, "Parental Divorce in Childhood and Demographic Outcomes in Young Adulthood," *Demography* 32 (1995): 299–316.

85 Age 33: Andrew J. Cherlin, P. Lindsay Chase-Lansdale, and Christine McRae, "Effects of Parental Divorce on Mental Health Throughout the Life Course," *American Sociological Review*, 63 (1998): 239–49.

85 Negative life trajectories: P. Lindsay Chase-Lansdale, Andrew J. Cherlin, and Kathleen E. Kiernan, "The Long-Term Effects of Parental Divorce on the Mental Health of Young Adults: A Developmental Perspective," *Child Development* 66 (1995): 1614–34.

85 Sara McLanahan: "Double the Trouble," *Psychology Today*, May/June, 1996, p. 18.

85 The major problem: Edward H. Thompson, Jr., and Patricia A. Gongla, "Single Parent Families: In the Mainstream of American Society," in *Contemporary Families and Alternative Lifestyles*, ed. E. D. Macklin and R. H. Rubin (Beverly Hills, Calif.: Sage, 1983), p. 111, quoted in Gallagher, *The Abolition of Marriage*, p. 91.

85 McLanahan and Sandefur: *Growing Up with a Single Parent*, p. 10.

85 Whitehead: "Dan Quayle Was Right."

85 What solo parenting and poverty entail: McLanahan and Sandefur, *Growing Up with a Single Parent*, chapter 8.

86 Children mourn: C. Jack Tucker, Jonathan Marx, and Larry Long, "'Moving On': Residential Mobility and Children's School Lives," *Sociology of Education* 71 (1998): 111–29.

86 Moving frequently: David Wood, Neal Halfon, Debra Scarlata, Paul Newacheck, and Sharon Nessim. "Impact of Family Relocation on Children's Growth, Development, School Function, and Behavior," *Journal of the American Medical Association* 270 (1993): 1334–38.

86 Poor, stable communities: R. J. Sampson, "The Community Context of Violent Crime," in *Sociology and the Public Agency,* ed. W. J. Wilson (Newbury Park, Calif.: Sage, 1993).

86 Douglas B. Downey: "The School Performance of Children from Single-Mother and Single-Father Families," *Journal of Family Issues* 15 (1994): 129–47.

86 Divorced parents are more educated: Census Briefs, "Children with Single Parents—How They Fare," September 1997.

87 McLanahan and Sandefur: *Growing Up with a Single Parent,* pp. 70–71, 81.

87 Comparisons of types of disrupted families: Ibid., pp. 30, 66, 77, and Douglas B. Downey and Brian Powell, "Do Children in Single-Parent Households Fare Better Living with Same-Sex Parents?" *Journal of Marriage and the Family* 55 (1993): 55–71. After analyzing National Educational Longitudinal Study data from 3,483 8th graders living with mother only and 409 living with father only, Downey and Powell concluded, "Of the 35 social psychological and educational outcomes studies, we cannot find even one in which both males and females benefit significantly from living with their same-sex parent." For further data on the frequency of behavioral and emotional problems in children of stepfamilies (despite their economic advantage over other single-parent families), see K. E. Kiernan, "The Impact of Family Disruption in Childhood on Transitions Made in Young Adult Life," *Population Studies* 46 (1992): 213–34.

87 "Children who grow up with only one parent": McLanahan and Sandefur, *Growing Up with a Single Parent,* p. 144.

87 Values and activities of single and married moms: Acock and Demo, *Family Diversity and Well-Being,* pp. 109, 123.

88 Patrick T. Davies and E. Mark Cummings: "Marital Conflict and Child Adjustment: An Emotional Security Hypothesis," *Psychological Bulletin* 116 (1994): 387–411.

88 Children of a widowed parent: McLanahan and Sandefur, *Growing Up with a Single Parent,* p. 77.

88 Edward Zigler: "Reinstituting the White House Conference on Children," *American Journal of Orthopsychiatry* 73 (1993): 334–36.

88 National Academy of Sciences: *Losing Generations: Adolescents in High-Risk Settings* (Washington, D.C.: National Academy Press, 1993), p. vii.

88 Urie Bronfenbrenner: "What Do Families Do?" *Family Affairs* 4 (winter-spring 1991): 1–6.

88 Amitai Etzioni: "How to Make Marriage Matter," *Time,* September 6, 1995, p. 76.

88 David Popenoe: "The Controversial Truth," *New York Times,* December 26, 1993.

88 Pepper Schwartz: "Peer Marriage," *Responsive Community,* summer 1998, pp. 48-60.

89 David Blankenhorn: *Fatherless America: Confronting Our Most Urgent Social Problem* (New York: Basic, 1995), pp. 23-24.

89 Marital satisfaction: Osnat Erel and Bonnie Burman, "Interrelatedness of Marital Relations and Parent-Child Relations: A Meta-Analytic Review," *Psychological Bulletin* 118 (1995): 108-32.

89 Paul R. Amato and Alan Booth: *A Generation at Risk: Growing Up in an Era of Family Upheaval* (Cambridge: Harvard University Press, 1997).

89 Less conflict better: Paul R. Amato, "Children's Adjustment to Divorce: Theories, Hypotheses, and Empirical Support," *Journal of Marriage and the Family* 55 (1993): 23-38.

89 Alan Acock and David Demo: *Family Diversity and Well-Being,* p. 231.

89 McLanahan and Sandefur: *Growing Up with a Single Parent,* p. 34.

89 Eleanor E. Maccoby: "Divorce and Custody."

89 Blankenhorn: *Fatherless America,* p. 169.

89 7 in 10 divorces: Amato and Booth, *Generation at Risk.*

90 Countries with high divorce rate: Carol L. Golm et al., "Culture, Parental Conflict, Parental Marital Status, and the Subjective Well-Being of Young Adults," *Journal of Marriage and the Family* 60 (1998): 319-34.

90 Dutch study: Ed Spruijt and Martijn de Goede, "Transitions in Family Structure and Adolescent Well-Being," *Adolescence* 32 (1998): 897-911.

90 New American research: Amato and Booth, *Generation at Risk.*

90 Martin E. P. Seligman: *Learned Optimism* (New York: Knopf, 1991), pp. 146-47.

90 Whether children cope well: Hetherington, Stanley-Hagan, and Anderson, "Marital Transitions." See also Hetherington and Clingempeel, "Coping with Marital Transitions."

90 William Galston: "A Liberal-Democratic Case," pp. 14-25.

90 Nicholas Zill: Quoted in Whitehead, "Dan Quayle Was Right."

91 Photos: Theodore H. Mita, Marshall Dermer, and Jeffrey Knight, "Reversed Facial Images and the Mere-Exposure Hypothesis," *Journal of Personality and Social Psychology* 35 (1977): 597-601. For a review of research on mere exposure and familiarity effects, see Robert F. Born-

stein, "Exposure and Affect: Overview and Meta-Analysis of Research, 1968–1987," *Psychological Bulletin* 106 (1989): 265–89.

91 Children feel angry: Hetherington, Stanley-Hagan, and Anderson, "Marital Transitions."

92 David Popenoe: "Fostering the New Familism," *Responsive Community* 2 (fall 1992): 31–39.

92 Whitehead: "Dan Quayle Was Right."

92 "Too little time": From a survey of 702 randomly selected 12- to 17-year-olds living in the District of Columbia, northern Virginia, and suburban Maryland conducted for the *Washington Post* (December 14, 1995) by ICR Survey Research Group of Media, Pa.

92 Nan M. Astone and Sara S. McLanahan, "Family Structure, Parental Practices, and High School Completion," *American Sociological Review* 56 (1991): 309–20.

93 Hewlett and West: *The War Against Parents,* pp. 47–48.

93 Robert Plomin and Denise Daniels: "Why Are Children in the Same Family So Different from One Another?" *Behavioral and Brain Sciences* 10 (1987): 1–60.

93 Adopted children: To be sure, most adopted children thrive under the care of nurturing parents who, unlike natural parents, are carefully screened. Although many adopted children face challenges, they more often are raised by two married parents. This suggests the potential benefits to children of encouraging unwed pregnant teens to consider adoption, reducing legal barriers to adoption, and protecting adoptive parents' rights. Only about 2 percent of unmarried mothers of newborns—though somewhat more among future-oriented mothers from advantaged families—relinquish their baby for adoption (Department of Health and Human Services report, http://aspe.os.dhhs.gov/hsp/cyp/xsteesex.htm).

93 Stunning findings: Judith Rich Harris, "Where Is the Child's Environment? A Group Socialization Theory of Development," *Psychological Review* 102 (1995): 458–89; David C. Rowe, "As the Twig Is Bent? The Myth of Child-Rearing Influences on Personality Development," *Journal of Counseling and Development* 68 (1990): 143–49, and *The Limits of Family Influence* (New York: Guilford, 1994).

94 Peter B. Neubauer and Alexander Neubauer: *Nature's Thumbprint: The New Genetics of Personality* (Reading, Mass.: Addison-Wesley, 1990), pp. 20–21.

94 Same sort of adults: Quoted from an article by Jerome Burne, *Manchester Observer,* April 1996.

94 Variation between solo-parent and two-parent family: Sandra Scarr, Patricia L. Webber, Richard A. Weinberg, and Michele A. Wittig, "Personality Resemblance Among Adolescents and Their Parents in Biologically Related and Adoptive Families," *Journal of Personality and Social Psychology* 40 (1981): 885–98.

94 David Rowe: *The Limits of Family Influence: Genes, Experience, and Behavior* (New York: Guilford, 1994), p. 163.

95 1996 study of 1,018 twin pairs: K. S. Kendler, M. C. Neale, C. A. Prescott, R. C. Kessler, A. C. Heath, L. A. Corey, and L. J. Eaves, "Childhood Parental Loss and Alcoholism in Women: A Causal Analysis Using a Twin-Family Design," *Psychological Medicine* 26 (1996): 79–95.

95 Vietnamese youth: Carl L. Bankston III, Stephen J. Caldas, and Min Zhou, "The Academic Achievement of Vietnamese-American Students: Ethnicity as Social Capital," *Sociological Focus* 30 (1997): 1–16.

95 Mary Pipher: Quoted in Rhea K. Faberman, "What's Leading America Astray," *APA Monitor*, September 1997, p. 15.

96 Letter writer: Frank W. Drachman, *Detroit Free Press*, August 22, 1998.

96 David Lykken: "How Can Educated People Continue to Be Radical Environmentalists?" *The Edge* (www.edge.org), June 25, 1998.

96 Shared environment and religiosity: This is found in the Minnesota twin studies, and confirmed in International Social Survey Program data from 19,815 people in 15 nations. "In relatively secular nations [though less so in religious nations], family religiosity strongly shapes children's religious beliefs," note Jonathan Kelley and Nan Dirk De Graaf in "National Context, Parental Socialization, and Religious Belief: Results from 15 Nations," *American Sociological Review* 62 (1997): 639–59. Meg J. Rohan and Mark P. Zanna report general value similarity to parents among children of parents with democratic values. Children of right-wing authoritarian parents tend either to have values quite unlike their parents or quite similar—they either rebel against or identify with their parents ("Value Transmission in Families," in *The Psychology of Values: The Ontario Symposium*, ed. Clive Seligman, James M. Olson, and Mark P. Zanna, vol. 8 [Mahwah, N.J.: Erlbaum, 1996]).

96 Asian boat children: Nathan Caplan, Marcella H. Choy, and John K. Whitmore, *Children of the Boat People: A Study of Educational Success* (Ann Arbor: University of Michigan Press, 1992). See also Andrew J. Fuligni, "The Adjustment of Children from Immigrant Families," *Current Directions in Psychological Science* 7 (1998): 99–103. Noting that academic performance among such immigrants declines with years in the United States, Michael Medved disputes the idea that immigrants

are bad for America. One could, he suggests, better make a case that
America is bad for immigrants.

96 Harris: "Children Don't Do Things Half Way," *The Edge* (www.edge.org),
   July 10, 1999.

97 Parent-bashing books: Hewlett and West, *The War Against Parents,*
   p. 137.

97 Parenthood harder than in the 1950s: Sara McLanahan and Julia Adams,
   "The Effects of Children on Adults' Psychological Well-Being, 1957–
   1976," *Social Forces* 68 (1989): 124–46.

Chapter 5: Violence

p. 99 London *Times:* Kate Muir, "Human Life Means Nothing," *Times* (London), July 15, 1993.

100 Gallup Poll: *Gallup Poll Monthly,* June 1994, p. 38.

100 3.7 times: State and local police and corrections expenditures were $79.5
   billion in 1992, when the national defense budget was $298 billion
   (*Statistical Abstract of the United States, 1994,* Tables 333, 517).

100 *Money* survey: September 1994.

100 New Yorkers: *New York Newsday* poll reported in Adam Walinsky, "The
   Crisis of Public Order," *Atlantic,* July 1995, pp. 39–54.

100 Gallup Youth Survey: "Teens Often Live in a Climate of Fear, Uncertainty, and Danger," *Emerging Trends* (Princeton Religion Research
   Center), pp. 4–5.

100 Hillary Rodham Clinton: Quoted in Alan Ehrenhalt, *The Lost City* (New
   York: Basic, 1995), p. 17.

101 Lawrence Stone: Findings presented at the 1994 Social Science History
   Association meeting, Atlanta, and summarized by Fox Butterfield, *New
   York Times* (reprinted *Grand Rapids Press,* October 30, 1994). His-
   torical changes are also discussed by Butterfield in "Many Cities in
   U.S. Show Sharp Drop in Homicide Rate," *New York Times,* August 13,
   1995.

101 Murdered, raped, robbed, assaulted: FBI *Uniform Crime Reports.* The
   rates per 100,000 in 1960 and 1993, respectively, were: murder, 5.1 and
   9.5; rape, 9.6 and 40.6; robbery, 60.1 and 255.8; assault, 86.1 and 440.1.

101 Britain: Central Statistical Office, *Annual Abstract of Statistics: 1996
   Edition* (London: HMSO, 1996), Table 4.1.

101 1.6 million: FBI, *Uniform Crime Report: Crime in the United States, 1997.*
   In 1996, 3.3 million violent-crime victims were estimated from the

National Crime Victimization Survey (www.ojp.usdoj.gov/bjs/glance/4meastbl.txt).

101 Margaret Ensley: Quoted in Barbara Kantrowitz, "Wild in the Streets," *Newsweek,* August 2, 1993, pp. 40–46.

101 Police officers per crime: Walinsky, "Crisis of Public Order."

101 Security guards and security measures: "Cost of Crime: $674 Billion," *U.S. News & World Report,* January 17, 1994, pp. 40–41.

102 Dozen crimes: David T. Lykken, "How Can Educated People Continue to Be Radical Environmentalists?" *The Edge* (www.edge.org), June 25, 1998.

102 John Donohue and Steven Levitt: Unpublished research summarized in Andrew Sullivan, "Did Abortion Make the Crime Figures Fall?" *Times* (London), August 15, 1999.

102 Pressure on police: Fox Butterfield, "Possible Manipulation of Crime Data Worries Top Police," *New York Times,* August 3, 1998.

103 Rise with recession: Economic strength and crime rates have been inversely correlated over the past thirty years, note Eleanor D. Craig and Andrew T. Hill. For example, "the strong economic growth of the mid-1980s saw a significant decline in crime rates, the recession of the early 1990s sent crime rates up, and the sustained positive growth since then has lowered the criminal behavior" ("Economic Growth as Crime Deterrent," www.intellectual capital.com/issues/98/1217/icbusgraph.asp).

103 Rearrest: Among state prisoners released in 1983, 76 percent of those 17 or younger, 68 percent of those 18 to 24, and 40 percent of those 45 or older were rearrested by 1986 (Allen J. Beck and Bernard E. Shipley, "Recidivism of Prisoners Released in 1983," Bureau of Justice Statistics Special Report, revised February 19, 1997 [NCJ 116261]).

103 Countries with young, unmarried males: Christian G. Mesquida and Neil I. Wiener, "Human Collective Aggression: A Behavioral Ecology Perspective," *Ethology and Sociobiology* 17 (1996): 247–62.

103 Birth trends: *Statistical Abstract of the United States, 1994,* Table 90.

103 John DiIulio: Quoted in Maggie Gallagher, *The Abolition of Marriage* (Washington, D.C.: Regnery, 1996), p. 46.

104 25 percent less likely: Males were 9.5 percent of the 1980 population and 7.1 percent of the 1995 population (*Statistical Abstract of the United States, 1997*).

104 44 million: The 1993 National Crime Victim Survey of more than 115,000 people in nearly 60,000 homes led to an estimate of 43,622,000 crimes in America in 1993 (John J. DiIulio, "Crime in America: It's Going to Get Worse," *Reader's Digest,* August 1995, pp. 55–60).

104 6.6 million violent crimes: Bureau of Justice Statistics 1990 data, sum-
         marized in *U.S. News & World Report,* January 17, 1994, p. 27, and
         updated to 1992 for crime, report, and arrest data from *Statistical
         Abstract of the United States, 1994,* Tables 310, 315.

104 Gary F. Jensen and Maryaltani Karpos: "Managing Rape: Exploratory
         Research on the Behavior of Rape Statistics," *Criminology* 31 (1993):
         363-85.

104 Mary P. Koss: "The Underdetection of Rape: Methodological Choices
         Influence Incidence Estimates," *Journal of Social Issues* 48 (1992): 61-
         75. See also Mary P. Koss, "Rape: Scope, Impact, Interventions, and
         Public Policy Responses," *American Psychologist* 48 (1993): 1062-69.

105 Younger women: S. B. Sorenson, J. A. Stein, J. M. Siegel, J. M. Golding,
         and M. A. Burnam, "Prevalence of Adult Sexual Assault: The Los
         Angeles Epidemiologic Catchment Area Study," *American Journal of
         Epidemiology* 126 (1987): 1154-64.

105 David Lykken: "The American Crime Factory," unpublished manuscript,
         University of Minnesota, 1995.

105 John DiIulio: "What the Crime Statistics Don't Tell You," *Wall Street
         Journal,* January 8, 1997.

105 Nearly 800,000: Data are available in the annual *Statistical Abstract of the
         United States* and FBI *Uniform Crime Reports.* Sample data: in 1970,
         23,217 gun deaths (11,772 suicide, 9,039 homicide, 2,406 accident);
         31,001 gun deaths (15,396 suicide, 13,650 homicide, 1,955 accident)
         in 1980; 35,344 gun deaths (18,526 suicide, 15,377 homicide, 1,441
         accident) in 1991. Each year there was also a small number of undeter-
         mined gun deaths (364 in 1991).

105 Prisoners: In 1960, there were 333,000 prisoners (213,000 in state and
         federal prisons and 120,000 in local jails). At midyear 1998, the correc-
         tional population was 1,277,866 inmates in federal and state prisons,
         and 592,462 in city and county jails (*Statistical Abstract of the United
         States, 1998,* Tables 375, 377, updated with U.S. Department of Jus-
         tice, "Nation's Probation and Parole Population Reached New High
         Last Year," August 16, 1998, release, and "Prison and Jail Inmates at
         Midyear 1998," March 14, 1999, release). There were 3,261,888 people
         on probation and 685,033 on parole.

106 Tops other nations: "New Inmates Pouring into U.S. Prisons at a Record
         Pace, U.S. Study Reveals," *Grand Rapids Press,* December 4, 1995.
         The U.S. incarceration rate slightly exceeds that of the number-two
         nation, Russia, the Sentencing Project reports.

106 William Bennett and John DiIulio: *Body Count* (New York: Simon &
         Schuster, 1996).

106 Costs: I have slightly inflated the estimates in *U.S. News & World Report*, January 17, 1994, of $39 billion for police, $29 billion for prisons, and $10 billion for legal and judicial costs. Adding private protection, loss of life and work, crimes against business, stolen goods, fraud, drug abuse, and drunk driving, the estimated total annual cost of crime was $674 billion (pp. 40–41).

106 Costs $25,000: Bennett and DiIulio, *Body Count*, pp. 113–14.

107 7 to 10 times: Richard K. Lore and Lori A. Schultz, "Control of Human Aggression: A Comparative Perspective," *American Psychologist* 48 (1993): 16–25.

107 Arrest rates: Walinsky, "Crisis of Public Order."

107 Paul F. Secord: "Imbalanced Sex Ratios: The Social Consequences," *Personality and Social Psychology Bulletin* 9 (1983): 525–43.

107 Hector Millan: Quoted in Fox Butterfield, "As Inmate Population Grows, So Does a Focus on Children," *New York Times*, April 7, 1999.

107 Charles Conrad: Kantrowitz, "Wild in the Streets."

108 National League of Cities survey: Keith Henderson, "School Violence Rising in Cities, Suburbs," *Christian Science Monitor*, November 21, 1994, and Mimi Hall, "Violence Up in 38% of Schools," *USA Today*, November 21, 1994.

108 Juvenile homicide doubled: Centers for Disease Control and Prevention, "Homicides Among 15–19-Year-Old Males," *Morbidity and Mortality Weekly Report*, October 14, 1994. Teen arrests for murder actually rose 158 percent from 1985 through 1994, according to the FBI's *Uniform Crime Reports* on 1994 crimes. Thomas Hobbes quoted in James B. Hayes, "The New American Revolution: A Recommitment to the Needs of Our Children," *Vital Speeches of the Day*, April 15, 1995, pp. 399–401.

108 3 to 8 P.M.: James Alan Fox and Sanford A. Newman, "After-School Crime or After-School Programs: Tuning In to the Prime Time for Violent Juvenile Crime and Implications for National Policy," a report to the U.S. Attorney General, Department of Justice, September 10, 1997, cited in Sylvia Ann Hewlett and Cornel West, *The War Against Parents* (Boston: Houghton Mifflin, 1998), p. 49.

108 Home alone: Data from others reported in Hewlett and West, *The War Against Parents*, p. 49.

109 William Dement: *The Promise of Sleep* (New York: Delacorte, 1999), pp. 102, 118, 406.

109 "Ticking crime bomb": John DiIulio, quoted by Nancy Gibbs in *Time*, June 20, 1994, p. 28.

109 80 percent by 7 percent: Fredrick Goodwin, former director of the Alco-
     hol, Drug Abuse, and Mental Health Administration, quoted in Juan
     Williams, "Violence, Genes, and Prejudice," *Discover,* November 1994,
     pp. 93–102.

109 Kirsti Lagerspetz: "Modification of Aggressiveness in Mice," in *Aggres-
     sion and Behavior Change,* ed. S. Feshbach and A. Frczek (New York:
     Praeger, 1979).

110 Primates and humans: J. Asher, "Born to Be Shy?" *Psychology Today,*
     April 1987, pp. 56–64; D. Olweus, "Stability of Aggressive Reaction
     Patterns in Males: A Review," *Psychological Bulletin* 86 (1979): 852–75.

110 Temperament: Jerome Kagan, *Galen's Prophecy: Temperament in Human
     Nature* (New York: Basic, 1994).

110 Temperament endures: Randy J. Larsen and Ed Diener, "Affect Inten-
     sity as an Individual Difference Characteristic: A Review," *Journal
     of Research in Personality* 21 (1987): 1–39; R. S. Wilson and A. P.
     Matheny, Jr., "Behavior-Genetics Research in Infant Temperament:
     The Louisville Twin Study," in *The Study of Temperament: Changes,
     Continuities, and Challenges,* ed. R. Plomin and J. Dunn (Hillsdale,
     N.J.: Erlbaum, 1986).

110 Identical twins: J. P. Rushton, D. W. Fulker, M. C. Neale, D. K. B. Nias,
     and H. J. Eysenck, "Altruism and Aggression: The Heritability of Indi-
     vidual Differences," *Journal of Personality and Social Psychology* 50
     (1986): 1192–98.

110 Child at risk: American Psychological Association, *Violence and Youth:
     Psychology's Response,* vol. 1, *Summary Report of the American
     Psychological Association Commission on Violence and Youth* (Wash-
     ington, D.C.: American Psychological Association, 1993). See also
     Linda Mealey, "The Sociobiology of Sociopathy: An Integrated Evolu-
     tionary Model," *Behavioral and Brain Sciences* 18 (1995): 523–99.

110 Age 18: FBI *Uniform Crime Reports, 1996* reports that for aggravated
     assault the most frequently arrested group was 18-year-olds.

110 Cryogenic sleep: David Lykken, *The Antisocial Personalities* (Hillsdale,
     N.J.: Erlbaum, 1995), p. 93.

110 Testosterone research: This is reviewed by one of the leading researchers,
     James Dabbs of Georgia State University, in various scientific articles
     and a forthcoming book.

110 Alcohol unleashes: B. J. Bushman, "Human Aggression While Under the
     Influence of Alcohol and Other Drugs: An Integrative Research Re-
     view," *Current Directions in Psychological Science* 2 (1993): 148–52;
     S. P. Taylor and S. T. Chermack, "Alcohol, Drugs, and Human Physical

Aggression," *Journal of Studies on Alcohol,* supplement no. 11 (1993): 78–88.

110 Violent people: H. R. White, J. Brick, and S. Hansell, "A Longitudinal Investigation of Alcohol Use and Aggression in Adolescence," *Journal of Studies on Alcohol,* supplement no. 11 (1993): 62–77.

111 Half the violent crimes: A. Abbey, L. T. Ross, and D. McDuffie, "Alcohol's Role in Sexual Assault," in *Drug and Alcohol Abuse Reviews,* ed. R. R. Watson, vol. 5, *Addictive Behaviors in Women* (Totowa, N.J.: Humana Press, 1993); A. J. Reiss, Jr., and J. A. Roth, eds., *Understanding and Preventing Violence* (Washington, D.C.: National Academy Press, 1993).

111 Rapists and alcohol: Michael C. Seto and Howard E. Barbaree, "The Role of Alcohol in Sexual Aggression," *Clinical Psychology Review* 15 (1995): 545–66.

111 4 in 5 students: Cheryl A. Pressley et al., *Alcohol and Drugs on American College Campuses: Issues of Violence and Harassment* (Carbondale, Ill.: Core Institute, Southern Illinois University, 1997), pp. 3, 4.

111 65 percent of homicides: American Psychological Association, *Violence and Youth,* vol. 1.

111 Two ways alcohol affects: J. G. Hull and C. F. Bond, Jr., "Social and Behavioral Consequences of Alcohol Consumption and Expectancy: A Meta-Analysis," *Psychological Bulletin* 99 (1986): 347–60; C. M. Steele and L. Southwick, "Alcohol and Social Behavior I: The Psychology of Drunken Excess," *Journal of Personality and Social Psychology* 48 (1985): 831–46.

111 People who love numbers: Philip J. Cook and Michael J. Moore, "Violence Reduction Through Restrictions on Alcohol Availability," *Alcohol Health and Research World* 17 (1993): 151.

111 10 percent price increase: Frank J. Chaloupka, "Effects of Price on Alcohol-Related Problems," *Alcohol Health and Research World* 17 (1993): 46–53.

111 Bennett and DiIulio: *Body Count,* pp. 69–79.

111 Jesse Jackson: *U.S. News & World Report,* January 17, 1994, p. 38.

111 Arrest rates: Data from FBI, *Uniform Crime Reports, 1996.* In 1996, 82.8 percent of the population was white and 12.7 percent black. Although whites therefore outnumbered blacks 6.5 to 1, blacks were 43 percent and whites 55 percent of those arrested for violent crime. Thus, the odds of a black person being arrested for violent crime were roughly 5 times greater than a white person's.

111 7 percent in prison: Bureau of Justice Statistics report on prison popula-
         tion, released December 3, 1995.

112 District of Columbia: 1991 data, Walinsky, "Crisis of Public Order."

112 Race and justice in California: Fox Butterfield, "Study Examines Race
         and Justice in California," *New York Times,* February 13, 1996.

112 Deborah Prothrow-Stith: *Deadly Consequences* (New York: Harper-
         Collins, 1991), p. 163.

112 Collegians and prisoners: The college enrollment data are from *The
         Chronicle of Higher Education Almanac Issue,* August 25, 1993, p. 13.
         The *Statistical Abstract of the United States, 1993* (Tables 338 to 340)
         reported 525,000 black males in state prisons and local jails (close to
         50 percent of the prison population). Another 57,000 prisoners (of
         whom I assume a similar percentage were black) resided in federal
         prisons.

112 Race of perpetrator and victim: FBI, *Uniform Crime Reports, 1996.*

112 Asthma attack: *Monthly Vital Statistics Report* 46, no. 1 (September 11,
         1997), Table 11, projecting white asthma death numbers proportional
         to their 83 percent of the population.

112 Benjamin Chavis, Jr.: Quoted in Carl Rowan, North American Syndicate
         column, November 9, 1993 (*Grand Rapids Press*).

112 Jesse Jackson: Sonya Ross, Associated Press, *Grand Rapids Press,* Janu-
         ary 9, 1994; *Responsive Community,* summer 1994, p. 90, reprinted
         from *New Republic,* March 21, 1994.

112 "If that many blacks": Jesse Jackson, "You Can Get Rid of Guns in Your
         School—If You Want To," *Parade,* December 18, 1993, p. 8.

113 Frederick Goodwin: Quoted in Williams, "Violence, Genes, and Preju-
         dice," pp. 93–102.

113 Leonard Eron: with L. Rowell Huesmann and Nancy Guerra, "Poverty
         and Violence," in *Aggression: Biological, Developmental, and Social
         Perspectives,* ed. S. Feshbach and J. Zagrodzka (New York: Plenum,
         1997).

113 Joblessness and crime fell: Report of a study by Richard B. Freeman and
         William M. Rodgers III of low-wage men in 322 metropolitan areas,
         in Sylvia Nasar and Kirsten B. Mitchell, "Booming Job Market Draws
         Young Black Men into Fold," *New York Times,* May 23, 1999.

113 David Rowe, Alexander Vazsonyi, and Daniel J. Flannery: "No More than
         Skin Deep: Ethnic and Racial Similarity in Developmental Processes,"
         Psychological Review 101 (1994): 396–413.

114 Richard Lewontin: *Human Diversity* (New York: Scientific American
         Library, 1982).

114 National economy and crime: Urie Bronfenbrenner, Peter McClelland, Elaine Wethington, Phyllis Moen, and Stephen J. Ceci, *The State of Americans* (New York: Free Press, 1996), p. 30.

114 Homicide rates by culture: Richard E. Nisbett, "Evolutionary Psychology, Biology, and Cultural Evolution," *Motivation and Emotion* 14 (1990): 255–63.

115 Richard E. Nisbett: "Violence and U.S. Regional Culture," *American Psychologist* 48 (1993): 441–49. See also Richard E. Nisbett and Dov Cohen, *Culture of Honor: The Psychology of Violence in the South* (Boulder, Colo.: Westview Press, 1996), and Dov Cohen, "Culture, Social Organization, and Patterns of Violence," *Journal of Personality and Social Psychology* 75 (1998): 408–19.

115 Physical punishment and aggressiveness: G. R. Patterson, P. Chamberlain, and J. B. Reid, "A Comparative Evaluation of Parent Training Procedures," *Behavior Therapy* 13 (1982): 638–50; M. A. Straus and R. J. Gelles, *Behind Closed Doors: Violence in the American Family* (New York: Anchor/Doubleday, 1980).

115 Cultures with minimal child-father contact: Harry Triandis, *Culture and Social Behavior* (New York: McGraw-Hill, 1994).

116 Communities: Michael R. Gottfredson and Travis Hirshi, *A General Theory of Crime* (Stanford, Calif.: Stanford University Press, 1990), p. 103.

116 51 of 61 murdered: S. Johnson and C. McMahon, "Killing Our Children," *Chicago Tribune*, January 2, 1994, cited in Lykken, *Antisocial Personalities*, p. 197.

116 Ervin Staub: "Societal-Cultural, Familiar, and Psychological Origins of Youth Violence," paper presented at the American Psychological Association convention, Toronto, 1993.

116 Norman Dennis: "Boys to Men? England Asks for Trouble," *The Family in America* (Rockford Institute Center), August 1997, pp. 1, 5–7.

116 Lykken: *Antisocial Personalities*, pp. 210, 212.

117 David T. Lykken: "On the Causes of Crime and Violence: A Reply to Aber and Rappaport," *Applied and Preventive Psychology* 3 (1994): 55–58. In personal correspondence (December 21, 1995), Lykken reports that "this 70% figure is quite real and important. In St. Paul, Minn., last year 70% of 'baby truants'—elementary school children with more than 25 unexcused absences during the year—were living with single mothers; nationally, about 70% of high school dropouts live with single moms; Gerald Patterson reports that 70 to 80% of the antisocial boys he has studied live with single mothers."

117 Cynthia C. Harper and Sara S. McLanahan: "Father Absence and Youth
       Incarceration," paper presented at the American Sociological Asso-
       ciation meeting, 1998. See also William S. Comanor and Llad Phillips,
       "The Impact of Income and Family Structure on Delinquency," work-
       ing paper in economics no. 7-95R, University of California, Santa
       Barbara, Economics Department, February 1998.

117 Social bonds to family: Robert J. Sampson and John H. Laub, *Crime in the
       Making* (Cambridge: Harvard University Press, 1993).

118 Escalating delinquency: American Psychological Association, *Violence
       and Youth*, vol. 1; Hirokazu Yoshikawa, "Prevention as Cumulative
       Protection: Effects of Family Support and Education on Chronic
       Delinquency and Its Risks," *Psychological Bulletin* 115 (1994): 28–54.

118 Other findings: I describe these phenomena, and the research that estab-
       lishes them, at greater length in *Social Psychology*, 5th ed. (New York:
       McGraw-Hill, 1996). For more on violence in groups, see Ervin Staub
       and Lori H. Rosenthal, "Mob Violence: Cultural-Societal Sources, In-
       stigators, Group Processes, and Participants," in *Reason to Hope: A
       Psychosocial Perspective on Violence and Youth*, ed. L. D. Eron, J. H.
       Gentry, and P. Schlegel (Washington, D.C.: American Psychological
       Association, 1994).

119 Gang description: Arnold P. Goldstein, "Delinquent Gangs," in *Student
       Aggression: Prevention, Control, and Replacement*, ed. A. P. Goldstein,
       B. Harootunian, and J. C. Conoley (New York: Guilford, 1994).

120 70,000 vehicle deaths: The 1970 population of 203 million produced
       54,633 motor vehicle deaths. The 1994 population was 1.28 times
       greater (260 million), which should have produced 69,973 vehicle
       deaths (*Statistical Abstract of the United States*, 1996).

120 C. Everett Koop and George D. Lundberg: "Violence in America: A Pub-
       lic Health Emergency," *Journal of the American Medical Association*
       267 (1992): 3075–76.

120 220 million guns: *CBS Evening News*, January 2, 1999, updating Bureau
       of Alcohol, Tobacco, and Firearms report of 211 million guns in *USA
       Today*, December 29, 1993.

120 42 percent: *Statistical Abstract of the United States*, 1995, Table 419.

120 Phil Murphy and Charmaine Klaus: "Homes and Lives Were on the Line,"
       USA Today, December 29, 1993.

121 Handgun Control, Inc.: From their poster "God Bless America"
       (www.handguncontrol.org).

121 Neal Knox: Quoted in Erik Larson, "Harder Line Prevails as Neal Knox
       Gains Control over NRA," *Wall Street Journal*, October 25, 1993.

121 Vancouver and Seattle: J. H. Sloan, A. L. Kellermann, D. T. Reay, J. A. Ferris, T. Koepsell, F. P. Rivara, C. Rice, L. Gray, and J. Logerfo, "Handgun Regulations, Crime, Assaults, and Homicide: A Tale of Two Cities," *New England Journal of Medicine* 319 (1988): 1256–61.

121 2.7 times greater risk: Arthur L. Kellermann, Frederick P. Rivara, Norman B. Rushforth, Joyce G. Banton, Donald T. Reay, Jerry T. Francisco, Ana B. Locci, Janice Prodzinski, Bela B. Hackman, and Grant Somes, "Gun Ownership as a Risk Factor for Homicide in the Home," *New England Journal of Medicine* 329 (1993): 1084–91.

121 5 times more suicide: Gary Taubes, "Violence Epidemiologists Test the Hazards of Gun Ownership," *Science* 258 (1992): 213–15.

121 Other studies: Arthur Kellermann, "Comment: Gunsmoke—Changing Public Attitudes Toward Smoking and Firearms," *American Journal of Public Health* 87 (1997): 910–12.

121 Colt's ads: "Center Urges FTC to Curb Deceptive Gun Ads," *Legal Action Report,* Center to Prevent Handgun Violence, April 1996, pp. 1, 3.

122 Leonard Berkowitz: "Impulse, Aggression, and the Gun," *Psychology Today,* September 1968, pp. 18–22, "How Guns Control Us," *Psychology Today,* June 1981, pp. 11–12, "A Career on Aggression," in *The Social Psychologists: Research Adventures,* ed. C. G. Brannigan and M. R. Merrens (New York: McGraw-Hill, 1995), and "Guns and Youth," in *Reason to Hope,* ed. Eron, Gentry, and Schlegel.

122 Karen Curtner: Quoted in Peter Katel, "Ark. Boys Stole Family Guns," *USA Today,* March 26, 1998.

122 Harris poll: Reported by Reuters, May 27, 1998 (my.excite.com/news/ r980527/15/news-guns). A 1999 Pew Research Center poll found that Americans by better than 2 to 1 think it more important "to control gun ownership" than "to protect the right of Americans to own guns" (Will Lester, "GOP Women Switch on Gun Control," Associated Press, *Grand Rapids Press,* May 21, 1999).

122 NRA by 10 to 1: Between January 1, 1991, and June 30, 1993, the NRA gave $2,917,525 to Senate and House candidates, while Handgun Control, Inc., gave $287,185. Other pro-gun lobbies gave an additional $98,000 ("NRA Leads Gun-Lobby Spending," *USA Today,* December 29, 1993.)

122 CDC funding: *Congressional Record,* House of Representatives, July 11, 1996, H7280–87.

123 43 states: Mary McGrory, Universal Press Syndicate, *Grand Rapids Press,* July 12, 1998.

123 Amitai Etzioni: "Gun Control: A Vanilla Agenda," *Responsive Community,*
summer 1991, pp. 6–10.

123 $135 billion: "Shootings, Killings Cost the USA Untold Billions," *USA
Today,* December 29, 1993.

123 About half favor handgun ban: An April 3–12, 1993, poll by Louis Harris
found 52 percent of 1,250 adults supporting a ban on hangun sales, and
43 percent opposed (Associated Press, June 4, 1993, *Holland Sentinel*).
A December 2–5, 1993, *USA Today*/CNN Gallup Poll of 1,014 adults
found 39 percent in favor of banning handgun sales to all but "police
and other authorized persons" (*USA Today,* December 30, 1993).

123 Gun searches and seizures: Fox Butterfield, *New York Times,* reprinted
as "Street Searches, Seizures Used in Cities to Limit Guns," *Grand
Rapids Press,* November 27, 1994.

123 Moynihan: Quoted in George Will, Washington Post Writers Group,
Grand Rapids Press, April 4, 1993.

124 California's get-tough strategy: Quoted by David S. Broder from a Rand
Corporation report by Joan Petersilia of the University of California,
Irvine (Washington Post Writers Group, *Grand Rapids Press,* April 18,
1994).

124 John DiIulio: "Abolish the Death Penalty, Officially," *Wall Street Journal,*
December 15, 1997.

124 National Research Council: *Understanding and Preventing Violence*
(Washington, D.C.: National Academy Press, 1993).

124 Louis Freeh: Inaugural address as FBI director, September 1, 1993.

125 Marian Wright Edelman: *The Measure of Our Success: A Letter to My
Children and Yours* (Boston: Beacon, 1992), p. 87.

Chapter 6: Money and Misery

p. 126 Roper survey: *Public Opinion,* August–September 1984, p. 25.

126 Life quality and more money: Angus Campbell, *The Sense of Well-Being
in America* (New York: McGraw-Hill, 1981), p. 41. A seemingly less
scientific national survey asked Americans, "If you could change one
thing about your life, what would it be?" The number one answer was
wealth, mentioned by 64 percent (James Patterson and Peter Kim,
*The Day America Told the Truth: What People Really Believe About
Everything That Matters* [New York: Prentice-Hall, 1991]).

127 Gallup Poll: George Gallup, Jr., and F. Newport, "Americans Widely Disagree on What Constitutes 'Rich,'" *Gallup Poll Monthly,* July 1990, pp.
28–36.

127 Roper Poll: Reported in Juliet B. Schor, *The Overworked American* (New York: Basic, 1991), p. 15.

127 Survey of college freshmen: Alexander W. Astin, Kenneth C. Green, and William S. Korn, *The American Freshman: Twenty-Year Trends*, a report of the Cooperative Institutional Research Program sponsored by the American Council on Education (Los Angeles: Higher Education Research Institute, Graduate School of Education, UCLA, 1987). Post-1985 data in annual *American Freshman* reports by Astin and others from same source, and from the *Chronicle of Higher Education*, January 12, 1996, pp. A34–35.

127 R. Woodrow Wasson: Quoted in Dirk Johnson, "Never Easy on the Wrong Side of the Tracks, '90s Affluence Widens the Gap," *New York Times*, October 14, 1998.

127 Thomas H. Naylor: "Redefining Corporate Motivation, Swedish Style," *Christian Century* 107 (1990): 566–70.

128 Robert H. Frank: *Luxury Fever: Why Money Fails to Satisfy in an Era of Excess* (New York: Free Press, 1999). For a synopsis, see his "Our Climb to Sublime," *Washington Post*, January 24, 1999.

128 Robert H. Frank, Thomas Gilovich, and Dennis T. Regan: "Does Studying Economics Inhibit Cooperation?" *Journal of Economic Perspectives* 7 (1993): 159–71.

129 16-nation study: Ronald Inglehart, *Culture Shift in Advanced Industrial Society* (Princeton, N.J.: Princeton University Press, 1990).

129 Chinese: Ed Diener and Shigehiro Oishi, "Money and Happiness: Income and Subjective Well-Being Across Nations," in *Subjective Well-Being Across Cultures*, ed. Ed Diener and E. M. Suh (Cambridge: MIT Press, in press).

129 Society of scarcity: Ronald Inglehart, *Modernization and Postmodernization: Cultural, Economic, and Political Change in Societies* (Princeton, N.J.: Princeton University Press, 1997), p. 64.

131 India: Michael Argyle summarizes data on India, and on the diminishing returns of increasing wealth, in "Causes and Correlates of Happiness," in *Understanding Well-Being: Scientific Perspectives on Enjoyment and Suffering*, ed. D. Kahneman, E. Diener, and N. Schwartz (New York: Russell Sage Foundation, 1999).

131 Inglehart: *Culture Shift in Advanced Industrial Society*, p. 242.

131 David T. Lykken: *Happiness* (New York: Golden Books, 1999), p. 17.

131 Mihaly Csikszentmihalyi: "If We Are So Rich, Why Aren't We Happy?" *American Psychologist*, January 2000.

131 Ed Diener: with J. Horwitz and Robert A. Emmons, "Happiness of the Very Wealthy," *Social Indicators* 16 (1985): 263–74.

132 J. Paul Getty: John Pearson, *Painfully Rich: The Outrageous Fortune and Misfortunes of the Heirs of J. Paul Getty* (New York: St. Martin's, 1995).

132 Warren Buffett: "Does Money Buy Happiness?" *Forbes,* April 21, 1997, p. 394.

132 Athina Roussel: *USA Today,* October 28, 1998.

132 People with disabilities: Kathleen Chwalisz, Ed Diener, and Dennis Gallagher, "Autonomic Arousal Feedback and Emotional Experience: Evidence from the Spinal Cord Injured," *Journal of Personality and Social Psychology* 54 (1988): 820–28. See also A. L. Allman and Ed Diener, "Measurement Issues and the Subjective Well-Being of People with Disabilities," Department of Psychology, University of Illinois, 1990; R. M. Bostick, "Quality of Life Survey Among a Severely Handicapped Population," Ph.D. diss., University of Houston, 1977; and Susan D. Decker and Richard Schulz, "Correlates of Life Satisfaction and Depression in Middle-Aged and Elderly Spinal Cord-Injured Persons," *American Journal of Occupational Therapy* 39 (1985): 740–45.

132 Friends agree with their perceptions: A. L. Allman, "Subjective Well-Being of Students With and Without Disabilities," paper presented at the Midwestern Psychological Association Convention, Chicago, May 1989.

132 Richard Kammann: "Objective Circumstances, Life Satisfactions, and Sense of Well-Being: Consistencies Across Time and Place," *New Zealand Journal of Psychology* 12 (1983): 14–22.

132 4,000-square-foot houses: This example was suggested by Robert Frank at the Understanding Quality of Life: Scientific Perspectives on Enjoyment and Suffering conference, Princeton University, November 1–3, 1996.

133 Making $50,000: Robert Frank offers evidence for this comparison in *Luxury Fever,* pp. 129, 163. I discuss social comparison dynamics at length in *The Pursuit of Happiness* (New York: Avon, 1992).

133 Daniel Gilbert: with E. C. Pinel, T. D. Wilson, S. J. Blumberg, and T. P. Wheatley, "Immune Neglect: A Source of Durability Bias in Affective Forecasting," *Journal of Personality and Social Psychology* 75 (1998): 617–38.

133 41 and 39 percent: Merck Family Fund poll, 1995, reported in Juliet B. Schor, *The Overspent American* (New York: Basic, 1998), pp. 17, 7.

133 William Bennett: Quoted by *Grand Rapids Press* wire services, December 14, 1990.

134 Pete Incaviglia: Quoted in *Life,* January 1991, p. 23.

134 Lottery winners: Philip Brickman, Dan Coates, and Ronnie J. Janoff-Bulman, "Lottery Winners and Accident Victims: Is Happiness Relative?" *Journal of Personality and Social Psychology* 36 (1978): 917–27; and Michael Argyle, *The Psychology of Happiness* (London: Methuen, 1986).

134 Frank Capaci: Peter Annin, "Big Money, Big Trouble," *Newsweek,* April 19, 1999, p. 59.

134 Inglehart: *Culture Shift in Advanced Industrial Society,* p. 212.

134 Robert Frank: *Luxury Fever.*

135 Richard Ryan: Quoted in Alfie Kohn, "In Pursuit of Affluence, at a High Price," *New York Times,* February 2, 1999. See also Tim Kasser and Richard Ryan, "Further Examining the American Dream: Differential Correlates of Intrinsic and Extrinsic Goals," *Personality and Social Psychology Bulletin* 22: 280–87.

135 1940 housing: Census Bureau report, "Tracking the American Dream," summarized by Associated Press (*Grand Rapids Press,* September 13, 1994).

135 $200 billion: Data from 1963 and 1995 *Statistical Abstract of the United States.* In 1992, Americans spent $200.2 billion in eating and drinking places, 12.43 times the $16.1 billion spent in 1960. Dividing 12.43 by the 3.37-fold consumer price increase and 1.4-fold population increase over this time period yields increased per person spending of 2.4 times (or, I estimate, about 2.5 times as of 1995).

135 Appliances: *Statistical Abstract of the United States, 1978* (Table 1383) and 1998. Technical note: Table 1383 reports 15 percent "room" air conditioners in 1960, which apparently accounted for virtually all air conditioning. Tables 1073 and 1074 of the 1963 *Statistical Abstract of the United States* report that 6,584 of 58,326 housing units—11 percent—had air-conditioning. The 15 percent estimate may therefore be high.

135 2,000 square feet: *Statistical Abstract of the United States, 1995,* Table 1214. This table reports that 21 percent of new homes had more than 2,000 square feet in 1970. Tracking that figure back as far as possible in earlier editions, the earliest data available were the 1966 figure.

136 Dora Costa: Summarized in "Fun for the Masses," *Economist,* August 2, 1997, p. 62.

136 Zoë Baird: She cited the statistics in this paragraph in a presentation to the Third Annual White House Conference on Character Education, June 1996 (drawing them, she tells me, from published reports).

137 "Pretty well satisfied": National Opinion Research Center surveys reported by Richard Gene Niemi, John Mueller, and Tom W. Smith, *Trends in Public Opinion: A Compendium of Survey Data* (New York: Greenwood, 1989).

137 Martin E. P. Seligman: "Explanatory Style: Predicting Depression, Achievement, and Health," in *Brief Therapy Approaches to Treating Anxiety and Depression,* ed. Michael D. Yapko (New York: Brunner/Mazel, 1989).

138 Gerald L. Klerman and Myrna M. Weissman: "Increasing Rates of Depression," *Journal of the American Medical Association* 261 (1989): 2229–35. See also Cross-National Collaborative Group, "The Changing Rate of Major Depression," *Journal of the American Medical Association* 268 (1992): 3098–3105.

138 Garrison Keillor: Quoted in Martin Marty, *Context,* May 15, 1989.

138 William Bennett: "Redeeming Our Time," *Imprimis,* November 1995, pp. 1–8.

138 Richard Ryan: Quoted in Kohn, "In Pursuit of Affluence." See also Kasser and Ryan, "Further Examining the American Dream."

138 Tim Kasser: "Two Versions of the American Dream: Which Goals and Values Make for a High Quality of Life?" in *Advances in Quality of Life: Theory and Research,* ed. E. Diener and D. Rahtz (Dordrecht, Netherlands: Kluwer, in press).

138 H. W. Perkins: "Religious Commitment, Yuppie Values, and Well-Being in Post-Collegiate Life," *Review of Religious Research* 32 (1991): 244–51.

139 Robert Wuthnow: *God and Mammon in America* (New York: Free Press, 1994).

139 What's the point: Evolutionary psychologists would say there *was* a point. Men compete for mates by acquiring resources that females desire for themselves and their offspring. Psychologist David Buss explains: "Women who selected men who were able to invest resources in them and their offspring would have been at a considerable advantage in survival and reproductive currencies compared to women who were indifferent to the investment capabilities of the man with whom they chose to mate" (David M. Buss, "Sexual Conflict," in *Sex, Power, Conflict,* ed. D. M. Buss and N. M. Malamuth [New York: Oxford University Press, 1996], p. 302). Because (according to this view) guys come from a long line of men who successfully attracted mates, we carry genes that predispose us to want to accumulate more and more resources. In this theory one hears an echo of Freud: it all comes down to sex.

    Mind you, little of this is conscious. Donald Trump isn't asking, "How can I—by accumulating wealth and trophy wives—maximize the number of genes I leave to posterity?" Rather, say evolutionary psychologists, our natural yearnings are our genes' way of making more genes.

139 16 percent to 24 percent: Sylvia Ann Hewlett and Cornel West, *The War Against Parents* (Boston: Houghton Mifflin, 1998), p. 81.

139 Sylvia Ann Hewlett and Cornel West: Ibid., p. 66.

140 Usually happens: "The Census Bureau reports that the distribution of income tends to become more unequal during expansions. Gini coefficients for household income [an index of income inequality] have risen in every year since 1968, except three: 1974, 1980 and 1990, all of them years of recession," reports John C. Weicher ("Changes in the Distribution of Wealth: Increasing Inequality?" *Review* [Federal Reserve Bank of St. Louis], January–February 1995, pp. 5–23).

140 Kurt Vonnegut: Quoted in Robert H. Frank and Philip J. Cook, *The Winner-Take-All Society* (New York: Free Press, 1995), chapter 11.

140 Countries with large income inequality: From a study of subjective well-being in 55 nations by Ed Diener, Marissa Diener, and Carol Diener, "Factors Predicting the Subjective Well-Being of Nations," *Journal of Personality and Social Psychology* 69 (1995): 851–64.

141 Richest fifth: "Historical Income Tables—Households. Table H-2, Share of Aggregate Income Received by Each Fifth and Top 5 Percent of Households (All Races): 1967 to 1997" (www.census.gov/hhes/income/histinc/ho2.html).

141 Richest 5 percent: "Historical Income Tables—Households. Table H-3, Mean Income Received by Each Fifth and Top 5 Percent of Households (All Races): 1967 to 1997" (www.census.gov/hhes/income/histinc/ho3.html).

141 Glenn Loury: "Tenuous Trickle-Down," *New York Times,* May 29, 1999.

141 From 59 percent to 50 percent: George J. Church, "Are We Better Off?" *Time,* January 29, 1996, pp. 37–40.

141 Worth 185 factory workers: A 1993 survey indicated 143 to 1 (Holly Sklar, "Losing Ground on Jobs, Wages: Profits Are Rising, But the Benefits Haven't Trickled Down," *Asbury Park Press,* September 3, 1995). *Time* updated that to 185 to 1 (Jill Smolowe, "Reap as Ye Shall Sow," February 5, 1996, p. 45).

141 IBM CEO: *Time,* September 4, 1995, p. 21.

141 1995 CEO salaries: *Wall Street Journal,* April 11, 1996.

141 British and American medical costs and longevity: M. I. Roemer, *National Health Systems of the World,* vol. 1, *The Countries* (New York: Oxford

University Press, 1991); R. Fein, "Health Care Reform," *Scientific American,* November 1992, pp. 46–53; *Information Please Almanac.*

141 Michael Jordan: *Forbes,* December 18, 1995, p. 212.

141 Michael Eisner's income: Holly Sklar, "For CEO, 'Minimum Wage' Means Millions," *Holland Sentinel,* April 16, 1999.

142 Richest 1 percent: Data from Edward N. Wolff, *Top Heavy: A Study of the Increasing Inequality of Wealth in America* (New York: Twentieth Century Fund, 1995), pp. 7, 22, 24, cited in Hewlett and West, *The War Against Parents,* p. 83. A 1996 United Nations report indicated that the world's 358 wealthiest people have assets equal to the combined income of 2.3 billion of the world's people, nearly half the global population (*Human Development Report, 1996,* published for the UN by Oxford University Press).

142 Piazza's pay: Bob Becker, "Don't Cry for Owners, Fans Are Victims," *Grand Rapids Press,* October 29, 1998.

142 Kevin Phillips: *The Politics of Rich and Poor: Wealth and the American Electorate in the Reagan Aftermath* (New York: Random House, 1990), p. 10.

142 Newt Gingrich: "I Am Not in a Teaching Job," *Time,* December 25, 1995, pp. 84–85.

142 You have to wonder: What system would you prefer if you had to choose before knowing your outcome in the genetic lottery? Would it be a system that concentrates wealth in the pockets of relatively few winners? Or would it be a system that, while rewarding initiative, equitably values the contributions of all workers with a family-supportive wage? Philosopher John Rawls presumes that if we were all behind a "veil of ignorance" regarding who we are, we would agree on two principles of justice: (1) the greatest freedom compatible with a like freedom for others, and (2) equality, except for inequalities attached to positions open to everyone and which work out in the long run to benefit all, including those least well off.

142 African-American inequality: In 1996, the top and bottom fifths received 51 percent and 3 percent, respectively, of all black income, and 48 percent and 4 percent of white income (www.census.gov/hhes/income/histinc/).

142 Gertrude Himmelfarb: "The National Prospect," *Commentary,* November 1995, pp. 65–66.

143 Milton Schwebel: Letter to *APA Monitor,* June 1998, p. 5.

143 Lester Thurow: "Why Their World Might Crumble," *New York Times,* November 19, 1995.

143 Robert H. Frank: "The Victimless Income Gap?" *New York Times,*
     April 12, 1999.

143 George Soros: *The Crisis of Global Capitalism* (New York: Public Affairs,
     1998), pp. 115, 208, 235, xxvii.

144 Chicago South Side: Alan Ehrenhalt, *The Lost City: Discovering the For-
     gotten Virtues of Community in the Chicago of the 1950s* (New York:
     Basic, 1995).

144 National Research Council: Panel on High-Risk Youth, Commission
     on Behavioral and Social Sciences and Education, *Losing Genera-
     tions: Adolescents in High-Risk Settings* (Washington, D.C.: National
     Academy Press, 1993), p. 236.

144 Children's Defense Fund: Arloc Sherman, *Wasting America's Future: The
     Children's Defense Fund Report on the Costs of Child Poverty* (Boston:
     Beacon Press, 1994).

144 Woody Allen: Quoted in Hal Lancaster, "Needs or Greedy? How Money
     Fits into Job Satisfaction," *Wall Street Journal,* July 1, 1998.

145 Greg J. Duncan: with Jeanne Brooks-Gunn and Pamela Kato Klebanov,
     "Economic Deprivation and Early Childhood Development," *Child
     Development* 65 (1994): 296–318.

145 What women desire: David Buss, *The Evolution of Desire: Strategies of
     Human Mating* (New York: Basic, 1994).

145 African-American males and marriage: M. Belinda Tucker and Claudia
     Mitchell-Kernan, eds., *The Decline in Marriage Among African Ameri-
     cans: Causes, Consequences, and Policy Implications* (New York: Sage,
     1995).

145 Lillian B. Rubin: " 'People Don't Know Right from Wrong Anymore,' "
     Tikkun 9 (1995): 13–18, 83–87.

145 Doubled joblessness and female heads: Hewlett and West, *The War
     Against Parents,* p. 77.

146 Benton Harbor: Mitchell Landsberg, "Benton Harbor Leads Single Par-
     ent Parade," Associated Press (*Grand Rapids Press,* September 19,
     1994).

146 Father joblessness and family breakup: *Trends in the Well-Being of
     America's Children and Youth, 1996* (Washington, D.C.: Department
     of Health and Human Services), p. 290.

146 Living family wage: The term originated in Australia as rationale for mini-
     mum wage for men, and informed early minimum wage laws in Britain
     and the United States (Allan S. Carlson, "Gender, Children, and Social
     Labor: Transcending the 'Family Wage' Dilemma," *Journal of Social
     Issues* 52 [1996]: 137–61).

146 William Bennett: Quoted in Doug Bandow, "Can 'Unbridled Capitalism' Be Tamed?" *Wall Street Journal,* March 19, 1997.

147 George Soros: "The Capitalist Threat," *Atlantic,* February 1997, pp. 45–58.

147 Bryce Christensen: "Far More than a Health Club: How the Family Guards Health and Alleviates Sickness," *Family in America,* April 1998, pp. 1–7.

147 John Paul and bishops: Michael Sean Winters, "Old Faithful," *New Republic,* February 9, 1998, pp. 16–17.

147 National Conference of Catholic Bishops: "Putting Children and Families First: A Challenge for Our Church, Nation, and World," pastoral letter, November 1991.

148 Robert Frank: *Luxury Fever.* See also "Timmy's Range Rover," *New York Times,* December 22, 1998. Frank doesn't include charity in his draft consumption formula, but he tells me he agrees it could be there. It could, he says, be a deductible expense. Although the tax-free savings plan would still likely divert some giving into savings, some of the much larger estates people would leave would result in sharply increased donations out of estates. Charitable giving through estates may be low, but it's higher than with year-to-year charitable giving, and might become even higher with bigger estates.

As Frank argues, the progressive consumption tax (beginning, say, with a 20 percent tax rate on annual consumption beyond $30,000 for a family of four and rising to 70 percent for consumption over $500,000) offers many advantages over our present taxation of income:

- It promises to free more people from luxury fever than has the voluntary simplicity movement. People who would have bought a $30,000 BMW Z3 may now adjust, with no less happiness, down to a $23,000 Mazda Miata.

- It taxes luxury spending without political debate over what are luxuries (each family can decide for itself what to spend its untaxed money on).

- Unlike sales tax and value-added taxes, it can be made progressive—placing the burden on those who consume the most. (Conservative economists such as Milton Friedman and liberals such as Lester Thurow similarly advocate a consumption tax, but they disagree on how progressive to make it.)

- By allowing people to completely shelter their savings and investment, savings will surge—and so, therefore, will productivity and economic growth. With economic growth, democratic values and social harmony will be more secure and more funds will become available to clean up the environment, care for underclass children, and support the common good.

- Families would be strengthened by diminishing the incentives for workaholic behavior. If less driven to earn and consume, we would also have more time for healthy sleep and exercise.

148 Jack Kemp: "A Cultural Renaissance," *Imprimis*, August 1994, pp. 1–5.

149 Hewlett and West: *The War Against Parents*, p. 97.

150 43 percent: Eugene Steuerle, "The Tax Treatment of Households of Different Size," in *Taxing the Family*, ed. R. G. Penner (Washington, D.C.: American Enterprise Institute, 1983), p. 75, cited in Allan Carlson, "Toward a Family-Centered Theory of Taxation," *Family in America*, January 1998, pp. 1–8.

150 Dan Quayle: "At Last We Agree: Fix the Family," *USA Today*, April 14, 1994.

150 C. Eugene Steuerle: Remarks at the Communitarian Teach-In on the Future of the Family, Rayburn Office Building, Capitol Hill, November 3, 1993.

150 James Alm and Leslie A. Whittington: Reported in Richard Morin, "Unconventional Wisdom," *Washington Post*, March 10, 1996.

150 Marriage encouragement policy: *Family Research Report*, September–October, 1994, pp. 1–2, cited in Paul C. Vitz, *Family in America*, June 1998, pp. 1–8.

150 Council on Families in America: *Marriage in America: A Report to the Nation* (New York: Institute for American Values, 1995).

151 President Reagan: Quoted in David S. Broder, "GOP Makes Sure Rich Keep Getting Richer," Washington Post Writers Group, *Grand Rapids Press*, September 24, 1995.

151 Robert Rector: "Requiem for the War on Poverty," *Policy Review*, summer 1992, p. 40, quoted in R. J. Sider and H. Rolland, "Correcting the Welfare Tragedy: Toward a New Model for Church/State Partnership," in *Welfare in America: Christian Perspectives on a Policy in Crisis*, ed. S. W. Carlson-Thies and J. W. Skillen (Grand Rapids, Mich.: Eerdmans, 1996), p. 459.

151 Dan Coats: *The Project for American Renewal* (Washington, D.C.: U.S. Senate, 1995).

151 More than $8,000 per child: Quayle, "At Last We Agree."

151 Exemption and credit proposals: William R. Mattox, Jr., "Government Tax Policy and the Family," in *The Family, Civil Society, and the State*, ed. Christopher Wolfe (Lanham, Md.: Rowman & Littlefield, 1998), p. 193.

152 $600 child allowance: The $600 amount comes from "A Communitarian Position Paper on the Family," Communitarian Network, Washington, D.C. The $1,000 suggestion comes from "A Call for Family-Supportive Tax Reform," from the Institute for American Values and various signatories (www.americanvalues.org/thestatement.htm).

152   Allan Carlson: "Toward a Family-Centered Theory."

152   10 percent to 50 percent: Carlson, "Gender, Children, and Social Labor."

152   Katha Pollitt: Quoted in Molly Ivins, "How About the Welfare Fathers?"
        Creator's Syndicate, *Grand Rapids Press,* January 25, 1995.

152   Mandatory identification: Support for this idea comes from the Clinton
        welfare reform proposal (*Time,* June 20, 1994, p. 30) and Senator Bill
        Bradley ("Civil Society and the Rebirth of Our National Community,"
        Responsive Community, spring 1995, pp. 4–10).

152   Irwin Garfinkel: "Child Support Assurance," Communitarian Teach-In
        on the Future of the Family, Rayburn Office Building, Capitol Hill,
        November 3, 1993. Also, Census Bureau data reported in Nicholas Zill
        and Christine Winquist Nord, *Running in Place: How American Fami-
        lies Are Faring in a Changing Economy and an Individualistic Society*
        (Washington, D.C.: Child Trends, 1994), pp. 7–8.

153   Council on Civil Society: *A Call to Civil Society: Why Democracy Needs
        Moral Truths,* Council on Civil Society, University of Chicago Divinity
        School, and Institute for American Values.

154   Jay Belsky: "Effects of Infant Day Care, 1986–94," address to the British
        Psychological Society section on developmental psychology, Ports-
        mouth, England, September 4, 1994.

154   European and American paid leave policies: Amitai Etzioni, remarks
        to the White House Conference on Character Education for a Civil,
        Democratic Society, May 19, 1995.

154   Janet Shibley Hyde: with Marilyn J. Essex, Roseanne Clark, Marjorie H.
        Klein, and Janis E. Byrd, "Parental Leave: Policy and Research," *Jour-
        nal of Social Issues* 52 (1996): 91–109.

155   Profits depend on cutting costs: This point is well made in Hewlett and
        West, *The War Against Parents,* p. 73.

155   Jeremy Rifkin: C-Span broadcast presentation to the Federal Highway
        Administration, April 2, 1996. See also Jeremy Rifkin, *The End of
        Work: The Decline of the Global Labor Force and the Dawn of the
        Post-Market Era* (New York: Putnam's Sons, 1995).

155   National survey: S. Grover and K. J. Crooker, "Who Appreciates Family-
        Responsive Human Resource Policies: The Impact of Family-Friendly
        Policies on the Organizational Attachment of Parents and Non-
        Parents," *Personnel Psychology* 48 (1995): 271–88.

156   Kellogg: John P. Beck, "Kellogg's Six-Hour Day," *Michigan History Maga-
        zine,* June 1997, p. 49; see also Benjamin Kline Hunnicutt, *Kellogg's
        Six-Hour Day* (Philadelphia: Temple University Press, 1996).

156   Marilynne Robinson: "The Way We Work, the Way We Live," *Chris-

tian Century, September 9–16, 1998, pp. 823–30. See also Marilynne Robinson, *The Death of Adam: Essays on Modern Thought* (Boston: Houghton Mifflin, 1998).

157 Herman Miller: Executive Compensation Committee Report, in notice of Annual Meeting of Shareholders, 1995. See also C. Davenport, "America's Most Admired Corporations," *Fortune,* January 30, 1989, pp. 68–94, and Max De Pree, *Leadership Is an Art* (New York: Doubleday, 1989).

157 Playing the free agent market: The number of CEOs who have been with their companies for less than three years grew by almost 50 percent from the early 1970s to the early 1990s (Frank and Cook, *Winner-Take-All Society,* p. 70).

157 Task Force: Hewlett and West, *The War Against Parents,* Appendix A.

158 Martin Luther King, Jr.: "Where Do We Go from Here: Chaos or Community?" in *A Testament of Hope: The Essential Writings of Martin Luther King, Jr.,* ed. J. M. Washington (New York: Harper & Row, 1986).

158 African-American families intact: Andrew Billingsley, *Climbing Jacob's Ladder* (New York: Simon & Schuster, 1992), p. 36.

159 Calcutta: Jonathan Alter, "The Name of the Game Is Shame," *Newsweek,* December 12, 1994, p. 41.

159 Immigrant families: Recent Asian-American immigrants are a case in point. See N. Caplan, M. H. Choy, and J. K. Whitmore, "Indochinese Refugee Families and Academic Achievement," *Scientific American,* February 1992, pp. 36–42.

159 Mexican immigrants: Javier L. Escobar, "Immigration and Mental Health: Why Are Immigrants Better Off?" *Archives of General Psychiatry* 55: 781–82.

159 Marian Wright Edelman: "Introduction: Cease Fire! Stopping the Gun War Against Children in the United States," *The State of America's Children Yearbook, 1994* (Washington, D.C.: Children's Defense Fund, 1994).

Chapter 7: Individualism and Community

p. 162 *"The* theory": Elizabeth Fox-Genovese, *Feminism Without Illusions: A Critique of Individualism* (Chapel Hill: University of North Carolina Press, 1991), p. 7.

162 "Whatever you please": Mary Ann Glendon, *Rights Talk: The Impoverishment of Political Discourse* (New York: Free Press, 1991), p. 9.

162 116,000 employees: G. Hofstede, *Culture's Consequences* (Beverly Hills, Calif.: Sage, 1980).

162 Alexis de Tocqueville: *Democracy in America,* ed. J. P. Mayer (New York: Knopf, 1991), pp. 506–8, quoted in William E. Hudson, *American Democracy in Peril: Seven Challenges to America's Future* (Chatham, N.Y.: Chatham House, 1995), p. 72.

162 "Prefer himself": Tocqueville, *Democracy in America,* p. 506.

163 "Radical individualists": Hudson's term for egoists in *American Democracy in Peril.*

163 "Alike and equal": Tocqueville, *Democracy in America,* p. 692.

163 Andrew Greeley: "Habits of the Head," *Society,* May–June, 1992, pp. 74–81.

163 Robert N. Bellah, Richard Madsen, William M. Sullivan, Ann Swidler, and Steven M. Tipton: *Habits of the Heart: Individualism and Commitment in American Life* (Berkeley, Calif.: University of California Press, 1985), p. 6.

164 Harry C. Triandis, Richard Brislin, and C. Harry Hui: "Cross-Cultural Training Across the Individualism-Collectivism Divide," *International Journal of Intercultural Relations* 12 (1988): 269–89. See also Harry C. Triandis, *Culture and Social Behavior* (New York: McGraw-Hill, 1994).

165 Carl Rogers: Quoted in Michael A. Wallach and Lise Wallach, "How Psychology Sanctions the Cult of the Self," *Washington Monthly,* February 1985, pp. 46–56.

165 Dennis Rodman: *Bad As I Wanna Be* (New York: Dell, 1996), p. 11, and *Walk on the Wild Side* (New York: Delacorte, 1997), jacket.

165 Self-esteem legislation: James L. Nolan, Jr., "Esteeming the 'Responsible' Self," *Responsive Community,* fall 1998, pp. 36–43.

166 Other psychologists: William Damon, *Greater Expectations: Overcoming the Culture of Indulgence in America's Homes and Schools* (New York: Free Press, 1995); Robyn Dawes, *House of Cards: Psychology and Psychotherapy Built on Myth* (New York: Free Press, 1994); Mark R. Leary, "The Social and Psychological Importance of Self-Esteem," in *The Social Psychology of Emotional and Behavioral Problems,* ed. R. M. Kowalski and M. R. Leary (Washington, D.C.: APA Books, in press); and Martin Seligman, *What You Can Change and What You Can't* (New York: Knopf, 1994).

166 Self-serving bias research: I document this in my texts *Psychology,* 4th ed. (New York: Worth, 1995), and *Social Psychology* (New York: McGraw-Hill, 1996).

166 Robyn Dawes: "The Social Usefulness of Self-Esteem: A Skeptical View,"

Harvard Mental Health Letter, October 1998, pp. 4–5. See also Dawes's informed and iconoclastic *House of Cards.*

166 Threatened self-esteem: Roy Baumeister, "Esteem Threat, Self-Regulatory Breakdown, and Emotional Distress as Factors in Self-Defeating Behavior," *Review of General Psychology* 1 (1997): 145–74.

166 Brad Bushman and Roy Baumeister: "Threatened Egotism, Narcissism, Self-Esteem, and Direct and Displaced Aggression: Does Self-Love or Self-Hate Lead to Violence?" *Journal of Personality and Social Psychology* 75 (1998): 219–29.

166 Facing failure: G. Agostinelli, S. J. Sherman, C. C. Presson, and L. Chassin, "Self-Protection and Self-Enhancement Biases in Estimates of Population Prevalence," *Personality and Social Psychology Bulletin* 18 (1992): 631–42; J. D. Brown and F. M. Gallagher, "Coming to Terms with Failure: Private Self-Enhancement and Public Self-Effacement," *Journal of Experimental Social Psychology* 28 (1992): 3–22.

167 Roy Baumeister: "Should Schools Try to Boost Self-Esteem? Beware the Dark Side," *American Educator* 20 (1996): 14–19, 43.

167 Mark Leary: "Social and Psychological Importance of Self-Esteem."

168 Rollo May: Quoted in William Doherty, "Bridging Psychotherapy and Moral Responsibility," *Responsive Community,* winter 1994–95, pp. 41–52.

168 Fritz Perls: "Gestalt Therapy (interview)," in *Inside Psychotherapy,* ed. Adelaide Bry (New York: Basic, 1972), p. 70.

168 Students in Japan and China: Harry C. Triandis, "The Self and Social Behavior in Differing Cultural Contexts," *Psychological Review* 96 (1989): 506–20, and "Cross-Cultural Studies of Individualism and Collectivism," in *Nebraska Symposium on Motivation, 1989,* vol. 37, ed. J. J. Berman (Lincoln: University of Nebraska Press, 1989).

168 Autobiographies and family histories: F. L. K. Hsu, cited in Triandis, *Culture and Social Behavior.*

168 Magazine ads: S.-P. Han and S. Shavitt, "Persuasion and Culture: Advertising Appeals in Individualistic and Collectivistic Societies," *Journal of Experimental Social Psychology* 30 (1994): 326–50.

169 President Clinton: State of the Union address, January 1996, and a subsequent speech in Long Beach, California, which in 1994 began requiring uniforms for the 60,000 children in its 70 elementary and middle schools. By late 1997, uniforms were required in most public schools in Cleveland, Chicago, Miami, and Boston (Tamar Lewin, "Public Schools Becoming Uniform in Their Dress Codes," *New York Times,* September 25, 1997).

169 Collectivists more often respond: S. E. Cross, M.-H. Liao, and R. Josephs, "A Cross-Cultural Test of the Self-Evaluation Maintenance Model," paper presented at the American Psychological Association convention, 1992.

169 University students in Hong Kong: Ladd Wheeler, Harry T. Reis, and Michael H. Bond, "Collectivism-Individualism in Everyday Social Life: The Middle Kingdom and the Melting Pot," *Journal of Personality and Social Psychology* 57 (1989): 79–86.

169 Feeling good: Shinobu Kitayama, Hazel R. Markus, and H. Matsumoto, "Culture, Self, and Emotion: A Cultural Perspective on 'Self-Conscious Emotions," in *Self-Conscious Emotions: The Psychology of Shame, Guilt, Embarrassment, and Pride,* ed. J. P. Tangney and K. W. Fisher (New York: Guilford, 1995).

169 Maintaining harmony: Shinobu Kitayama and Hazel R. Markus, "Construal of the Self as Cultural Frame: Implications for Internationalizing Psychology," in *Becoming More International and Global: Challenges for American Higher Education,* ed. J. D'Arms, R. G. Hastie, S. E. Hoelscher, and H. K. Jacobson (Ann Arbor: University of Michigan Press, in press).

169 Child on back: Hazel Markus and Shinobu Kitayama, "Culture and the Self: Implications for Cognition, Emotion, and Motivation," *Psychological Review* 98 (1991): 224–53.

169 What parents want: Duane F. Alwin, "Historical Changes in Parental Orientations to Children," in *Sociological Studies of Child Development,* ed. N. Mandell, vol. 3 (Greenwich, Conn.: JAI Press, 1990).

170 Jessica Dubroff's mother: Associated Press, *Grand Rapids Press,* April 12, 1996.

170 Asian parents: C. Harry Hui, "West Meets East: Individualism Versus Collectivism in North America and Asia," invited address, Hope College, 1990.

170 "Daughter of individualism": Fox-Genovese, *Feminism Without Illusions,* p. 241.

170 Barbara Dafoe Whitehead: *The Divorce Culture* (New York: Vintage, 1997).

170 Fox-Genovese: *Feminism Without Illusions,* pp. 8, 241.

171 Chodorow, Miller, and Gilligan: Nancy J. Chodorow, *The Reproduction of Mothering: Psychoanalysis and the Sociology of Gender* (Berkeley: University of California Press, 1978); Nancy J. Chodorow, *Feminism and Psychoanalytic Theory* (New Haven, Conn.: Yale University Press, 1989); Jean Baker Miller, *Toward a New Psychology of Women,* 2d ed. (Boston: Beacon Press, 1986); Carol Gilligan, *In a Different Voice:*

Psychology Theory and Women's Development (Cambridge: Harvard University Press, 1982); Carol Gilligan, N. P. Lyons, and T. J. Hanmer, eds., *Making Connections: The Relational Worlds of Adolescent Girls at Emma Willard School* (Cambridge: Harvard University Press, 1990).

171 Girls' play: J. Lever, "Sex Differences in the Complexity of Children's Play and Games," *American Sociological Review* 43 (1978): 1178–87.

171 Spend time: M. M. Wong and M. Csikszentmihalyi, "Affiliation Motivation and Daily Experience: Some Issues on Gender Differences," *Journal of Personality and Social Psychology* 60 (1991): 154–64.

171 Men's and women's self-esteem: R. A. Josephs, H. R. Markus, and R. W. Tafarodi, "Gender and Self-Esteem," *Journal of Personality and Social Psychology* 63 (1992): 391–402; J. E. Stake, "Gender Differences and Similarities in Self-Concept Within Everyday Life Contexts," *Psychology of Women Quarterly* 16 (1992): 349–63.

171 In conversation: Deborah Tannen, *You Just Don't Understand: Women and Men in Conversation* (New York: Morrow, 1990).

171 In groups: K. Dindia and M. Allen, "Sex Differences in Self-Disclosure: A Meta-Analysis," *Psychological Bulletin* 117 (1992): 106–24; Alice H. Eagly, *Sex Differences in Social Behavior: A Social-Role Interpretation* (Hillsdale, N.J.: Erlbaum, 1987).

171 "Help others": Linda J. Sax, Alexander W. Astin, William S. Korn, and Kathryn M. Mahoney, *The American Freshman: National Norms for Fall 1998* (Los Angeles: Higher Education Research Institute, UCLA, 1998).

171 Twins: David Lykken, from the University of Minnesota twins study, in *Happiness* (New York: Golden Books, 1999), p. 25.

171 Care for aging parents: J. Aronson, "Women's Sense of Responsibility for the Care of Old People: 'But Who Else Is Going to Do It?'" *Gender and Society* 6 (1992): 8–29; L. E. Troll, "Mother-Daughter Relationships Through the Life Span," in *Family Processes and Problems: A Social Psychological Analysis,* ed. S. Oskamp (Newbury Park, Calif.: Sage, 1987).

171 Gifts and cards: L. Destafano and D. Colasanto, "Unlike 1975, Today Most Americans Think Men Have It Better," *Gallup Poll Monthly,* February 1990, pp. 25–36; Hallmark Cards, cited in *Time,* fall 1990 special issue on women.

171 Visiting friends: In a DDB Needham Life Style consumer survey, 40 percent of women and 33 percent of men agreed (Robert D. Putnam, *Bowling Alone* [New York: Simon & Schuster, 2000]).

171 Photos: S. M. Clancy and S. J. Dollinger, "Photographic Depictions of the

Self: Gender and Age Differences in Social Connectedness," *Sex Roles* 29 (1993): 477–95.

172 Women's charity: National Council for Research on Women, "Women and Philanthropy Fact Sheet," *Issues Quarterly* 1, no. 2 (1992): 9.

172 Democratic party support: "Women, Men, Marriages, and Ministers," *American Enterprise,* January–February 1992, p. 106.

172 54 percent of women: *Wall Street Journal*/NBC News Poll, December 1–5, 1995, *Wall Street Journal.*

172 Gender and empathy: N. Eisenberg and R. Lennon, "Sex Differences in Empathy and Related Capacities," *Psychological Bulletin* 94 (1983): 100–131.

172 Judith Hall: "On Explaining Gender Differences: The Case of Nonverbal Communication," *Review of Personality and Social Psychology* 7 (1987): 177–200, and Judith Hall, *Nonverbal Sex Differences: Communication Accuracy and Expressive Style* (Baltimore: Johns Hopkins University Press, 1984).

172 Greater responsiveness: M. Grossman and W. Wood, "Sex Differences in Intensity of Emotional Experience: A Social Role Interpretation," *Journal of Personality and Social Psychology* 65 (1993): 1010–22; S. Sprecher and C. Sekikides, "Gender Differences in Perceptions of Emotionality: The Case of Close Heterosexual Relationships," *Sex Roles* 28 (1993): 511–30; J. M. Stoppard and C. D. G. Gruchy, "Gender, Context, and Expression of Positive Emotion," *Personality and Social Psychology Bulletin* 19 (1993): 143–50.

172 Friendships with women: Lillian B. Rubin, *Just Friends: The Role of Friendship in Our Lives* (New York: Harper & Row, 1985); L. A. Sapadin, "Friendship and Gender: Perspectives of Professional Men and Women," *Journal of Social and Personal Relationships* 5 (1988): 387–403.

173 Kazuo Kato and Hazel Markus: "Development of the Interdependence/Independence Scale: Using American and Japanese Samples," presentation to the American Psychological Society, 1993.

173 Hazel Markus and Shinobu Kitayama: "Culture and the Self."

173 Triandis explains: Triandis, *Culture and Social Behavior.*

174 Colonization: Triandis, "Cross-Cultural Studies of Individualism and Collectivism."

174 Assess people's helpfulness: Robert V. LeVine, T. S. Martinez, G. Brase, and K. Sorenson, "Helping in 36 U.S. Cities," *Journal of Personality and Social Psychology* 67 (1994): 69–82.

174 Other studies confirm: A. Hedge and Y. H. Yousif, "Effects of Urban Size,

Urgency, and Cost on Helpfulness: A Cross-Cultural Comparison Between the United Kingdom and the Sudan," *Journal of Cross-Cultural Psychology* 23 (1992): 107–15; N. M. Stebley, "Helping Behavior in Rural and Urban Environments: A Meta-Analysis," *Psychological Bulletin* 102 (1987): 346–56.

174 Born since 1950: Putnam, *Bowling Alone*. See also Ronald Inglehart, *Modernization and Postmodernization: Cultural, Economic, and Political Change in Societies* (Princeton, N.J.: Princeton University Press, 1997).

175 Mary Pipher: *The Shelter of Each Other: Rebuilding Our Families* (New York: Putnam, 1996), p. 232.

175 Soldiers: G. H. Elder, Jr., and E. C. Clipp, "Wartime Losses and Social Bonding: Influences Across 40 Years in Men's Lives," *Psychiatry* 51 (1988): 177–97.

175 Experiments illuminate: See the last chapter of my *Social Psychology*, 5th ed.

175 Margaret Mooney Marini: "The Rise of Individualism in Advanced Industrial Societies," paper presented at the Population Association of America annual meeting, 1990.

175 Francis Fukuyama: *The Great Disruption: Human Nature and the Reconstitution of Social Order* (New York: Free Press, 1999).

175 Ivan Boesky: Quoted in Charles Colson, *Breakpoint*, January 1996, p. 26.

176 Gallup polls: Virginia A. Hodgkinson and Murray S. Weitzman, *Giving and Volunteering in the United States* (Washington, D.C.: Independent Sector, 1990 and 1992).

176 Increased to 30 percent: Susan Jacoby, "Why Do We Donate? It's Personal," *New York Times*, December 9, 1997.

176 Malcolm Forbes: Stephanie Coontz, *The Way We Never Were* (New York: Basic, 1992), p. 95.

176 Don Eberly: *Restoring the Good Society* (Grand Rapids, Mich.: Hourglass Books, 1994), p. 20.

176 George Will: Cited in ibid., pp. 61–62.

176 Daniel Bell: Adapted from *Time*, February 19, 1996, p. 27.

177 Russell Kirk: Cited in Eberly, *Restoring the Good Society*, p. 62.

177 Ruut Veenhoven: "Quality-of-Life in Individualistic Society: A Comparison of 43 Nations in the Early 1990s," *Social Indicators Research*, in press.

177 Triandis: *Culture and Social Behavior.*

178 Singapore: Jay Branegan, "Is Singapore a Model for the West?" *Time*,

January 18, 1993, pp. 36–37; Henry Kamm, "In Prosperous Singapore, Even the Elite Are Nervous About Speaking Out," *New York Times*, August 13, 1995.

178 Accompanying our individualism: David Popenoe, "The Evolution of Marriage and the Problem of Stepfamilies: A Biosocial Perspective," in *Stepfamilies: Who Benefits?* ed. Alan Booth and Judy Dunn (Hillsdale, N.J.: Erlbaum, 1994); Harry C. Triandis, R. Bontempo, M. J. Villareal, M. Asai, and N. Lucca, "Individualism and Collectivism: Cross-Cultural Perspectives on Self-Ingroup Relationships," *Journal of Personality and Social Psychology* 54 (1988): 323–38.

178 Ed Diener: with Marissa Diener and Carol Diener, "Factors Predicting the Subjective Well-Being of Nations," *Journal of Personality and Social Psychology* 69 (1995): 851–64.

178 Suicide and homicide rates: David Lester, "Subjective Well-Being, Suicide, and Homicide," *Psychological Reports* 83 (1998): 234.

178 Declining social connections and support: James S. House, "Social Support and the Quality and Quantity of Life," in *Research on the Quality of Life*, ed. F. M. Andrews (Ann Arbor: University of Michigan Press, 1986).

178 Live alone: In 1940, 8 percent of households involved Americans living alone. Today, 25 percent do. The Census Bureau (in a May 3, 1996, release) predicts that by 2010, 27 percent will. Because those 25 percent of households have fewer people per household, they account for 12 percent of all adults (24.9 million in 1996).

178 Participation is waning: Ron Grossman and Charles Leroux, "Nation of Strangers: A New Silence," *Chicago Tribune*, December 29, 1995, and Robert Wuthnow, *Loose Connections: Joining Together in America's Fragmented Communities* (Cambridge: Harvard University Press, 1998).

179 Bowling leagues and PTA: David Blankenhorn, "The Possibility of Civil Society," in *Seedbeds of Virtue: Sources of Competence, Character, and Citizenship in American Society,* ed. Mary Ann Glendon and David Blankenhorn (Lanham, Md.: Madison Books, 1995), p. 274. See also Robert D. Putnam, "Bowling Alone: America's Declining Social Capital," *Journal of Democracy* 6 (1995): 65–78.

179 Roper data: Putnam, *Bowling Alone.*

180 Everett C. Ladd: *The Ladd Report on Civic America* (New York: Free Press, 1999).

180 Imprecisely measured: Referring to question order effects described in "Measuring Misanthropy" (http://www.icpsr.umich.edu/GSS/news/trendtab.htm).

180 Gallup Poll: *Gallup Poll Monthly,* July 1994, p. 35.

180 Prudential Insurance: William Galston, remarks to the Third Annual White House Conference on Character Education, June 8, 1996.

180 54 percent: Lynne Casper and Loretta Bass, "Hectic Lifestyles Make for Record-Low Election Turnout, Census Bureau Reports," Census Bureau Press Release 280, August 17, 1998.

180 Ron Grossman and Charles Leroux: "Nation of Strangers."

180 Education and civic engagement: The proportion of adults who completed four years of high school or more increased from 41 percent in 1960 to 81 percent in 1994 (*Statistical Abstract of the United States, 1995,* Table 238). For a careful analysis of these trends, see Robert D. Putnam, "The Strange Disappearance of Civic America," *American Prospect,* winter 1996, pp. 34–48.

181 Daniel Yankelovich: "The Affluence Affect," in *Values and Public Policy,* ed. H. J. Aaron, T. Mann, and T. Taylor (Washington, D.C.: Brookings Institution, 1994).

181 William Butler Yeats: Quoted in Frank S. Pepper, ed., *The Wit and Wisdom of the Twentieth Century* (New York: Peter Bedrick Books, 1987), p. 74.

182 Martin E. P. Seligman: *Learned Optimism* (New York: Knopf, 1991), pp. 284–85.

182 Roy F. Baumeister: *Escaping the Self: Alcoholism, Spirituality, Masochism, and Other Flights from the Burden of Selfhood* (New York: Basic, 1991), p. 7.

182 Two-thirds of Americans: 1992 Yankelovich Clancy Shulman survey for *Time* and CNN, and 1994 National Opinion Research Center survey, respectively; reported in *The American Enterprise,* July–August 1995, p. 104. Awareness of the effects of divorce may be increasing, however. A 1998 *Washington Post*/Kaiser Foundation/Harvard University survey (using altered wording, making comparison difficult) found 50 percent disagreeing that "A couple that is unhappy should get divorced even if they have young children." Moreover, 62 percent say that divorce should be harder to obtain than it now is (data presented by *Washington Post* polling director Richard Morin at the Communitarian Summit, Washington, D.C., February 1999).

183 Bernard Farber: "The Future of the American Family: A Dialectical Account," *Journal of Family Issues* 8 (1987): 431–33.

183 "Freedom of one spouse": Norval Glenn, "Values, Attitudes, and the State of American Marriage," in *Promises to Keep: Decline and Renewal of Marriage in America,* ed. David Popenoe, Jean Bethke Elshtain, and David Blankenhorn (Lanham, Md.: Rowman & Littlefield, 1996).

183 Divorce in collectivist countries: See Triandis, *Culture and Social Behavior; Statistical Abstract of the United States, 1995,* Table 1366; and the United Nations' *Demographic Yearbook.*

183 Collectivists demand less romance: Karen K. Dion and Kenneth L. Dion, "Individualistic and Collectivistic Perspectives on Gender and the Cultural Context of Love and Intimacy," *Journal of Social Issues* 49 (1993): 53–69; Elaine Hatfield and Susan Sprecher, "Men's and Women's Preferences in Marital Partners in the United States, Russia, and Japan," *Journal of Cross-Cultural Psychology* 26 (1995): 728–50.

183 "Keeping romance alive": "Women, Men, Marriages, and Ministers," *American Enterprise,* January–February, 1992, p. 106.

183 After two years: T. L. Huston and A. F. Chorost, "Behavioral Buffers on the Effect of Negativity on Marital Satisfaction: A Longitudinal Study," *Personal Relationships* 1 (1994): 223–39.

183 The divorce rate peaks: Helen Fisher, "The Nature of Romantic Love," *Journal of NIH Research,* April 1994, pp. 59–64.

184 Usha Gupta and Pushpa Singh: "Exploratory Study of Love and Liking and Type of Marriages," *Indian Journal of Applied Psychology* 19 (1982): 92–97.

184 Autonomy and attachment: John D. Cunningham and John K. Antil, "Cohabitation and Marriage: Retrospective and Predictive Comparisons," *Journal of Social and Personal Relationships* 11 (1994): 77–93.

184 Partnership as self-actualization: David R. Hall, "Marriage as a Pure Relationship: Exploring the Link Between Premarital Cohabitation and Divorce in Canada," *Journal of Comparative Family Studies* 27 (1996): 1–12.

184 Saving individuals: Quoted in Albert Martin, *One Man, Hurt* (New York: Ballantine, 1975), p. 244, cited in Whitehead, *The Divorce Culture,* p. 71.

184 Individualists' frustrations with marriage: John Scanzoni, Karen Polonko, Jay Teachman, and Linda Thompson, *The Sexual Bond: Rethinking Families and Close Relationships* (Newbury Park, Calif.: Sage, 1989), p. 117.

185 Warren Beatty: Quoted in Jonathan Alter, "Beatty and Bening," *USA Weekend,* October 7–9, 1994, pp. 4–6.

185 Garrett Hardin: "The Tragedy of the Commons," *Science* 162 (1968): 1243–48.

186 Julian J. Edney: "The Nuts Game: A Concise Commons Dilemma Analog," *Environmental Psychology and Nonverbal Behavior* 3 (1979): 252–54; Julian J. Edney, "The Commons Problem: Alternative Perspectives," *American Psychologist* 35 (1980): 131–50.

186 Adam Smith: *The Wealth of Nations* (Chicago: University of Chicago Press, 1776/1976), p. 18.

187 Fukuyama: *The Great Disruption.*

187 Parapsychology founders: James E. Alcock, "Parapsychology: The 'Spiritual' Science," *Free Inquiry,* spring 1985, pp. 25–35; John Beloff, "Science, Religion, and the Paranormal," *Free Inquiry,* spring 1985, pp. 36–41.

187 Germany and astrology: Vernon Padgett and Dale O. Jorgenson, "Superstition and Economic Threat: Germany, 1918–1940," *Personality and Social Psychology Bulletin* 8 (1982): 736–41.

187 Russian pseudoscience: S. Kapitza, "Antiscience Trends in the U.S.S.R.," *Scientific American,* August 1991, pp. 32–38.

187 Former medium: M. L. Keene, *The Psychic Mafia* (New York: Dell, 1976), p. 10.

187 Amitai Etzioni: "A Communitarian Response," *Responsive Community,* fall 1992, pp. 78–79.

187 Pope John Paul II: Speaking at a morning mass at Oriole Park in Baltimore, quoted in *Christian Century,* October 25, 1995, p. 980.

188 Vaclav Havel: *Disturbing the Peace* (New York: Knopf, 1990), p. 10.

188 Aleksandr Solzhenitsyn: *Warning to the West* (New York: Farrar, Straus and Giroux, 1976), pp. 130–31.

188 Charles Colson: *Against the Night: Living in the New Dark Ages* (Ann Arbor, Mich.: Servant Publications, 1989), pp. 36, 178.

189 Universal Declaration of Human Responsibilities: *Responsive Community,* spring 1998, pp. 72–77.

189 National Commission on Civic Renewal: Quote from executive director, William A. Galston, at National Press Club briefing, June 24, 1998.

189 John W. Gardner: "Rebirth of a Nation," address to the Forum Club of Houston, Texas, February 17, 1993.

189 Robert N. Bellah: "Community Properly Understood: A Defense of 'Democratic Communitarianism,'" *Responsive Community,* winter 1995–96, pp. 49–54.

190 Amitai Etzioni: "The Community in an Age of Individualism" (interview), *Futurist,* May–June 1991, pp. 35–39. Japan remark in his address to the Communitarian Summit, Washington, D.C., February 1999.

191 Barry Freundel: "What Do American Jews Believe?" *Commentary* 20 (August 1996), p. 35.

191 Walker Percy: Quoted in A. J. Bacevich, "On the Right Side of History," *America,* February 14, 1998, pp. 24–25.

191 Maggie Gallagher: "The Moral Logic of No-Fault Divorce," in *The Family, Civil Society, and the State,* ed. Christopher Wolfe (Lanham, Md.: Rowman & Littlefield, 1998), p. 131.

192 James Q. Wilson: *The Moral Sense* (New York: Free Press, 1993), p. 13.

192 Roy F. Baumeister and Mark R. Leary: "The Need to Belong: Desire for Interpersonal Attachment as a Fundamental Human Motivation," *Psychological Bulletin* 117 (1995): 497-529.

193 "Most people mention": Ellen Berscheid, "Interpersonal Attraction," in *The Handbook of Social Psychology,* ed. G. Lindzey and E. Aronson (New York: Random House, 1985).

193 Less likely to die prematurely: Sheldon Cohen, "Psychosocial Models of the Role of Social Support in the Etiology of Physical Disease," *Health Psychology* 7 (1988): 269-97; J. S. House, K. R. Landis, and D. Umberson, "Social Relationships and Health," *Science* 241 (1988): 540-45.

193 Leukemia and heart disease survival: E. A. Colon, A. L. Callies, M. K. Popkin, and P. B. McGlave, "Depressed Mood and Other Variables Related to Bone Marrow Transplantation Survival in Acute Leukemia," *Psychomatics* 32 (1991): 420-25; R. B. Williams et al., "Prognostic Importance of Social and Economic Resources Among Medically Treated Patients with Angiographically Documented Coronary Artery Disease," *Journal of the American Medical Association* 267 (1992): 520-24.

Chapter 8: Media, Minds, and the Public Good

p. 195 "F—— the bitch": 2 Live Crew's album, *As Nasty as They Wanna Be,* reportedly included 226 uses of the "F" word and 163 uses of "bitch."

195 Marian Wright Edelman: *The Measure of Our Success* (Boston: Beacon, 1992), p. 81.

195 James Garbarino: "Growing Up in a Socially Toxic Environment: Life for Children and Families in the '90s," *Nebraska Symposium on Motivation,* vol. 42 (Lincoln: University of Nebraska Press, 1995).

196 *Washington Post:* Megan Rosenfeld, "Father Knows Squat," *Washington Post,* November 13, 1994, cited in Sylvia Ann Hewlett and Cornel West, *The War Against Parents* (Boston: Houghton Mifflin, 1998).

196 Hewlett and West: *The War Against Parents,* pp. 130, xii.

196 Newton Minow: Quoted in Newton N. Minow and Craig L. LaMay, *Abandoned in the Wasteland: Children, Television, and the First Amendment* (New York: Hill and Wang, 1995), p. 95.

197 Evening dramas: George Gerbner, "Women and Minorities on Television:

A Study in Casting and Fate," report to the Screen Actors Guild and the American Federation of Radio and Television Artists, June 1993.

197 Violence data: George Gerbner, N. Morgan, and N. Signorielli, "Television Violence Profile No. 16: The Turning Point from Research to Action," Annenberg School for Communication, University of Pennsylvania, 1993.

197 National Television Violence Study: *National Television Violence Study* (Thousand Oaks, Calif.: Sage, 1997).

197 Fistfights: Observation by director Stuart Gordon based on Chicago emergency room experiences, reported in Sean Mitchell, "Gore Galore," *USA Weekend*, July 13-14, 1991.

197 73 percent: From a 1995 University of California, Santa Barbara, study of 2,500 hours of programming on 23 channels over 20 weeks (*National Television Violence Study: Executive Summary, 1994-1995,* and *National Television Violence Study: Scientific Papers, 1994-1995* [Studio City, Calif.: Mediascope, 1996]).

197 End of elementary school: A. C. Huston, E. Donnerstein, H. Fairchild, N. D. Feshbach, P. A. Katz, and J. P. Murray, *Big World, Small Screen: The Role of Television in American Society* (Lincoln: University of Nebraska Press, 1992).

197 Premium cable more violent: From a 1995 University of California, Santa Barbara, content analysis, reported in Alan Bash, "Industry-Funded Study Criticizes Violence on TV," *USA Today,* February 6, 1996.

197 *Die Hard 2* and MTV: Body count reported in *Newsweek,* April 1, 1991, p. 46; MTV violence "far exceeds that on commercial television," reports the American Psychological Association, *Violence and Youth* (Washington, D.C., 1993).

197 George Gerbner: "The Politics of Media Violence: Some Reflections," in *Mass Communication Research: On Problems and Policies,* ed. C. Hamelink and O. Linne (Norwood, N.J.: Ablex, 1994).

198 Unmarried versus married sex: C. Fernandez-Collado and B. S. Greenberg, with F. Korzenny and C. K. Atkin, "Sexual Intimacy and Drug Use in TV Series," *Journal of Communication* 28, no. 3 (1978): 30-37; E. O. Laumann, J. H. Gagnon, R. T. Michael, and S. Michaels, *The Social Organization of Sexuality: Sexual Practices in the United States* (Chicago: University of Chicago Press, 1994).

198 Only one was married: Caryn James, "A Baby Boom on TV as Biological Clocks Cruelly Tick Away," *New York Times,* October 16, 1991, cited in Maggie Gallagher, *The Abolition of Marriage* (Washington, D.C.: Regnery, 1996), p. 83.

198 Prime-time sex: Barry S. Sapolsky and Joseph O. Tabarlet, "Sex in Prime-

time Television: 1979 Versus 1989," *Journal of Broadcasting and Electronic Media* 35 (1991): 505–16.

198 Luke and Laura: Gerard J. Waggett, "Let's Stop Turning Rapists into Heroes," *TV Guide,* May 27, 1989, pp. 10–11.

199 TV and religion: T. Skill, J. D. Robinson, J. S. Lyons, and D. Larson, "The Portrayal of Religion and Spirituality on Fictional Network Television," *Review of Religious Research* 35 (1994): 251–67; F. E. Saad and L. McAneny, "Most Americans Think Religion Losing Clout in the 1990s," *Gallup Poll Monthly,* April 1994, pp. 2–4.

199 Blue collar: Gerbner, "Women and Minorities on Television."

199 Alcohol: "TV and Film Alcohol Research," *NCTV News* 9, no. 3–4 (1988): 4.

199 1945 Gallup poll: G. H. Gallup, *The Gallup Poll: Public Opinion, 1935–1971,* vol. 3 (New York: Random House, 1972).

199 98 percent (versus 94 percent with telephone service): *Statistical Abstract of the United States, 1995,* Table 897.

199 Nearly as many TVs as people: 0.814 TVs per person in the United States, versus 0.639 in the number-two TV-owning nation, Canada (*Statistical Abstract of the United States, 1995,* Table 1381).

199 *Baywatch:* D. McDougal, "Baywatch!" *TV Guide,* August 13–19, 1994, pp. 12–17.

199 7.24 hours per day: Or 50 hours 42 minutes per week, as reported in electronic correspondence from Anne Elliot, director of communications, Nielsen Media Research, January 18, 1996.

200 20,000 hours: Robert Putnam believes that increased TV viewing is a prime cause of declining civic engagement, from bowling leagues to voting: "Controlling for education, income, age, race, place of residence, work status, and gender, TV viewing is strongly and negatively related to social trust and group membership, whereas the same correlations with newspaper reading are positive. Within every educational category, heavy readers are avid joiners, whereas heavy viewers are more likely to be loners. . . . In short, television privatizes our leisure time." Such facts invite us "to ask whether we like the result, and if not, what we might do about it" ("The Strange Disappearance of Civic America," *American Prospect,* winter 1996, pp. 34–48).

A recent intensive study of the consequences of Internet use by 169 people revealed that heavy usage functioned much like television—reducing communication with family members, diminishing the size of one's social circle, and increasing depression and loneliness (Robert Kraut et al., "Internet Paradox: A Social Technology That Reduces Social Involvement and Psychological Well-Being," *American Psychologist* 53: 1017–31.

200 Victor Cline: with R. G. Croft and S. Courrier, "Desensitization of Children to Television Violence," *Journal of Personality and Social Psychology* 27 (1973): 360–65.

200 Blasé reaction: Ronald S. Drabman and Margaret H. Thomas, "Does Media Violence Increase Children's Toleration of Real-Life Aggression?" *Developmental Psychology* 10 (1974): 418–21; "Does TV Violence Breed Indifference?" *Journal of Communication* 25, no. 4 (1975): 86–89; and "Does Watching Violence on Television Cause Apathy?" *Pediatrics* 57 (1976): 329–31. See also Brendan G. Rule and Tamara J. Ferguson, "The Effects of Media Violence on Attitudes, Emotions, and Cognitions," *Journal of Social Issues* 42, no. 3 (1986): 29–50.

200 Charles R. Mullin and Daniel Linz: "Desensitization and Resensitization to Violence Against Women: Effects of Exposure to Sexually Violent Films on Judgments of Domestic Violence Victims," *Journal of Personality and Social Psychology* 69 (1995): 449–59.

201 George Gerbner and associates: "The Demonstration of Power: Violence Profile No. 10," *Journal of Communication* 29 (1979): 177–96, and "The Politics of Media Violence: Some Reflections," in *Mass Communication Research: On Problems and Policies,* ed. C. Hamelink and O. Linne (Norwood, N.J.: Ablex, 1994).

201 New York but not neighborhood: Linda Heath and J. Petraitis, "Television Viewing and Fear of Crime: Where Is the Mean World?" *Basic and Applied Social Psychology* 8 (1987): 97–123; Tom R. Tyler and F. L. Cook, "The Mass Media and Judgments of Risk: Distinguishing Impact on Personal and Societal Level Judgments," *Journal of Personality and Social Psychology* 47 (1984): 693–708.

201 7- to 11-year-olds: J. L. Peterson and N. Zill, "Television Viewing in the United States and Children's Intellectual, Social, and Emotional Development," *Television and Children* 2 (1981): 21–28.

201 Hillary Clinton: Judy Blume, "The First Lady Talks TV," *TV Guide,* November 13, 1993, p. 12.

202 Flyers feel fear: "Commercial Aviation," *Gallup Report,* March–April 1989, pp. 32–33.

202 Commercial flights: *Accident Facts* (Chicago: National Safety Council, 1991).

202 Fiction and judgment: Richard J. Gerrig and Deborah A. Prentice, "The Representation of Fictional Information," *Psychological Science* 2 (1991): 336–40.

202 Marital faithfulness and perceptions: Andrew M. Greeley, *Faithful At-*

traction (New York: Tor Books, 1991); Tom W. Smith, "Adult Sexual Behavior in 1989," General Social Survey Topic Report No. 18 (Chicago: National Opinion Research Center, University of Chicago, 1990); B. C. Leigh, M. T. Temple, and K. E. Trocki, "The Sexual Behavior of U.S. Adults: Results from a National Survey," *American Journal of Public Health* 83 (1993): 1400–1408.

202 University students: Gina Agostinelli and David Wyatt Seal, "Social Comparisons of One's Own with Others' Attitudes Toward Casual and Responsible Sex," *Journal of Applied Social Psychology* 28 (1998): 845–60.

203 Neil M. Malamuth and James V. P. Check: "The Effects of Media Exposure on Acceptance of Violence Against Women: A Field Experiment," *Journal of Research in Personality* 15 (1981): 436–46.

203 Social science consensus: C. Everett Koop, "Report of the Surgeon General's Workshop on Pornography and Public Health," *American Psychologist* 42 (1987): 944–45. For more information on the mixed evidence regarding rape myths, see Mike Allen, Tara Emmers, Lisa Gebhardt, and Mary Giery, "Exposure to Pornography and Acceptance of Rape Myths," *Journal of Communication* 45 (1995): 5–26.

203 View rape victims: Daniel G. Linz, Ed Donnerstein and S. M. Adams, "Physiological Desensitization and Judgments About Female Victims of Violence," *Human Communication Research* 15 (1989): 509–22; Daniel G. Linz, Ed Donnerstein, and Steven Penrod, "Effects of Long Term Exposure to Violent and Sexually Degrading Depictions of Women," *Journal of Personality and Social Psychology* 55 (1988): 758–68.

203 More likely to rape: Malamuth and Check, "Effects of Media Exposure on Acceptance of Violence Against Women."

203 Douglas T. Kenrick and Sara E. Gutierres: "Contrast Effects and Judgments of Physical Attractiveness: When Beauty Becomes a Social Problem," *Journal of Personality and Social Psychology* 38 (1980): 131–40.

204 Centerfold experiment: Douglas T. Kenrick, Sara E. Gutierres, and L. L. Goldberg, "Influence of Popular Erotica on Judgments of Strangers and Mates," *Journal of Experimental Social Psychology* 25 (1989): 159–67; J. B. Weaver, J. L. Masland, and D. Zillmann, "Effect of Erotica on Young Men's Aesthetic Perception of their Female Sexual Partners," *Perceptual and Motor Skills* 58 (1984): 929–30.

204 Viewing pornography: Dolf Zillmann, "Effects of Prolonged Consumption of Pornography," in *Pornography: Research Advances and Policy Considerations*, ed. D. Zillmann and J. Bryant (Hillsdale, N.J.: Erlbaum, 1989).

204 Feeling homely: J. D. Brown, N. J. Novick, K. A. Lord, and J. M. Richards, "When Gulliver Travels: Social Context, Psychological Closeness, and Self-Appraisals," *Journal of Personality and Social Psychology* 62 (1992): 717–27; B. Thornton and S. Moore, "Physical Attractiveness Contrast Effect: Implications for Self-Esteem and Evaluations of the Social Self," *Personality and Social Psychology Bulletin* 19 (1992): 474–80.

204 Wendy Stock: "The Effects of Pornography on Women," in *The Price We Pay: The Case Against Racist Speech, Hate Propaganda, and Pornography*, ed. L. J. Lederer and R. Delgado (New York: Hill and Wang, 1995).

204 Priming mountain climber: E. Tory Higgins, William S. Rholes, and C. R. Jones, "Category Accessibility and Impression Formation," *Journal of Experimental Social Psychology* 13 (1978): 363–78.

204 Doug McKenzie-Mohr and Mark P. Zanna: "Treating Women as Sexual Objects: Look to the (Gender Schematic) Male Who Has Viewed Pornography," *Personality and Social Psychology Bulletin* 16 (1990): 296–308.

205 Friendliness as come-on: Richard J. Harris, "The Impact of Sexually Explicit Media," in *Media Effects: Advances in Theory and Research*, ed. J. Bryant and D. Zillmann (Hillsdale, N.J.: Erlbaum, 1994).

205 Rock music videos: Christine H. Hansen and Randy D. Hansen, "Priming Stereotypic Appraisal of Social Interactions: How Rock Music Videos Can Change What's Seen When Boy Meets Girls," *Sex Roles* 19 (1988): 287–316; Christine H. Hansen and Randy D. Hansen, "Rock Music Videos and Antisocial Behavior," *Basic and Applied Social Psychology* 11 (1990): 357–69.

205 Dolf Zillmann and Jennings Bryant: "Effects of Massive Exposure to Pornography," in *Pornography and Sexual Aggression*, ed. N. Malamuth and E. Donnerstein (Orlando, Fla.: Academic Press, 1984).

206 15 sexual innuendoes and acts: Sapolsky and Tabarlet, "Sex in Primetime Television."

206 George Gerbner: "Society's Storyteller: How Television Creates the Myths by Which We Live," University of Pennsylvania, 1992.

206 Sir David Puttnam: Foreword to Julian Wilson, *Complete Surrender* (East Sussex, U.K.: Monarch, 1996), pp. 9–10.

206 Third-person effect: Julie M. Duck and Barbara-Ann Mullin, "The Perceived Impact of the Mass Media: Reconsidering the Third Person Effect," *European Journal of Social Psychology* 25 (1995): 77–93; J. M. Innes and H. Zeitz, "The Public's View of the Impact of the Mass

Media: A Test of the 'Third Person' Effect," *European Journal of Social Psychology* 18 (1988): 457–63.

207 Drano: Brad J. Bushman, "Individual Differences in the Extent and Development of Aggressive Cognitive-Associative Networks," *Personality and Social Psychology Bulletin* 22: 811–19.

207 208 prison convicts: *TV Guide*, January 26, 1977, pp. 5–10.

207 Violent TV diet and aggression: Leonard D. Eron, "The Development of Aggressive Behavior from the Perspective of a Developing Behaviorism," *American Psychologist* 42 (1987): 425–42; C. W. Turner, B. W. Hesse, and S. Peterson-Lewis, "Naturalistic Studies of the Long-Term Effects of Television Violence," *Journal of Social Issues* 42, no. 3: 51–74.

207 William Belson: *Television Violence and the Adolescent Boy* (Westmead, England: Saxon House, Teakfield, 1978). See also G. Muson, "Teenage Violence and the Telly," *Psychology Today*, March 1978, pp. 50–54.

207 Leonard D. Eron and L. Rowell Huesmann: "Adolescent Aggression and Television," *Annals of the New York Academy of Sciences* 347 (1980): 319–31; "The Role of Television in the Development of Prosocial and Antisocial Behavior," in *Development of Antisocial and Prosocial Behavior,* ed. D. Olweus, M. Radke-Yarrow, and J. Block (Orlando, Fla.: Academic Press, 1985).

208 Chicago-area and Finnish youngsters: L. Rowell Huesmann, K. Lagerspetz, and Leonard D. Eron, "Intervening Variables in the TV Violence-Aggression Relation: Evidence from Two Countries," *Developmental Psychology* 20 (1984): 746–75.

208 Criminal records: Leonard D. Eron and L. Rowell Huesmann, "The Control of Aggressive Behavior by Changes in Attitudes, Values, and the Conditions of Learning," in *Advances in the Study of Aggression,* ed. R. J. Blanchard and C. Blanchard, vol. 1 (Orlando, Fla.: Academic Press, 1984).

208 Brandon Centerwall: "Exposure to Television as a Risk Factor for Violence," *American Journal of Epidemiology* 129 (1989): 643–52; see also *Journal of the American Medical Association,* June 10, 1992, p. 3059.

208 Doubled playground aggression: T. M. Williams, ed., *The Impact of Television: A Natural Experiment in Three Communities* (Orlando, Fla.: Academic Press, 1986).

208 Leonard Eron and APA Youth Commission: "Televised Violence and Kids: A Public Health Problem?" *ISR Newsletter* (University of Michigan), February 1994, pp. 5–7, and "Media Violence: How It Affects Kids and What Can Be Done About It?" address to the American Psychological Association, 1995.

208 Effect greatest with hostile individuals: Brad J. Bushman, "Moderating
      Role of Trait Aggressiveness in the Effects of Violent Media on Ag-
      gression," *Journal of Personality and Social Psychology* 69 (1995):
      950–60.

208 Mortal Kombat: The game also has been found to increase arousal and
      feelings of hostility as college men play it. See Mary E. Ballard and
      J. Rose Wiest, "Mortal Kombat: The Effects of Violent Videogame
      Play on Males' Hostility and Cardiovascular Responding," *Journal of
      Applied Social Psychology* 26 (1998): 717–30.

209 Rape rates increased: John H. Court, "Sex and Violence: A Ripple Effect,"
      in *Pornography and Sexual Aggression,* ed. N. M. Malamuth and
      E. Donnerstein (New York: Academic Press, 1985).

209 Japan: Milton Diamond and Ayako Uchiyama, "Pornography, Rape, and
      Sex Crimes in Japan," *International Journal of Law and Psychiatry* 22
      (1999): 1–22.

209 Larry Baron and Murray A. Straus: "Sexual Stratification, Pornography,
      and Rape in the United States," in *Pornography and Sexual Aggression,*
      ed. Malamuth and Donnerstein.

209 Adolescent pornography use: Robert Bauserman, "Sexual Aggression and
      Pornography: A Review of Correlational Research," *Basic and Applied
      Social Psychology* 18 (1996): 405–27.

210 Ontario rapists and molesters: William Marshall, "Pornography and Sex
      Offenders," in *Pornography: Research Advances and Policy Con-
      siderations,* ed. D. Zillmann and J. Bryant (Hillsdale, N.J.: Erlbaum,
      1989).

210 Kenneth Hunter: Quoted in Jim O'Connell, "Child Porn Bust Nets
      Priests, Cop," Scripps Howard News Service (*Grand Rapids Press,*
      May 10, 1996).

210 Los Angeles Police: R. Bennett, "Pornography and Extrafamilial Child
      Sexual Abuse: Examining the Relationship," unpublished manuscript,
      Los Angeles Police Department Sexually Exploited Child Unit, Febru-
      ary 1991. There is no contradiction between finding that 30 percent of
      child pornography consumers sexually abuse children, and 62 percent
      of child sexual abusers consume pornography.

210 Serial killers: R. K. Ressler, A. W. Burgess, and J. E. Douglas, *Sexual
      Homicide Patterns* (Boston: Lexington, 1988).

210 John Money: *Gay, Straight, and In-Between* (New York: Oxford Univer-
      sity Press, 1988).

210 Ted Bundy: Interview with James Dobson, *Detroit Free Press,* January 25,
      1989.

210 Ed Donnerstein: "Aggressive Erotica and Violence Against Women," *Journal of Personality and Social Psychology* 39 (1980): 269-77.

211 "In laboratory studies": E. P. Mulvey and J. L. Haugaard, Office of the Surgeon General, "The Surgeon General's Workshop on Pornography and Public Health," prepared by August 4, 1986.

211 Albert Bandura: with D. Ross and S. A. Ross, "Transmission of Aggression Through Imitation of Aggressive Models," *Journal of Abnormal and Social Psychology* 63 (1961): 575-82.

211 Leonard Berkowitz and Russell Geen: "Film Violence and the Cue Properties of Available Targets," *Journal of Personality and Social Psychology* 3 (1966): 525-30.

212 Ithiel de Sola Pool: Quoted in Minow and LaMay, *Abandoned in the Wasteland.*

212 Margaret Loesch: Quoted in J. Kaplan, "Why Kids Need Heroes," *TV Guide,* March 4-10, 1995, pp. 25-30.

212 Delinquent boys: R. D. Parke, L. Berkowitz, J. P. Leyens, S. G. West, and J. Sebastian, "Some Effects of Violent and Nonviolent Movies on the Behavior of Juvenile Delinquents," in *Advances in Experimental Social Psychology,* vol. 10, ed. L. Berkowitz (New York: Academic Press, 1977); J. P. Leyens, L. Camino, R. D. Parke, and L. Berkowitz, "Effects of Movie Violence on Aggression in a Field Setting as a Function of Group Dominance and Cohesion," *Journal of Personality and Social Psychology* 32 (1975): 346-60.

212 National Institute of Mental Health: *Television and Behavior: Ten Years of Scientific Progress and Implications for the Eighties* (Washington, D.C.: Superintendent of Documents, 1982).

212 Chris J. Boyatzis: with G. M. Matillo and K. M. Nesbitt, "Effects of 'The Mighty Morphin Power Rangers,' on Children's Aggression with Peers," *Child Study Journal* 25 (1995): 45-55.

213 Norway incident: J. Blucher, "Tuning In to Violence: Are 'Power Rangers' and Other TV Shows Making Children More Aggressive?" *Anchorage Daily News,* October 27, 1994.

213 Convergence of evidence: For reviews of all studies see Susan Hearold, "A Synthesis of 1,043 Effects of Television on Social Behavior," in *Public Communication and Behavior,* ed. G. Comstock, vol. 1 (Orlando, Fla.: Academic Press, 1986), and Wendy Wood, F. Y. Wong, and J. G. Chachere, "Effects of Media Violence on Viewers' Aggression in Unconstrained Social Interaction," *Psychological Bulletin* 109 (1991): 371-83.

213 Emotional spillover: Dolf Zillmann, "Cognition-Excitation Interdependencies in Aggressive Behavior," *Aggressive Behavior* 14 (1988): 51-64;

"Aggression and Sex: Independent and Joint Operations," in *Handbook of Psychophysiology: Emotion and Social Behavior,* ed. H. L. Wagner and A. S. R. Manstead (Chichester: John Wiley, 1989).

213 Sexual passion: E. M. Palace and B. B. Gorzalka, "The Enhancing Effects of Anxiety on Arousal in Sexually Dysfunctional and Functional Women," *Journal of Abnormal Psychology* 99 (1990): 403-11.

213 Disinhibition by violence priming: Leonard Berkowitz, "Some Effects of Thoughts on Anti- and Prosocial Influences of Media Events: A Cognitive Neoassociation Analysis," *Psychological Bulletin* 95 (1984): 410-27; Brad J. Bushman and Russell G. Geen, "Role of Cognitive-Emotional Mediators and Individual Differences in the Effects of Media Violence on Aggression," *Journal of Personality and Social Psychology* 58 (1990): 156-63; W. L. Josephson, "Television Violence and Children's Aggression: Testing the Priming, Social Script, and Disinhibition Predictions," *Journal of Personality and Social Psychology* 53 (1987): 882-90; Eunkyung Jo and Leonard Berkowitz, "A Priming Effect Analysis of Media Influences: An Update," in *Media Effects: Advances in Theory and Research,* ed. J. Bryant and D. Zillmann (Hillsdale, N.J.: Erlbaum, 1994).

213 $29 billion: 1996 broadcast television revenue, reported in "Communications Industry's Annual Revenues Near $350 Billion, Census Bureau Reports," Census Bureau release, January 13, 1999.

214 *The Kiss:* Cited by Bryan Strong and Christine DeVault in a December 1, 1992, draft chapter of their human sexuality text.

214 Every four minutes: Sapolsky and Tabarlet, "Sex in Primetime Television."

214 Louis Harris: "Sexual Material on American Network Television During the 1987-1988 Season," conducted by Louis Harris and Associates for Planned Parenthood Federation of America, January 26, 1988.

214 90 times: Sapolsky and Tabarlet, "Sex in Primetime Television."

214 220 scenes: Robert S. Lichter, Linda S. Lichter, and Stanley Rothman, *Prime Time: How TV Portrays American Culture* (Washington, D.C.: Regnery, 1994), p. 39, cited in Robert Lerner and Althea K. Nagai, "Family Values and Media Reality," in *The Family, Civil Society, and the State,* ed. Christopher Wolfe (Lanham, Md.: Rowman & Littlefield, 1998), p. 178.

214 David Elkind: *Ties That Stress: The New Family Imbalance* (Cambridge: Harvard University Press, 1994), pp. 157-58.

215 MTV examples: Bob DeMoss, "Do You Know What Your Kids Are Watching?" *Focus on the Family,* August 1994, pp. 2-5.

215 32 to 1: B. S. Greenberg, J. D. Brown, and N. L. Buerkel-Rothfuss, *Media, Sex, and the Adolescent* (Cresskill, N.J.: Hampton Press, 1993), cited in

R. J. Harris, "The Impact of Sexually Explicit Media," in *Media Effects: Advances in Theory and Research,* ed. J. Bryant and D. Zillmann (Hillsdale, N.J.: Erlbaum, 1994).

215 New Zealand research team: *British Medical Journal,* 1998, quoted in Jane Brody, "Teen-Agers and Sex: Younger and More at Risk," *New York Times,* September 14, 1998.

215 Jane Brody: "Teen-Agers and Sex."

215 68 percent: Nick Ravo, "A Fact of Life: Sex-Video Rentals Gain in Unabashed Popularity," *New York Times,* May 16, 1990.

215 9.8 million: 9,823,000 as of July 1999. This does, however, include pages devoted to Super Bowl XXX and America's Cup XXX.

215 *Kill the Bitch,* etc.: Among titles that Gail Dines found at her neighborhood pornography shop ("Pornography and Advertising: Cultural Representations of Violence Against Women," paper presented to the American Psychological Association convention, August 1991).

215 David F. Duncan: "Violence and Degradation as Themes in 'Adult' Videos," *Psychological Reports* 69 (1991): 239–40.

215 Hans-Bernd Brosius: with James B. Weaver III and Joachim F. Staab, "Exploring the Social and Sexual 'Reality' of Contemporary Pornography," *Journal of Sex Research* 30 (1993): 161–70.

216 Susan Brownmiller: *Against Our Will: Men, Women, and Rape* (New York: Simon & Schuster, 1975), p. 394.

217 Letter writer: Norman H. Kessler, "Porn Could Have Positive Side Effects," *Holland Sentinel,* August 4, 1991.

217 2 to 1 margin: Richard G. Niemi, John Mueller, and Tom W. Smith, *Trends in Public Opinion: A Compendium of Survey Data* (New York: Greenwood, 1989), p. 199.

217 Nadine Strossen: Quoted in Nathan Seppa, "Psychologists Protest Screening of Flynt Film," *APA Monitor,* March 1997, p. 11.

217 William Griffitt: "Females, Males, and Sexual Responses," in *Females, Males, and Sexuality: Theory and Research,* ed. K. Kelley (Albany: State University of New York Press, 1987).

217 Theater patrons: Stephen L. Black and Susan Bevan, "At the Movies with Buss and Durkee: A Natural Experiment on Film Violence," *Aggressive Behavior* 18 (1992): 37–45.

217 Recipe for sexual aggression: Neil M. Malamuth, Daniel Linz, Christopher L. Heavey, Gordon Barnes, and Michele Acker, "Using the Confluence Model of Sexual Aggression to Predict Men's Conflict with Women: A 10-Year Follow-Up Study," *Journal of Personality and Social Psychology* 69 (1995): 353–69.

218 Parental fights and child abuse: N. M. Malamuth, R. J. Sockloskie, M. P. Koss, and J. S. Tanaka, "Characteristics of Aggressors Against Women: Testing a Model Using a National Sample of College Students," *Journal of Consulting and Clinical Psychology* 59 (1991): 670–81.

218 Michael Medved: "Popular Culture and the War Against Standards," *Imprimis* 20, no. 2 (February 1991): 1–7.

218 Edelman: *The Measure of Our Success,* pp. 52–53.

218 Ellen Goodman: "Parents Battle Culture to Protect Kids," Washington Post Writers Group, *Holland Sentinel,* August 17, 1991.

218 Children's sexual scripting via TV: Huston et al., *Big World, Small Screen,* pp. 47–48.

218 MTV quotes: Bob DeMoss, "Do You Know What Your Kids Are Watching?" *Focus on the Family,* August 1994, pp. 2–4.

218 Jack Valenti: "Don't Blame TV When Parents Don't Take Control," *Los Angeles Times* syndicated commentary, *Grand Rapids Press,* October 10, 1993.

219 Phil Donahue: CBS News, *48 Hours,* June 2, 1993, quoted in Minow and LaMay, *Abandoned in the Wasteland,* pp. 24–25.

219 Minow and LaMay: Ibid., pp. 25, 138.

219 Agree/disagree callers: Michael Medved, "It's Safe to Go Back in the Dark," *USA Weekend,* March 18–20, 1994.

219 Culture in decay: Phil Donahue quoted in Jane Hall, "Farewell Phil," *Tacoma News Tribune,* May 5, 1996. Geraldo Rivera quoted in Robert Wright, "The False Politics of Values," *Time,* September 9, 1996, pp. 42–45.

220 Ann Landers: Creators Syndicate, February 20, 1992.

220 Stephanie Coontz: *The Way We Never Were: American Families and the Nostalgia Trap* (New York: Basic, 1992), p. 277.

220 Ellen Goodman: "Hollywood Needs to Reel in Higher Quality," Washington Post Writers Group, *Grand Rapids Press,* 1995 (date unknown).

220 Robert Dole: At least Dole did not hold up Schwarzenegger as a model for human relations. After Schwarzenegger in the first few minutes of *Terminator 2* drove a long-bladed knife through a man's shoulder, pinning him to a pool table, and frying another man's hands and face on a restaurant griddle, George Bush gave him an honored guest position on the platform when accepting the 1992 Republican nomination (*Time,* August 31, 1992, p. 27).

221 Minow and LaMay: *Time,* June 26, 1995, pp. 25, 70.

221 Ice Cube: Quoted in Jean Bethke Elshtain, "On Moral Outrage, Boycotts, and Real Censorship," *Responsive Community,* fall 1992, pp. 9–13.

221 Time Warner CEO: Cited in Minow and LaMay, *Abandoned in the Wasteland,* p. 108.

221 27,000 scripts: Michael Medved, interview by Michael G. Maudlin, *Christianity Today,* March 8, 1993, pp. 22–29.

221 Roger Rosenblatt: Letter to the editor, *New York Times Book Review,* March 29, 1992, p. 16.

221 Curtail smoking: "There is no question in my mind that the government is seeking an all-out prohibition on cigarettes," said a prototypical smoker in an R. J. Reynolds full-page newspaper ad. "And once we've let them achieve their goal they'll be free to pursue other targets. They'll go for liquor and fast food and buttermilk and who knows what else. There's a line of dominoes a mile long" (*Grand Rapids Press,* June 27, 1994).

221 People for the American Way: "Taking Aim at Freedom," *Broadcasting and Cable,* November 8, 1993, quoted in Minow and LaMay, *Abandoned in the Wasteland,* p. 107.

222 Amitai Etzioni: *The Spirit of Community: Rights, Responsibilities, and the Communitarian Agenda* (New York: Crown, 1993), p. 177.

222 *Time*/CNN poll (by Yankelovich Partners): *Time,* June 12, 1995, p. 26.

222 All Americans favor: A 1995 *Newsweek*/Gallup poll found 92 percent of Americans in favor of banning the "sale or rental of video cassettes featuring sexual acts involving children" and 3 in 4 people favoring banning films and magazines showing sexual violence, but only 29 percent wanting to ban nudity in magazines (George Gallup, Jr., August 14, 1986).

222 Elizabeth Fox-Genovese: *Feminism Without Illusions: A Critique of Individualism* (Chapel Hill: University of North Carolina Press, 1991), p. 111.

222 Oliver Stone: In response to Bob Dole's May 31, 1994, speech in Los Angeles, as reported by Associated Press (*Grand Rapids Press,* June 1, 1994).

222 Paul Simon: Remarks to the Television/Film Meeting on TV Violence, Los Angeles, August 2, 1993.

222 *New York Times* editorial: "A Damaging Remedy for Sex Crimes," April 13, 1992. Stephen Carter finds it "both amusing and sad to hear liberals who have fought against the portrayal of vicious racial stereotypes in the media now saying that portrayals of sex and family life in the media affect nobody's behavior" ("Becoming People of Integrity," *Christian Century,* March 13, 1996, pp. 296–301).

223 Mark Fowler: Cited in Fred M. Hechinger, "About Education," *New York Times,* February 28, 1990.

223 11 hours per week: Dorian Friedman, "The Politics of Children's TV," *Family Life*, December–January 1993–94, p. 99, cited in Hewlett and West, *The War Against Parents*, p. 148.

223 Minow and LaMay: *Abandoned in the Wasteland*, p. 103.

223 Adam Smith: Quoted in ibid., p. 118.

223 James Wall: Quoted in Tom Maurstad and Beth Pinsker, "TV Cozies Up to Sex," *Dallas Morning News*, reprinted in *Detroit Free Press*, September 28, 1995.

224 Canada: "Obscenity Redefined in Canada Porn Law Ruling," *New York Times*, reprinted in *Grand Rapids Press*, February 28, 1992, and Sarah Lyall, "Canada's Porn Laws Inconsistent at Best, Booksellers Argue," *New York Times*, reprinted in *Grand Rapids Press*, December 19, 1993.

224 Smelly garbage, etc.: Fox-Genovese, *Feminism Without Illusions*, p. 98.

224 William Galston: "A Liberal-Democratic Case for the Two-Parent Family," *Responsive Community*, winter 1990–91, pp. 14–26.

224 Etzioni: *The Spirit of Community*, p. 48.

225 Robert Coles: Quoted in Richard Zoglin, "Chips Ahoy," *Time*, February 19, 1996, pp. 58–61.

225 Brad Bushman and Angela Stack: "Forbidden Fruit Versus Tainted Fruit: Effects of Warning Labels on Attraction to Television Violence," *Journal of Experimental Psychology: Applied* 2 (1996): 207–26.

225 1998 survey: Telephone poll of 1,007 adults taken February 20–24, 1998, by ICR of Media, Pa., reported by Howard Goldberg, Associated Press (*Grand Rapids Press*, March 2, 1998).

225 John Grisham: Quoted from his magazine the *Oxford American* in Elizabeth Gleick, "A Time to Sue," *Time*, June 17, 1996, p. 90.

225 Wendy Kaminer: "Of Second Amendment Rights and Responsibilities," *Intellectual Capital*, November 12, 1998 (www.intellectualcapital.com).

226 V-chip cost and technology: *USA Today*, July 10, 1995, and *Time*, February 19, 1996, pp. 58–61.

226 Richard Cotton and Howard Stringer: Quoted in Richard Zoglin, "Chips Ahoy," *Time*, February 19, 1996, pp. 58–61.

226 Marty Franks: Associated Press, "Cable Executives Support Rating System," *Holland Sentinel*, January 22, 1994.

226 Lucie Salhany: Quoted in Minow and LaMay, *Abandoned in the Wasteland*, p. 110.

226 $38 billion: "Communications Industry's Revenues Surpass $322 Billion

in 1996, Census Bureau Reports," U.S. Census Bureau release, June 15, 1998.

227 Racial behavior and attitude change: See David G. Myers, *Social Psychology,* 5th ed. (New York: McGraw-Hill, 1996).

227 38 percent: David Whitman, "Was It Good for Us?" *U.S. News & World Report,* May 19, 1997, pp. 57–64. See also Robert Lerner, Althea Nagai, and Stanley Rothman, *American Elites* (New Haven, Conn.: Yale University Press, 1996).

228 Marijuana use: From the annual government-financed survey of high school senior drug use conducted by Lloyd Johnston and others at the University of Michigan's Institute for Social Research.

228 Cigarette smoking decline: Frank Newport, "One-Fourth of Americans Still Smoke, But Most Want to Give Up the Habit," *Gallup Poll Monthly,* June 1996, pp. 2–6.

228 1990s Hollywood smoking: *CBS Evening News,* November 24, 1996. High school smoking data from Centers for Disease Control and Prevention study, reported by the Associated Press (*Holland Sentinel,* May 24, 1996).

228 Smoking 10th graders: Percentage who smoked cigarettes in previous 30 days, from University of Michigan's annual "Monitoring the Future" survey, conducted by Lloyd D. Johnston, with data released on December 19, 1996, by University of Michigan News and Information Services.

228 Too much violence: David W. Moore and Lydia Saad, "Public Says: Too Much Violence on TV," *Gallup Poll Monthly,* August 1993, p. 18.

228 76 percent: *U.S. News & World Report* commissioned poll, reported in Jim Impoco, "TV's Frisky Family Values," April 15, 1996, pp. 58–62.

228 Network violence decreasing: Gerbner, Morgan, and Signorielli, "Television Violence Profile."

228 Hollywood executives: Based on a possibly unrepresentative sample of 570 respondents to a survey mailed to 6,059 Hollywood executives, reported in Impoco, "TV's Frisky Family Values." Actually, this self-justification is not so incredible. As noted in Chapter 7, a powerful phenomenon called "self-serving bias" taints much human thinking, causing people routinely to shuck responsibility for their harm doing. Thus drivers usually deflect responsibility for their accidents. Divorcees nearly always blame their spouse. And facing failure, managers routinely blame workers. I describe self-serving bias at length in *Social Psychology,* 6th ed. (New York: McGraw-Hill, 1999).

228 Scott Sassa: Quoted in Lynn Elber, Associated Press, *Grand Rapids Press,* January, 15, 1999.

229 Leonard Eron and Rowell Huesmann: "Control of Aggressive Behavior."
     For more on media education, see Daniel Linz, Barbara J. Wilson, and
     Edward Donnerstein, "Sexual Violence in the Mass Media: Legal Solu-
     tions, Warnings, and Mitigation Through Education," *Journal of Social
     Issues* 48 (1992): 145-71.

229 Commercials and children: R. P. Adler, G. S. Lesser, L. K. Meringoff,
     T. S. Robertson, and S. Ward, *The Effects of Television Advertising on
     Children* (Lexington, Mass.: Lexington, 1980); Seymour Feshbach,
     "Television Advertising and Children: Policy Issues and Alternatives,"
     paper presented to the American Psychological Association conven-
     tion, 1980; E. L. Palmer, and A. Dorr, eds., *Children and the Faces
     of Television: Teaching, Violence, Selling* (New York: Academic Press,
     1980).

230 Norma Feshbach: "The Child as 'Psychologist' and 'Economist': Two Cur-
     ricula," paper presented at the American Psychological Association
     convention; 1980; also S. Cohen, "Training to Understand TV Adver-
     tising: Effects and Some Policy Implications," paper presented at the
     American Psychological Association convention, 1980.

230 Carnegie Council on Adolescent Development: *Great Transitions: Pre-
     paring Adolescents for a New Century* (New York: Carnegie Corpora-
     tion, 1995).

231 Peggy Noonan: Quoted in Minow and LaMay, *Abandoned in the Waste-
     land*, p. 8.

231 Marian Wright Edelman: "Introduction," *The State of America's Children
     Yearbook, 1994* (Washington, D.C.: Children's Defense Fund, 1994).

231 The Clintons: Blume, "First Lady Talks TV"; Bill Clinton, interview with
     Barry Golson and Peter Ross Range, "Clinton on TV," *TV Guide*,
     November 21, 1992.

231 DeLores Tucker: Sonya Ross, "Hip-Hopping Mad: Crusader Targets
     'Gangsta' Rap," Associated Press (*Grand Rapids Press*, September 5,
     1995).

231 Time Warner holdings: Robert Peters, "Time Warner Still in the Porn
     Business," *Morality in Media*, September-October 1998, pp. 3-4.

231 Forum for Responsible Advertisers: Brian Steinberg and Tara Parker-
     Pope, "Giant Sponsors Plan Campaign to Clean Up TV," *Wall Street
     Journal*, September 4, 1998.

232 President Clinton: Associated Press, *Holland Sentinel*, December 16,
     1993.

232 Mediascope: Carnegie Council on Adolescent Development, "Connect-
     ing the Media and Adolescent Development Professionals," in *Great
     Transitions*, pp. 121-22.

233 Gregg Easterbrook: "Watch and Learn," *New Republic,* May 17, 1999.

234 Joseph Lieberman: "Three U.S. Senators Speak Out," *American Enter-prise,* March–April 1999, p. 34.

234 Edward Donnerstein, Daniel Linz, and Steven Penrod: *The Question of Pornography* (New York: Free Press, 1987), p. 196.

Chapter 9: Educating for a Moral Compass

p. 236 James Madison: In *Federalist* 55—"Republican government presupposes the existence of [virtues] in a higher degree than any other form," quoted in William A. Galston, "Liberal Virtues and the Formation of Civic Character," in *Seedbeds of Virtue: Sources of Competence, Character, and Citizenship in American Society,* ed. Mary Ann Glendon and David Blankenhorn (Lanham, Md.: Madison, 1995), p. 55.

236 James Q. Wilson: "Liberalism, Modernism, and the Good Life," in *Seedbeds of Virtue,* ed. Glendon and Blankenhorn, p. 19.

236 Theodore Roosevelt: Reported in Sarah Glazer, "Teaching Values," *CQ Researcher,* June 21, 1996, pp. 529–52.

236 Benjamin Franklin: Quoted in "Points of Discussion" working paper for the White House Conference on Character Building for a Democratic, Civil Society, Communitarian Network, July 1, 1994.

236 Thomas Lickona: "Comments for Panel Discussion on Character Education," paper for the 2d Annual White House Conference on Character Education for a Democratic, Civil Society, May 19, 1995. See also Thomas A. Lickona, *Educating for Character* (New York: Bantam, 1991).

236 Plato: Quoted in Derek Bok, "Ethics, the University, and Society," *Harvard Magazine,* May–June 1988, p. 40.

236 Wannsee Conference: D. Patterson, *When Learned Men Murder* (Bloomington, Ind.: Phi Delta Kappan Publishers, 1996).

237 Ralph Waldo Emerson: Quoted in Robert Coles, "The Disparity Between Intellect and Character," *Chronicle of Higher Education,* September 22, 1995.

237 Mandatory schooling: Stephen L. Carter, *The Culture of Disbelief: How American Law and Politics Trivialize Religious Devotion* (New York: Basic, 1993), p. 204.

237 McGuffey's readers: Michael A. Rebell, "Values Engagement and the Schools," Institute for American Values Working Paper 39 (New York: Institute for American Values, September 1993).

237 Francis Fukuyama: *The Great Disruption: Human Nature and the Reconstitution of Social Order* (New York: Free Press, 1999).

237 National Education Association: Quoted in Morton L. Hunt, *The Compassionate Beast* (New York: Morrow, 1990), p. 216.

238 William A. Galston: Remarks to the White House Conference on Character Education for a Democratic, Civil Society, July 29, 1994.

238 1996 Gallup survey: " 'Values' in the Coming Election," *Emerging Trends* (Princeton Religion Research Center), October 1996, p. 1.

238 Cheating: 24th Annual Survey of High Achievers by Who's Who Among American High School Students (Associated Press, *Grand Rapids Press,* October 20, 1993). In the 29th annual survey, 80 percent admitted to some form of cheating during high school (France Griggs, Scripps Howard News Service, *Grand Rapids Press,* November 27, 1998).

238 Josephson Institute of Ethics survey: www.josephsoninstitute.org/98-Survey/98survey.htm. See also Karen Thomas, "Teen Ethics: More Cheating and Lying," *USA Today,* October 18, 1998.

238 Cheat sheet: F. Schab, "Schooling Without Learning: Thirty Years of Cheating in High School," *Adolescence* 26 (1991): 839–47.

238 College cheating: Survey by Rutgers University professor Don McCabe, reported in Dennis Kelly, "Cheating Up on Campuses with Honor Codes," *USA Today,* March 11, 1996.

238 Connie Shepard: " 'Good Morning, Teacher' Is Ancient History," *Los Angeles Times,* April 18, 1993.

238 Louis Raths, Merrill Harmin, and Sidney Simon: *Values and Teaching: Working with Values in the Classroom* (Columbus, Ohio: Merrill, 1966).

238 New Jersey high school: A story told by William Bennett as recounted in Ben Wildavsky, "Can You *Not* Teach Morality in Public Schools?" *Responsive Community,* winter 1991–92, pp. 46–54.

238 James Q. Wilson: *The Moral Sense* (New York: Free Press, 1993), p. 6.

239 Merrill Harmin: "Value Clarity, High Morality: Let's Go for Both," *Educational Leadership,* May 1988, pp. 24–30.

239 New York State Regents: Quoted in Wildavsky, "Can You *Not* Teach Morality in Public Schools?"

239 Sweden, Japan, and Russia: Judith Torney-Purta and John Schwille, "Civic Values Learned in School: Policy and Practice in Industrialized Nations," *Comparative Education Review* 30 (1986): 30–47.

239 William A. Galston: "Liberal Virtues and the Formation of Civic Character."

240 Robert McAfee Brown: Quoted in Martin Marty, "Graceful Prose: Your Good Deed for the Day," *Context,* December 1, 1988, p. 2.

241 Community dialogue: Michael A. Rebell of New York City's Center on
       Values, Education, and the Law reports the ingredients of a consensus-
       building process in "Values Engagement and the Schools."

241 Three in four Americans: *Wall Street Journal*/NBC poll, reported in
       Gerald F. Seib, "Americans Feel Families and Values Are Eroding But
       They Disagree over the Causes and Solutions," *Wall Street Journal*,
       June 11, 1993.

241 Fayetteville: Tim Stafford, "Helping Johnny Be Good," *Christianity
       Today*, September 11, 1995, pp. 34–39.

241 Antelope Trails: Reported to me by principal Judith Casey, and in "Ante-
       lope Trails Character Education Program," Antelope Trails Elementary
       School, Colorado Springs, Colo.

241 William Damon: *The Youth Charter: How Communities Can Work
       Together to Raise Standards for All Our Children* (New York: Free
       Press, 1997).

241 Gallup poll: "Most People Want to See Basic Values Taught in the Public
       Schools," *PRRC Emerging Trends*, December 1993, pp. 1, 3.

241 Gallup poll: Reported in *Phi Delta Kappan* and in William Damon,
       *Greater Expectations: Overcoming the Culture of Indulgence in
       America's Homes and Schools* (New York: Free Press, 1995), p. 96.

242 1996 Gallup poll: George H. Gallup, Jr., *Religion in America: The 1996
       Report* (Princeton Religion Research Center, 1996).

242 Criminals: From a study of London males by David Farrington and
       Donald West, reported in Wilson, *The Moral Sense*, p. 11.

242 1993 Parliament: "Towards a Global Ethic," 1993 Parliament of the
       World's Religions, Chicago, Illinois.

242 Character Counts Coalition: A project of the Josephson Institute of
       Ethics, Marina de Rey, Calif.; supporting statistics provided by per-
       sonal correspondence, March 14, 1996. Organizations belonging to
       the coalition include the YMCA, Boys and Girls Clubs of America,
       Big Brothers/Big Sisters of America, the National Urban League, the
       National Association of Secondary School Principals, and the National
       Association of State Boards of Education.

243 Empathy and impulse control: Psychologists, communitarian sociologist
       Amitai Etzioni, and conservatives William Bennett and John DiIulio
       concur on these two ingredients of character. Bennett and DiIulio, for
       example, describe "the twin character scars left by moral poverty—
       lack of impulse control and lack of empathy" (*Body Count* [New York:
       Simon & Schuster, 1996], p. 57).

243 Delay of gratification: D. C. Funder and J. Block, "The Role of Ego-

Control, Ego-Resiliency, and IQ in Delay of Gratification in Adolescence," *Journal of Personality and Social Psychology* 57 (1989): 1041–50; W. Mischel, Y. Shoda, and P. K. Peake, "The Nature of Adolescent Competencies Predicted by Preschool Delay of Gratification," *Journal of Personality and Social Psychology* 54 (1988): 687–96; and W. Mischel, Y. Shoda, and M. L. Rodriguez, "Delay of Gratification in Children," *Science* 244 (1989): 933–38.

243 Statewide initiatives: Remarks by Secretary of Education Richard Riley to the Third White House Conference on Character Education, June 8, 1996.

243 48 states: Lynn Nielsen, "New Study Shows States Returning to Character Education," *Character Educator* (from Character Education Partnership), summer 1998, p. 9.

243 Maryland: Mary C. Aranha and Stephanie T. Taymen (Maryland State Department of Education), *Character Educator,* summer 1998, pp. 1, 4.

243 In Britain: John O'Leary, "Man Who Wants Schools to Focus on Right and Wrong," *Times* (London), July 6, 1996, p. 8.

243 Principals: Hunt, *The Compassionate Beast,* pp. 215–18.

243 Schools as moral communities: The phrase is the title of a book by Michael Schulman, to be published by the Jewish Foundation for Christian Rescuers of the Anti-Defamation League, New York.

244 Community service opportunities: Several recent national reports connect the "service learning" movement to character education. A 1997 report available from the Council of Chief State School Officers observes, "Many teachers have watched children deepen their character when they take the risk of seeing things from someone else's perspective, or when they have shouldered responsibility for things as they are and set to work to change them" (Bruce O. Boston, *Their Best Selves: Building Character Education and Service Learning Together in the Lives of Young People*). A 1996 report available from the Institute for Global Ethics describes service learning as "a cycle of learning which involves, first, preparation for the service."

"Service Learning Is a Heavy Hitter," reports New York University psychologist Susan Anderson (in an address to the 1999 Communitarian Summit). Research shows several benefits of engaging youth in responding to community needs through service that's integrated into the curriculum and accompanied by personal reflection. When youths tutor, clean up the environment, do social service projects, and so forth they become more convinced of their ability to make a difference. Their desire to serve deepens. They become more accepting of diverse people. Their sense of personal competence increases. And their rates of absenteeism, dropout, and teen parenthood all diminish. Given that all this happens without any harm to academic achievement, why not encourage more service learning, especially during the high-risk after-school hours? Yale law school professor Stephen Carter (also in remarks to the Communitarian Summit) offers a way to give incentives for service learning without coercing participation. As we take "badness" into consideration when meting out punishment, why not assess "goodness" when handing out rewards? For example, add some definition of goodness (perhaps defined partly by service to others) to the list of criteria used in college admissions.

244 Thomas Lickona examples: "Combatting Violence with Values: The Character Education Solution," *Law Studies* 19 (1994). For many more practical examples, see Lickona's compendium of ideas and resources in *Educating for Character*.

244 San Ramon study: Reported in Glazer, "Teaching Values."

245 Mark Lipsey: Quoted and summarized in Charles C. Mann, "Can Meta-Analysis Make Policy?" *Science* 266 (1994): 960–62.

245 Arnold Goldstein: *The Prosocial Gang: Implementing Aggression Replacement Training* (Thousand Oaks, Calif.: Sage, 1994), and *Student Aggression: Prevention, Management, and Replacement Training* (New York: Guilford, 1994).

245 Deborah Prothrow-Stith: "Building Violence Prevention into the Curriculum," *School Administrator* 51 (April 1994): 8–12.

245 Dan Olweus: "Bullying or Peer Abuse at School: Facts and Intervention," *Current Directions in Psychological Science* 4 (1995): 196–200.

245 W. Rodney Hammond: Reported in the APA *Monitor,* April 1996, p. 20.

245 RCCP: Reported in *A Fine Line: Losing American Youth to Violence,* Special Report of the Charles Steward Mott Foundation, Flint, Mich., 1994.

246 David Johnson and Roger Johnson: "Teaching Students to Be Peacemakers: Results of Five Years of Research," *Peace and Conflict: Journal of Peace Psychology* 1 (1995): 417–38.

246 Other programs: Edward Zigler, Cara Taussig, and Kathryn Black, "Early Childhood Intervention: A Promising Preventative for Juvenile Delinquency," *American Psychologist* 47 (1992): 997–1006; Morton Deutsch, "Educating for a Peaceful World," *American Psychologist* 48 (1993): 510–17.

246 Patrick Friman: Posted by e-mail (Frimanp@BoysTown.org), and on the Teaching in Psychology network, December 15, 1994, as edited by Friman on March 20, 1996.

247 Phyllis Schlafly: Quoted in Tamary Henry, "Growing Debate Centers on Who Teaches Values," *USA Today*, March 20, 1996.

247 Charles Colson: "The Coming Crime Wave," *BreakPoint*, 1996, no. 60112.

248 James Davison Hunter: "Religious Freedom and the Challenge of Modern Pluralism," in *Articles of Faith, Articles of Peace*, ed. James Davison Hunter and Os Guinness (Washington, D.C.: Brookings Institution, 1990), p. 69.

248 Hillary Rodham Clinton: *It Takes a Village* (New York: Simon & Schuster, 1995), p. 174. On May 30, 1998, the president reaffirmed that "nothing in the U.S. Constitution requires schools to be religion-free zones, where children must leave their faiths at the schoolhouse door" (Reuters release, May 30, 1998).

248 President's request: See "Remarks by the President on Religious Liberty in America," James Madison High School, Vienna, Virginia, July 12, 1995, and Secretary of Education Riley's letter to school superintendents.

248 Stephen Carter: *The Culture of Disbelief*, pp. 52, 179.

250 David Popenoe: "Pro-Family Proposition for Consideration" at the Communitarian Network National Family Project meeting, August 6, 1994.

250 Centers for Disease Control: "Sexual Behavior Among High School Students—United States, 1990," *Morbidity and Mortality Weekly Report*, January 3, 1992, pp. 885–88.

250 Peggy Brick and Deborah M. Roffman: "'Abstinence, No Buts' Is Simplistic," *Educational Leadership*, November 1993, pp. 90–92.

250 Debra W. Haffner: "Toward a New Paradigm on Adolescent Sexual Health," *SIECUS Report*, December 1992–January 1993, pp. 26–30.

250 Full range: Debra Haffner, "Safe Sex in Teens," *SIECUS Report*, September–October 1988, quoted in *Sexual Health Update*, Medical Institute for Sexual Health, fall 1996, pp. 1–2.

250 Diana Baumrind: "Comment on Williams' and Silka's Comments on Baumrind," *American Psychologist* 37 (1982): 1402–3.

251 Sex education effects: Gilbert J. Botvin, Steven Schinke, and Mario A. Orlandi, "School-Based Health Promotion: Substance Abuse and Sexual Behavior," *Applied and Preventive Psychology* 4 (1995): 167–84. See also Douglas Kirby, *A Review of Educational Programs Designed to Reduce Sexual Risk-Taking Behaviors Among School-Aged Youth in the United States* (Springfield, Va.: National Technical Information Service, 1995, document no. PB96108519), and Kristin A. Moore et al., "Beginning Too Soon: Adolescent Sexual Behavior, Pregnancy, and Parenthood: A Review of Research and

Interventions," U.S. Department of Health and Human Services (http://aspe.os.dhhs.gov/hap/cyp/xsteesex.htm).

251 Centers for Disease Control: "Sexual Behavior Among High School Students."

251 Tenfold reduction: Steven D. Pinkerton and Paul R. Abramson, "Condoms and the Prevention of AIDS," *American Scientist* 85 (1997): 364-73.

251 98 percent of parents oppose children's smoking: From the 1993 National Household Education Survey.

251 Alfred McAlister: with C. Perry, J. Killen, L. A. Slinkard, and N. Maccoby, "Pilot Study of Smoking, Alcohol, and Drug Abuse Prevention," *American Journal of Public Health* 70 (1980): 719-21.

251 Other research teams: R. I. Evans, C. K. Smith, and B. E. Raines, "Deterring Cigarette Smoking in Adolescents: A Psycho-Social-Behavioral Analysis of an Intervention Strategy," in *Handbook of Psychology and Health: Social Psychological Aspects of Health,* vol. 4, ed. A. Baum, J. Singer, S. Taylor (Hillsdale, N.J.: Erlbaum, 1984), and B. R. Flay, K. B. Ryan, J. A. Best, K. S. Brown, M. W. Kersell, J. R. d'Avernas, and M. P. Zanna, "Are Social-Psychological Smoking Prevention Programs Effective? The Waterloo Study," *Journal of Behavioral Medicine* 8 (1985): 37-58.

252 6th to 8th grade role play: R. S. Hirschman and H. Leventhal, "Preventing Smoking Behavior in School Children: An Initial Test of a Cognitive-Development Program," *Journal of Applied Social Psychology* 19 (1989): 559-83.

252 Another study: P. L. Ellickson and R. M. Bell, "Drug Prevention in Junior High: A Multi-Site Longitudinal Test," *Science* 247 (1990): 1299-1305.

252 Dajahn Bievens: Quoted in Jane Gross, "Sex Educators for Young See New Virtue in Chastity," *New York Times,* January 16, 1994.

252 Abstinence-only curricula: Andres Tapia, "Abstinence: The Radical Choice for Sex Ed," *Christianity Today,* February 8, 1993, pp. 25-29.

253 Little effect, 50 states, and $6 million: Brian L. Wilcox and Jennifer Wyatt (University of Nebraska Department of Psychology), "Adolescent Abstinence Education Programs: A Meta-Analysis," paper presented at the 1997 Joint Annual Meeting of the Society for the Scientific Study of Sexuality and the American Association of Sex Educators, Counselors, and Therapists.

253 Successful efforts: "Eye-Opening Information on the 'Success' of 'Safe Sex' Programs and Exciting News About Abstinence Education Programs," *Sexual Health Update,* Medical Institute for Sexual Health, spring 1998, pp. 1-4.

253 Jefferson Junior High: Reported in Thomas Lickona, "Character Edu-
      cation," paper presented to the Second White House Conference on
      Character Education for a Democratic, Civil Society, May 19, 1995,
      and in Glazer, "Teaching Values."

253 Sarah Brown: Remarks to the Third Annual White House Conference on
      Character Education, June 7, 1994.

253 Jeffrey S. Luke and Kathryn Robb Neville: "Curbing Teen Pregnancy: A
      Divided Community Acts Together," *Responsive Community,* summer
      1998, pp. 62–72.

254 Outreach programs: Joseph P. Allen, Susan Philliber, Scott Herrling, and
      Gabriel Kuperminc, "Preventing Teen Pregnancy and Academic Fail-
      ure: Experimental Evaluation of a Developmentally Based Approach,"
      Child Development 64 (1997): 729–42.

254 Stephen Carter: *The Culture of Disbelief,* pp. 201–2.

254 Abstinence and sex education: "Values and Choices" (from the Search
      Institute in Minneapolis) provides an example of an abstinence-
      advocating comprehensive sex education program for middle school
      students. It is "values-based," yet comprehensive enough to be on the
      SIECUS recommended list. Here in Michigan, liberals and conser-
      vatives from groups such as Planned Parenthood and the Michigan
      Family Forum have formed the Michigan Abstinence Partnership, to
      follow Maryland's lead in developing a curricular and media campaign
      that encourages 9- to 14-year-olds to save sex for marriage.

254 Supporting the teaching of abstinence: "Most People Want to See Basic
      Values Taught in the Public Schools," *PRRC Emerging Trends,* Decem-
      ber 1993, p. 1, 3.

254 Joys of saved sex: In the National Opinion Research Center's recent
      national sex survey of 3,432 18- to 59-year-old Americans, women who
      reported always having orgasms ranged from 22 percent among the
      nonreligious to 32 percent among commitment-oriented conservative
      Protestants (see Edward Laumann et al., *The Social Organization of
      Sexuality* [University of Chicago Press, 1994]). The survey also found
      that married men have twice as much sex as single men and report
      more physical and emotional satisfaction with their sex lives.

254 Chicago schools: Ray Quintanilla, "Schools Find Motherhood Lesson
      Well Learned," *Chicago Tribune,* May 12, 1999.

255 David Popenoe: *Life Without Father: Compelling New Evidence that
      Fatherhood and Marriage Are Indispensable for the Good of Children
      and Society* (New York: Free Press, 1996), p. 187.

255 Allen Verhey: "The Holy Bible and Sanctified Sexuality: An Evangelical

Approach to Scripture and Sexual Ethics," *Interpretation* 49 (1995): 31–45.

256 Maggie Gallagher: *Enemies of Eros* (Chicago: Bonus, 1989), pp. 270–71.

Chapter 10: Faith and Society

p. 257 Hillary Rodham Clinton: Quoted in Michael Kelly, "Saint Hillary," *New York Times Magazine,* May 23, 1993, pp. 22–25, 63–66.

257 Lee Atwater: with Todd Brewster, "Lee Atwater's Last Campaign," *Life,* February 1991, p. 67.

258 Al Gore: *Earth in the Balance* (Boston: Houghton Mifflin, 1992), p. 367; announcement speech in Carthage, Tenn., Maureen Dowd, "The God Squad," *New York Times,* June 20, 1999.

258 Daniel Bell: *The Cultural Contradictions of Capitalism* (New York: Basic, 1976), p. 28.

258 Aleksandr Solzhenitsyn: *A World Split Apart* (New York: Harper & Row, 1978).

258 Jesse Jackson: Associated Press, "Jackson: Family Ethics Will End Violence," *Holland Sentinel,* September 6, 1993.

258 Anna Quindlen: "Missing in New America: Meaning in Our Lives," New York Times News Service, *Grand Rapids Press,* 1993.

259 Norman Lear: Address to the National Press Club, December 1993, quoted in Cal Thomas, "Crime Laws Won't Solve Crime Problem," Los Angeles Times Syndicate, *Grand Rapids Press,* December 17, 1993.

259 Michael Lerner: *The Politics of Meaning* (Reading, Mass.: Addison-Wesley, 1996), p. 4.

259 Vaclav Havel: *Disturbing the Peace* (New York: Knopf, 1990), p. 11.

259 Robert W. Fogel: Quoted in John J. DiIulio, Jr., "The Lord's Work: The Church and Civil Society," in *Community Works: The Revival of Civil Society in America,* ed. E. J. Dionne, Jr. (Washington, D.C.: Brookings Institution Press, 1998), p. 58.

259 Chris Evert: Quoted in Christopher Whipple, "Chrissie," *Life,* June 1986, pp. 64–72.

260 Ronald Inglehart: *Culture Shift in Advanced Industrial Society* (Princeton, N.J.: Princeton University Press, 1990), p. 180.

260 George H. Gallup, Jr.: "A Nation in Recovery," *PRRC Emerging Trends,* December 1994, pp. 1–2.

260 54 percent to 82 percent: "Remarkable Surge of Interest in Spiritual Growth Noted as Next Century Approaches," *Emerging Trends,* December 1998, p. 1.

260 87 percent: Quote from pollster Daniel Yankelovich, cited in *A Call to Civil Society*, Council on Civil Society, Institute for American Values, 1998, p. 4.

260 Overreport church attendance: C. Kirk Hadaway and Penny Long Marler, "Did You Really Go to Church This Week? Behind the Poll Data," *Christian Century*, May 6, 1998, pp. 472–75.

260 96 percent believe in God: Matches 96 percent belief recorded by Gallup 50 years earlier, in 1944 (*PRRC Emerging Trends*, January 1995, p. 5).

261 More than a million people: *Time* religion editor Richard Ostling, on *MacNeil-Lehrer News Hour*, April 5, 1996. See also Tamala M. Edwards, "Get Thee to a Monastery," *Time*, August 3, 1998, pp. 52–54.

262 NFL services: Tom Weir, *USA Today*, January 27, 1999.

262 Six prime-time programs: CBS *60 Minutes*, November 9, 1997. See also the series of *TV Guide* articles on religion on television in the March 29, 1997, issue.

262 *TV Guide* poll: Joanne Kaufman, "Tuning in to God," *TV Guide*, March 29, 1997, pp. 33–35.

262 New science-religion courses: The odds of the universe being born with just the right amount of matter and force to neither collapse back on itself nor explode into a soup too thin for stars, and of intelligent life then forming, are so infinitesimal—making the universe seem so welcoming toward us—as to provoke some thinkers to presume a providential First Cause, "to which everyone gives the name of God," said Aquinas. Gregg Easterbrook explores this theme in *Beside Still Waters: Searching for Meaning in an Age of Doubt* (New York: Morrow, 1998).

262 John Templeton: John Templeton Foundation Advisory Board Meeting, October 7, 1998.

263 Alma Daniel, Andrew Ramer, and John Randolph Price: Ruth Shalit, "Quality Wings," *New Republic*, July 20 and 27, 1998, pp. 24–31.

264 Astrology: See, for example, S. Carlson, "A Double-Blind Test of Astrology," *Nature* 318 (1985): 419–25.

264 1 in 4 Americans: "Fear of Dying," *Gallup Poll Monthly*, January 1991, pp. 51–59.

264 Past-life regression studies: Nicholas P. Spanos, "Past-Life Hypnotic Regression: A Critical View," *Skeptical Inquirer* 12 (1987–88): 174–80; also N. P. Spanos, E. Menary, N. J. Gabora, S. C. DuBreuil, and B. Behwirst, "Secondary Identity Enactments During Hypnotic Past-Life Regression: A Sociocognitive Perspective," *Journal of Personality and Social Psychology* 61 (1991): 308–20.

265 Historians of science: R. Hooykaas, *Religion and the Rise of Modern*

Science (Grand Rapids, Mich.: Eerdmans, 1972); Robert K. Merton, *Science, Technology, and Society in Seventeenth-Century England* (New York: Fertig, 1938, reprinted 1970).

265 J. B. S. Haldane: *Possible Worlds and Other Papers* (Freeport, N.Y.: Books for Libraries Press, 1928, reprinted 1971).

265 Carl Sagan: *The Demon-Haunted World* (New York: Random House, 1995).

266 Founders of parapsychology: James E. Alcock, "Parapsychology: The 'Spiritual' Science," *Free Inquiry*, spring 1985, pp. 25-35; J. Beloff, "Science Religion and the Paranormal," *Free Inquiry*, spring 1985, pp. 36-41.

266 Richard Dawkins: "The Emptiness of Theology," *Free Inquiry*, spring 1998, p. 6.

266 Shalom H. Schwartz and Sipke Huismans: "Value Priorities and Religiosity in Four Western Religions," *Social Psychology Quarterly* 58: 88-107.

267 Christopher Beem: "Civil Is Not Good Enough," *Responsive Community*, summer 1996, pp. 47-57.

267 George Carey and James Wolfensohn, "Closing Statement by the Co-Chairs," World Faiths and Development Dialogue, London, February 18-19, 1998.

267 Common Ground: "A Call to the Common Ground for the Common Good," issued June 8, 1993, by the National Council of the Churches of Christ, USA, the Synagogue Council of America, and the United States Catholic Conference.

267 Os Guinness: *The American Hour: A Time of Reckoning and the Once and Future Role of Faith* (New York: Free Press, 1993), p. 30.

267 Good without God?: Charles Colson, "Can We Be Good Without God?" *Imprimis* (Hillsdale College, Mich.), April 1993, pp. 1-4.

267 Gallup: "Can Atheists Live Virtuous Lives?" *PRRC Emerging Trends*, December 1994, p. 4.

267 Madeleine L'Engle: *Walking on Water: Reflections on Faith and Art* (Wheaton, Ill.: Harold Shaw, 1980), p. 59.

268 Richard Dawkins: Quoted in Garth Wood, "The Final Blow to God," *Spectator*, February 20, 1999, pp. 12-13.

269 Voltaire: Quoted in James Q. Wilson, *The Moral Sense* (New York: Free Press, 1993), p. 219.

269 E. O. Wilson: *Consilience* (New York: Knopf, 1998), p. 244.

269 William Damon: *Greater Expectations: Overcoming the Culture of Indulgence in America's Homes and Schools* (New York: Free Press, 1995), pp. 25, 81, 82.

269 National Commission on Children: *Beyond Rhetoric: A New Ameri-can Agenda for Children and Families,* Final Report of the National Commission on Children, 1991.

269 Religion, delinquency and drugs: Michael J. Donahue and Peter L. Ben-son, "Religion and the Well-Being of Adolescents," *Journal of Social Issues* 51 (1995): 145–60; Richard L. Gorsuch, "Religious Aspects of Substance Abuse and Recovery," *Journal of Social Issues* 51 (1995): 65–83. For earlier reviews see C. Daniel Batson and W. Larry Ventis, *The Religious Experience: A Social-Psychological Perspective* (New York: Oxford University Press, 1982); Bernard Spilka, Ralph W. Hood, Jr., and Richard L. Gorsuch, *The Psychology of Religion: An Empirical Approach* (Englewood Cliffs, N.J.: Prentice-Hall, 1985). Lindon Eaves (personal communication, October, 1996) also is finding that delin-quency, drunkenness, and marijuana use are several times more likely among North Carolina adolescent twins who say religion is "not impor-tant" rather than "very important." This difference is partly mediated by the peer group associations of religious versus nonreligious trends.

270 Out-of-wedlock attitudes: University of Michigan Survey Research Cen-ter data from the *Monitoring the Future* national surveys, reported in Urie Bronfenbrenner et al., *The State of Americans* (New York: Free Press, 1996), p. 10.

270 Schwartz and Huismans: "Value Priorities and Religiosity."

270 Seymour Martin Lipset: Remarks to the Communitarian Spirit and Contemporary America symposium at the Communitarian Summit, Washington, D.C., February 1999.

270 U.S. Values Survey: Reported in Margaret Mooney Marini, "The Rise of Individualism in Advanced Industrial Societies," paper presented at the Population Association of America annual meeting, Toronto, 1990.

270 Provo, Utah: See R. Start, C. Kent, and D. P. Doyle, "Religiosity and Delinquency: The Ecology of a Lost Relationship," *Journal of Re-search on Crime and Delinquency* 7 (1982): 83–98. At the time of this study, 97 percent of people in Provo and 28 percent of those in Seattle were church members. To this day, Provo has about a third the crime rate of Seattle, or even smaller, richer, neighboring Bellevue (and Provo has lower average income than either Seattle or Bellevue). Data provided in *County and City Data Book,* 12th ed., U.S. Department of Commerce.

270 Dennis Prager: Quoted in *BreakPoint with Chuck Colson,* 1996, no. 60212, p. 12.

271 Religion-prejudice studies: See David G. Myers, *Social Psychology,* 5th ed. (New York: McGraw-Hill, 1996).

271 Jonathan Swift: *Thoughts on Various Subjects*, 1727.

271 Religious roots of philanthropy: "America's Most Generous," *Fortune*, January 13, 1997, p. 96.

272 Churchgoing and charitable contributions: Virginia A. Hodgkinson and Murray S. Weitzman, *Giving and Volunteering in the United States: Findings from a National Survey* (Washington, D.C.: Independent Sector, 1990).

272 Two-thirds of all giving: Virginia A. Hodgkinson, Murray S. Weitzman, and A. D. Kirsch, "From Commitment to Action: How Religious Involvement Affects Giving and Volunteering," in *Faith and Philanthropy in America: Exploring the Role of Religion in America's Voluntary Sector*, ed. Robert Wuthnow, Virginia A. Hodgkinson et al. (San Francisco: Jossey-Bass, 1990).

272 Contributions from individuals: The American Association of Fund-Raising Counsel Trust for Philanthropy estimated that of the $122.6 billion contributed during 1990, $7.1 billion came from foundations, $5.9 billion from corporations, $7.8 billion from individuals' bequests, and $101.8 billion from individuals' gifts.

272 Congregational giving: Gallup Organization, *From Belief to Commitment: The Activities and Finances of Religious Congregations in the United States* (Washington, D.C.: Independent Sector, 1988).

272 Gallup on volunteerism: George Gallup, Jr., "Commentary on the State of Religion," *Religion in America: Gallup Report No. 222*, March 1984, pp. 1–20.

273 Follow-up Gallup survey: Diane Colasanto, "Americans Show Commitment to Helping Those in Need," *Gallup Report*, November 1989, pp. 17–24.

273 1992 volunteering: Hodgkinson and Weitzman, *Giving and Volunteering in the United States*, p. 162.

273 Virginia survey: 29 percent of those never attending church reported doing volunteer work, as did 61 percent of those who reported attending more than weekly (Center for Survey Research, reported in Everett Carll Ladd, "Volunteering in America," *Philanthropy*, May–June 1999, pp. 24–28).

273 Responsibility to the poor: Robert Wuthnow, *God and Mammon in America* (New York: Free Press, 1994).

273 Adoptive parents: Anu R. Sharma, Matthew K. McGue, and Peter L. Benson, "The Psychological Adjustment of United States Adopted Adolescents and Their Nonadopted Siblings," *Child Development* 69 (1998): 791–802.

273 Paul G. Schervish: "Wealth and the Spiritual Secret of Money," in *Faith and Philanthropy in America,* ed. Wuthnow and Hodgkinson et al.

274 Gregg Easterbrook: "Science Sees the Light," *New Republic,* October 12, 1998, pp. 24–29.

274 Dennis L. Krebs and Frank Van Hesteren: "The Development of Altruism: Toward an Integrative Model," *Developmental Review* 14 (1994): 103–58.

274 Four chaplains: Drawn from my *Social Psychology,* 5th ed. (New York: McGraw-Hill, 1996), pp. 552–53; sources include Rabbi Goode's daughter, L. Elliott, "Legend of the Four Chaplains," *Reader's Digest,* June 1989, pp. 66–70, and V. M. Parachin, "Four Brave Chaplains," *Retired Officer Magazine,* December 1992, pp. 24–26.

275 Partners for Sacred Places: Peter Steinfels, "Beliefs," *New York Times,* November 1, 1997, and T. J. Billitteri, "Deterioration of Church Facilities Said to Endanger Social Services," *Chronicle of Philanthropy,* November 13, 1997.

275 David L. Ostendorf: "Exploiting Immigrant Workers," *Christian Century,* May 5, 1999, pp. 492–93.

276 Frank Emerson Andrews: *Attitudes Toward Giving* (New York: Bureau of Social Research, 1953), p. 85.

276 Held back the night: Charles Colson, *Against the Night: Living in the New Dark Ages* (Ann Arbor: Servant Publications, 1989), p. 133.

277 Martin Luther King, Jr.: Quotes from King's early sermon "The Transformed Nonconformist" (quoted in Don Eberly's *Restoring the Good Society* [Grand Rapids: Hourglass Books, 1994], p. 76), and from Kay Coles James, *Transforming America from the Inside Out* (Grand Rapids: Zondervan, 1995), pp. 47–48. (James's book was also inspired by discussion of Wilberforce, aided by other sources.)

277 Walter Lippmann: *The Good Society* (Boston: Little, Brown, 1937), p. 382.

277 Le Chambon: F. Rochat, "How Did They Resist Authority? Protecting Refugees in Le Chambon During World War II," paper presented at the American Psychological Association convention, 1993.

278 Ignacio Martin-Baro: Arthur Aron, "A Tribute to Ignacio Martin-Baro (1942–1989)," SPSSI *Newsletter,* April 1990, p. 4.

278 Oscar Romero: Doris Donnelly, quoting Jorge Lara-Braud ("Joy: The Delight of Longing," *The Living Pulpit,* October–December, 1996, p. 6).

278 Laszlo Tokes: Jill Schaeffer, "Romania: The Eighth Circle of Hell," *Perspectives,* May 1990, pp. 4–6.

278 Marian Wright Edelman: *Publishers Weekly,* October 2, 1995, quoted in
      Martin E. Marty, *Context,* January 1, 1996, p. 1.

278 Andrew Billingsley: *Climbing Jacob's Ladder: The Enduring Legacy
      of African-American Families* (New York: Simon & Schuster, 1992),
      p. 349. Billingsley also reported on the T. J. Jemison address to the
      National Baptist Convention.

278 Don S. Browning: "Altruism, Civic Virtue, and Religion," in *Seedbeds of
      Virtue: Sources of Competence, Character, and Citizenship in Ameri-
      can Society,* ed. Mary Ann Glendon and David Blankenhorn (Lanham,
      Md.: Madison, 1995), pp. 123, 126, updated by personal correspon-
      dence, April 1, 1996.

279 Robert L. Woodson: Quoted in William Raspberry, "The Power of Spiri-
      tuality," *Washington Post,* December 7, 1992. See also Robert L.
      Woodson, Sr., *Listening to Joseph: How Today's Community Healers
      Can Revive Our Streets and Neighborhoods* (New York: Free Press,
      1998).

279 Cornel West: *Race Matters* (Boston: Beacon, 1993), p. 14.

279 Richard B. Freeman: "Who Escapes? The Relation of Churchgoing and
      Other Background Factors to the Socioeconomic Performance of
      Black Male Youths from Inner-City Poverty Tracts," in *The Black Youth
      Employment Crisis,* ed. R. B. Freeman and H. J. Holzer (Chicago:
      University of Chicago Press, 1986).

279 Single arrest: Sylvia Ann Hewlett and Cornel West's report on the 1995
      Million Man March in *The War Against Parents* (Boston: Houghton
      Mifflin, 1998), pp. 206–11.

279 40 studies: Byron R. Johnson, Spencer D. Li, David Larson, and Mike
      McCullough, "A Systematic Review of the Religiosity and Delinquency
      Literature: A Research Note," *Journal of Contemporary Criminal
      Justice,* in press.

279 Their own analyses: Byron R. Johnson, Spencer D. Li, Sung Joon Jang,
      and David Larson, "The 'Invisible Institution' and Urban Delinquency:
      The African-American Church as an Agency of Local Social Con-
      trol," *Criminology,* in press; Byron R. Johnson, David B. Larson, Sung
      Joon Jang, and Spencer D. Li, "Escaping from the Crime of Inner
      Cities: Churchgoing Among At-Risk Youth," *Justice Quarterly,* in press;
      Byron R. Johnson, Sung Joon Jang, David Larson, and Spencer D. Li,
      "Does Adolescent Religious Commitment Matter? A Reexamination
      of the Effects of Religiosity on Delinquency," *Journal of Research on
      Crime and Delinquency,* in press.

280 Eugene Rivers: "High Octane Faith," in *Community Works: The Revival
      of Civil Society,* ed. E. J. Dionne, Jr. (New York: Brookings Institution

Press, 1998), pp. 59–63. See also Joe Klein, "In God They Trust," *New Yorker*, June 16, 1997, pp. 40–48.

280 John DiIulio: "The Coming of the Super-Preachers," *Weekly Standard*, June 23, 1997, pp. 23–25; "The Lord's Work: The Church and Civil Society," in *Community Works*, ed. Dionne; "Go Directly to Jail" (interview), *Sojourners*, September–October 1997, pp. 16–22. See also Mary Ann Meyers, "DiIulio Gets Religion," *Pennsylvania Gazette*, October 1997, pp. 23–29.

280 *Washington Post:* Jon Jeter, "A Homespun Safety Net: Michigan Community Finds Jobs for All on Welfare," October 8, 1997.

281 States and churches: Adam Cohen, "Feeding the Flock," *Time*, August 25, 1997, pp. 46–48; Joseph P. Shapiro, "Can Churches Save America?" *U.S. News & World Report*, September 9, 1996, pp. 46–53; and Isaac Kramnick and R. Laurence Moore, "Can the Churches Save the Cities? Faith-Based Services and the Constitution," *American Prospect*, November–December, 1997, pp. 47–53.

281 Ronald J. Sider and Heidi Rolland: "Correcting the Welfare Tragedy: Toward a New Model for Church/State Partnership," in *Welfare in America: Christian Perspectives on a Policy in Crisis*, ed. S. W. Carlson-Thies and J. W. Skillen (Grand Rapids, Mich.: Eerdmans, 1996); Stephen V. Monsma, "Overcoming Poverty: The Role of Religiously Based Nonprofit Organizations," in *Welfare in America*, ed. Carlson-Thies and Skillen.

281 John DiIulio: "PRRAY: Some Key Ideas and Principles," presented to John Templeton Foundation meeting, October 1997.

281 Tillie Burgin: Joe Klein, "Can Faith-Based Groups Save Us?" *Responsive Community*, winter 1997–98, pp. 25–39.

281 Charles Colson: "The New Criminal Class," *Wall Street Journal*, January 24, 1996. A recent study in four New York State prisons found more mixed results: Those participating in Prison Fellowship programs were as likely as those not to be rearrested. However, those most active in Bible studies were less likely to be rearrested (Byron R. Johnson, David B. Larson, and Timothy C. Pitts, "Religious Programs, Institutional Adjustment, and Recidivism Among Former Inmates in Prison Fellowship Programs," *Justice Quarterly* 14 [1997]: 145–66).

282 Paul Wellstone and Bob Kerrey: Quoted in Klein, "In God They Trust."

282 President Clinton: "Fighting Juvenile Crime," *Christian Century*, July 29–August 5, 1998, p. 710.

282 George Carey and related quotes: "Carey's Moral Crusade Upsets Schools," "Society Shaken by an 'Assault on Traditional Values,'" and

"Carey Urges Parents and Teachers to Set an Ethical Example for All,"
Times (London), July 6, 1996, pp. 1, 9.

282 Jonathan Sacks: "Therapy Instead of Morality," *Times* (London), July 5,
1996, p. 20.

283 Martin Luther King, Jr.: *Where Do We Go from Here: Chaos or Community?* (New York: Harper & Row, 1967).

283 Bill Clinton: Remarks to the 86th Annual Holy Convocation of the
Church of God in Christ, Mason Temple Church of God in Christ,
Memphis, Tenn., November 13, 1993 (Washington, D.C.: White House
Office of the Press Secretary).

283 Progressive evangelicals: Jim Wallis, on behalf of "The Cry for Renewal,"
Religion News Service release by David E. Anderson ("Religious
Moderates Seek to Assert Voice in Political Affairs," May 22, 1995).

283 William James: *The Varieties of Religious Experience* (New York: Mentor,
1902, reprinted 1958), p. 264.

283 George Zabelka: "I Was Told It Was Necessary," *Sojourners,* August 1980,
pp. 12–15.

283 Faith and happiness: What explains these positive links between faith
and well-being? Is it the supportive close relationships often enjoyed
by those active in one of America's 350,000 faith communities? Is it
the sense of meaning and purpose that many people derive from their
faith? Is it the hope that faith offers when people face what social psychologists Sheldon Solomon, Jeffery Greenberg, and Tom Pyszczynski
call "the terror resulting from our awareness of vulnerability and
death"? Such proposed explanations await further exploration.

284 Martin Gardner: Kendrick Frazier, "A Mind at Play: An Interview with
Martin Gardner," *Skeptical Inquirer,* March-April 1998, pp. 34-39.

285 87 percent: From two 1995 Gallup surveys, one of which found 30 percent saying religion was fairly important "in your own life" and 58
percent saying it was "very important." The other found 22 percent
answering "fairly important," 32 percent "very important," and 32 percent "extremely important" (*Gallup Poll Monthly,* September 1995, pp.
33, 40).

285 Transforming faith: "Levels of Religious Commitment," *Emerging Trends*
(Princeton Religion Research Center), June 1996, p. 5.

285 Belief follows behavior: For much more on this, see Chapter 4, "Behavior and Attitudes," in my *Social Psychology,* 6th ed. (New York:
McGraw-Hill, 1999).

286 Torturers: Ervin Staub, *The Roots of Evil: The Origins of Genocide and
Other Group Violence* (Cambridge: Cambridge University Press,
1989).

286 Soren Kierkegaard: *For Self-Examination and Judge for Yourself,* trans. W. Lowrie (Princeton, N.J.: Princeton University Press, 1944), p. 88.

286 Pascal: *Thoughts,* trans. W. F. Trotter, in *World Masterpieces,* ed. M. Mack (New York: Norton, 1965), 2:38.

286 C. S. Lewis: *Mere Christianity* (New York: Macmillan, 1960), book 3, chapter 9.

287 Educational research on group amplification: A. W. Chickering and J. McCormick, "Personality Development and the College Experience," *Research in Higher Education,* no. 1 (1973): 62–64; K. A. Feldman and T. M. Newcomb, *The Impact of College on Students* (San Francisco: Jossey-Bass, 1969); R. C. Wilson, J. G. Gaft, E. R. Dienst, L. Wood, and J. L. Bavry, *College Professors and Their Impact on Students* (New York: Wiley, 1975).

287 David G. Myers and George D. Bishop: "Discussion Effects on Racial Attitudes," *Science* 169 (1970): 778–89.

287 Clark R. McCauley and Mary E. Segal: "Social Psychology of Terrorist Groups," in *Group Processes and Intergroup Relations: Review of Personality and Social Psychology,* ed. C. Hendrick (Newbury Park, Calif.: Sage, 1987).

288 Robert Wuthnow: "Evangelicals, Liberals, and the Perils of Individualism," *Perspectives,* May 1991, pp. 10–13.

288 Apart from any church or synagogue: George Gallup, Jr., as summarized in Richard Morin, "The Church of Public Opinion," *Washington Post National Weekly Edition,* November 6–12, 1995, p. 37.

288 Robert Bellah: with Richard Madsen, William M. Sullivan, Ann Swidler, and Steven M. Tipton, *Habits of the Heart* (New York: Perennial, 1985), p. 221.

288 N. J. Demerath III: "Cultural Victory and Organization Defeat in the Paradoxical Decline of Liberal Protestantism," *Journal for the Scientific Study of Religion* 34 (1995): 458–69.

289 David O. Sears: "Life Stage Effects Upon Attitude Change, Especially Among the Elderly," manuscript for Workshop on the Elderly of the Future, Committee on Aging, National Research Council, Annapolis, Md., May 3–5, 1979; "College Sophomores in the Laboratory: Influences of a Narrow Data Base on Social Psychology's View of Human Nature," *Journal of Personality and Social Psychology* 51 (1986): 515–30.

289 Bennington women's voting: D. F. Alwin, R. L. Cohen, and T. M. Newcomb, *Political Attitudes Over the Life Span: The Bennington Women After Fifty Years* (Madison: University of Wisconsin Press, 1991).

289 Howard Schuman and Jacqueline Scott: "Generations and Collective
        Memories," *American Sociological Review* 54 (1989): 359–81.

290 Marian Wright Edelman: *Guide My Feet: Prayers and Meditations on
        Loving and Working for Children* (Boston: Beacon, 1995), pp. 154–55.

290 Ellen and Dana Charry: "Send a Christian to Camp," *Christian Century*,
        July 14, 1999, pp. 708–10.

291 Gandhi: November 19, 1931, quoted in ibid., p. 200.

Epilogue

p. 292 *Boston Quarterly Review:* Quoted in Herman Lantz, Martin Schultz, and
        Mary O'Hara, "The Changing American Family from the Preindus-
        trial to the Industrial Period: A Final Report," *American Sociological
        Review* 42 (1977): 406–21.

292 *Look:* Reported in Arlene Skolnick, *Embattled Paradise: The American
        Family in an Age of Uncertainty* (New York: Basic, 1991), pp. 1–2.

293 *Time's* family projection: Claudia Wallis, "The Nuclear Family Goes
        Boom!" *Time*, fall 1992 special issue "Beyond the Year 2000." The odd-
        est projection is a large number of active bisexuals, whose numbers
        have been and remain almost infinitesimal—less than 1 percent of
        adults in national surveys (see David G. Myers, *Psychology* [New York:
        Worth, 1995]).

293 Ellen Goodman: "Two Sides Speak to Family Crisis: Man, Woman,"
        Washington Post Writers Group, *Grand Rapids Press*, September 22,
        1994.

293 Winston Churchill: Quoted by Carnegie Council on Adolescent Develop-
        ment president David Hamburg in Steve Wulf, "Generation Excluded:
        A Report Chides America for Neglecting Adolescents," *Time*, Octo-
        ber 23, 1995, p. 86.

293 1800s: James Q. Wilson briefly describes the early 1800s in "Liberalism,
        Modernism, and the Good Life," in *Seedbeds of Virtue*, ed. Glendon
        and Blankenhorn.

294 Aleksandr I. Solzhenitsyn: *A World Split Apart* (New York: Harper &
        Row, 1978), p. 61.

Index